LETTERS IN A

Letters in a Suitcase

Douglas, Dorothy & Muriel Heelas

Edited by Arthur Harris

YOUCAXTON
PUBLICATIONS

ISBN 978-1-915972-27-9
Published by YouCaxton Publications 2023

YouCaxton Publications
www.youcaxton.co.uk

This book is dedicated to the Heelas family and my wife Yenny, also Will and Aisha for all their help in completing this work.

Contents

Family photo left to right, Newton Heelas, Douglas, Mabel, Muriel and Dorothy

INTRODUCTION

This is a book of letters that were mainly written to Mrs Mabel Heelas and her husband by their son Douglas and daughters Dorothy and Muriel.

The reason I have these letters is rather odd.

In 1972, when I first came to London at the age of 18 straight from living in a remote old house in Cornwall, I got a job with Stanley Gibbons of the Strand London, philatelic dealers. While growing up I used to collect stamps, I think everybody did in those days a long time ago (including Muriel). I worked for Stanley Gibbons for about 10 years, until I lost interest in stamps, and turned instead to dealing in antiques.

Sometime in the early 1990s on a Thursday at 6 a.m. in the morning I went off to Merton Abbey Mills. Every Thursday there was a small antique market there. I would have set off from home in West London on my Vespa scooter in search of items to sell on a stall I ran in Portobello Road every Saturday morning. Arriving at the market probably about 6.30 a.m.. I proceeded to walk around the small hall where the dealers were setting up to sell their wares. I walked round and round until 8 a.m. when I had to leave in order to get back home to take my son to school. I had to be back by 8.30 so my wife could go to work and I could cycle with my son to school 2 ½ miles away.

I never bought much at Merton Abbey Mills. In fact, I can't remember what I bought on that particular morning, apart from one thing. On a stall at the end of the hall was a dealer who did house clearances. I walked past it on probably my sixth time circling the hall. All antique dealers are rather like vultures circling from above looking for their prey. As I passed this stall with mixed ephemera on it I saw a suitcase. It was open and in it were a lot of old envelopes.

I quickly looked through the suitcase on the stall. Most of the envelopes were of no value just with 1 ½ d to 2 ½ d George V1 stamps on them, not worth anything to postal history collectors, but there were quite a few postcards sent from England to Thailand during the Second World War which had censors' post marks on them and Japanese red marks. They were all addressed to a British Prisoner of War Camp in Thailand, and there were probably 20 or 30 of these. The suitcase was £30 with the contents, so I bought them and strapped the case on my scooter and returned home. I emptied the letters and cards into a small cardboard box. I put the box in a cupboard and left it there. On that Saturday I must have filled up the suitcase with other items I had purchased during the week and taken them to Portobello. I think I sold the empty suitcase for around £15. There has always been a demand for old suitcases as display items.

The next time I looked at the box was about 20 years later when I retired. I thought most of the letters were from the same person, as they were all marked on the back from D Heelas, so I put them all in date order and eventually started to read through them. I soon realised that most of the letters before 1945 were from Douglas Heelas and the later ones from Dorothy Heelas.

At first I didn't pay any attention to Dorothy's letters, as the Second World War seemed much more interesting. I started with Douglas's letters, typing them up on the computer. They started from his school days, and after I had been doing it for about a year or more I had typed all of them. First I didn't type everything, but when I reached the end I went over them and redid it all in full. I thought they might make a book so I looked up Douglas Heelas on the computer and I gradually found bits of information about him but couldn't find out if he had any living relatives. One day I drove down with my wife to Shrewsbury House School, where he went as a boy, and asked them if they had any information, but they did not. I had found a few Heelases on Facebook and written to one I thought might be a relative but no reply. Many months later I got a message from the school that Douglas's sons, David and Jeremy, and daughter Baie, had been in touch with them, and they gave me their details so I could contact them. So over the next while I sent them copies of all the letters that I had typed out.

Douglas was born in 1919 and was known as Dug. He had two sisters: Dorothy (born 1911) known as Dar, and Muriel (born 1906) known as Boss, who was a school secretary and music teacher. Their parents Mabel and Newton were born 1874 and 1864 respectively. Newton was the vicar of St Peter's Norbiton. They also had two other girls: Winifred, who was born in 1903 and died probably during the flu pandemic in1918, and Kathleen in 1907 who died as a baby.

So it wasn't until a while later that I started to look at Dorothy's letters, and then proceeded to type those up.

It appears the suitcase was in the property belonging to Muriel and after her death in 1985 the family had taken most of the personal effects away, but this suitcase had been inadvertently left and was later bought with other furniture by the house clearance people. Luckily it wasn't bought by a philatelist who would probably have sorted out the rarer postal history of the various envelopes to sell separately, and disposed of the rest as a cheap lot.

The book that follows is not intended to be the history of Douglas, Dorothy and Muriel's lives but a short look at periods of their lives, the majority from 1939 to the 1940s. The letters are predominantly to their parents, and personal in nature, but reflect the social history of the time.

My thanks go to Douglas's children who gave me other family papers relating to Douglas which included some of Douglas's diary plus various photographs which have been included in the pages of this book.

You will notice that some of the letters use '&' instead of 'and'. '&' is used when they are writing by hand and 'and' when the letter is typed. Similarly '@' is used by hand, and 'at' is used in a type-written letter.

It is a deep regret that Douglas's sons David Heelas and Jeremy Heelas have passed away since I started to compile this book.

Part 1

Chapter 1

1929 - August 1939

Douglas's letters start in 1929.

In January 1929 Douglas aged 9 was sent to board at Shrewsbury House School in Surbiton. On 17th Febuary 1929 he writes to his parents that on Saturday he saw that parts of the Thames had frozen. News reports show that on 14th Febuary the Thames froze and a ground temperature of 25 degrees of frost which was equal to the lowest recorded temperature since 1895 when the Thames was blocked and ice skating was allowed in some of the lakes in the Royal Parks.

Douglas wrote on 28th Jan 1931

The greatest day of the whole of the year THURSDAY JAN 28th 1931 From 7.30 to 8.50. At 7.30 one of the boys of our dormitory said that there was a lot of wind, matron came in and one of the other boys said he could see flames in the ventilator. Our dorm went down stairs, ring a ling ring a ling the fire engine came up. We had breakfast and we heard the fire men at work, it was only a chimney on fire, we finished breakfast then went out and saw the engine. On the roof were some firemen, they were waving to us, they were by the chimneys then loaded up the engine and we waved to them until they were out of sight, it was very thrilling. Look in the Surrey Comet on Sat under Surbiton or Long Ditton.

It obviously was a very memorable day, which he remembered for a long time

Muriel the oldest sister nicknamed Boss starts a new job as secretary/music teacher and writes to the family from Port Regis, Broadstairs, Kent

Muriel

22nd Sept 1932

Thanks awfully for all your letters. It is jolly nice to get them. I am absolutely bored stiff with nothing to do. I have typed out a few lists, and only done two letters for Mr Evans, since I have been here. Yesterday he went to London for the day, and left me with nothing to do, and to-day he has gone to London to fetch the boys back, and they don't arrive until to-night, so I have another empty day before me. All the staff have now arrived, so I will give you a description of them all.

Mr Hooper. He is the youth who came on Sunday. Very tall, rather like Ar Beats' Mike. Not bad. We have been for several drives, and played ping-pong a lot together, before the others came back, as he seems to have nothing to do.

Mr Harker. Aged about 22. Dreamy sort of youth. Frightfully musical, he comes and forks me out to play high-brow duets. He and Mr Cooper share a car.

Mr Thorn. Quite oldish. His hair seems to radiate from one given point in the middle of his head. No parting anywhere. Quite a mystery,(the hair). Nothing particular about him.

Mr Drew. About my age. Tall and very broad. New this term. Seems very la-di-da. I should think just from Oxford. Wrote to Mr Evans to know what was the approximate position of his bedroom, so I imagine he is rather a fop. He only came last night, so I don't know much about him. He says he is going to buy a car at the "end of the scholastic year"!!!!

Miss Garing. The housekeeper. About 40 ish. Quite nice.

The Matron. About 30 ish. Not bad, but rather like Edie Densham.

Miss Didsworth. The Maths; mistress. Tries to look 20, but I don't suppose she will ever see 40 again. I think her hair is dyed.

Miss Thompson. The kindergarten mistress. About 35. She is perfectly sweet. I am going for a walk with her this morning.

I don't know much about the females, as they only came yesterday morning. Mr Evans is a funny bloke. Frightfully clever, is always going to the pictures. He knows millions of celebrities, especially Actors and Actresses. Spends all his holidays in Paris etc. His car won't go, so he goes to London by lorry. They have one for the boys. He looks so funny togged up in his best going out in this lorry.

My car is quite the Boh Bouche!!! The Earl of Durhams' two sons are here. Also tell Dar that Harold Craxtons' boy is here, and that I have got to teach him music. This is a very expensive school, much more than Duggers. Everything is frightfully up to date. The dishes we have our grub on is fixed to a power plug so it keeps hot.

I went to see the Alison's after super the other night. I shall go again this afternoon. They go on Saturday or Monday. Mr is awfully nice.

I don't have that sitting room all to myself. It is for the female staff.

Could you send me my hot-bottle. It is so cold at nights. I think it leaks.

Mr Evans never tells me a thing, so I don't know when I can get off. I do hope I shall get a night off now and again. I have got to play the organ for Sunday evening services, as Mr Evans takes the service. They have a chaplain in the morning. They are very high church.

My office is a muggy little hole. It evidently was a cloak room, as there is a door through leading to a Wesleyan Chapel. I have a desk, like Daddy's, and a typewriter on a table, and a piano. It is long and narrow, and a long window right high up so I can't see out at all, which is rather a blow.

My asthma is better until I try to go for a walk, and then I get awfully bad.

Surtees and Marjorie wrote to thank us for having them. I enclose Majorie's letter for Dar to see.

If you think this letter would interest Ar beat, you might send it along, as I can't be dished to write another long one.

I don't type as badly as this generally, just in case you thought. To Dar.

The type writer is an Underwood. Quite nice Mr E. dictates fearfully slowly. Thank goodness. He talks at a fearful lick, and takes breathes in the middle of sentences in a loud, onerous way. Sounds so funny. Aren't lists horrible to type?

Letter from Douglas who attends Marlborough College Wilts

To Mummy, Daddy & Dar From Douglas

19th July 1936,

How are the car lessons going? Hope you haven't killed yourself yet? I hope you are getting on well. We shall have fun when the girls are away and with you driving Daddy, shan't we!!! Love the thought of Llandudno again, is it settled yet? I would like to lend you the £6 that you want for the car.

We had the orders for (Aldershot) camp given us, so here they are Week – Days: - 6.30 p.m. reveille 7.30 Breakfast, 9.00 Parade, 1.15 lunch, 2.30 Demonstrations, 5.00 Tea, 6.30 Guard mounting, 7.45 Sing-song, 9.00 Prayers, 9.15 Supper, 9.30 1st Post, 10.00 Last Post, 10.15 Lights out.

Sunday. 7.30 Reveille, 8.00 H.C. 8.30 Breakfast. 10.30 Church parade. 11.15 Inspection of Camp. 1.15 Dinner. 2.15 Sports. 6.30 Tea. 7.15 Guard Mounting. 8.0 Service. 8.15 Supper. 9.30 1st Post. 10.0 Last Post. 10.15 Lights Out.

I am looking forward to it, we go by train to Aldershot (camp army training), I have offered my services for guard mounting. What you do is you have 2 hrs between 7.30 p.m. and 6 a.m. & have to guard the approaches to camp during the night. You have 2 hours each and the next day you get off, 2 hours parade & so you don't do badly. I think it is only one night during the week & it would be rather fun if you were at the time when the sun was rising.

Could I have my usual end of term money for my fare from camp home & could I borrow the rest because I have run out again. This term I have spent about £2 altogether, I don't mind much because it was mostly on fruit, which I don't get during other terms. Could I have the money sometime during the week. I will send you my camp address when I know it definitely. They say the food is rotten at camp except for porridge and potatoes, but a lovely canteen you can buy anything from chops to bulls eyes. Yesterday was the worst day we have this term. It rained solidly from morning till night & the wind was simply terrible. We had an athletics, match v Wellington, we won by one point.

The Bishop of London preached to-day usual things no teeth usual sort of sermon, mediocre. I think he's rather a sweet old boy. Exams begin tomorrow.

This afternoon I am going to pick raspberries, I found a place the other day about 2 miles away lovely ones. To-night the old Bish comes to our house and sits on our beds.

13th Dec 1936

Thank you for the 10 shillings, I will thank Daddy shall I ? He or you say that you will send £1 for my journey when I want it, would you please send it on Friday, so that it catches the post at Kingston not later than 4.30 p.m.home by Friday latest post at Kingston 4.30 p.m. It will reach me 1st post on Saturday & I shall buy the ticket on Saturday. It is no use writing to me after the last post from Kingston on Friday night because I start from the college at 6.45 a.m. on Monday Dec 21st.

I shall not want my bank – book, it was very kind of Daddy to give me the 10/- I can tell you it was very welcome. I think perhaps you will agree that I did not fritter the money that I have spent this term, I think I have grown out of that habit.

Today I am trying to write to the people who usually have a letter a term what a fag!!! Blinkers etc. he usually writes to me and it looks very funny when I answer after I have got one every term practically so I shall get one in first. Ask D.D. to forgive me writing to her please. I got a very nice letter from Ar Beet* on Wednesday.

I do admire Edward, don't you? After that speech of his on the wireless, poor man I thought it was terribly pathetic, saying that "he did not feel he could carry on the duties of Kingship without the woman he loved by his side" I was deeply moved at those words and the way he spoke about his mother & brother & Mr Baldwin.

I wish now he was still our King, before I did not want him after the beginning of the crisis but now my opinion has totally altered and I hope he lives a happy life with the woman he loves. I expect you listened in to his speech. I see that he is taking away with him his favourite picture of his father in one of his 43 trunks!

PS. Keep all the papers about Edward & George etc. I am keeping them but I shall cut them up to put in my scrapbook.

7.45 p.m.

Mr Cornwell is writing to you this evening. He told me go to-night so it will be all right. I did not ask him about it he just told me.

I see in London they are selling mementoes of King Edward his coronation mugs etc. Could you buy something for me to remember him by. Could you also KEEP an unused GEORGE V stamp.

*Aunt Beet is Mabel's sister Beatrice who was born in 1865, they have a sister Aunt Jessie born 1875

Chapter 2

World War II

Douglas with his Mother & Father

Dug joins the Royal Artillery at Aldershot and the war is approaching. On 23rd August 1939 Germany signed the Non-Aggression pact with the Soviet Union and on 1st September 1939 Germany invades Poland, 3rd September Britain and France declare war on Germany.

On 27th August 1939 Douglas writes,
Please excuse my writing but yesterday the whole regt (including me) was inoculated against typhoid, incase we go abroad, & I can't use my left arm, it makes me feel a bit funny. I had lunch with Pastes to-day & would have stayed to tea only we are not

allowed to leave the barracks for long then we have to be near here.

We are all very busy (doing nothing much).

How are you all ? I don't think I shall be able to come home on Wed.

Then on the 30th August 1939

Things are just about the same, great preparations. We don't think there will be war.

I will try & come over after duty on Friday night I would arrive @ Surbiton at 5.30, could I be met ? Let me know if you are going out though. I may not be able to come & shan't know till 4.30 p.m !! as many things turn up at the last minute.

Tomorrow (Thurs) Daddy & Ma must go to photographer & have their photographs taken together the same size I am sending you, a decent photographer I paid £1 1s for 3, as they were cheap I had 6 little ones done one each for my sisters and others to ? My Godmother? Ar Nellie ? Ar J.B. ? Blinkers ?

When Boss goes home she & Dar must have their photos taken only if war comes I shall want to take an up to date one with me of you all.

As result of the calling out of army reserve I regret I can't come home tomorrow, could you come over here for an hour or two either at 5.30 p.m on Saturday or 3.30 p.m on Sunday. Sat would suit me best. If you can come meet me where I pointed out – on the opposite side of the road to my room.

Have you been to the photographer? I am sure you would not like me to go to the war without an up to date photo of you both.

The next letter from Douglas is 13th September saying that the troops are at Farnham Surrey and are getting fed up waiting to go off to war.

From Douglas 23rd Sept 1939 12 noon. 2nd Lt D.E.N.Heelas,
21st Anti-Tank Regiment R.A.
I am not absolutely positive but everything points to us going off to-day. Don't you worry I shall look after myself!! I will send

the field postcard to Boss at Broadstairs as I don't know your Broadstairs address, I think it will be better that way then she can communicate to you wherever you are.

4.15 p.m. What a nice lot of letters you are getting from me !! My address from now on is 2nd Lt D.E.N.Heelas, BB Battery, 21st Anti – Tank Regiment R.A., c/o Army Post Office.

We leave here early tomorrow (Friday) morning.

I will write again as soon as allowed.

Telegraph office in London, tell them to send parcel of papers twice a week so I always see every paper starting from last Saturdays you can pay for them it won't cost much. Only I don't want you to send them as as if they do they will reach me much quicker.

I will write again when I have time.

At this time Dorothy was working in the Auxiliary Territorial Service and applied for a job driving in France, but she did not get the job and continued working for the A.T.S. in London throughout the war.

The next letters from Douglas to his parents were all written with his address as 'Somewhere in France' since if they were intercepted the Germans wouldn't have the address of the soldiers.

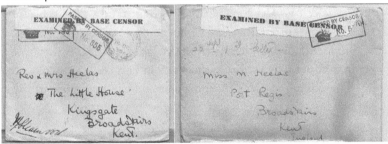

Envelopes with censor marks

9

23rd Sept 1939 Saturday 3 p.m. Somewhere in France
We arrived France this morning after an uneventful crossing the sea was a little bit choppy and the boat rolled quite a lot. I slept the night under a table in the saloon. We continued our journey this evening. We have been looking around the place all day and changing our money into French.

I don't seem to have heard from you for some time so hope you write soon and tell me where you are.

I am sending this letter to Muriel, so ring Ma & Pa up if they are still at Teddington and tell them that I am fit and enjoying my continental holiday!!

26th Sept 1939 Tuesday. Somewhere in France
We arrived here on Sunday and are billeted again on the French.

I had never realised they were so backward in sanitary arrangements. There are no baths what so ever and all their lavatories are like Ar Jessie's was at Hampden.

I am enjoying myself very much and I think everybody is as well, there is quite a lot of work to do so I am not board. The weather is absolutely perfect sun the whole day long but very cold at night.

At some military shops they sell canvas baths about two feet wide & two feet long with a wooden stand will you please purchase one & send it.

I have not had any letters from you yet but probably they will come soon actually no one has had any in France.

There is a great lack of newspapers so will you write to the Daily.

2nd Oct 1939 Monday Somewhere in France
I am so sorry for not having written before, but we have been on the move a bit and it has been very difficult to write & as we are not allowed to post letters from ordinary post boxes, it has been very difficult (in fact impossible to post anything).

First I had better put your minds at rest we are in no danger at all where we are in fact just as safe as you in England. When I left England I thought I would never see a bed again, or have any good food, but this must be a very queer war, I have never slept one night without a bed and you know how comfortable the beds in France are. We are as I said before billeted with French people. They are awfully kind to us and make us as comfortable as they possibly can and most of them tell us of their experiences in the last war!!

For food the men get excellent stuff cooked by the regiment cooks etc. The officers we go usually to a restaurant or hotel in the village or town where we are, but when we get settled a bit, as I think we are now we shall probably set up an officer's mess. All the other officers are awfully nice and we all seem to get on very well together, there are no "flies in the ointment" at all. The men in our battery are all terribly nice and they all seem very happy and contented, although some of their sleeping places have been very bad.

As we have not been able to send mail likewise we have not received any since last Thursday but I got a letter from you which you posted on the Friday before, put the date on them please. In answer to your letter:-

I don't mind Bernard having my bicycle a bit I am sorry it was smashed in transit.

A franc is worth 1 1/2d not 3 1/2d, we get a beautiful (what adjectives I use) evening dinner cost 20 francs (2s6d) four or five courses in these hotels & restaurants.

Answer to Daddy's letter which came in the same envelope. There is no marching behind bands singing Tipperary, I wish there were!! Hope you enjoyed yourself at Tetbury I expect by the time you get this letter you will be at Broadstairs.

I was amused by Daddy's remark "Mr Stuges will be very much missed, he did all the church accounts" Is that all he will be missed for ?? That made me laugh no end.

On our drives through towns & villages all the inhabitants come out and cheer and throw fruit to us, if we are going slow enough, the fruit is very abundant and if you walk even down the street of a village, you are given peaches pears & apples & we are often told in orchards where we stay to take as much fruit as we want. The hedges along the road are crammed with blackberries the natives don't seem to eat them. We have had two or three blackberry and apple pies.

It is very difficult to say much because we are not allowed to mention names of places. I could mention many where we have been through on our many holidays. I am aching to let you know where I am now and I don't think it would be against the rules if I told you we are near where mother & I went for that little trip a year or two ago alone and coming along the road to-day I saw the actual thing that we came to see when we both got soaked to the skin. But this information is secret & you must not mention to anybody the actual name of the place.

I have had a nasty cold for the last few days & it won't clear up, it has not had much chance lately. The weather up till now has been perfect sun all day and everyday. But the wind here is awful. I believe there is a big bag of mail for us so I expect I shall hear from you in it. Naturally don't mention in any letters to me the name of the place I am near, we are about 10 miles out of it. It is alright to tell you the information about it which I have given you as I have asked a competent authority but it is SECRET.

Send this on to Aunt Beet & Aunt Jessie I will write to them when I have got time.

If possible I will write 2 letters a week to you but don't get worried if you don't get them & there won't always be much to say.

With much love Don't worry about me.

Dug's letter of the 6th October from somewhere in France is addressed to his parents who are staying with Boss in Broadstairs Kent. In it he says 'I am relieved to know you are safe in Boss's hands if I were you I should stay they should stay there until I come back after the war'.

On the Sunday they had a church parade and about 250 men turned up, the singing was terrific, there was no music and the service lasted about 25 minutes.

Douglas's letter had a list of things he wanted (Carbolic soap, torch batteries) because as he put it 'the French govt have taken them over', he also suggests 'How about knitting me a khaki pullover for winter!' and also some boxes of 50 Players cigarettes.' Also he wants a new photograph of Ma & Pa together in a folding traveling frame with celluloid as glass and one which folds over about double the size of a postcard.

In the first budget of the war on 27th Sept 1939 Sir John Smith had increased income tax from 5s6d to 7s6d in the pound, and in Dug's letter of

12th Oct 1939

I am sorry to hear the I/Tax is 7s 6d in the £1, that will hit the dividends rather hard. I have added it up & you will be about £20 poorer p.a. If you are ever short just let me know as I think I shall have a lot spare.

Could you send me a large bottle of aspirins, small will do only I get a head-ache now & again from my cold, which is better but I can't get rid of the cough I should like some lozenges too because of a tickle in my throat what a lot of complaints. But I am very well, not much to do though. Send me a 6d book every fortnight or 3 weeks, sort of thriller, not too thrilling!

15th Oct 1939

The weather here is awful it rains a lot & the mud is terrible, I was very glad I bought those gum boots in England. The last few days we have been putting bricks down where our vehicles are & it is great fun although I don't do much! The wind is awful too. When you go out on your walks on the cliff mind you don't go to near the edge. If you are driven into Margate every day you won't have much petrol left. What do you mean by "awful war" You wouldn't know there was a war on here. I am glad Dar has got a nice job in London, does she like it?

I think it is very unlikely I will get any leave before March but I don't really know.

On the 16th Dug got the job of censoring the men's letters and said they write reams! He says he hates the job and it is very monotonous. It had been raining a lot 'The Church service was cancelled yesterday because it rained & they didn't want the troops to get wet marching there, it was rather disappointing'.

There is no news at all. It has rained solidly day & night for the last two days. There are strong rumours that leave starts next month, how true they are I don't know but it is something to look forward to. It is wonderful what an influence letters have on the men especially me. So write (as you do) every other day without fail, also send some writing paper.

This is important.

As you know I have worn my army jacket everyday for 6 months & needless to say it is getting a bit shabby, so I suggest you write to J.G.Plumb & Son (116?) Victoria Street London, and order one to be made as soon as possible & send out direct. They are £6 10s, but I feel it is worth it because I want to look nice when I come on leave etc. I also want an S.D. cap R.A. they will have those in stock and also my size so tell them to send one off now. I think I shall be paid quite soon now. Tell them to be quick with my jacket.

Try & sell back my tail coat etc. to Barkers if you can because when the war is over I shall go straight to theologic college & thence to the army & shall wear evening uniform in the army. I am still quite happy and enjoying myself. Hope you are all the same.

22nd Oct 1939

I have not had any letter from you in five days, it is not your fault because nobody in the regiment has, but I am getting a bit feed up about it. This afternoon I went for a 4 mile walk with the Major to reconnoiter a gun position.

The weather has been a bit better last two or 3 days but of course mud is still awful.

When the mail does come I expect to have heaps of letters (saved up) from you.

The paper does not come round this way except one who sells the continental Daily Mail, which is two pages. Tell Dar I have started to use her cigarette case.

Don't bother to send cigarettes now as we can get them @ 20 for 6d unless Ar J.B. sends them.

I want some thick pants because I don't think I have got any.

We read in the papers how these organisations give cinema & variety shows to the troops in England, it makes me sick we get nothing like that. Troops in England can go to a cinema there easily. There is a filthy little cinema here but it is crowded with troops French films and the dearest is only 4 francs = 6d, the cheapest is 2d.

I am looking forward to the mail coming then I will answer your letters.

Much love Still very happy & well. Hope you are all the same.

27th Oct 1939

Thanks you very much for:-

(i) Soap (ii) Picture Post (iii) 2 letters Oct 21st Sat & Thurs not dated presumably 19th which came after 21st one. (iv) aspirins, cascara etc (v) chocolates (vii) Torch from Dar (vii) Book from Boss (viii) 2 Daily Sketch. I think that is all I have or am or I am enjoyed them all. The chocs were a bit stale but quite nice.

Don't talk about rain! We seem to have it all day & every day & I wade about in my gum boots more than ankle deep in mud, they are the greatest friend here!!! It must be lovely for you to see the ships and also I always love a really rough sea

I will now explain about Lloyds Bank. I quite agree I was very sorry to leave Lloyds Teddington because they were so nice. But as soon as I transferred to Cox & Kings they paid me without any forms to fill in, which I have found out was holding up my pay & I have authorised them to pay my Mess Bills also which they will do & also they will see that I am paid regularly and will see I get all my allowances & everything like that. So I feel I have done the right thing & also here I can draw 800 francs from the field cashier three times a month ie. 2,400 francs a month well if I don't draw all that as I don't, they will see that I am credited it to their bank as it should be which is very difficult for Lloyds Teddington to do. The only alternative is which I think is quite a good idea keep a deposit account at Teddington & save up some money because I spend very little out here. If you think that is a good idea I will do it, let me know. Another alternative is to send a cheque on Cox's every now & again to Lloyds Tedd & use them for out going cheques & keep Cox's for incoming money only.

But I hope you see my point about transferring & I think it will turn out better in the end because I am assured of getting paid what is due to me &the army don't give you your pay they make it as hard as possible for you!! Write to Lloyds Tedd for me & tell them to cancel the Mess Bills I do not intend to pay the mess till I get paid. I hope they are not offended at me leaving them as you rather make out in your letter, I wrote a very kind letter & explained how things stood.

Don't worry about pocket money for me I can get more than I want. But if Daddy is ever short don't hesitate to write to me and I will send him a cheque by return because I am a rich man!! I told you in a letter which you must have got by now that I have been paid £49-9-0. As I said in another letter don't bother about cigs any more as they are dirt cheap 50 cigs cost 1s 3d (about).

They have opened a N.A.A.F.I. canteen here & we can buy almost anything chocolate, tinned fruit, sherry, soap, toothpaste, razor blades, biscuits everything else one needs except torch batteries.

I have read a lot of English newspapers lately which seem to me would startle some people who had sons or husbands in the B.E.F., most of what I read as far as I know are not true, so take everything you read with a pinch of salt. I am quite safe and happy & enjoying myself and I think the men are too, except we would rather be at home. Lets hope there will be some leave soon as I am sure there will be. What a long letter. I am just off to have dinner (7.30 p.m.) so will end. I hope you are all very well & still enjoying yourselves I am expecting a letter from Boss give her my love.

I hope to play football tomorrow or Sunday & go to church.

30th Oct. 1939

I am sending you some razor blades as I can send them by post they are rather late for your birthday but you will have to excuse that. Thanks for the 50 cigs from Mrs Allison I will write & thank her, today I had a letter from Ar J.B. and also 50 cigs so I am well stocked, we have an issue of 50 per week, but they don't last long. Thank you also for the writing paper I like this so much now that I don't want to change.

To-day has been the first fine day we have had for 3 weeks sun all day but very cold.

I think I shall be seeing you all within the next few months as rumour is very strong that we are getting leave soon. It is important in this respect to keep me informed of your whereabouts as I expect I shall only be able to give you an approx day of my arrival.

2ⁿᵈ Nov 1939

This will be a v. short letter, thanks for your letter. I have sent my batman out to buy eggs and all he says is oofs he gets them, when I go I pronounce it properly but oofs is quite enough. I am enclosing a photograph* of the people I am billeted on, she is much fatter than you she is 62 & he is 68, he used to be the station master here, 3 trains per day. She is the sweetest old French woman I have met & is always laughing, I call her my second mother when I have a tear in my coat or button off I always take it to her & in the evening a Capt & I have dinner which she cooks three courses for about 2/- inclusive of drink, then after dinner he & I go to the kitchen listen to the news & then talk to them in French, I am trying to teach them English too. Will write again when I get your letter this afternoon.

French couple Douglas stays with

3rd Nov 1939

My new address instead of c/o army Post Office, British Expeditionary Force. The rest is the same. Thank you v. much for letter dated 28 Oct. enclosing all Dar's letters she seems to be enjoying herself. Can't imagine her sweeping out cloak rooms though.

I am sorry you are having such awful weather, I think it is wise that you are going back to Teddington because you are both prone to colds and there won't be any worry there now for you for which I am glad, but if there is one air raid on London go back to Broadstairs. I'd like & that is a plum cake made by you. I suggest you put it in a round tin and sew it round with white cloth. Lots of parcels come like that it is a special kind of cloth & in a tin it would not be stale. I think I shall get leave next month, but have not been told for certain.

4th Nov 1939

Thank you v. much for your letter of Oct:30 (last Monday) You said you were sending it by air mail but I expect that was not possible. Thanks also for 4 pairs of socks & chocolate please remember though that I dislike plain chocolate intensely & had to give it away, I should have thought Boss knew that, my favourite is nut milk choc. But the box you sent it in was not good and half torn away, it was a boot box.

You seem to pay a fabulous price for butter, would you like me to send you out some, it is about 1/1d per lb here & I don't think I have to pay the postage.

We are having a church parade tomorrow @ 10.30 a.m. followed by H.C. which I shall attend. One of the men plays the piano very well.

5th Nov 1939 "BB' Battery 21st Anti Tank Regt RA, British Expeditionary Force.

Thank you v. much for your letter of Tues 31/10/39. It seems to take just 5 days. I am enclosing a little present for Ma this makes up all the 2/6d's per week which I have missed. Will you please buy Daddy 100 cigarettes with it. I would like to pay what I owe Daddy so let me know. This is part of the thanks for the affection you both show to me in your letters and the rest is my affection for you (if you can understand that last sentence you will be lucky because I can't, but you know what I mean).

I have not yet heard when I shall get leave.

Now about the soap question, you say I was quite snuffy. Here is the full story. I wrote to you for some soap, which you sent and it was just what I wanted. In a letter in the box you said as it cost so much to send can't you buy it out there, so I wrote back and said I could. So Bah! To you.

When I come home we are going out to the Palace Theatre one matinee aft, in the best seats but I will let you know details of that later.

We had a church service to-day a padre came named Bird who is a parson near Epsom. He is not much good as an army chaplain, but quite a nice service.

8th Nov 1939

You ask about my billet, I have a room next to the Majors in a big chateau a very nice bed etc. This house is not the same as the place where the couple who's photograph I sent live, but I can't explain how but I shall go back to there soon. My batman looks after me and does everything, I send my washing to the village every week which is very nice. I sacked the batman I came out of England with as he was too young & no good. I got another but he did not like the job. I have now got a very nice one who used to be a major's batman in another regt for 5 years, but I believe he is leaving us for another regt, but I hope he will not have to. The capt and I don't sleep in the same place together now, but I see him quite often.

Thank you for the hair-raising books I have not started them yet. I'm afraid I can't keep up with acknowledging all the parcels I have thanked for them all. You do amuse me I receive some socks one day and two days after you say I have not thanked for, how could you have got the letter in that short time, or perhaps I am wrong & it was the parcel before with socks & choc, but I know I thanked for them because I said the chocs were stale. I could do with some more handkerchiefs please, do you knit hanks!!! You be very careful on a bicycle, I don't feel very happy about you riding but if Boss thinks it is alright you can, but if she lets you be very careful. If I was there I would not let you.

Tomorrow I am going to dig some gun pits. About me being so rich. We have rations just like the men do and we make them do for breakfast lunch & tea, and we always go out for dinner which costs 18 francs 2s per day including drink. At Aldershot I had to pay 3/6d a day. Laundry a month costs about 8/6d, at Aldershot it was 18/6d. There are no Mess charges here at Aldershot it was £2 a month. So you see I am much richer and there are no entertainments to go to. At Aldershot I went to the pictures at least three times a week in 2/- seats. There are no train fares home here, at Aldershot I came home to Kingston nearly every week that cost 5/-, so you see I am a rich man. I am just going to have a bath 6.30 p.m., will finish this when I am clean.

I have just finished my bath 7.15 p.m. & feel nice & clean the first proper one for nearly a month.

I have just put Ar J.Y's pullover. I think how she measured it, is to try it on Ar Beat & hope I am the same size. Evidently I am ½ as big as Ar Beat I should think it would fit an elephant!! Lets hope yours is smaller. You are lucky having such nice cheap fish. I have not had any sardines since I left Blighty. I shall love some mittens which I hear DD is going to make, I hope I get them before next summer.

I am going to send you cheese during the next few days as the major says it is the most delicious he has tasted. I did not like it.

We are having great does on Sat next Nov 11th We are having poppies to start with then 5 men from our battery & some from other regts are going to parade in the market square round the war memorial (not this war) and the French are going to parade opposite them and then wreaths will be laid. In the afternoon we are having a tea party in the other village (my idea this) and we are asking all the village people and the soldiers, after ten we are going to have songs then end up with the Marseillaise & Nat Anthem. The place is going to be decorated with French & English flags all the men are going to pay 5 francs each and the officers will pay 100 each. In the evening we are going to have a dinner party of other officers & listen to the Queen's speech..

You must be careful with your lights or else you will be fined. About the bank at one time I was overdrawn 14/- as they wrote & told me, so send the copy of the letter which they sent you & send them as I have forgotten what I said & you said it was very nice.

I am sending this cutting out of the continental Daily Mail, relatives of personnel serving with the B.E.F. can apply for them to be sent home on leave on compassionate grounds, just in case you want me for serious illness.

I have not heard definitely when I am going on leave but leave starts on Dec 17th and is for 10 days port to port. 12 ½ % of the battery can go at one time but I expect there will be a special rota for officers so there is quite a chance I may be back for Xmas.

10th Nov 1939

No letter today from you it is not your fault as there is very little mail to-day. Consequently there is no news. I have done a lot of digging the last two days & feel quite thin now.

I think it is very doubtful if I get leave for Christmas as I think they send married ones first which I think is very logical. I am looking forward to our party tomorrow (Nov:11) I will tell you how it goes in the next letter. I have got a poppy.

Buy a small present Not more than 3/6 each from my £5 for Boss & Dar if you can from me.

12th Nov 1939

I am sending off the cheese which I promised you at the same time as this letter. It is only for you two and Boss & Dar (if they are there) but nobody else, so when anybody else comes in hide it unless of course you don't like it. Let me know if you have to pay duty or anything on it, if nothing or a little and you like the cheese I will send a box every week because it is only 4 francs = 6d. I have sent a box to the Aunts at Bloomfield. I like the writing pad you sent very much but I have found this writing paper and like it better.

I received my tunic and cap from Plumbs on Friday I think I must have another pair of slacks could you order them from Plumbs please tell them to match my tunic and about ½" smaller round the waist. The tunic is very nice indeed. Send me the bill

21

and I will pay as I had my monthly a/c from Lloyds (Cox) to-day & I have got £60-8-0 in it. I still owe my mess bill £18 and your cheque £5 and about £9 which I have spent here in francs to be deducted. So that leaves £28-8 and so I can afford it all right and the bill will only be about £10 and then I can start saving. I get about £18 per month. I got paid for Oct very promptly as I bank at Coxes.

It is very warm (for the time of year) here and I expect it is the same with you so I should certainly stay till the end of this month but be careful and keep Daddy well wrapped up and also yourself. I hope you got the razor blades all right. Thanks for Sunday Graphic please send it every week, I still get the D.Tele every day, I am going to write to my Godmother again this evening.

We also no Guy Fawkes here on the 5/11/39!!!

Yesterday we had a parade round the French war memorial the Major of the town laid a wreath followed by a high army rank officer, last post, 2 mins silence rev, that was all naturally it rained. In the aft we had our own tea party of the villagers nearly 200 turned up. In the evening us officers (us 3) had a party of our own and asked in two others, the menu was Hors d'oeuvre, soup, entrée of cauliflower (?), Lobster, chicken peas etc fruit & cakes excellent dinner. Afterwards the family of the house came in and we danced for a bit. I danced once with the maid!! and trod on her toes a lot.

Must end now. I am still very well & happy no colds or other diseases!!

16th Nov 1939

Thanks for the 20 fcs in the chocs. Thank you very much. I don't know if you made a mistake in my likes of chocolate but I DON'T like PLAIN choc. There is a N.A.A.F.I here & I can get any kind of choc. I bought a toothbrush there to-day, I have taken to smoking a pipe again. Tobacco is very cheap (English) because we get it without duty. The pants you sent are very nice indeed.

Did you hear the concert Broadcast Gracie Fields gave to the troops in France yesterday evening two of our battery went and said it was absolutely marvellous, they went to the actual show.*

I remember (now you say) how we were sitting at that restaurant & bought a paper & it showed the floods at Kingston, I have not been there again.

Yesterday & to-day the weather has been awful, wind & rain the whole time.

I wish you would hurry with that that photograph. A week after you receive this letter you are to send me a photo of you both together, one which is new.

I had a good mail to-day, a letter from you one from Ar Beat another from Canon Anderson and one from Mrs Aked-Davis who said she had just sent off a parcel to me, it has not arrived yet though she said 'I shall always remember your kindness to Geoffery at Paddington Station and Geoffery carrying a colossal suitcase and you (that's me) always so nobly coming to help him" I have written to Geoffery & he gave his mother my address, awfully nice of her I thought.

I am not staying with couple who's photograph I sent you at the moment, but as Daddy said at a chateau we have the English news every evening at 9 pm but there is never anything new. I am glad Boss mucks in with my letters but she is not to muck in with the letters you send me !! Dar is very good at writing I get about one a fortnight it is about time I wrote her again.

*The first overseas show given by ENSA was headed by Gracie Fields 15th Nov 1939 in Douai, France.

19th Nov 1939

Thank you very much for the pants, Punch, Sunday Graphic & cake. We are going to have the cake for tea, the major has one sent out nearly every week which I share so he will share mine. Also thanks for the milk whipper walnuts, they are very good. It is very nice not having to put a stamp on my letters. It is 'San fairy ann' not as you said 'an fairy ann' in French it is 'Ce n'est pas rien' no is not I don't know what is it.

Could you please get me 6 darts as the major had a dartboard sent out a fortnight ago and the darts are wearing out. Quite good ones about 2/- for 6 is the right price. I think I am quite good at darts. Last night I went to dinner with my Scotch friend & we played vinqt-et-un, I won 10 francs not bad eh! This evening I am going to a drinking party at 6 p.m. to meet a Brig-General quite a nice chap I think from what I knew of him in England. I don't think we had a church service to-day anyway I did not go. The weather to-day is awful terrific wind and rain. I had my hair cut also'.

21st Nov

I was reading to-day statistics of road deaths in Britain, & 60% of the people killed on roads after dark were over 60 years old, so neither of you are to go out at all after dark, Boss you are to see this is strictly enforced. I will write again when I get your letter to-morrow. I am delighted to hear you are both so well. I am also very well & happy but longing to come home.

22nd Nov 1939

Thank you v. much for letter 17/11/39 and also handkerchiefs which I got to-day, will you also send 2 or 3 tins of elastoplast from any chemist as I am always cutting my hand on corrugated iron or such like and a major who was in the last war says that this soil is dangerous if it gets into cuts etc. I have two doses of anti-tetanus serum so should be fairly all right. I can't afford to send anymore cheese as it costs me too much to send, the cheese itself cost 4 francs and 7 francs postage which seems to me to be too much. Have you found that any of my letters are opened at Base? I tell you what I would like for a Christmas present and that is Punch sent every week you might start now, it would be better if you bought it yourselves then read it then posted it to me. I would like two special copies one of the Christmas number which is 1/- & the other I think 21/10/39 it is a number compiled of a lot of cartoons of the last war probably you will have to write direct to Punch for that. Could I also have a box of Simpson's Iodine Soap. I use about a tablet every 6 days. I have seen one or two Bosche airplanes here and one I saw brought down the one day. I have been doing a lot of digging lately, which I enjoy very much. We often have Soles here probably not Dover and they are really delicious cooked by the French when we have dinner in the evening.

24th Nov 1939

Your letters always take five days to reach me. The Daily T. only takes 3 days but it is posted in the early hours of the day 12.45 a.m. Generally which really is not bad. Don't mention any names of French places please in your letters any more I mean near here I think it is killing Dar having to do drill, when you next write thank her for her last letter which I have never answered. She seems to enjoy herself going to pictures etc. . Yesterday & day before it was real winter weather, white frosts and to-day it was much warmer and rained all day and to-night there is a very clear moon, so think to-morrow will be cold again. I am sure now I shall like the helmet when it comes! I heard DD was making me mittens will they be finished before next summer? I doubt it myself!!! I get up every morning at about 7.45 a.m. have breakfast at 8.15 a.m. and go to parade about 8.45 then dig till lunch at about 1.15, then muck about (specially for Daddy's benefit) till tea, then play darts & write letters, have a wash then go to dinner at 8 p.m. bed 10.15. I have seen a wireless & don't know whether is waste of money to buy it, it is a beautiful one worked from electric light, 880 francs about £4 10s, it seems rather a waste to me as we can get papers. I wouldn't mind so much if it was portable. See if you can get a cheap portable for me and if they (the people you get it from) think it is possible send it out here , otherwise keep it till I come on leave. I feel it is rather waste if I buy this electric because if we go away from electric it is useless & I can get the battery charged up for nothing. I will write again soon.On second thoughts don't bother about the wireless It would be more trouble than it is worth carting it about.

28th Nov 1939

Thanks for chocolate & torch battery, I should very much like another cake please. I also thought my clothes from Plumbs were v. expensive. Our battery had two tickets to hear Gracie the other day and it was decided by votes.

To-day has been a lovely day sun all day but a sharp wind; yesterday & the day before were awful rain & wind all day. If I were you I were you I should stay where you are till just before Christmas because it is 1000-1 against me being home much before the end of Febuary or beginning of March, it then rather depends on the state of the war but I am NOT quite sure of this. I can't really say when I shall be back because we had not had any details of leave for officers.

Why do you send a rug to be brushed in Scotland haven't you got a clothes brush yourself? Boss will like going to Wales if the school moves I expect. If there is an air raid warning when I come on leave I refuse to go down any shelter, when the Bosche flies over here I just stand & look, and I shan't waste ½ hour of my 10 days on leave & if I am with you, you won't go down either.

I am glad you like the cheese I send, I will bring some more when I come on leave, also about 12lbs of butter as well. There is no more news to tell you. I am going to my 2nd mother on Friday.

6th Dec 1939

At the moment we are 9 in the mess (reason secret). Some of our chaps went to the Leslie Henson concert the other day and they were rather disappointed because the two leading ladies Binnie Hale & Vi Loraine were in a car accident that evening. I was told that I can go to a film which is being specially shown on Friday at 5.30 p.m. I must have some riding breeches & will you write to Plumbs or somebody & have them made the cheapest they can & also a large pair of puttees, R.A. style I expect I shall have to pay £4 or 5 but it will be money well spent & if Plumbs have not started my slacks tell them to cancel that order. I want them in the shortest possible time, as the battle - dress which we have to wear is in my opinion quite useless. One of our men saw the king yesterday*, where mother & I know well. We have bought a pig for the men for Christmas, us 3 officers are giving it as a present to them. It cost 450 frs and coming tomorrow, we have a lot of swill which we can feed it on, and we are debating whether to give it gentle exercise, if so I hope to get a bit of string & walk it down the village street. There is the most beautifully kept British cemetery here which I am going to see more closely to-morrow & the keeper of it is English & lives in the village he has a French wife. I ordered 30 lbs of Christmas Pudding yesterday from a N.A.A.F.I. for the men, we are going to do them really well, they deserve it & as far as that goes do ourselves as well too. They carry the blackout too far in England, here they are not nearly so particular, the shops have their front lights on etc slightly blacked, but they don't bother about chinks of light, which is quite logical as you can't see chinks from the air, you tell that to the next ARP man who goes to you. I normally get up at a ¼ to 8 in the mornings. We play darts every evening and we are all a very happy party, call each other by Christian names, the 2nd Lieuts don't call Majors by theirs, but the Majors call us by ours, which is right I think.

When I come on leave I don't want to see or go to parties to anyone outside the family, there are exceptions D.D. is one, the other I want to ask in to supper are Russell Whites, and a few friends from school I want to see ie Desmond, Aked etc perhaps Canon Anderson he write regularly to me & Blinkers. I shall go & see Tate & Mrs Howard. We shall go to the theatre and I am looking forward to it we are all going to have a marvellous time. I shall bring back plenty of butter as I see that rationing comes in on 8/1/40. Will you excuse me if I don't send Christmas presents to you as it is awfully difficult. Let me know where you will be for Christmas?

* George V1 made a visit to B.E.F. in France from 5th Dec, the visit was kept a secret, his Majesty spent several days in France to inspect front line positions. He was accompanied by the Duke of Gloucester Sir Alexander Hardinge (his private secretary).

10th Dec 1939

Thank you very much for your box of soap, darts etc which came yesterday, they are all just what I wanted. Also thanks for the many letters & Sunday Graphic & News Review. I had a parcel from Mrs Thorpe also sending mittens scarf & socks which was v. kind of her. I am so busy this week I that I don't know when I shall have time to write & thank her we have an exercise on Wednesday, about 1 ½ hours to censoring every evening, working outside all day & I have to prepare two lectures for Thursday, one on camouflage. But I will try & write to her to-morrow. We had a church service this evening at 5.15, 7 men attended, the Major

& myself. I went to the cinema yesterday and saw an English film called "Night Flight" 7 years old, then had dinner in a big town near then walked home.

12th Dec 1939

Don't bother to send me any more batteries for my torch as I can get them easily out here now. I bought a lot of Christmas cards today and yesterday I bought about 12 from the Regt which I like the best one will come to you next post.

I shall be able to let you know the time of my arrival by telegram from the port of disembarkation I know where I land and where I arrive but can't tell you in a letter.

13th Dec 1939 B.E.F. Christmas card 1939

16th Dec 1939

I had a lot of books sent me to-day by Blinkers, which was very nice, 4 penguin series books. We have decided not to give the pig exercise he just eats & sleeps all day & is getting fatter. We have also ordered the 30lbs of Christmas pudding and about 12 geese.

I was sorry I did not see the King. I got the box of darts thanks. Could you please send as soon as possible some leads for the pencil you gave me.

When is my balaclava coming, the cold is frightful here, it is freezing hard this evening a biting wind & the clouds look full of snow, it has tried hard to snow all day. I watched our battery play football this afternoon and my ears were frozen

I hope you have a very happy Christmas because we shall have one out here. Our program for the 25th is this, Troop football matches in the morning, men's dinner at 2 p.m. which we attend. In the evening there is to be a men's concert which I expect us officers will attend. Boxing day we attend sergeant's mess dinner, but we ourselves will probably dine quietly with a couple of turkeys & pudding etc, but that is how I like it. I hope you all have a lovely Christmas and prosperous New Year and I shall be back with you soon after so cheer up. I am very happy & well but am looking forward to my balaclava. All my love to you both for many more years of happiness & prosperity.

22nd Dec 1939

The cold here is awful there was a beautiful white frost this morning & fog, the fog cleared about 11 a.m. and the sun shone all day but it did not thaw at all and it is still cold to-night, but my bed is very nice & warm. The men have two fires in their room so should be alright.

27th Dec 1939

Thank you ever so much for your lovely presents, I am wearing Daddy's now and have half eaten Mother's, I liked the pigs very much. We had a marvellous Christmas here, we all enjoyed ourselves very much indeed. I will relate our programme of the week-end. We had quite a white Christmas not snow but plenty of frost. On Sunday 24/12/39 at 11 a.m. we had our Christmas service, we started with 'Hark the Herald' and for other hymns we had 'while shepherds watch their flocks', 'Good King Wenceslas', 'First Noel' ended up with the King. I have never heard such lusty singing, the men seemed to thoroughly enjoy themselves H.C. after. Then read most of the afternoon at 6.30 p.m. we had a concert arranged by a warrant officer which was very well done. In the evening we walked to a nearby town to have our own Christmas dinner, the streets were terribly icy. We had an excellent dinner asparagus, soup, turkey etc, then walked back and went to bed by then 3 a.m.!! On Christmas morning I helped the Capt with the men's dinners decorating the room and tables etc, at noon we three officers went to have a drink with the sergeants in their mess (as is the custom on the 25th Dec). We had our own dinner of cold turkey. We let our batmen go off all day so had to do our meals ourselves. At 2 p.m. we went to see the men have their dinners consisting of goose, Brussels, roast spuds, pork and Christmas pudding. We had bought some beer for them, and then found that Guinness's had give enough bottles of beer to B.E.F. for everyman, so they had both, we had some crackers and also put the King and Queen's Christmas cards on the table one for each man. Then at 3pm I went to hear the Kings speech across the road. The Colonel had given us four bottles of Champagne and I had 5 glasses and did not feel to well in the aft. At 3.30 p.m. the Colonel himself came to visit. In the evening I helped get the dinner ready and went to bed 11.30 p.m.

Are you licensing the car this quarter if not here's what to do, license it at the end of January, so you can obtain the petrol, then we shall have that and Feb's petrol and I may be able to get 300 miles worth myself, but I am not sure as the car is not registered in my name you might try & find out about that if I can't have the petrol can you register the car in my name for a bit. Also tell Boss to get some petrol out of Sir Milson for me. I thought we would have one trip to Ar Beets one to Ar J.B's calling at Marlboro' on the way so we want as much as poss and one trip to Aunt Nelly and then muck about. I had some cigarettes from D.D.

We might also when I come on leave go to Broadstairs & spend the night if Boss can't possibly leave. I got all my presents from you Boss & Dar on the 23rd Dec which was very nice. I have many more letters to write so must stop. I am glad Daddy is so well and you also I hope. No going out after dark or in the cold wind. I am very well & happy. I am open to a cake any time now. P.S. I enclose the Kings Christmas card for you to see. Look after it and don't loose it keep it till I come home.

28th Dec 1939
To night it is snowing hard and there is already about 3" of snow on the ground so that won't improve things. I hope you all had a happy Christmas and hope you will have a merry new year. I am

glad you will have plenty of petrol for me when I come on leave. What I would like is for you to meet me at Victoria having come by train and Dar meet us at Teddington sta with car that will save some petrol but I will leave it to you. Ar J.Y. sent me a diary which is very nice so really don't want another I hope Daddy enjoyed himself at Ar J.B.'s and that he arrived home safe & sound but he must not go there again when there is so much dark about. I wear Daddy's pullover every day now & it is very nice & warm.

1st Jan 1940

Many many happy returns of the day. May you and Daddy live many more years in happiness & comfort and continue as you have been an inspiration to your children. We have all shared your joys and sorrows and in what ever trouble you have been in, you have always come out on top trusting in Gods great love and I know how much hope and strength it has given you. I am writing this letter listening to the wireless on the student songs, and they are singing "Little Brown Jug" which I know you like very much, I remember you singing it now & again. May this year will bring you joy & happiness and every success in the world to you both, and also I hope that this year will bring us peace and that we shall all join our loves again, and that I shall be home for good from another war to end wars.

I saw the old year out by having an evening with some friends (officers) just down the road, I retired to bed 2 a.m. this morning. Thanks for the walnuts etc they are lovely and I am having a party to-night and the menu is, soup, Russian salad, chicken, peas, spuds, mushroom omelettes and if there is any more room your walnuts. After that we shall play Vingt-et-un which is an excellent game. I had a letter with the bill of 3 guineas for my breeches, how cheap they were I thought.

You wrote on Christmas aft, I agree with you I liked the quotation the King said will you cut it out of a newspaper & send it me please. I drove a truck today on very icy roads, the snow thaws during the day & freezes at night which is of course bad.

I am going to write to Russel White to have my favourite hymns when I come on leave.

I am sending you a small present to spend on yourself. When are you both going to have your photos taken, when they are done buy a leather traveling case to put them in you know what I mean.

With all my love for a very happy birthday and many more years of a good righteous life which you have both led and lets hope the time is near when I come home for good.

4th Jan 1940

The day before yesterday we had 15 degrees of frost, so you can imagine how cold it was, and now I have a bad cold. So I am having some tea with Rum and two aspirins in bed this evening.

I will write again when I feel a bit better not that I feel ill but you know how a cold feels.

6th Jan 1940

I am feeling much better to-day as a result of Rum & tea for the last two nights just before bed & my cold has practically disappeared.

It has thawed hard all day to-day & looks like rain but there is quite a cold wind.

Here is a temporary program of my leave.

Feb 2nd Friday, Arrive home D.D. comes in evening. (in this program Ma & Pa & self are always in it & others if specified).

Sat 3rd Go to the Palace theatre with Dar and Boss in 10s6d seats (matinee), preceded by good lunch at the Strand Palace.

Sun 4th Go to Twickenham to church.

Mon 5th Go to Ar Beats leaving Tedd at 10 A.M. stay for good lunch & leave arriving back before dark.

Tues 6th Tea party Miss Chenwells, Mrs Attfield Supper at The Russel White (Rev & Mrs only)

Wed 7th Matinee London theatre provisional only. Ar Beet & J.Y. stay for 2 nights.

Thurs 8th Rest at home with Beet etc.

Fri 9th Go to Reading Aunt Nelly's for lunch where Ar J.B. will meet us.

Sat 10th ? .

Sun 11th Church at Twick .

Monday 12th ? .

13th Leave for France.

What do you think of this program.

I am having my supper alone this evening and am eating an omelette intermittently writing this letter.

While I am at home Ma is to do NO work whatever Mrs Howard must come on the day I arrive & work like a Wednesday, I am glad you are getting a whole time servant, I think it is better for you.

10th Jan 1940

I am so sorry to hear about Darr's cold, I hope she is alright now, I am glad you got your monkey up with them. How is the new maid? Tell Darr I doubt whether she gets shot as a deserter. When will Boss's pullover come? I wear two always and when really cold another one in bed. I hope Boss does not make it too big like Ar Jessie Y, who says the pattern was yours. It is very cold again freezing day & night but it was a lovely sunny day to-day. I come home in 3 weeks to-morrow, not long now.

I think it would be best if Boss did not meet me at Dover then I can catch the first leave train, only she is not allowed on the quay or platform & it might be difficult, so she must get the weekend off, is that easy? I will write again soon, will Dar be able to get a nice lot of time off.

13th Jan 1940

I am glad you like your new maid so much. I am thrilled Dar is going to be an officer. I congratulate her, when will it come through, if the women's army is like the army it will be about six weeks or two months. My cold is over now but still have a cough in the mornings. The weather is lovely & terrible! We have beautiful sun all day but the cold is awful, freezing all day & all night, here is an example, I wash in my basin one night at 7.30 p.m., when my batman comes in the morning it is one solid block of ice, my sponge & loofa are always frozen stiff, but I am beautifully warm in bed. There were 18 degrees of frost the night before last & even more the night before that. The wind has been bad the last day or two. But I always wear Dar's scarf and Daddy's pullover, so it's not too bad.

15th Jan 1940

It has not been nearly so cold to-day but it is freezing again to-night. I did not have a chance to go to church yesterday as I had to cancel it because I was too busy. I expect you have heard they have got another scare on & leave has been suspended, I don't yet know how this will affect me.

When are you sending the gloves as I am urgently in need of them, also the Balaclava. I also need another pair of socks from Mrs Bicknell.

17th Jan 1940

I am so sorry you have asthma & hope it is all right by now did you go to bed? I have heard officially that I shall definitely go on leave on the 1st Feb & arrive day after. Leave started again to-day, I am paying for the theatre tickets & nothing less on than 10s 6d will suit me! I think it will be best to wait till I return before booking as there might be another disappointment at the last minute.

When we woke up yesterday morning the ground was lightly covered with snow, in the afternoon we had a terrific blizzard which lasted about ½ hour, it has all frozen this morning & the roads were terrible the wind was biting & it was freezing all day, although there was bright sun the wind has dropped this evening but it is still freezing.

22nd Jan 1940

I have heard no news how mother is for three days this is slightly excusable because there was no maill to-day, but when there is anybody ill I expect to hear every day. It snowed the whole of yesterday and most of the night, and this evening it is freezing. I have got chilblains on my left foot it is my fault because I came in with them wet from the snow and then aired them by the fire, to-morrow the doctor is going to put something on for me.

I have first written to Mr Russell White to ask him if I can have my favourite hymns in church when I come on leave. I have told him that you are going to ask him & Mrs in to a meal when I am come home.

23rd Jan 1940

I am delighted to hear you are all right now. Only 7 more days before I leave here. I am glad that Boss would not let you get up, it was evidently what you wanted. It must be awkward not having a bath because of the water, but here we have no baths and no lavs that pull, so we are in the same boat. I hope the bath will work when I come home because that is the thing I want most.

I still don't know what time my boat sails.

It has thawed a little bit to-day but it is freezing again to night! I don't think I will be able to bring much in the way of presents back as they have tightened up customs regs, but I will bring 8lbs of butter and some sugar.

To Dorothy

One thing I forgot will you book seats for the matinee of "Under Your Hat" at the palace on Sat Feb 3rd for Ma, Pa, Boss you and me. I hope Boss will be able to come. 10/6 seats or more nothing less I will pay. Book NOW because a returning leave chap says they could not book any 5/- seats for two months.

If a box is not too dear get that & not too high in the air I think stalls are best.

25th Jan 1940

I took the temperature outside at 8.45 a.m. today it was -12° C. that is 22° of frost but people say that after a full moon which is to-night the weather changes, rain is more preferable to this cold. To-day however was the most beautiful day I have ever seen, the trees were covered to top to bottom with frost, there was snow covering the whole ground & brilliant sun shinning all day. Could we have one of the Aunts (Ar JY & Beet) to stay one at a time when I am home. Have Ar JY first to be there when I arrive if possible.

Now be careful of your two selves and BE SENSIBLE. Don't run any risks however slight they may seem. I think I had better lay down the law. Unless it is really warm neither of you are to come to Victoria to meet me. Is that understood. Dar is to see you carry out this order.

Still very well & happy & longing to see you all again. Be very careful of the weather.

27th Jan 1940

I heard Winston Churchill's speech* on the wireless at 2.35 p.m. this afternoon very good I thought. I am so glad to hear by letter to-day that you are so much better, but both of you must be careful. I quite agree with you about the waste of money in theatre tickets, so don't bother about them. Re petrol I have just seen an order saying that I personally have to apply to the nearest recruiting office. So Dar can make enquires at her barracks. It has rained all day to-day and was beautifully warm but to-night its freezing again. The gloves Dar sent me are lovely.

You can expect me on FEB: 3rd SATURDAY at about 7 P.M. at Victoria.

*3 ½ months before becoming prime minister 'Come then let us to the task to the battle and the toil'

28th Jan 1940

I arrive at Victoria about 6.15 p.m. On Sat Feb 3rd

30th Jan 1940

Please excuse my hitherto scrappy letters but on account of the weather they have now definitely postponed leave, I did not realise you were having it such bad weather in England. There is about 4" of ice on the roads out here & it is raining to-night & freezing at the same time. When leave reopens I hope to come about 3 days after I heard to-day that I was going to leave here on Sat arrive home on Sun but of course all that is altered now.

I have not been very well myself these last few days I was very foolish on Sat, I had a bath & then went over to my cold office to do some work and evidently caught flu' anyway since then I have an awful cough and throat culminating to-night by not being able to talk as I have lost my voice. I stayed indoors all yesterday and am really v.much better to-day. I have medicine & a gargle from the Dr & a hot brick as water bottle in my bed every evening and tea & rum so I should have been all right to come on leave but now I shall be more all right.

I must stop now as my tea & rum is nearly ready (9.45 p.m.).

I heard on the wireless that they are temporarily rationing coal to 2 cwt per week, will you have enough for yourselves?

So don't take any risks you two and don't go out at all if it is cold.

I am very happy and longing to come home but don't worry I am not really ill.

1st Feb 1940

Arrive Victoria if cancellation is finished at about 11.45 a.m. on Sat NOT 6.15 p.m. as stated before.

17th Feb 1940 sent on paper from, Grand Hotel, Dover, Kent I met Boss to-day @ 11.15, and we have come here and are just going to have lunch. She had to come by train. I forgot to give you the petrol coupons so here they are. Neither of you are to go out doors when the snow is on the ground.

Give my love to the aunts Dar & D.D. Thank Ar JY for coming to Vic.

19th Feb 1940 (from somewhere in France) Monday 5.45 P.M. It has been quite warm to-day & it is thawing hard. When I got back I found 4 or 5 letters from you waiting for me & written from 29 Jan - 2nd Feb (approx). I had my wireless on last night in bed & also when I got up this morning, I do love it so, the Major seemed very pleased that I had brought one back. There is no more news as you can imagine. I hope you are all very well. What I told about leave is correct & I should be home (War Permitting) about the middle of June.

26th Feb 1940 Monday

Thank you v much for three letters of 18th 20th 21st one was a joint one. You may have seen in the papers that there was a Rugby football match between French army & British army in Paris (yesterday Sunday). I was allowed to go to it & also stay the night there. I went with my Scotch friend, a Major & a Capt. We had a marvellous time, we got there for lunch yesterday, then went off to the match, which we enjoyed, it was a beautiful afternoon, then we had tea & a bath, then a sandwich dinner, then went to a show and saw Maurice Chevalier (he was in it). This was a bit curious, we were in the fourth row of the stalls and about 10 mins after it started 4 people two men & two girls came & sat in the front row. I said to my Scotch friend who sat next to me, that man looks like Noel Coward*, he said the other man looks like Leslie Howard, anyway in the interval I went out and they were sitting in the vestibule drinking and so I took up my program & gave the back of it to Leslie to sign & then to Noel, they both seemed delighted and the Major & my friend came up and we all talked, I offered Leslie and Noel a cigarette, which they both had and then Noel gave us a drink all round, the Major talked to Leslie most of the time & I talked to Noel, we were with them about a quarter of an hour, they were awfully nice. Then we all shook hands and said good-bye, & Noel Coward said to me, if you get leave in Paris again ring me up and come and have a drink, he gave me his telephone number, & they both wished us all luck. I am sending the autographs for Dar, tell her to keep them for me. This morning we had a walk in Paris before the train went, and had lunch on the train. It was such a nice break and very enjoyable, I wish it could happen regularly.

NOW to answer your letters. You never told me if you got the petrol coupons I sent from Dover. Elliots sent my boots which I got to-day, they look v. nice. Will you send me the bill or let me know how much they were, also Plumbs sent the bill for breeches. I did not actually put £15 in my a/c at Teddington but I am sending you a cheque for £15, which they will cash all right.

I will write again soon.

P.S. We stayed in a lovely hotel, bedroom private bathroom & lav attached and only 89 francs for bed and breakfast = about 10s, it was a lovely hotel.

*Noel Coward volunteered for war work, running the British propaganda office in Paris.

Leslie Howard went to Paris in January 1940 to find an actress for the film 'The Man Who Lost Himself'. Leslie's biographies suggest he had several meetings with Noël Coward.

3rd Mar 1940

Thank you ever so much for the lovely rug which arrived this afternoon, it feels beautifully warm. The Major admired it, I opened it in the Mess so he saw it. I have not had a proper letter from Ma for about 3 days. I got the Marlburian letter which she put a few words in yesterday, I got one from Daddy yesterday, one from Ar Beet to-day and also the wireless battery from Bentalls, my other battery has not yet run down but when it does I shall not be without, as it is such a God send. We have had beautiful weather the last two or three days, sun and the wind has dropped to-day although it has been freezing every night. I went to church this morning, a poor sermon. After lunch I went for an hours walk then I sat outside with the interpreter in the sun & we had the wireless on, it was really quite hot. The birds are beginning to sing and it feels really like spring. In the morning I came down for breakfast opened the window just by me and can hear the birds singing & there is a nice view, what a change after the winter we have had!

Thank Dar for the "Lady Vanishes" just the sort of book I like, see if you can get me "Four Feathers" I am hard up for literature but I don't like murders books now they are all the same.

The spring coming makes me so pleased with life. Spend all the money you want to and if you are short apply to me. Don't forget that you have not got to pay all the rent this quarter only about £2.

7th Mar 1940 10.15 pm. Thursday

I am writing this letter in bed and have my wireless on listening to "Lord Haw Haw"*. Thank you very much for your letter to-day and for Punch from Dar. I had a parcel from Mrs Russel White with socks & scarves, she said she heard from Sydney & he was also at the Paris match. I forgot to ask Noel Coward about his grandfather living @ Teddington. Any time will do to pay me back the £15 I am in no hurry what ever. I am relieved for your sake that May has gone but do get another maid NOW. Thank you v.much for the pencil which I got yesterday. When I wrote & said I was going on the spree, I did not know if I could mention the name of the place, but the next day it was all over the Continental D. Mail. So I thought it was alright to tell you. I shan't be able to write to you again until Monday or Tuesday so don't expect a letter.

*German propaganda radio broadcast

11th Mar 1940

I have just come back from where ever I have been & am very tried so I will write a nice long letter to-morrow. Hope Dar is all right now.

12th Mar 1940

When it is cold at night I use your rug on my bed, but it will come in more useful when I have to sleep out of doors.

It has been very windy to-day and some rain this afternoon but it has cleared now & is very nice.

How did Dar get measles? Is she all right now? Boss saw me off at Dover, we sailed at 2.45 p.m. and got the other side about 4.30 p.m., where I had to meal, the train left about 6.15 and I stayed the night somewhere and arrived at the battery about 12 noon on the Sunday. I had a nice letter from Boss which was a surprise, she is making me a present of the B.E.F Radio Times, which will be very nice.

I am back with my old Madame for a few days but shall be back again at the end of this week, I think our Captain has left us to command another battery.

17th Mar 1940

Yes you have told me in every letter before and the two since that Dar has got German measles!! I am glad she is all right now, I never thought however that she would ever go to a dentist. Last Thursday was a terrible day, it rained all morning the gale was dreadful and in the afternoon there was a blizzard (snow) and I had to be out in it all the time, when I got back I found that the gale had blown in a wall of straw, all over our vehicles. Fortunately the damage was less than I first imagined & it turned out slight.

To-day it has rained all the morning & it is still raining now (2 p.m.) but it is quite nice & warm. I am sitting in the mess with the wireless on.

22nd March (?) 1940 Friday (Envelope opened by examiner and
date cut from letter)
No letters from you have yet come but I am living in hopes that I shall soon get one. I have got plenty of books to read & I play chess with my Major nearly every day, I beat him twice to-day. Cigarettes are 50 for 1s8d & I find I smoke less than I used. The food is magnificent. I can't think of anything more to-day

30th Mar 1940 Field Post Card Service
I am well
I have received your letter dated 24/2/40
Letter follows at first opportunity Douglas

31st Mar 1940
I got a letter to-day from the B.B.C. (they got my address from me being sent the R.Times by Boss) and asked me if I would report on the popularity among the troops of some programs, so I told them I will do it. I can't send it as the letter enclosing came 14 days late as they put the wrong address.

I shan't want another cake for 10 days as the Major was sent two the other day & we only have one at a time on the table & I have not touched yours yet.

I think the battery of my wireless is failing & shall soon have to put the new bats in, which I have got.

The weather lately has been v.bad, we had an awful snow storm on Thursday, rain on Saturday rain this morning but this evening was very nice. I am with my old madame for a day or two, she is still very well.

3rd April 1940
I have not received any 6d books to read & have nothing to do. Have you had your photographs taken yet, I wish you would hurry up getting them taken by a good London firm, I will pay if you have not enough money but get it done soon. I think it would

be nice to take a flat in Brighton, but get a maid to do the work then you can all be out all day. You have not sent any letters by airmail yet. We have as much butter & food as we like here. Nice for Dar to have her photograph in the paper.*

650,000 IN CALL-UP

A.T.S. Clerks Aid
Register of 23's
650,000 of the 25 and
26 classes are to
register within a
month. Here are some
of the 23 class being
" signed on " by A.T.S.
clerks yesterday. Story,
Page Three.

Dar in Photo Second from left

7th April 1940

Thank you very much for the lovely cake I got yesterday. We have only just started the first one you sent & it is delicious. Thank you for the letter written last Wednesday. Enclosing Ar J.B's letter. Your letter was unstamped but I have not had to pay on it. I put a new battery in my wireless to-day. This morning I played a game called medicine ball, with three warrant officers & two sergeants. It is a game in which you have some sacking and inside some earth & rags to make it weigh about 7 lbs, then you have a net & play like tennis except you throw to one another, we played from 11.15 a.m - 1 p.m. It is very good exercise. This afternoon the Major & I sat outside in the sun reading & had the wireless on it was a beautiful day nice & warm etc, the first fine day for about a fortnight. After tea I went out on a motor bike to deliver a letter, that took an hour, then (as every Sunday) I listened to the service broadcast to the forces at 7 p.m. We have not had a service here since Easter day H.C. I like the BBC services much better anyway. Killing about Dar being stopped by a bobby.

9th April 1940

I am writing this letter in bed waiting to hear the 12 o'clock news, the day of the invasion of Norway etc*. Thank you for the two books you sent yesterday. They are just the kind I like. This evening I went to dinner with my Scotts friend. This evening the weather has been awful rain & wind terrific.

*Germany invaded neighbouring Denmark on 7 April, and the Danes surrendered after two days. Denmark provided a land route to neutral Norway, which was invaded on 9 April. The small Norwegian army mounted fierce resistance, with the help of 12,000 British and French troops. The campaign in Norway ended when the German invasion of France and the Low Countries changed the focus of the war.

11th April 1940 Thursday 9.30 p.m.

Thank you for your letter which I got yesterday. I can't find it now so can't answer it, I read it all right & thank Dar for her letter & books very nice. I hope you are enjoying yourselves wherever you are. Our Navy & Air Force seem to be doing well.

There is no more to say.

14th April 1940 Field Service Post Card

I am quite well.

16th April 1940 Tuesday

Thank you for your two letters which I got yesterday from Bournemouth. The B.E.F notepaper is not provided & you can only buy it from French shops. My batman returns from leave to-morrow, which will be nice. This evening we heard Gracie Fields on the wireless, I did not think much of her. I had a letter from Ar J.Y. the day before yesterday she told me Miss Leaney was dead. I am glad to hear you are going to get a maid. It is rather late (11p.m) and I am tired so will stop.

17th April 1940

Field Service Post Card
   I am quite well.

19th April 1940

Thank you for your letter written on 12th which I got yesterday enclosing a photo of you & Boss. I had a cake from DD the day before yesterday which was very nice. I want a nice photograph of Ma & Pa done properly in a leather traveling case I have been asking for this for five months but has not yet come, have an expensive one done properly.

21st April 1940 Sunday 12 noon

How are you all? Thank you for your letter which I got yesterday written on 15th Monday. To-day is a perfect day sunny and very hot, the pear blossom is on the verge of coming out and the trees and hedges look delightful. I have had bad luck lately with my things, the other day my watch refused to go, so I took it to a shop near here and they said it wanted cleaning, then I dropped my nice pencil you gave me and the lead won't always come out now. Yesterday we heard the 1 o'clock news on my wireless then it suddenly failed, I tuned it on again at 2 and listened a bit then tuned it on later & it refused to go, so I took it to a shop near here they said the valve had gone, so I was going to send a telegram to Bentalls this morning for another valve, but when I came down for breakfast this morning I tuned it on and it went and is now going beautifully, so it must just be a faulty connection somewhere, & it may die anytime again.

As it is so hot now I have been thinking of summer underclothes and to-day I packed up a parcel to you there are a lot of socks which are either too small or have been mended such a lot that they are no more good. I also sent a pair of pyjamas which are too hot, and three summer pants of which two seem to be alright but seem to want new elastic but I will leave that to you if they are all right send them back but one of them is thread bare, also I am sending one pair of winter pants. I have forgotten what I have got at home in the way of summer things so perhaps you will sort them out for me. The following are the things I want:-

6 pairs of socks not wool ones as they are now too hot for summer you can get 2/6 a pair of khaki ones at Bentalls I think.

6 hand kerchiefs. 3 or 4 Towels

4 khaki collars size 16 ½" 2 ties (khaki)

summer vests& pants

pyjamas

The shirts I have got are I think all right for summer & winter aren't they? What I would like as well are some gym shoes. I had a letter from Blinkers yesterday. He has not got much to say for himself.

The two books you sent from Bournemouth are very nice & I have finished the one about the spy.

I saw an advert in the "Field" of March 9th of a book written by Montague Allwood it was 15/- and he had just had it published it seemed to be experiences & trips of life in general will you write to him & ask where it can be bought & send it to me. I was talking to an army padre the other day & he was telling me where he lived in his youth etc in the course of conversation he had lived at Tetbury for 10 years and it was he who advised Rossie Braybrooke to go into the church, he knew the Braybrooke's quite well but he left there about 1926. I am glad to hear your cough is much better. I expect Daddy enjoyed himself & the change. When you address my letters in future I think you better put under B.E.F. France, as there seem to be two B.E.F's now & I don't want the letters to go to Norway. I still have not been to church since Easter but I usually listen to the 7 p.m. forces service. You know I correspond with the B.B.C. I wrote to them the other day sending my form back & told them to get Russell White to take the 7 p.m. service & relay it out here one Sunday, I have not asked Russell White if he minds so you might mention it to him. I don't expect they will do it anyway but might.

I had £6 13s from field allowance in the Army transferred to Lloyds. Cox & Kings from Lloyds Teddington. Field allowance is 2/- a day, which one gets from being on active service over and above my 11/- a day wages, so it really comes in very useful. I am thinking of sending some clothes ie. Tunic & slacks & cap to you to be cleaned by Hardings as here they only do them in big towns & it is difficult to get to these towns.

This afternoon I shall sit outside in the sun with the wireless on as it it such a lovely day.

My ear is still troubling me a bit & I have had slight toothache, so if it continues I shall have to pay a visit to the dentist. I drink a lot of lemonade cordial out here, which I get from the N.A.A.F.I. it is like Kia-Ora, I usually mop about 4 bottles a week, a bottle costs 15 francs, so it is quite expensive, but I think it is worth it.

My wireless failed again this afternoon, I got an expert (a soldier) on wirelesses & he says it is the battery one of them is a dud, I wrote to Bentalls a week ago to send me some more batteries so they should be here soon. The expert in view of the fact that the battery had only been in use a fortnight said it might have got damp. What a long letter!! I shall have nothing to say for the rest of the week.

25ᵗʰ April 1940

On Monday I hired a car to take my wireless to a town to have it mended, and had to hire another car to fetch it back yesterday, evidently two wires were touching each other and this prevented it from going, also the man said 2 valves were weak so I am writing to Bentalls for two, because the volume is very bad.

My right ear has been very bad this week so I have been to the Dr every day. He says I have got an inflammation of the inner wall of the ear & he has given me stuff to take for it, but I have pains in it all day and can't sleep much at night. I feel quite all right otherwise & there no need to worry about it as it is not serious & it has not put me off my food.

Sunday Mon Tues were beautiful days & it was boiling hot but yesterday & to-day it has rained a lot. No more to say now.

Ring up Bentalls & authorise them to put a/c for valves on your bill & to send them immediately.

26ᵗʰ April 1940

I have not had a letter since I wrote to you two days ago. My ear is much better I have had to put hot fomentations on it and the Dr gave me some pills to take at night so I can sleep & they worked wonders last night. It has rained a lot again to-day but it will make the trees grow all the more. Write to Mr Wallis at Heelas,

Reading & find out how the budget* affects the dividends, from what I understand it will hit you rather hard as no bonus shares can be paid there are usually a lot of bonus shares but it may not effect us at all so write & see. There is no more to say for now, I will write again on Sunday.

*In April 1940 a new budget. The standard rate of income tax was increased from seven shillings to seven shillings and sixpence. An extra penny was added to the tax on a pint of beer. There were also extra taxes on tobacco. The most controversial measure was to increase postal charges. This especially upset members of the armed forces who were serving abroad as they feared it might reduce the number of letters they received from their families.

28th April 1940

I am writing this letter on Saturday 27 but wanted you to think I was writing on Sunday because I shan't have time to get it written before the mail goes. My ear is improving & nearly better now but I am still putting hot fomentation on it. I received my map board to-day which is lovely. How much did it cost? I expect you saw in the paper that Gen Sir J Dill* has got another job in England, it was only about a fortnight ago that I saw him & he shook hands with me. He is an awfully nice man.

*Returned from France April 1940 and appointed Vice Chief of the Imperial General Staff

Addressed to Dorothy Heelas

1st May 1940 10.40 p.m. Wednesday

My Darling Dar

Many happy returns of the day, how old are you now 29. I guess that's right isn't it. I am awfully sorry but I have not yet got you a present because we are in the depths of the country, but as soon as I get back to civilisation I will buy something (the same as Boss).

There is no more news as you see all my letters to Ma & Pa. Give my love to DD & Boss etc.

Lots of love & a happy birthday

Please excuse short letter but I got up at 5.30 this morning & am tired & post goes early to-morrow.

Addressed to Mother & Daddy

4th May 1940 Saturday

Will you please send me 2 large tins of elastoplast. I am glad to hear you have got somebody to come in & do the work for you. My misfortunes are better, watch goes now & wireless goes beautifully now I have put up an aerial, my ear is still not right although it does not hurt now at all. We had a thunderstorm the day before yesterday, on the whole the weather is not too bad.

Following the disastrous Norwegian campaign, Prime Minister Neville Chamberlain faced heavy criticism at home. By early May, Chamberlain had lost the confidence of the House of Commons. Labour ministers refused to serve in a national coalition with Chamberlain as leader, so he resigned. Churchill became prime minister on 10 May, the same day Germany invaded Holland and Belgium. The German army rapidly defeated France with a strategy called 'blitzkrieg', or 'lightning war', which used speed, flexibility and surprise to execute huge outflanking manoeuvres.

10th May 1940

Quite well and enjoying life. No more to say, I am in too much of a hurry. Don't worry I am quite safe.

22nd May 1940 Wednesday

I am awfully sorry I have not had a chance of writing you a letter for such a long time, but I can assure you it is not always easy! Don't worry too much about me the only danger I am in is from bombs which are rare and shells but we have a good slit trench & can assure you I am in that for a good part of the day, I am well out of the way of rifle & machine gun fire. I must say I wish this war would end soon, although we are all in good heart & cheerful. We get plenty to eat. I heard on the wireless last night that Arras and Ameis had fallen which sounds rather bad I thought, but the general opinion is that it is only a flash in the pan & that he will be driven back fairly soon. Thank you ever so much for the lovely photographs, I carry it in my pocket all the time & think they are very good. I was so sorry to hear that Dar did not get her commission better luck next time. I will stop now because I can get it away. I will try & write again to-morrow but don't worry if I am few & far between writing.

23rd May 1940 FSPC

I am quite well.

Letter follows at first opportunity

24th May 1940 Friday

I have not had no mail for about 5 days now, it is not your fault as it is not coming through, so don't worry if you don't hear from me for a long time. I am quite safe and happy. We are having beautiful weather, except yesterday when it rained for the first time for a fortnight. Will you please send me 1000 cigarettes as they are getting very scarce, go to a tobacconist & put the order thro' them then you get the cigs tax free, they will do as a reserve. No more to say for now don't worry at all.

All my love from your ever loving son.

Chapter 3

Back In UK

26th May 1940 to 4th June Allied forces were utterly overwhelmed by the German 'blitzkrieg' in France. Thousands of soldiers were trapped in a shrinking pocket of territory centred around the French seaside town of Dunkirk. The Royal Navy's Operation Dynamo succeeded in evacuating approximately 338,000 British and French troops in destroyers and hundreds of 'little ships' - volunteers who sailed to France in their own vessels - over a period of ten days, while under constant attack from the Luftwaffe.

1st June 1940 From Officers Mess, Watson Barracks,
Shrivenham, Berks

My Darling Mother Daddy & the rest of the family.

I hope you have not been too worried lately about me. I must say that once or twice I gave up all hope of getting away, but I was taken off the beach near Dunkirk at 3 a.m. yesterday morning and put in a destroyer. The navy were marvellous, the risks they ran getting us away and when we got on board they gave us hot drinks etc. I was nearly "all in" when I got on board as I stood in the sea waist high for 3 hours marshalling my men to the rowing boats, they just took us off on. Of course I have lost everything except your photograph and the clothes I stand up in although I lost my pants and socks, but a military tailor has come here & I am being fitted up little by little. The cashier is here & I shall get £5 off him. About leave, we have got to go to other centres after this to be reorganised and they hope to let us have leave from there but it won't be for sometime. If you like you can come & see me here or at Swindon, as I expect to be here at least until Wednesday, but perhaps it would be better to wait to see exactly where I am going to after & see me there. There is a lovely mess here & it is a joy to get something to eat because I have had only bully & biscuits for the last seven days, & there was not much of it then. I have had some glorious sleep here too. I have tried to telephone to you but the lines are blocked, but I shall try again to-morrow (Sunday). I have just bought some shoes, cap, shirt & underclothes! I lost my lovely wireless as it was impossible to carry it. On the beach at Dunkirk we were bombed, shelled & machine gunned, but I dug in to the sand & made some sort of hole to sit in. I had to toss up with my Capt who should stay & fight with the rear guard, I won & therefore have got away but I think he will be away in a day or two, our Colonel is there too.

Naturally there is a tremendous lot to tell you which I will do when I see you. I am very well & happy & am very lucky to have got away, it was due to the wonderful work of the navy and merchant fleet. Give my love to everyone.

All my love from your loving son Douglas

P.S. I am going to tea with the local Parson today he used to be vicar of Richmond & knows our name.

9th June 1940 Sunday

I am going north to-morrow (Monday), I don't know what time yet but I shall hear to-day. That means that I may be coming on leave one day this week. So you must be prepared to get Daddy back at any time. What about the car? Get all the necessary license, insurance etc ready & I can get extra petrol while on leave, but I should not actually pay for license until you hear from me. I will send a telegram as soon as I know. One trip we must do is to Great Missenden, also The Russell Whites must come for a meal.

No more to say but see that Daddy will be back & that the car is ready, of course I may not come home this week probably not but it is just possible. I will let you know my address as soon as possible.

If you get the car registered in my name I can get extra petrol.

20th June 1940 Thursday

I arrived back safely at 10.25 on Tuesday. I am sorry I have not written before but I have been so busy paying for billets that I did not know where I was. We had an air raid alarm at midnight last night, we all went down the cellar but got tired of it after 20 minutes so went to bed, the all clear did not go till 4 a.m., in the darkness I banged my head on a wall & got a gash over my right eye, I have got plaster over it now. I have just received 3 letters from you dated 20,28 & 30 May addressed to France. Don't write to this address anymore I can't tell you yet where I am going and don't know exactly when.

From Muriel to Mrs Mabel Heelas

20th June 1940 Blandford, Dorset
Thanks very much for your P.C. Don't fag to write if you're too busy or hot! Although I like hearing. I have no news at all. We spent 2 ½ hours last night- 12.30 a.m. – 3 a.m. under ground, so are all dog-tierd. Did you chaps have an alarm also?

From Douglas

30th June 1940
I am quite near to Mrs Chapman.We had two air raid warnings last week, but I couldn't be bothered to move so stayed in bed.

I went to the "Stump" Church this morning it is a very nice place inside.

This evening I am going to the pictures to see "100 men & a girl"

After all I want a flea bag so could you buy one again at Bentalls. I will try & write more frequently after this.

P.S I owe you a fiver & I will pay later.

30th June 1940 (Britain had taken the decision not to defend the Channel Islands in the event of a German invasion. As German forces overran France in June 1940, about 30,000 people were evacuated from the islands, with about twice that number choosing to remain. Jersey and Guernsey were bombed on 28 June with the loss of 44 lives. The German occupation began two days later. The Channel Islands were the only part of the British Isles to be occupied during the war.)
July –Sept 1940 The Battle of Britain

German attempt to gain air superiority over the RAF before starting a land invasion "Operation Sea Lion", the British managed to force Hitler to postpone and in the end cancel this

'Stay Where You Are' July 1940 Pre - Invasion Advice

6th July 1940 Monday (from c/o The Post Office, Boston, Lincs) I hope you sent my valise the quickest way as I am sleeping in a tent by the docks, which is quite pleasant. My address is,

"BB" Battery,

21st Anti-Tank Regt,

c/o Post Office,

Boston,

Lincs.

I shan't be staying here very long. Yesterday I went past Mrs Jacksons place. To-day I had 6 letters from you, which were addressed to France and about 12 Daily T

10th July 1940 (from Boston, Lincs)
Thanks for your letter which I got to-day, I have got a sort of bedstead which collapses every evening!! I have the same batman as in France. The house is unfurnished. It is just before you get to Boston dock, we left the dock side 10 days ago, it is 300 yards from the dock.. I went to Stump church last Sunday week. I went to Louth on Sunday & yesterday again. I went to tea with the "Stump" vicar, a canon, on Sunday. On my timing of rowing, I was 6 hours late owing to an unexpected strong wind. We had a terrific storm to-day thunder & rain.

There is really no more to say for now. I am hoping you will come & stay here in a few weeks time.

18th July 1940 5.45 pm. Thursday
I am awfully sorry you have not had a letter from me for ten days, but I have definitely posted two since then. I think it would be nice if you all came over & stayed for a few days in September. You see I never think it is so necessary to write very often as you & I are in the same country now, don't you agree? We had a military funeral on Tuesday of a man who was accidentally killed, I had the worst job as I had to meet his widow at the station. I went over to Lincoln yesterday I think that it is the nicest Cathedral in England.

I am going to supper with the parson Canon Cook on Sunday. My little puppy is rather sweet he is six weeks old, but if my Captain wants him I shall sell him, I bought it because it was lonely here without any animals, he sleeps in the summer house with his sister, that is my Majors dog & we have bought some wire to wire around the lawn to run about in.

26th July 6.50 pm Friday "BB" Battery, 21st Anti-Tank Regt.RA,
c/o 131st Infantry Brigade, Boston, Lincs.
Note my new address I am still in the same place though. The other day I was offered a wager from two of my Captains that I would not row down the river from Boston to Bardney (21 miles) and (21 miles) back in 24 hours. The two Captains offered me £5 each and I had a side bet with one 5-1 in £'s that I would not get there & back. So I saw a boatman he hired me a boat painted it up

etc. & I started at 3.45 a.m. yesterday (Thursday) morning, about 8am the wind & blew against me, anyway I arrived there at 2.15 p.m. had something to eat & started back at 3.30 p.m. had more to eat ½ way back 8pm & arrived here at 2 a.m. this morning none the worse. I got my money this aft £15 of which £3 goes for the hire of the boat, they were all very surprised I managed it & congratulated me. I have slept nearly all to-day

12th Aug 1940 Monday Addressed to Ailisa, Knowle Road,
Budleigh-Salterton, South Devon
I wrote to you last Thursday so you should have got it on Friday. Now I have been posted to another regiment to wit, the 125th Anti-Tank Regt R.A. and go to Norwich on Thursday I am rather glad as I have got into a rut here with very little work to do. This means that I may NOT be able to go on leave on Monday in fact I think it is very doubtful wether I go on Monday but if I don't it doesn't matter I shall be home very soon after, but anyway I will try my best to get home on Monday, so don't be disappointed.

17th Aug 1940 Saturday "D" Battery 125th Anti-Tank Regt RA,
Norwich, Norfolk.
I am so sorry I have not written to you for such a time, but it was a bit of an upheaval moving here. Naturally I hate it because I had so many friends in the 21st. All the Officers in my new battery are rather com, some very com, but prospects here are better than in the other place in respect of promotion. But I expect in time I may like it. I had thought of joining the R.A.F. as an army co-operation pilot, but I suppose you wouldn't like that, let me know if you don't mind. I don't know when I will go on leave, I shall start dropping hints soon. There is plenty of work to do as this regiment is Territorial & they know literally nothing. They were formed in Sunderland & all come from there. No more for now.

20th Aug 1940 Thursday
Thank you very much for your letter & P.C. from Daddy. I am settling down very well now & like it as I have plenty of work to do. We are sleeping under canvas, which is quite pleasant. I hope one day soon to go over to Boston & see all my friends there. The

officers mess is in a big village hall. There was another officer who came here with me from the 21st & he & I go out into Norwich every other evening, we are going out to-night, he is a Captain.

We have about 5 or 6 air raid alarms every 24 hours. We have had quite a lot of rain just lately.

27th Aug 1940 Addressed to My Darling Mother & Daddy Boss

Dar

I am glad you all enjoyed yourselves in Devon, I was very disappointed I could not come but I think I am coming on leave the week after next. Thank you for two letters & a picture P.C. which I got to-day. I have given up the idea of R.A.F. after strong opposition from you all. I am settling down very well now & like the officers very much & the men as well. Yesterday I met Charles Bunting, you may remember when we once passed through this town we had tea at Buntings Ltd he was a friend at school. We had a bit of fun last Wednesday aft, the air-raid alarm went & about 10 mins the Hun dropped 8 eggs* about 100 yards from where I was standing, I fell then when I heard the whistle, fortunately no-one was hurt. I saw in the paper to-day that the Hun claims he has bombed Kingston, in view of this fact coupled with the bombings in the home area, I order you to go & live at Ar Beets in future you are to take up residence as soon as possible.

*slang for bombs

2nd Sept 1940 Monday

Thank you for your two letters which I received to-day one dated 28 Aug & 30 Aug which have taken a long time to get here. I am glad you had a good journey down from Devon. I hope Boss & Dar will be at home when I come on leave next Monday, have all my civvies ready please. I suggest you make Daddy's study into a strong room a brick wall in front of the windows & supports in the room itself, I will do it all when I come home on leave if you like as I have had quite a lot of experience in that sort of thing, of course it will cost a bit, but I will help with the expense. There is no more to say for now. My old Colonel has been awarded the

D.S.O. I went over to Boston yesterday for a special reason which I will tell you when I go on leave.

13th Sept 1940 Friday "B" Battery, 125 Anti Tank Regt, Norwich

I arrived safely at 6.45 p.m last night, 25 minutes late, we had one air raid alarm during the journey, I sat in the restaurant car all the time & also had tea. There was much evidence of the Hun outside London. When I arrived @ Norwich I went to the Hotel & there had dinner, then came on I saw the Colonel he wanted to know all about the London raids etc. I am attached to another battery for about three weeks. I had a lovely nights sleep last night, no airplanes about at all. I will write again to-morrow. I hope Boss had a good night. NOTE new address B NOT D Bty

15th Sept 1940 Sunday

I sent you a telegram because I did not think you would get my letter before Monday. I hope you are alright because I saw a picture in the Mirror yesterday of a house on fire @ Kingston & the BBC says a lot of bombs were dropped in the South West of London, don't take any risks and if things get "hot" go to Ar Beets. You tell me to write on both sides of the page but what is there to say? I have not been back down into the town since I came back. There is nothing more to say. Hope you are all O.K. I am going to write to the Paskes & Ar Beet

19th Sept 1940 Thursday

I have not had a word from you since Tuesday I hope you are all OK. On Monday I was out in the country & machine-gunned by a Bosche plane. A sergeant about 15yards away was badly hurt.

I had a letter to-day from the 21st A/T you know when I was at Leeds I find I shall get 8/6d per day extra. It has been raining all this afternoon but is nice & fine now. I really can't think of anything to say.

21st Sept 1940

Thank you very much for your letter. I am quite alright & not a bit worried about the machine-gunning, he was not one of our men but one from another regt. I am still longing to get back to 21st so have written to ask if they will claim me back. We are having indifferent weather. Must hurry to catch post. Will write longer letter to-morrow.

22nd Sept 1940 Sunday 12.25

Thank you for the two letters which you sent the other day. I am still in the land of the living, and we don't get much air activity round here, quite a lot of sirens but nothing more.

How has Boss been getting on with her air raids? I am still waiting to get out of this regt & have written to the 21st once or twice to suggest they might get me back.

29th Sept 1940

I have not been into Norwich since I came back off leave I am quite satisfied to sit in the mess during the evenings and also it is difficult to get into town and also I waste money.

I am rather worried about you all as the newspapers say that bombs were dropped in S.W. London. I saw that Bosche planes were brought down at Kingston, Esher, Twickenham & Richmond, so if it is too hot there you will have to go down to Ar Beets, things are very quiet here, once or twice we hear Bosche planes flying over but not very often.

I have still not yet heard from my old Battery Comd from the 21st about the "feelers" I put out to return to the regt. Will you look in the London telephone book & find out the address of the Bishop of Woolwich as I have forgotten the address to write to Desmond.

Did you see in the paper that Percy Fear's son had been killed, he was a 2nd Lt in an A.A. regt & was killed owing to enemy action, so I shall write to him to-day.

9th Oct 1940

I have decided now to stay in this regt. My old Colonel wrote to this Colonel and he said he did not want me to go as there were so many things wanting doing here. So I said "all right". I was very disappointed at first but perhaps I shall get promotion quicker here. Also my battery comdr has gone away for 5 weeks and they have put me in command of the battery for that period, which I think is a great honour because there are a number of Captains who they could have put in command.

Our nights here are very quiet and we have no alarms during the day (touch wood).

I hope Daddy had a nice birthday, what did you do with him.

13th Oct 1940 Sunday

I am so sorry I have not written for so long but I have been really busy just lately. Thank you very much for the cheque for £3. I am saving money but I was very broke paying all my Dunkirk bills.

On Thursday evening I went to the theatre here & saw Phyllis & Zena Dare in "Full House". It was killing, that was the first time I have been out on the spree since I was home on leave. Thanks for Daddy's two letters.

Yesterday I was passing through & had tea in the costal town where we spent a summer holiday a few years ago actually the place where I heard that I had passed school certificate.

Things are very quiet here thank goodness, how are they with you? I went to church this morning it was dull but quite nice hymns.

I bought a camp bed the other day for the winter will you please send me some sheets.

20th Oct 1940 Sunday 12.45.

We have a new Major named Francis and he is a regular, & extremely nice & very efficient so will brighten the place up tremendously which is certainly wanted here.

There is very little news from here. We have very few alarms about one during the daytime and two after dark which last about 1 hour each. I have been very busy during the last week, and this afternoon I am going down to the coast.

27th Oct 1940

How would you like to come & spend the weekend here the week after next come on Friday aft. & stay till Monday morning, I can fix up an hotel, only you will have to let me know early as I have to get a permit for you.

There has been more enemy activity lately, bombs dropping for the last two nights but they were a very long way away. The sirens have just gone 12.45 p.m. It will only last about ¼ hr. I should think.

7th Nov 1940

I have been quite busy lately doing different things. I heard from Alec Bingham a Marlboro' friend yesterday he is training to be an officer, he lives opposite to one of our majors of the 21st who when we returned from France was invalided out of the army & they evidently know each other.

13th Nov 1940

I am so sorry I have not written for a week, but I have been on a course here and two instructors teach us how to instruct, it is most interesting but there is a tremendous amount of work to be done & I don't get much time off as I have to write up notes every evening, the course does not end till next Saturday so I may not have a chance of writing until then.

I am sleeping in a big house on a camp bed. Thank Dar for all the clothes they fit beautifully I can't pay you for them yet & also I owe you about £8. I don't know if I told you but I have got Cox and Kings to buy me £2 worth of Nat Savings Certificates per month so that after the war I shall have something put by in case I need it.

You keep blowing me up for not writing long enough letters but what can I say? I have to be just as careful in security as I was in France

I have just been to the evening service at the village church here (4.30) which was quite nice. This evening there is a concert with the Royal Artillery band of 35 men, which I am going to.

20th Nov 1940 Wednesday 8 A.M.

Thank you very much for your nice long letter which I got on Monday afternoon. I am still terribly busy taking driving instruction & giving lectures etc. We finished our course last Saturday & the major who ran the course an instructor in gunnery told me confidentially that he had recommended me for promotion to Captain but of course that does not necessarily mean I shall get it & at present there is not a vacancy, but that is a great step in the right direction.

The weather has been very bad lately & we have not been worried by the enemy much either.

I don't know whether I shall get any leave this winter but I am due for my second 7 day leave in January & it will be lovely to go to Louth.

I have got the job of officers mess secretary which means arranging for meals, wines, cigarettes, bills and accounts etc, which is of course quite a job.

3rd Dec 1940 Tuesday

There is an officer here who lives in Twickenham & he said you had a very bad time last Friday from the Bosche.

I have been terribly busy just lately because we have a general's inspection & I had to get everything in my men just so, & on top of that had to get the Mess a/c's O.K.

8th Dec 1940 Sunday

I was glad to hear on the wireless this morning that you had had no air raids last nights, we are just the same, in fact it has been very quiet for about 4 weeks with one exception.

You must have had an awful night that Friday, what would you have done if Boss & I had been there? I know one thing & that is you would have been sitting down the cellar all the time.

It is very cold here but I manage to keep warm. No more to say for now I am very busy trying to wind up Novembers mess a/c.

Thank you v.much for your letter. I got back all right on Tuesday at 7.25, 1¼ hours late, there was a warning between Ipswich & Norwich so the train crawled along. We had a very pleasant Christmas here we had our own dinner at 2 p.m. Pheasant, spuds and Brussels and Christmas Pudden. The men had a very good one also Pork & beef, Pudden & 1 pint of Beer & 10 cigarettes each. I did not after all go away but stayed here the whole week. I went to church this morning, it was rather a dull service.

It must have been nice for Boss not to have air raids for 3 days on end. Thank you v.much for coming to see me off. I quite agree that it would be very expensive if you came down here to stay & it would not be worth while just to come for a week-end as I can only get 1 night out of 3 off, but of course if you do come I should be delighted to see you. I am glad to hear Daddy is better. Must stop to catch last post 5.30 p.m.

2nd Jan 1941
We have had snow here to-day & it's all over the ground & has frozen, so the roads are pretty bad. I am sorry to hear you are ill in bed, you are very naughty I told you you ought not to have gone out in those cold winds.

After all I think my mackintosh is good enough, £4 seems such a lot for a new one & the one I have got is quite good enough. So will you please send it back if it has come if you have not got my clothes from Plumbs will you hurry them up as I must have them immediately or anyway as soon as possible.

There is very little enemy activity here one or two sirens per day, how is Boss getting on with the raids?

I was vaccinated again on Tuesday!

5th Jan 1941 Sunday Addressed to My Darling Mother
Very many happy returns of the day. I hope this letter gets to you on the right day. I have got a bit of a cold and stayed indoors most of yesterday but to-day I went for a 1½ hours walk which was nice. We have had 5 air alarms to-day up to now (5.30 p.m.) but no enemy activity.

I don't know if you remember I told you that last January I had a bet of 1000 francs with my Battery Comdr in the 21st, he said the war would be over by December & I said it would not, anyway I had a letter from him on Friday enclosing a cheque for £5 which was very kind of him in payment of the bet. He has now been promoted to Lieut-Col and is somewhere in Scotland.

I got a bill from Plumb's £10-4-6 and I am rather pleased because all the other officers seem to have had to pay more for their kit, so after all I don't think I have done so badly. I hope I shall get the kit soon. Will you please send me the amount of money which I owe you for purchases at various shops as soon as possible, because I want to get all my debts settled.

Give my love to all the family.

12th Jan 1941 Sunday

Thank you for your letter which I got yesterday. I am so glad your cold is better. I have had an awful cold it started on Thursday night but started to clear up last night, but I still have to be careful & wear my greatcoat whenever I go out. We are shortly going up to Scotland but are not leaving the country this month. I got my tropical kit from Plumbs on Tuesday. I wrote to Plumbs paying their bill £10-4-6. I don't really need another Mackintosh as the one I have is quite good enough. The snow disappeared yesterday completely & this afternoon it is sunny.

Must hurry to catch post will write again soon.

14th Jan 1941 Tuesday

Thank you very much for the lovely identity disc for my wrist, which arrived to-day. I have been very busy to-night looking over my things and am afraid I have destroyed a lot of your letters, and other ones which I could not possibly keep. I am sending you the letters you asked for. I am enclosing a cheque for £7 for clothes Elliots repairs & batteries. I owe you another £8 but I can't pay that yet I am afraid but I will let you have a cheque before I go. Don't write anymore letters to this address I will send you my other address in Scotland as soon as I know. I cannot let you know when I am leaving here. I am going on a motor bicycle so shall have a lot of news for you then. My cold is nearly all right now and is almost cleared up. Everybody has gone to bed so I can think in peace.

I had the present from Mrs Thorpe the other day of 500 players wasn't it sweet of her? A catastrophe happened to-night you know that lovely leather writing case you gave me, I think I must have left the key of it at home somewhere so had to force it open, but have only damaged the lock & shall give it to my batman to try & get a new lock to-morrow in Norwich. I hardly know what an air raid siren sounds like as we have not had one for about 4 days or nights. I must stop now as it is quarter past midnight & I must write to Mrs Thorpe.

P.S. I am sending a lot of receipts for safe custody.

My new address is "D" Battery, 125 Anti Tank Regt R.A. 18 DIVISION, Home Forces.

Moving to-morrow Thursday will write if possible every evening.

17th Jan 1941 10.30 p.m. In Bed From Doncaster I am staying the night here in a house with charming people. Last night we stayed at Peterbough. I was riding a motorcycle yesterday & in view of the intense cold ice & snow it made my cold worse. So to day I was told travel in a vehicle & it has helped. We arrive at our destination on Sunday night. Longing to go to sleep so will stop. Will describe everything in next letter.

19th Jan 1941 Sunday Catterick Camp We reached Catterick Camp yesterday afternoon about 3.45 p.m. It started snowing about 4 p.m. & we were going to start off this morning at 8 a.m. but we are stranded as there are drifts further North & so have to stay. It snowed all night & all day to-day & is still snowing (5 p.m.). We are quite happy but have no idea when we shall be able to move.

My cold is much better but not quite right although it does not now make me feel ill. I had a temperature I think when we were at Peterborough but I have not had one since. Catterick as you probably know is the Aldershot of the north. Everybody is extremely kind to us here & put themselves out to make the men & officers comfortable. The clouds are very heavy with snow so we may be here some time. My wireless brightens things up & we have a lovely fire.

I can't get any of your letters till we rejoin the Regt who mostly went by train so I shall try & ring you up once or twice.

We are going to the officers club this evening for a drink it is about ½ a mile away.

I will write again to-morrow or Tuesday

21st Jan 1941 Tuesday

We are still snowed up here at Catterick, it has started thawing now but it is thought that it will freeze to-night, so even then the roads will be quite impossible. It is rather dull here and I have not been out on a spree but am going out in a few minutes 5.30 p.m to the officers club to have a bath and supper. It has been very dull here not much to do.

I must stop now as they are nagging at me to get started.

26th Jan 1941 Sunday "D" Battery,
125 Anti-Tank Regt, Langton House Camp,
Duns, Berwickshire.

Thank you very much for all your letters which I got when I arrived here on Thursday night. We left Catterick on Thursday morning at 8 a.m. and arrived at 8.15 p.m. 135 miles passing through Darlington & Newcastle etc, I did not ride a motorcycle again after the first day, & my cold has practically disappeared now. We are (the officers) billeted in private houses in the town which is not too bad but I prefer to be in a mess. It is a very small one, I can't say I like it much. Yesterday I saw the Colonel about me being promoted as I am getting fed up with hearing about other officers being promoted who are junior to me in other regts & there has been no movement of officers from this unit, he says he will see the Brigadier & if I then don't get satisfaction I shall personally ask to see the General. I had a lovely pen knife as Christmas present from Ar J.Y. We are feeding in a hotel here and I found out to-day that we are supposed to pay 3/- a day out of our own pockets for food etc, so I am going to kick up a row about that to-morrow. I hope you enjoyed yourself at Blandford & that Daddy enjoyed himself at Tetbury I bet he didn't!! I know

now why all your letters are so long it came out when I received all the weeks letters at once & that it you repeat yourself all the time, so that accounts for my letters being so short. I will try & send you a wire to-morrow giving address.

P.S. Make a note of my address as above.

2nd Feb 1941 Sunday

I went to the pictures three times last week, as there does not seem to be anything else to do here.

You will be glad to hear that I am in the throws of promotion & I am nearly a Lieutenant, but you must not address me as such until I let you know officially, that is when I am allowed to put up another pip which I expect will be one day this week, but I shall be paid as from 1st Jan 41 and get 2/- per day more, which isn't really too bad, but I am not satisfied with that and shall go on for promotion to Capt.

I am now feeding in my billet where I sleep, the owners are very nice indeed and Mrs cooks for us. Anyway that stopped having to pay 3/- a day at the hotel, which was ridiculous. I am going to pay my person 10/- a week as she is very kind and gives us extra food of her own. I have just been adding up how much I have got in the bank and it is £22 which isn't really too bad and then I have £10 of travellers cheques in my pocket.

There was some talk here (in my billet) of going to Edinburgh one night, it's about 46 miles from here. Will you send me Uncle Walters address for me as I might ask to go away from here for the afternoon one day & I would go & see him. I went for a walk this afternoon by an old castle & lake, this place must be lovely in summer time, about 2 miles out you get on to the moors & they are delightful, heather woods & streams. I shall probably go to Berwick one night this week to the pictures its only 16 miles

We are had a sing song last night here and went to bed very late! We have had no more information as to what is going to happen with us. When you write to Ar J.Y. thank her for the penknife I will write to her soon.

6th Feb 1941 Thursday

You can call me Lieut on your letters I heard last night there were quite a lot of us who got it and I shall get pay as from 1st Jan 2/- p.d extra 13/- in all. My landlady paid you a great compliment the other day she said to me you must have a nice mother. We went out in the country all day to-day on an exercise which was quite nice, it was beautifully sunny. It snowed the whole day yesterday from 9 a.m. till 9.45 p.m. & to-day I am told many roads were blocked, it thawed all to-day and it is freezing to-night, whats the weather like with you?

I am just going out for the evening 8 p.m. to my major's billet so had better stop.

12th Feb 1941 Wednesday

Thank you v.much for the letters which I got yesterday congratulating me on the 2nd pip.

There was a great thrill in town here to-day because during the night they had the 7th air raid warning of the war!

16th Feb 1941 125 Anti-Tank Regt R.A.,
c/o Army Post Office 890

I will write again tomorrow I think when I get the other side I will send all my letters by air mail, so you had better do the same. I can't say what day I am going but it is in the immediate future. I have not yet received any parcels of clothes or wireless batteries, but tomorrow will not be too late. We have been having the most lovely weather here , birds singing, flowers coming out etc. The aircraft went passing over when they raided Glasgow the other night. Take care of yourselves. Don't worry about me, I shall look after myself when I get to my final destination.

19th Feb 1941 Wednesday

I was out on an exercise all Monday & Tuesday it was terribly dull. It was nice talking to you on the telephone last week, I will make it a weekly show as it only costs 1s/2d a time, I will try perhaps on Saturday. I went out last Sunday to a party singing & games, it was great fun, the people here are awfully kind & nice,

I sometimes take the local policeman's daughter to the pictures, she is about 20 & is very nice.

The weather is awful, it started raining on Saturday afternoon, poured all Sunday, started snowing in the early hours of Monday morning & has not yet stopped 7.30 p.m. it is now 2 feet deep already a great many roads are quite impassable. This afternoon the whole battery had a snow ball fight, which was great fun I was very wet at the end but I enjoyed it.

Could you please send me the picture which was hanging up in my room called "IF" by R.Kipling.

I don't think it is possible for you to come here for more than a week-end and just for that short time I don't think it is worth the money, if we stay in this country much longer they will re-start leave and rumour has it that we are not going before the middle of April, so I shouldn't come anyway yet if there are indications of going I will send you a wire and then you can come for a few days, but it seems a waste if you come & then find I can come home.

You must be more careful and not go out in the evenings when the guns go.

The snow drops here are lovely all over the hillsides. On Sunday afternoon I went for a drive with the person I am billeted on, we went to a place called Ayton & had tea, I paid for the tea, it was very nice seeing everything we saw St Abbs Head Lighthouse, which you have no doubt heard of, the coast is very rugged, also we passed Eyemouth a small fishing town which had a bad fishing disaster in 1881, about 200 men killed, perhaps you remember hearing about it when you were a little girl. What a good idea to get a job as a censor perhaps my Godmother might be able to help you.

They had an audit of all accounts the other day & mine passed O.K. the officers mess I mean.

23rd Feb 1941 Sunday

I tried to telephone you on Friday evening but there was 4 hours delay, so I gave it up as hopeless. I told you it began snowing last Monday, it finished on Friday and there was 3 feet of snow in all parts. Every road out of Duns was impassable and now it has started to freeze. The inhabitants say it is the worst fall of snow they have had for 36 years, but of course not so cold as it was last winter. We shan't be in this place much longer but we are going to another place in Scotland, I can't say why in the letter, but there is no indication of moving right away so worry about that when I know the new address I will send it but continue to write here till I say.

27rd Feb 1941 "D" Battery, 125 Anti-Tank Regt R.A.,
The Haining, Selkirk, Roxburghshire
Note my new address, I moved here yesterday, but did not like the place at all. It is a bigger town 4000 inhabitants, one cinema, two hotels and a number of pubs. We are living in a mess. I do miss not being in a civilian billet after Duns, & also shall miss taking out the policeman's daughter, she was very nice indeed. Please excuse the pencil but my pen has not much ink & I must write another letter which requires ink.

We had more snow & frost during the night but this afternoon it started to thaw again, so perhaps soon we shall be all right again. Selkirk is built on a hill & is in a valley with very high hills all round.

I have decided to send you monthly the difference in pay between 2nd Lieut & Lieut ie. 2s a day that is £3 a month as from 1st Jan 41 but the first instalment will have to be the repayment of £8 which I borrowed from Ma, & that will come when my back pay is credited to me. If I can afford it I will send more than £3.

I will try & phone regularly but it is sometimes difficult to get thro'.

2nd Mar 1941 Sunday
How nice to hear your voice on the telephone yesterday. It is nice because we have an outside telephone in the mess. The mess is an hotel, which has been requisitioned by the military, & soon if you want to you will be able to ring me up, but that part has not been fixed yet.

I am thrilled to hear about Dar she is lucky, does she want to go? There is every indication, which I cannot mention in a letter, that we shall not be going abroad for a very considerable time.

6th Mar 1941 Thursday

I'm in bed with a touch of the flu, we were on exercises on Tuesday out all night & most of yesterday & I was freezing cold & last night evidently I didn't look well & the Dr said I was not to get up to-day.

After all the encouragement I have recently given you on the fact that I am not going abroad, will shock you, as we are going almost immediately, the news came through very unexpectedly yesterday. Why I said we were not going was because 48 hours leave was starting and we were losing some of our guns. All I can say is I shall not be here in 10 days time. I don't think you had better come up here as we shall be so terribly busy, it will be difficult. But if you ring up on the phone as I will when I get up DON'T mention my going abroad. No more to say for now.

16th Mar 1941 Sunday

Please note my new address it is:-125 ANTI-TANK REGT R.A.c/o ARMY POST OFFICE 890

I will write again to-morrow. I think when I get the other side I will send all my letters by air mail so you had better do the same.

I can't say what day I am going but it is in the immediate future. I have not yet received any of the parcels of clothes or wireless batteries but to-morrow will not be too late. We have been having the most lovely weather here these last few days birds singing flowers coming out etc. The aircraft went passing over when they raided Glasgow the other night. Take care of yourselves. Don't worry about me, I shall look after myself when I get to my final destination I am allowed to tell you where I am. I will again to-morrow.

17th Mar 1941 Monday

To My Darling Mother & Daddy & Dar

Now you mustn't worry about me, you know I joined the army to fight for my King & country and YOU & if the authorities say I can fight better abroad I must go abroad. We shall not be happy until we have won this war and then we can all live in peace & happiness. You must look forward to the day when we are all re-united again as a family. I am very happy & looking forward to my experiences & the knowledge that what ever happens I shall have done something to help my country. My only regret is I am leaving you but I know that you will be good and won't worry about me, that is the only thing that consoles me, so don't worry about me under any circumstances, I brought myself back from France so I shall bring myself back this time. I can give you my full address when I get my destination so you will know where I am. We are off to-morrow early in the morning & all your letters and parcels will get forwarded on to me. I will write as soon as poss, but don't expect any letters for some time because there are not pillar boxes in the sea, but as soon as I can I will send you a cablegram if it is allowed. I expect I shall have another chance of posting you a letter again. I don't know where we are going to-morrow.

I have got your two photographs in my pocket but just in case I loose it will you send me some more as soon as possible.

You must be very careful of yourselves and avoid the bombs like poison !! When Dar goes you had better go & live near Boss.

?? Mar 1941 (date cut out by censor) Somewhere,
125 Anti-Tank Regt, c/o A.P.O. 1635

We are on a ship thats all I can say about that. I have a cabin to myself & a bed with a light over the bed which is all very nice. I am very well & enjoying life. I never bought any stockings in the end but shall probably be able to get some on board or somewhere. The food is very good just the same as the last trip. Tell Boss that I bought Whitakers Almanac with the voucher she gave me for my birthday. I hope you got my last letter all right from on land. No more news for now, this will probably be the last letter for some time. I hope you ......(back of where date cut..) all right & not worrying about me.

19th Mar 1941 Wednesday

I am still very well & quite happy, I hope you are just the same. I am now on board a ship but I can give you no further details, very good food & a nice place to sleep.

I just can't think of anything to say. Everybody seems very happy & contented. I am just going to start reading the book you sent me sometime ago "Black Record" then I am going to sleep.

22nd Mar 1941 Saturday

Things still the same as when I wrote yesterday. There is still nothing to say, we are all a very happy party & we do P.T. which is very good exercise. It is not quite so hot to-day. In the evening I sometimes play cards or read a book. No more to say for now. Don't worry about me.

10th April 1941 Tuesday, 125 Anti – Tank Regt.
RA. c/o A.P.O. 890

I arrived back safely at 9.30 on Tuesday morning, three hours late. We had an air raid alarm at 9 that night and it lasted all the way until 6.30 in the morning, there was A.A. fire & Bosch over the whole time. They had a blitz here on that night too. We are helping with fire – watching here which is quite good fun.

I went to the pictures on Tuesday night & saw the "Farmers Wife" which is awfully good and I heard the doorman say "My lot".

13th April 1941 Sunday A.P.O.

I have not received any letters from you since I came back. I expect you will be very pleased to hear that it will be many months before I go away, everything seems to have been cancelled and we are moving further south during the week. I am very feed up with being "mucked" about and I am going to put in an application to return to the 21st & I shan't be satisfied until I get back there, so I am going to try like hell !! The weather here has been very bad lately. There have been no air raid alarms since I have been back. The moon has always been hidden by cloud. I went to church this morning, the vicar is a Canon Brerton, a very nice service.

20th April 1941 Sunday, 6 Brownsville Road,
Heaton-Moor, Stockport, Cheshire

We arrived here at 4 a.m. yesterday morning. It is a residential area. We have got a house as a mess, there are only four of us at present. Then we have five other homes and a hall for the men. It is very nice district about 2 miles from Stockport and 7 miles from Manchester. We have no idea what is going to happen to us but imagine we shall go right away next month the reason we did not go on the other thing was there was somebody who was more necessary & so they are going.

I thought of you all during the two very heavy blitzes lately the last one being last night. I hope you are all quite all right poor Boss! How she must have enjoyed them. Cigarettes are impossible to buy here so could you send me 100 players a week please. I bought a pipe yesterday & I have considerably cut down my cigarette smoking.

24th April 1941 Thursday

Thank you ever so much for all the letters & the 40 cigarettes you sent. I put in my application to return to the 21st but think it has been rejected. I could if I wish go further and see somebody at the War Office but I don't think I shall, I will be content and hope something interesting will happen. I went to church here last Sunday evening but it was a rotten service & I shall go the Methodist next.

I am going to be attached to the infantry very soon for some unknown duration to teach them how we work. I will let you know my new address when I go, it is some where near Wolverhampton.

27th April 1941 Sunday

Thank you ever so much for the last 40 cigarettes. I am glad you have got the £12 that is evidently the money I borrowed from you. I am going to-morrow to the Infantry somewhere in Staffordshire in the country which will be nice. So don't write again until I send you my new address I don't know yet how long I shall be away from the Regt. The night before last I went to

Manchester terrific havoc in parts, I just managed to get batteries for my wireless.

We had a noisy night last night guns going a lot but nothing dropped near us.

The situation in Greece does not seem too good to-day I am afraid it will be another "Dunkirk" but we may be able to get some equip away although I don't think the war in the Balkans will decide anything. I am looking forward to hearing Churchill tonight*. I went to the Methodist this morning, it wasn't too bad.

*Churchill's speech 27/04/41 Report on the War "A Difficult Time"

30th April 1941. Wednesday 125 Anti-Tank Regt R.A. 1/5 Bu
Sherwood Foresters, attchd Teddersley Hall, Parkridge, Staffs
I arrived here the day before yesterday. It is a lovely mansion but 2 ½ miles to the nearest village which is only small. Stafford itself is about 5 miles away. I brought my batman along with me. The officers here are a very nice lot. I hope you got the telegram which I sent off to-day. Cigarettes are very scarce I sent my batman to every shop in Stafford yesterday but he could not get any at all, but I have cut down smoking a lot. You can get them at Hambridges in Kingston. I will send you a cheque soon for the money you spend. Don't bother to send the Times any more as they have it in the mess here all right. There is no more news for now.

4th May 1941 Sunday
Thank you ever so much for the 100 cigs which I got to-day also for the 20 Rhodian, I will give the 20 to my batman as you say.

I am thoroughly enjoying myself here the officers are really charming. It is a bit of an ordeal to come to a strange mess and not know one of them but they have really made me feel at home. I have been on 4 exercises and today (this morning) we attacked the home guard and I was going about putting gas bombs in the middle of Stafford, which I enjoyed, also I saw the new "Queens messenger convoys" they are lovely affairs and were giving the troops free coffee & sandwiches.

Yesterday I went into Stafford & spent the afternoon & had tea went to Smiths & got some wireless batteries. It is delightful

74

here real country birds singing & trees & hedges sprouting out. I wish the officers of the 125 were as nice as these here.

8th May 1941

I had a letter from Geoffrey A-Davies to-day he seems to be very well. Also Watson my friend in the 125th wrote & said 3 of our men had been killed while fire watching in Liverpool, one of them I knew & he was an awfully nice chap.

12th May 1941 Monday

Thank you very much for the cigarettes which I got to-day and the letter written on Saturday.

I hope you are all right after Saturday nights raid*. It seems a pity about the Houses of Parliament & W. Abbey because the were such imposing buildings. To-day duty took me to Chester I thought of Daddy there, & had a little time for shopping and enjoyed going on the ropes of the shops so to speak. Last night I walked into Stafford 4 ½ miles for exercise & air. I was out all night last week on an exercise which was quite good fun, & I am doing the same this week as an umpire. I asked for and got a truck for myself the other day from 125 so things are much easier now.

*Westminster Abbey, the Houses of Parliament were hit but the main fabric of the buildings were saved 10th May.

18th May 1941 Sunday

I am thoroughly enjoying myself here and shall have been here three weeks to-morrow. I had orders from the Infantry c/o yesterday to another battalion, but this adjutant rang up & asked if I could stay another week. I think they must like me.

I go out shooting with some who shot here in the grounds, I just look on as I could never hit anything and most evenings we play poker for very small stakes, I am in pocket though. Next week-end I am going to another battalion the Beds & Herts, they are very nice I believe. Last Friday I went over to Stockport to see my Battery because my Battery Commander (who put in an application for a transfer and was successful) was leaving to go to his new Regt, Anti Aircraft, he was Major Francis and one of the few gentlemen in the regt,

Next week-end I shall go and see my new Battery Commander, he is an ex-yeoman so should also be a gentleman, I am a snob!

I went on a Home Guard Exercise this morning, and this evening I went to a little village Church quite near which had a very nice service.

I am hoping for 100 cigarettes on Tuesday as usual. Everything is very dry & we need rain badly. There is nothing more to say for now

28th May 1940 Tuesday 125 Anti Tank Regt,
Merevale Camp, Atherstone, Warwickshire
I hope you are all right and that Daddy enjoyed himself at Tetbury. I was over at Stockport during the week-end, we are now living under canvas and the weather is very bad it rains every day most of the time. The news was good about the sinking of the Bismark*. I am just going out on a 3 day exercise.

*27/05/41 Bismark sunk 111 men saved and over 2000 lost.

31st May 1941 Saturday
Thank you very much for the nice long letter and cigs and P.O.book. We are living in tents here which is quite pleasant but it is terribly wet, it has rained every day for the last week. I am trying very hard to get back to my Regt, as I feel that I now I am rather wasting my time. It is possible that I may want my tin box the situation changes such a lot in different parts of the world that I maybe wanted anywhere at any time. My new Battery Comdr is Major Wylie who used to be our 2nd in command, he is very nice & his brother is a master at Marlboro' whom I knew slightly when I was there. I find I have to pay £3 a month income tax instead of £1 before.

If I were you I should keep Mrs Little at 15/- p.w. & let my money when it comes pay her as you shouldn't do the work. If you will have her I will start paying you the money now. I am not near Warwick the place is in Warwickshire. To-morrow I am going to North Wales for two nights to watch some shooting. I have forgotten the name of the place but it should be quite interesting.

Tell Dar I should love some Penguins for the men if she can send some, I will tell her when as I don't want them now, when I return to the Battery.

I have just received your letter written yesterday. The sun is out this afternoon & it is lovely, very hot sitting in a tent all afternoon. I have been sitting here tearing up all old letters etc, mostly yours, I am sorry but I have not room to put them if not. I came here by road in the truck which I have got & am going to N.Wales in it to-morrow till Tuesday morning. I have no camp bed but a lilo

3 Jun 1941. Tuesday 8.15 A.M. Officers Mess,
R.A. Practice Camp, Trawsfynydd

I have been here since Sunday & am just going back, the weather has been lovely huge lovely hills all round you know we can almost see Snowdon from here. I came through Festiniog and am going back via Dolgellau.

Don't write any more letters to Warwickshire all letters now should be to Stockport as I return on Wednesday or Thursday.

4th June 1941. 125 A.Tk Regt R.A. 13 Clifton Road,
Stockport, Cheshire

I expect you have by now got my letter from N.Wales. A most curious thing happened on my way back. I stopped for lunch at Shrewsbury and went to an hotel and sat at a table for two, soon after a man came & sat opposite he started talking after a bit & asked me the way out of the town to Wales (Llandudno). He said he had come a long way, I said where, he said Swindon, I keep an hotel there he said it was the Great Western. So I said it is exactly a year ago that my mother & father came & stayed there when I returned from Dunkirk & told him you were quite friendly with his wife. He was going to Llandudno to his son who had also came back from Dunkirk, who had developed something wrong with his feet. He gave me his address & I gave him yours as he said he thought his wife would like to write to you. We also discussed the damage done to his hotel by the troops who were there and the rows he had with the army. He wrote to the Times about it in November & it was published. I am going back to Stockport to-morrow Thursday. Could you add to my requirements by sending some blue Gillette razor blades, as I can't get them for love or money here. Its raining here. I am giving 2 lectures here before I go.

8th June 1941 Sunday

Thank you for the 50 cigs & socks v.nice. Will you tell Dar to send the books now please. My new Bty Comdr makes us & himself do P.T. in the morning at 6.30 a.m. I don't mind it, it is quite nice. Next Sunday I am going away again for 10 days to be attached to an armoured unit. I am glad we have invaded Syria as I think we shall get many of the French to join our forces. Thanks for the razor blades, but they are no good because you sent green, only Gillette blue will fit my razor so will you try again please. I went to church this morning not bad, this afternoon I am going to do a little gardening & shall buy some flowers. The weather is dull. No more to say.

12th June 1941 Thursday

I went to Manchester on Tuesday night with my friend Irving Watson & saw the play "Nutmeg Tree" with Y.Arnaud and Fredrick Leister (of Housemaster) the play is going to London next month. Next week is a new play of Noel Coward.

16th June 1941 Monday Attached 9th Royal Lancers, Tidworth, Hants

We are having lovely weather here very hot to-day living in tents. I forgot to tell you when I was with the Beds and Herts in Warwickshire the padre there lived at Wisbech & knew the reputation of your father, he said he was very much loved there & is spoken of still as a great man. Evidently he used to preach & tell the people to beware of drink because of the state he was in himself etc.

6th July 1941 Sunday

I am sorry I have not written before, but we have been out on exercise last week, we went out early Tuesday morning & didn't return till late on Thursday night. It was very pleasant we were up in Yorkshire near Ilkley, lovely country and the weather was perfect.

14th July 1941 Monday

The weather is still very bad here rain & clouds all the time. Tomorrow we are going out on a three day exercise which should be quite interesting. I got my wireless back on Friday it only cost 10/- to repair & goes beautifully now so I am very pleased. There is no more news for now that I can think of.

21st July 1941 Monday

I got back here all right at 9.30 on Thursday. Had a nice tea & dinner on the train soup, rissole veg & jelly coffee beer 5/- for everything. I took a taxi from the station & we have moved the mess to another house a few doors away, it is a much nicer house in every respect.

27th July 1941 Sunday

Thank you very much for the cigs for my birthday they were v.nice also for the two greetings telegrams, couldn't quite make out why it was 2 but they were both very welcome. I got the hair brush & cheque book etc all right. Daddy sent me a P.O. for 5/- D.D. some cigarettes, my Godmother the usual 30/- and a compendium from Ar Beet.

Yesterday evening Major Wylie (my Battery Comdr), Irvine Watson who came over & me went to Manchester first to a new theatre then to the Midland hotel and had a very good meal. Thanks for sending all the Times. The weather is lovely I am going down to our new place to-morrow week on the advance party to get the place ready, it is very nice just near Lichfield, about 8 miles away with quite a good bus service. The name of the village is Rugeley in Staffs.

3rd Aug 1941 Sunday

I had been away all the week on an exercise we had a lovely time , it was down in S.Wales and Hereford, lovely country & scenery & except for the first day (when it poured) very nice weather. I got my new service dress to, which fits beautifully, I tried it on the 1st time to-day. To-day we had a Non-conformist preacher, very good indeed he is the senior chaplain to the division.

I hear on the wireless to-day that we have bombed Berlin again, so I am afraid you will get it too. The Russians seem to be doing very well, I am surprised.

Thank Boss & Dar very much for me for their birthday presents.

11th Aug 1941 Monday. Officers Training School,
Trevalyn Manor, Rossett, Nr Wrexham.

I hope you received my telegram all right. I arrived here to-day for 10 days course messing officers course to learn all about the administrative and practical side of cooking. I complained that I had no interest and did not wish to come here & they said that I needn't come but they had to send someone in the end & I was the only one available, but still it will be 10 days holiday.

Last Wednesday I took an advance party of 20 men to our new billets and cleaned the place out etc and the main body arrived on Saturday afternoon.Our new place is a huge neglected house with a very big tower. I had the whole house distempered by the men I took down there.

14th Aug 1941 Thursday

Thank you for two letters which I have just got & two packets of cigarettes from Daddy. I am enjoying myself very much here. Yesterday & the day before it was lectures & this morning we went to Wrexham to see an infantry depot, the equipment they use for cooking etc. I was very bored at that, but there was a sidelight while we were waiting, the A.T.S. were on marching drill & it was better than a pantomime. I am going to see to-day what the trains are like to Lincolnshire on Saturday as I am thinking of going there for the week-end as we are free after we have cooked & eaten! our own lunch till Monday morning, that is if I can eat mine!! We have two A.T.S. officers on the course & I shall try & get their help. I am wondering what Attlee is going to say this afternoon. I have heard a rumour that we are going to declare war on France, but I think this is doubtful.

15th Aug 1941 Friday

Still enjoying myself here. The weather has been awful here lately rain all the time. I went to Chester this afternoon went to the pictures had a hair cut and tea & returned by bus.

We had to cook our own lunch to-day in mess tins & four others had to cook sea pie and rice & sultanas, I was chief cook & it was worth eating, very good in fact.

25th Aug 1941 Monday D Bty 125 A/T, c/o P.O.
Armitage, Nr Rugeley, Staffs

I hope you got my telegram all right to-day. I am so sorry I did not write mid-week last week. I got back here all right on Friday evening after a very pleasant time. On Friday afternoon we had an exam, which was very easy I shall be interested to hear when it is published how many marks I got. I hope you have heard from the Prodigal & that she hasn't involved herself too fully*. I was going to ask if I could this week-end off, but most of the others are going away to a firing camp & I shall be one of the only ones left so I don't feel justified, but I will try the following week-end. Blue Gillette Blades required urgently.

* Dorothy marriage surname changed to Newson

30th Aug 1941 Saturday

My Darling Mother & Daddy & Boss

Thank you for your letter this morning. I am sorry to hear Dar has been such a fool but I didn't expect they will be together for long.*

To-day has been lovely sunny etc but every other day this week it has rained.

The mess is lovely a glorious view of the country side all round with the main London- Manchester railway line about 400 yards away & whilst we eat we can see trains. The master of the house

Mr Bailey is a great chess man & I went in the night before last & played. On Wednesday Mrs Bailey asked the Major & myself into tea. They are charming people pots of money, 5 cars & in normal times 6 maids, but very generous. I think they are Roman C.

Cheer yourselves up it isn't such a terrible thing & don't be miserable when I come home. We will discuss your future.

P.T.O That blade you sent is all right so perhaps all green labels are the same, ask if they are slotted they are O.K. if only 3 holes NOT O.K.

P.S. I shall grow a beard if you don't hurry with the blades. (crossed out)

* Dorothy's marriage was later annulled.

24th Sept 1941 Wednesday

Thank you for your letter which I got to-day written on Monday. I am sorry I am so bad at writing. I am afraid I have some bad news. We are again going abroad in the near future but I think it is certain we shall get leave before then. To-morrow we are going on an exercise in the South of England somewhere. I will write now & again, I shan't receive any of your letters till our return on 4 or 5 October. If you hear in the papers or wireless of a big exercise you will know it is me. Don't worry about me going abroad again it might turn out the same as last time.

3rd Oct 1941. Friday In the field,
near Fenny, Stratford

I am sorry I have not written before, but it is very difficult when fighting battles as we have been moving a lot. This has been the biggest military exercise the country has ever held and a lot of big people have seen it including Churchill & the heads of all the foreign countries in this country. We started the exercise on Monday & it finished this morning, we went South of Newbury to Fenny Stratford which is on Watling St. I had hoped to be nearer Ar Beet but no luck, I imagine there was first the same activity near her (pen has run out), tanks aeroplanes, gas & all were out & I estimate there must have been over 500,000 men taking part. The weather has been variable we have had rain fog cold & sun, but it has been a good holiday. When we return we are going back to Stockport but I shall be staying at Armitage a day or two longer to have the place cleaned up & hand it over. I will let you know when to change my address back. I hope to be back on leave the week after next (I forget the date).

22nd Oct 1941 Wednesday

Thank you very much for your letters respectively and for the invoice from N.A.A.F.I., I am very sorry to have troubled you about it. I had a great honour to-day I was one of the three subalterns out of about 16 to be chosen to take some men for a demonstration of shooting for the King. We had to go some miles from here but he came very close to me & he did look nice but our Col mentioned to me afterwards & said he looks as though he tans his face with brown, just what you said. The King did not speak to me. All my clothes must reach me soon. I will send a wire to-morrow about that. I arrived back here all right on Sunday night about 10 pm. We had a warning on Monday night whilst they were raiding Liverpool, and there is one on now but there has only been one lot of gunfire.

About the King my photograph was taken standing behind a gun by movie tone news, so you may see me if you go to the flicks.

Chapter 4

Leaving England

From diary of events written after the war:

October 1941 We left Heaton Moor, Stockport, about 10 p.m. on Sunday 26th October, by train and arrived at Avonmouth at 4.30 a.m. 27th October. We then embarked on the "ORANSAY", about 20,000, tons - a very nice clean ship with a big officers' lounge. I had a cabin to myself. The ship had been damaged earlier by bombing off Narvik. The officers' food was excellent - but, according to them, the troops' was rather poor.

We sailed about noon on Tuesday, 28th October, with an escort of one Anti-Aircraft cruiser, the "CAIRO". During that night there were German aircraft overhead.

We arrived off Gourock in the Clyde about 5 p.m. on Wednesday, 29th October, and anchored; there were a number of other ships forming the convoy already there,

At 10.30 p.m. on Thursday, 30th October, in company with other ships we sailed: on the following morning we were joined by two more ships from Liverpool. Among the others were the RENO DEL PACIFICO; ANDES; ORONTES. We had an escort of 6 destroyers and the A.A. Ship CAIRO.

I was doing the job of assistant messing officer, and we had P.T., a little military training etc., and boat drill. A.A. Guns (2 Bofors and many Brens) were constantly manned for the first 3 or 4 days; however nothing unusual occurred.

On Sunday, 2nd November, I was awakened at dawn by the noise of aircraft and rushed on deck to find U.S.A. fighters flying round the convoy. One plane flew very low and dropped a message on each ship for the Captains.

We went down for breakfast and going back on deck there was the most wonderful sight - the sun shining on warships. They were American warships, and consisted of one Aircraft Carrier, one Battleship, three Cruisers and about seventeen Destroyers - and they were escorting a number of oil tankers. Our British escort then turned back, and the Americans took over. It amused us at the time, having such a big escort to take us over the safest part of our Atlantic crossing. It was known by now that we were bound for Halifax, to travel on U.S.A. boats - the first time any British troops had travelled on them. The Atlantic was very calm, considering the time of year - but for 36 hours we rolled a bit.

Early on Saturday, 8th November, going on deck, we saw land. It appeared like the Yorkshire moors, rather barren. We then entered Halifax harbour.

> Nov 1941. 125 Anti-Tank Regt R.A. c/o Army P.O.
> 1635 (just before going to India)

Thank you for the £1 note for stockings I am afraid I haven't bought them yet. Thanks also for the shirt and vests, the latter I received this evening. Well I am sorry to say we go before Monday so in future address all my letters to the above address. Everything is ready packed & lots of things have gone. The sirens have just gone 8.35 p.m. I am going to write a lot of letters to-day, I haven't written any that I should have done for some long time. (9.25 p.m.) We have had a short burst of gun fire & nothing else touch wood. I hope you are all v.well, have you gone to Blandford yet? You must get well & stay well. I will write again on the ship but don't expect you will get the letter for sometime after I have gone. Don't forget to number all the letters you write me & keep a note of the dates sent & I will acknowledge them all. Also send letters now & again by air-graph. I must stop now we are all going to church to-morrow. I am assuming that you promised not to worry about me, so don't, will you give my love to everybody.

I enclose cheque for £5 in part payment of articles bought on leave.

I have sent my wireless home as it is more a liability than asset, it requires repairing. I am also sending home new batteries bought from Bentalls unused, suggest you get them credited

7th Nov 1941. Letter No.1.(on the way to India)
I am very well & happy & enjoying life. I have not been sea sick up to now thank goodness. They gave me the job of messing officer on the ship, so have been quite busy all the time which is preferable to walking round the decks doing nothing. I have not had any mail yet but hope to in the near future, of course I can't tell you anything at all, it will all have to wait till the war is over which I hope won't be long. I have read a few books but otherwise can't really account for my spare time. We are having good food & I have got a lovely bed.

I am writing to Muriel, so expect you will hear from her. Number as I have done all your letters then we shall know if any are missing.

I am afraid this is very short. I went to H.C. on Sunday at 7.30 A.M. & morning service at 10.45 in the officers mess. No more for now. Don't worry about me I am quite safe & very well.

7th Nov 1941 To Boss

Darling Boss
I am still quite all right and enjoying life. Where I am and what I am doing I can't tell you of course, but the time will come when eventually I can tell you of all my experiences. There is very little which I can say in a letter so this letter will be short. Up to now thank goodness I have not suffered at all from sea sickness. I expect you will be very glad to get home for the Christmas holidays and out of the way of a lot of screeching kids; now Dear I must close.

I have written to Ma & Pa. Take care of them both. Much love Douglas

Letter from Mr Heelas to Douglas

10th Nov 1941
My Dear Douglas. Thank you for the letters which I see and which I don't see. I hope you are quite fit and well, and that the climate fits you, and I hope that you do not have to encounter many various beasts! You want to be like Diogenes if you are assaulted - turns the lion's tail outside and keep him there!

We go on the same old way day after day, it gets rather monotonous, but perhaps it is good for us. Hoping to hear from you soon, and may God bless you and protect you.

From Douglas To Boss

15th Nov 1941

I am still very well and enjoying life. A few days ago we started to dress in thin clothes as the heat is absolutely awful. I go about in tropical shirt and shorts and with no tie or jacket. We shall be arriving very soon in our second port of call. We get some very refreshing drinks on board such as ices and lemonade so that helps to keep one cool.

Give my love to Ma & Pa and all at home. I hope you are looking after them all right.

From Douglas To Mother & Father

17th Nov 1941. Letter No.2. (on the way to India)

I am enjoying myself. We have now got into our tropical kit but I am still very hot even with it on. I wear a tropical shirt and shorts. The sea is beautifully blue and we are having glorious sunshine. At night it is much too hot to have any clothes on. I am now sitting in the officers lounge with all the windows open and sea all around, I wish you could see the sight. The sea is beautifully calm. We are expecting to arrive in our second port of call in a day or so. We changed ships at our last port of call, of course I can't tell you any more information about us but when I come home for good I will unravel everything. Number your letters to me.

I am messing officer which entails quite a lot of work in the heat but it is very nice to have something to do. In the evening I usually go & stand out on deck and get the evening breezes & have also been reading quite a lot of books. The food on the ship is quite good but in this heat one doesn't want much, I drink gallons of water though & they have got ices and lemonade so we are very lucky. I have written to Muriel so expect you will be hearing from her. Give my love to the Aunts & Dar. Take care of yourselves it won't be long before I am home.

From diary of events November 1941 written after the war.

We transferred with all our stores to the U.S.S. JOSEPH T. DICKMAN (about 13,000 tons), carrying about 1,200 troops. I was appointed messing officer. It was a clean ship. I shared the cabin with three others - it was rather crowded, but had a private bathroom etc. The officers had a small lounge in a U shape - but there was not much deck space. The troops had wire beds in tiers and fed on a cafeteria system. This was preferable to the British troop ships, where they sleep in hammocks and feed from tables in the same place. The food on the DICKMAN was magnificent - mainly American. The officers fed with the American officers and had some negroes waiting on them. No drink was allowed on board. The ship used to be called PRESIDENT ROOSEVELT.

Also in convoy were WEST POINT (ex American, 36,000 tons): the troops on this ship (about 5,000) did not have a very good time - MOUNT VERNON: WAKEFIELD (with Div. Staff on board). I was working hard, as we had to supply cooks and other kitchen personnel, and there were about 5 or 6 Americans who supervised.

Relations between the British and American officers were formal, and we heard later that the Captain had forbidden fraternisation between troops. However, it was very friendly and all over the ship one saw one or two Americans with crowds of our troops round them. The Americans were very surprised to see us, as they had not been told who was going on board - their favourite bet was taking Canadians to England.

There was a Canadian Division (I believe 1st Armoured Div) in Halifax going to England on ships we left. The Canadians were helping us in contacting American officers.

I, as messing officer, was taken to see the supply officer who was amiable. One of the first questions he asked was "Who is paying for the food - is it paid by lease-lend Act? This tickled me a lot - asking a very junior officer a question about international finance.

There was a soft drinks fountain, which sold ices, lemonade, etc, and also a canteen selling American cigarettes and other necessities.

It was curious seeing the town lit up after so long of black-out.

In the evening a film was shown on deck and about midnight we pulled out and anchored in the stream to allow another ship to load up.

On the ship was 196 Field Ambulance, under Colonel Houston; R.E. Field Park was under Major Noble, and Ordnance troops and a few others. Colonel Dean was O.C. Ship. The Executive officer and Captain were rather difficult about many things - especially water tight doors. About once every five or six days I was Guard officer, which meant going round all the sentries who were on water tight doors day and night. The feeding took about two hours per meal, and the men had to go down a very steep iron ladder and queue up. Breakfasts started at 6.30 a.m. lunch at 11a.m. and supper at 3.30 p.m. I made friends with an American dentist, and used to play chess with him in the evenings.

At about 8.30 a.m. on Monday 10th November, we sailed. We had the same escort as previously. After two or three days it began to get very hot and we changed into tropical kit. On 11th November we untied and sailed round the harbour, while they tested the degaussing gear (anti-magnetic mine device), and did not tie up again until the afternoon. Also on 11th the troops had very special food, including chicken, to celebrate Armistice Day.

We used to have church services on board the ORONSAY and DICKMAN, and concerts, about once a week on the DICKMAN, and every afternoon we used to have lectures on different military subjects (I usually went to sleep). Part of my job was censoring men's mail - this was very boring. Most evenings on the DICKMAN I used to play cards, and later in the evenings we had coffee and sandwiches in the dining room.

On the DICKMAN we used to wear shirts and shorts all day, but changed to slacks, collar and tie and tunic.

17 - 19 November Trinidad

Nothing unusual occurred during this trip and we arrived in TRINIDAD about a week later, having shed some of our escort on the way. The entrance to Port of Spain is very beautiful, surrounded by hills and palm trees on top. We anchored about six miles off the shore, and spent the next two days taking on stores, refuelling etc. We were not allowed ashore, but a few official people went to send mail, buy things for people etc.

We then sailed on, and a fast oil tanker came with us. When we were opposite DAKAR our escort was increased slightly. We had the ceremonial crossing the line celebrations. I got off fairly lightly, as I said my words quickly before getting ducked too much. We had a very uneventful trip from then on.

From Douglas To Mother & Father

30th Nov 1941. Sunday Letter No.3.
(on the way to India)

I hope you are both very well, and neither of you have been ill lately. I have not had any news, since I left England and isn't much chance for quite a long time. We have now called at two ports and I am writing this in anticipation of arriving at our third fairly soon.

Some time ago we crossed the equator and went through the ceremony when King Neptune "comes aboard", it was great fun. I expect you know all about it the main thing is being ducked in a big tank of water.

The heat has been terrific at times but lately it has cooled down quite a lot. Many of the men have been in the sun and are very sun burnt, but I have kept out of it as much as possible. After a fortnight on this boat I was relieved of my duties as messing officer so now am having a good rest, with eating & sleeping as the main features of every day. We have had three or four concerts on board given by the men including my batman who plays the violin beautifully. Also there have been many boxing contests. We have got a C of E padre on board and we had a very nice service this morning.

I am hoping to be able to send you a cable at the next port of call just to let you know that all's well with me. I have had prickly heat which starts from perspiration and the whole of my body was covered in heat spots, but they have practically disappeared now. I have felt very fit indeed up to now. Don't worry about me but look after yourselves.

We had scares of U Boats now and again, and destroyers dropped depth charges, but we think it was only whales. Rumours were rife as to where we were going, but we were eventually told CAPE TOWN. A few days out from there we ran into very bad weather one night, unexpectedly, and nothing had been tied down, so a considerable amount of damage was done in the hospital and kitchens - breaking glasses, cups, plates etc. A safe in the office went through a wall. The storm only lasted a few hours.

We had to go 300 miles south of CAPE TOWN before entering because of enemy forces in the vicinity, and it got so cold that we changed our clothing back to winter clothes.

War with JAPAN was declared on 8th December, Pearl Harbour attack was 7th December.

At about 11 a.m. on 9th December we again sighted land, and could see Table Mountain. The alarm bells rang and we were at action stations for about an hour. We never found out whether this was just because of minefields or enemy ships. At about 4.30 p.m. we tied up on the dock side.

Cape Town 9th -13th December,. The quay-side had a number of natives on it, and people threw money and cigarettes etc. to beggars. We were allowed leave from 7 p.m. till 2 a.m., and given an advance of £5 S.A. The arrangements made for our reception were terrific - all along from the docks hundreds of cars were waiting to take troops to families for meals and sight-seeing. This went on every day, and the people were very kind. I went out that evening with some friends - John Watts and others. We went to a restaurant and had some drinks and a meal, and then went on to a dance specially arranged for British and American officers. I did not dance, but later on we were told that a high personage was going to make a speech - and who should walk in but General Smuts. He passed within a few yards of me. He got a terrific reception and made a speech. The gist of it was "The only good thing the Japs had done for the world was to bring America into the War" - at which there was terrific applause - not much appreciated by the Yanks.

I left about midnight and came back to the ship by train.

The next day, 10th December, after breakfast, we went for a route march, which took about two hours. Then I met Ken Rubin and we had lunch in a restaurant and had a look around the shops. Everything seemed very expensive. We then took a tram outside the town and went and looked at the Cecil Rhodes Memorial - it is fairly high up and one gets a beautiful view. On one side you see the South Atlantic, and on the other the Indian Ocean. Near the memorial was a small tea shop where we had tea. We returned to the tram stop and two people in a car asked us if we would like to see the sights. They took us round a coast road for about 1 1/2 hours drive, and then went to their cottage on the coast and had drinks - it was a lovely drive. The weather was fine and warm during our stay in CAPE TOWN. They drove us back to the town and we had a quiet dinner and returned to the ship.

On 11th December I was on duty - on guard at the gangway of the ship. In the evening they showed a film "Pygmalion". A very noticeable thing was the fraternisation between British troops and Yank sailors - a number of them went out together.

On 12th December we went for a route march in the morning, and then George Prestige and I went out to lunch and then took a tram on the way to Table Mountain, the tram terminus - but we found no one going as there was too much wind, and we were too lazy to walk up. But it was worth going there if only to get a view of Cape Town bay and all the shipping. We went back by tram into town, had tea and learned of the sinking of the PRINCE OF WALES and the REPULSE. We then walked around the shops.

I asked some question from a troops sightseeing bureau, and the lady in charge asked us if we were doing anything, and as we were not, she invited us out to dinner and spend the evening - so we went in her car to her house, about 6 miles out, met her husband and daughter and then went to a hotel for dinner. She asked us if we would like to go to a dance with her daughter or have a quiet evening - we said the later, and they drove us to some high point above Cape Town and looked at the lights of town. We then drove back to their house, had light refreshments and talked till about 11 p.m. We signed our names in their visitors' book, just under a number of names from the PRINCE OF WALES, and they said they would write home to our people. They then drove us back to the docks and we went aboard ship. At Cape Town I bought two books which were very expensive - one was Cavalcade and the other Stalky and Co., by Kipling.

One thing I have always regretted was not having sent parcels of food and clothes, as I thought I was not allowed to do so - but find others did.

At about midday on 13th December we sailed again. After about two days we were told to change our address to Middle East Forces, but the next day this was cancelled, and the MOUNT VERNON and another ship left us. The MOUNT VERNON went straight to SINGAPORE and the other ship to MOMBASA to undergo a repair. Our course was altered and we headed straight for BOMBAY. On Christmas Day we went to church early, then went and saw the men's food, which included chicken and plum pudding. The Americans gave gifts of cigarettes etc., and everybody had a new card, nicely decorated. In the afternoon there were carols, and after that a concert.

24th Dec 1941. Wednesday Letter No.4. (at sea)
I hope you received my last cablegram all right from our last port of call & I hoped it would arrive in time to be a nice Christmas present.

At this port of call we had a magnificent time. I meet a friend from another boat one who used to go about with Irvine Watson & I and lives at Twickenham. The first night I went with some friends to a hotel & drank beer till I had had too much!! & then we went by taxi to a dance which was arranged for officers and arrived back at 1.15am to the boat. The next morning we went for a 2 hours route march which was lovely having ones feet on "terra firma" again after such a long time on the boat. We had lunch on board then I met this friend from Twickenham & we went and looked at the shops, lovely things no rationing there except ½ lb butter per person per day and NO white bread all brown, after that we went to a beauty spot by bus (troops don't have to pay on buses or trams). We saw the beauty spot and were waiting for a bus back when a car pulled up and asked if we would like a drive along the sea and see some more beauty spots so they took us for about 3 hours drive, brought us back to their house and gave us the best brandy I have ever tasted, much better than France. They dropped us in the town & we had dinner and then to bed on board. The next day I was on duty so had to stay on board. The last day I went out with another friend who lives near Oxford, a parson's son. We first did some shopping I bought a tie and some stockings frightfully expensive 6/6d a pair, cheapest they had. I then bought some books Stalky & Co by Kipling & Cavalcade then we had some tea and then some kind lady asked us if she & her family could entertain us for the evening so we accepted. We went for another car drive then to a hotel for a lovely dinner then another drive (you'd think I must have been tired of drives) then we went to their house and had a "family" evening sitting & talking & play with their three lovely cats. About 11 p.m. they drove us back to the docks. Well that's my shore leave and I thoroughly enjoyed it. The last people who took us out have got your name and address & they are going to write to you, they were both elderly 60-65. The arrangements and expense these town people went to make everybody happy was wonderful. Arrangements were mostly for the men as opposed to officers and as one came out of the dock gates there was one long line of cars waiting for the troops, the people would take the troops for a drive then supper and then to a dance or pictures etc, of course everybody wants to go back to this particular place!! (no names can be mentioned)

It is Christmas eve & as I sit here I can hear them practicing for a carol service for to-morrow. I have never felt so un-Christmas like in my life. What with having great difficulty in trying to keep cool etc, instead of having snow or ice on the ground. We are still at sea but nearing our destination. We have plenty of entertainment P.T. tugs of war all sorts of deck games and a concert per week, and I think everybody is enjoying life especially me.

To-morrow Christmas day I shall be thinking of you I shall go to H.C. in the morning at 7 o'clock. All the men are having turkey & plum pudding & I expect they will put up some decorations of sorts. I hope you are all right at home & enjoying yourselves, no air raids I hope. Naturally we have received no mail yet & so I am longing to hear all about you. The sea has been & still is as calm as a mill pond, except for one night when it "cut up rough" and all chairs & tables etc went flying!! I had to give a lecture to the officers of the regt a few days ago on messing, it went down all right I think. Every officer had to give a lecture & could choose his subject. Well this letter will have to keep you all going for a bit. I am very fit, well and happy, but I am longing for the day when we shall all be re-united, lets hope it won't be long. My love to Dar the Aunts D.D & everybody else interested. Write to my Godmother & give her my love, I will write to her soon. I expect you have heard of my correspondence with Boss. Take care of yourselves, I will too.

Telegram from Douglas to Mr & Mrs Heelas

31st Dec 1941

All well New address Put name of Regt c/o G.P.O Bombay India Cable to me.

Happy Birthday Douglas Heelas

From diary of events written after the war. 29th December

On 29th December we entered BOMBAY harbour about 8 p.m. and tied up at the docks. Bombay is a lovely sight - huge white buildings - from the sea.

The first evening I was Guard officer so could not go ashore. We had no idea why we had been brought to India, but the next morning we were told we were going up country about 100 miles.

On 30th December I went with some friends in a car in the morning and saw some of the sights. We went to the Royal Yacht Club for lunch - a very good meal, and on to a bathing pool by the sea in the afternoon and had tea there. For dinner we went back to the Yacht Club and stayed there for the evening.

The city is the dirtiest place I have yet seen - with people begging all the time, and at night Indians sleeping on the pavements or in the gutter.

On 31st December we went to the Yacht Club for lunch, and in the afternoon went shopping. I bought some chocolates and a suitcase - everything dirt cheap. In the evening we went to the Taj Mahal Hotel for dinner - a very bad and expensive one. I went back to the ship early and went to watch night service. Next morning, 1st January, we were up early and went down to the station. Our train was not due to leave till 6 p.m. We were allowed in the town in the morning, and Major Wylie and I did some shopping and then went to lunch in the Yacht Club. There is a beautiful view from there of the bay, with one or two warships, and a large number of yachts. We then returned to the station and waited for the train.

At 6 p.m. we left. The carriages have bunks which are let down from the roof to lie on, and have wash basins attached to each compartment, which holds four. I shared a compartment with a padre. We arrived at our destination, Ahmednagar, at about 6 a.m., where there was breakfast. We stopped on the way at Poona.

2nd - 22nd January Ahmednagar

I drove by truck from the station to the cantonment, and as I was messing officer for the Regiment, started to get things organised for feeding. I walked to the dairy and ordered milk; then went in a bullock cart with Sergeant Cook to the contractors' place to buy rations - as only dry rations are supplied by the R.I.A.S.C. I vowed I would never travel by that method again, as it was very bumpy and slow, and the roads were bad.

For our stay there I was very busy as messing officer. Things were difficult - meat was very tough and there were a lot of complaints about food generally.

We sleep in small one-storied brick houses, with fans, electric lights, but no up-to-date lavatories or washing arrangements. I slept on my lilo on the floor.

Now and again I went to a small cinema. For newspapers we got the Times of India. In the mess we employed an Indian to do the cooking - he was expensive and the food was not good. The days were hot and the nights cool, so that was pleasant.

The Battery did a lot of training and route marches, but I did not partake. Rumour was rife as to our destination, some even saying we were going home - other rumours said we were staying in India. However we got orders move back to Bombay. Most of the Division left a few days before, and we left in the evening of 22nd January and arrived in Bombay early next morning. Going through the outskirts of Bombay conditions looked terrible - goats and other animals walk in and out of the houses, and the people were in rags.

We pulled in next to the ship and then had breakfast. We loaded the ship and embarked ourselves at about 10.a.m.

23rd January Empress Of Asia

We all got a shock when we saw the boat - a C.P.R. boat of about 17,000 tons - it looked, and was dirty and old. A very old coal burning ship, with 3 funnels due for scrapping. I shared a cabin with 2 other officers. There was a good but small officers' lounge. The men's quarters were filthy and food was awful - some of the meat and bread was bad, and the heat was terrific. The crew told us that on one of their trips some New Zealand airmen were taken on board, and walked off again, refusing to travel on such a ship. They did not give us much chance to walk off, as we sailed at 3 p.m. in company with two other ships and a destroyer, for an unknown destination. Later off Ceylon, we picked up some more ships and a bigger escort etc, for an unknown destination, still.

On 3rd February we passed through the straits of Sunda in the early morning, and at 2 p.m. a large part of the convoy turned to enter Batavia, Java. Five ships went on, destined for Singapore. Amongst our escort was the cruiser "EXETER" and one or two Dutch cruisers and destroyers.

We received a message to say that our destination depended on availability of fighter escort (needless to say we never saw a fighter). We were also escorted by a seaplane, which flew around all day. Up to now we had an uneventful trip.

22nd Jan 1942 Telegram from Douglas to Mr & Mrs Heelas
All well Douglas Heelas

Chapter 5 Douglas

Missing In Action

St. Stephen's Church
(East Twickenham)
"The Lord watch between me and thee, when
we are absent one from another."

Name ...Douglas.........................

PRAYER

O Almighty God, Who art a stronghold to all those
who put their trust in Thee, keep this our loved one
in Thy safety; In danger give him deliverance, in
temptation keep him true to Thee, in loneliness comfort
him, and at all times keep him and us conscious of Thy
Presence and resting in Thy love and protection.

Bring him home in safety and give him, and us all,
a deeper knowledge of Thyself as our Saviour and King;
through Jesus Christ our Lord.   Amen.

ADVICE TO THE RELATIVE OF A MAN WHO IS MISSING

In view of the official notification that your relative is missing, you will naturally wish to hear what is being done to trace him.

The Service Departments make every endeavour to discover the fate of missing men, and draw upon all likely sources of information about them.

A man who is missing after an engagement may possibly be a prisoner of war. Continuous efforts are made to speed up the machinery whereby the names and camp addresses of prisoners of war can reach this country. The official means is by lists of names prepared by the enemy Government. These lists take some time to compile, especially if there is a long journey from the place of capture to a prisoner of war camp. Consequently " capture cards " filled in by the prisoners themselves soon after capture and sent home to their relatives are often the first news received in this country that a man is a prisoner of war. That is why you are asked in the accompanying letter to forward at once any card or letter you may receive, if it is the first news you have had.

Even if no news is received that a missing man is a prisoner of war, endeavours to trace him do not cease. Enquiries are pursued not only among those who were serving with him, but also through diplomatic channels and the International Red Cross Committee at Geneva.

The moment reliable news is obtained from any of these sources it is sent to the Service Department concerned. They will pass the news on to you at once, if they are satisfied that it is reliable. It would be cruel to raise false hopes, such as may well be raised if you listen to one other possible channel of news, namely, the enemy's broadcasts. These are listened to by official listeners, working continuously night and day. The few names of prisoners given by enemy announcers are carefully checked. They are often misleading, and this is not surprising, for the object of the inclusion of prisoners' names in these broadcasts is not to help the relatives of prisoners, but to induce British listeners to hear some tale which otherwise they could not be made to hear. The only advantage of listening to these broadcasts is an advantage to the enemy.

The official listeners can never miss any name included in an enemy broadcast. They pass every name on to the Service Department concerned. There every name is checked, and in every case where a name can be verified, the news is sent direct to the relatives.

There is, therefore, a complete official service designed to secure for you and to tell you all discoverable news about your relative. This official service is also a very human service, which well understands the anxiety of relatives and will spare no effort to relieve it.

Advice To Relative Of A Man Who Is Missing

Letter From Mother and Father to Douglas

24th Jan 1942

This morning your letter dated Nov 30th No3 has just arrived, we have had the two other letters, I am very sorry I haven't numbered mine. I lost count with airmail coming and I didn't always have my account book by me. I have sent at least – 8 by post – 6 air mail & one air graph on Dec 15th, my last air mail was on Wed last – 21st Jan This is all according to my account book. I shall be glad to hear when you get a letter, how & where! Also thank you very much for the Cable received on Thursday the 2nd We've had – Assuming you having a visit – from King Neptune – I wonder if you have shaved too with – a good razor. My brother Napier was home as I was in bed for a week with the bronchial asthma again & got lots food, he & Dorothy bought me a delicious chicken, so we had a good feed! I am afraid of telling you the same news in most of my letters! We used to have a joke against my mother she wrote to the family time & again that " Napier was bringing a monkey home"! I am very interested in all your letters I will touch on the points that you'll remember which it was. You say, we have called at 2 ports & now are arriving at our 3rd fairly soon also it had been so hot & you had prickly heat, am glad its gone, you are not to get in the sun too much, wish we could though. I am glad you had a change from messing officer – must be a responsibility. Still having the concerts & you would feel proud of your bat-man playing the violin.

We haven't seen DD for a week as the snow and frost has been very sever, she will come next week and I will give her your message (love to DD) they haven't had a maid for 2 months, it's difficult to get help. We still have our woman Mrs Wright, she's 10/- a week which is quite good, and I give her bits of food over, for which she is always most grateful. We have a fire in our bedroom & have been sitting in it too since Boss went back last Monday as it is colder in the drawing room and it saves the coal (we shan't suffer from prickly heat!). Today all the snow was cleared off and it is not so cold I am thankful to say. We shall go to Tetbury next month - Feb- for a week or two Aunt J B is well in health, in her mind worse. I've written at great length on her so won't repeat it in this letter. I think I told you her heart is rather feeble & she will be 81 in April, one can't expect much. Aunt Beet & Aunt J are very well, they've let another room for 7/- a week so they are getting 37/- & the lodgers pay for everything, the light & cooking heat, not bad for the depths of the country. Bush let me have a 2lbs jar of mince meat this week. I'm quite fussy over it and shall make some pies for Boss, she loves them, I wish I could send you some. I wonder if you get fruit bananas and oranges etc.

I'm going out to send a cable this afternoon – I wonder how long they take.

Good my dear old boy, we think of you such a lot, I am glad you had a padre on board & so were able to have services – keep it – up if you can "it's a link" with us too-

With dearest love from Daddy & me – your loving Mother

The above letter was returned by Home Postal Centre 3rd March 1943, delivery could not be effected.

HPC.R.E. Ref:- HPC/G/RLB/CAS HOME POSTAL CENTRE, ROYAL ENGINEERS, NOTTINGHAM. 3 MAR 1943

Dear Madam

It is regretted that, although the accompanying letter was forwarded overseas, delivery could not be effected.

Air transmission could not be provided at the time because of the demands on available aircraft capacity for military traffic but dispatches were made by surface transport for as long as possible.

Postage stamps for...1/1 ½........ representing the difference between the ordinary postage and the air postage paid is accordingly enclosed herewith.

.........Mother........ writer of a letter addressed to ....Lieut Heelas ....

D. ROSS Lt. Colonel, Officer Commanding

From Diary

4th February 1942 at about 11 a.m., going through Bangka Straits in line ahead, with the EXETER leading, we were the last of the transports. We saw on the starboard side, very high, 27 aircraft. We naturally thought they were ours, but soon the alarm gong went. The drill was for all officers to go to the mess decks, except for one per unit to go to the officers' lounge, which was the Report Center, and all W.Os and Serge's. to their cabins.

The planes started bombing us and straddled the ship, doing a little damage to the officers' dining room and holing some lifeboats. The heavier attack was on the EXETER: there were no casualties and only slight damage to the convoy. The escort put up a heavy barrage and so did all LMGs on transports. After the attack the O.C. Troops changed the drill by saying no W.Os or Sergeant's would stay in their cabins - and this eventually proved a great blessing.

We were expecting other attacks all day, but none came.

On 5th February I was up on deck early and could see vast fires burning in Singapore. There were only two destroyers as escorts - the others had turned back in the night.

At about 11.15 a.m., when 15 miles off Singapore, the alarm bells rang and we all went to action stations until after the all clear went - only to be followed by the alarm again. The planes started attacking then. They singled us out - probably because we had three funnels. We were in one of the forward mess decks, with the troops singing and playing violins etc. The first bomb (oil) burst in the officers' lounge - the second burst further aft, near the hospital, and they both penetrated two or three decks.

After about 1/2 hour smoke was coming into our mess deck through the ventilator shafts and we evacuated from there. The noise of A.A. from the destroyers and our ship was terrific. On one of the landings, about half way up there was a noise like the sound of bombs, which turned out to be the anchor being dropped. We all dropped to the ground until told by a sailor, and then got up looking sheepish! When we eventually got on deck we saw the whole bridge ablaze. We all went to the fore peak where they were lowering the wounded into the water on rafts. Although planes were still flying around, and there were crowds of troops on the fore peak, they did not attempt to machine gun us.

Aft of the ship a destroyer had tied up, and troops were walking off. The hospital was cut off as the fire had spread, and the Doctor was getting the patients out of the port-holes. After getting them all out he managed to get out himself (although he was fat). He was awarded the M.C.

In the officers' lounge three officers were never found, and some were badly burned.

After being on the fore peak for some time the O.C. Troops, (Lt.-Col. Dean) ordered all those who could swim overboard. I went over and started swimming to a landing stage, but the current was too strong, so I went round the front and after about half an hour was picked up by a small motor-boat. (Boats were all over the sea picking people up.) After picking up some more we were put on a sort of steamship boat (about 2,000 tons), where we were given drinks, cigarettes etc. We then moved towards the harbour. The Asia was ablaze from stem to stern and we heard we had anchored 10 yards from a minefield.

We landed about 4 p.m. and were given tea and cakes and moved off in a lorry. Before going over the side I had taken off my boots and socks, and when landing only had a pair of shorts and a shirt. We were driven by lorry to some empty houses in Branksome Road.

5th February Singapore

Branksome Road was near the airport. We had a meal and settled for the night.

On Friday, 6th February, they started re-equipping us. We were given rusty rifles which had been salvaged from up-country, and needed considerable cleaning up. There were many Jap planes about - they came over in formations of 27.

On Saturday, 7th February, about 11 a.m., 27 planes dropped bombs on the aerodrome about ¼ - ½ mile away - no casualties.

On 8th February we went on a recce of the area, taking all afternoon, but we never occupied the area. Sitting on the verandah that night we heard terrific barrages of guns, and the sky was lit up with flashes; it was the Nips landing on the island.

On Monday, 9th February, we heard on the B.B.C. that the Japs had landed - this was the first official news.

In the afternoon of 10th February we moved to Tel Palu and took up defensive positions, but about 5 p.m. we had to move to Seletar aerodrome, where we sent out patrols all night. It was very quiet.

The buildings were in a bad mess - people had looted and meat was going bad, maggots etc.

11th February, Wednesday. Left Seletar at about 11 a.m. Two Nip aircraft came over very low to have a look. Owing to lack of transport we had to leave most of our kit behind. We moved to a hill near Thompson Road, and prepared to dig in, but were withdrawn to Battery H.Q. just before dark.

12th February, Thursday. Took up positions in same area where we stayed all day. No casualties in Battery up to now.

13th February, Friday. Moved onto Graves Hill in the early morning, only about ¼ mile away. We were shelled by mortars when arriving and had some casualties. Took Battery H.Q. into position at the bottom of the hill near Thompson Road. Then I walked up to R.H.Q. to get some rations and returned. Mortared all day intermittently. No more casualties.

14th Febuary, Saturday. In the same position - mortar fire continued. Paid periodic visits to Battery H.Q. One man got shell shock.

15th February, Sunday. About 3.30 p.m. the C.O. came round and told of the capitulation, and that at 4 p.m. we were to pile our arms and hang white towels over them. Talked with Major Wylie until late.

PRISONERS OF WAR - CHANGI 17th February - 3rd April

16th February, Monday. Collected some kit, and played cards etc.

17th February, Tuesday. In the afternoon started marching to Changi (15 miles). Late that night, within about 6 miles of Changi, we were so tired that we slept. Fireflies on the road lit it up, and the natives gave us coconuts and drink.

18th February, Wednesday. We arrived at Changi early in the morning.

ROBERTS BARRACKS, CHANGI was used as POW camp

At Roberts Barracks 18th February - 4th March

1. Food. We were living on very short rations of bully, biscuits, milk, tea, flour etc. One by one these items ran out and we came down to rice diet, one pound of rice per day, curry powder and some vegetables. It was a time of hunger. Cigarettes were very short.

2. Accommodation. The officers were living on the balcony and the men inside the concrete three storied barracks. These held 88 in peace time - we got about 1,000 in each.

3. News. Wireless sets were forbidden, but there were a number of illicit ones - although at this time on never heard the news. The Nips issued to H.Qs The Syonan Times*, and we got a certain amount from that.

4. Church. On 22nd February we had an outdoor church service (memorial) for the whole of 18 Division R.A. Afterwards the salute was taken by the C.R.A.
5. Medical. This was adequate, I think.
6. General Treatment. We did not see many Nips, but some people were slapped for minor breaches.
7. Work. A lot of time we spent digging latrines, and generally making ourselves as comfortable as possible.
8. Special Orders by Nips. (a) All Nip officers to be saluted by all ranks. (b) All officers to remove badges of rank and wear a star on their left pocket. (c) No trading with natives. (d) No going beyond the wire - which was about three miles away.

*Published in English formerly called 'The Straits Times' from 1845, was renamed 'The Syonan Shimbun' from 20th February 1942 until 4th September 1945.

20ᵗʰ March, 1942. The War Office, Casualty Branch, Blue Coat School, Church Road, Wavertree, Liverpool, 15

Madam, I am directed to inform you that according to the latest

information available in this office your son, Lieutenant D.E.N. Heelas, Royal Artillery, was serving in Malaya during the hostilities which terminated in the capitulation of Singapore on the 15ᵗʰ Febuary, 1942.

Every endeavour is being made though diplomatic and other channels to obtain information concerning him, and it is hoped that he is safe although he may be a Prisoner of War, It will be necessary, however, to post him as "Missing" pending receipt of some definite information.

Immediately any further information is obtained it will be sent to you, and I am to request you to be good enough to notify this Office of any change of your address. Should any news reach you from any other source or should you receive any card or letter from your son it will be appreciated if you will at once forward it to this Department.

I am,

Madam,

Your obedient Servant,

A.Williams

From Diary

4th March - 3rd April 1942

We had to move out of Roberts Barracks to make room for a hospital, as the Nips had ordered all wounded and sick out of Singapore. We went under canvas on a very pleasant raised piece of ground overlooking the Straits between the mainland and the island, seeing a lot of the Jap Navy.

The Japs wired us into areas - there were 18 Div Hospital Southern area, 1, 8 and 11 Div and Australian areas. To go from one to another we had to have a flag, and the approaches to each area (which were about 100 yards apart) were guarded by Indian guards - whom everybody had to salute.

The Black market started up and we could buy cigarettes at $1 for 10; tins of butter and bully at $3.50 each. Food became much worse.

All this time the wounded were coming in from Singapore - dysentery became rife.

There was not much work to do. About mid-March a party was called to work in Singapore, and a party of 3,000 went down. By this time we were able to get some extra kit from a dump.

4th April - 3rd August River Valley Camp

On 3rd April (Good Friday) our Regiment was ordered to go to River Valley Camp, Singapore, on a working party. We marched to Changi Jail early in the morning, and then were taken on by transport.

1. Food. This was much better, although still a rice diet - but we got more meat and vegetables. We could buy bread at 10 cents a small loaf, jam, and other things fairly cheaply. 29th April 1942 the Imperial Japanese Army gave a tin of pineapple to P.O.W.s in honour of the Emperor's birthday. We got an issue

of 10 cigarettes a week, and could buy Chinese cigs. which were awful.

2. Accommodation. We were housed in long huts (originally built for refugees from up-country). There were two platforms for sleeping, one on top of the other, made of boarding. The sides were of matting, and attar roofs, and also electric light.

3. News. We were allowed to buy the Syonan Times. Jon Watts also brought in a wireless set by bits in food tins, and set it up under his bed. It worked from the light, and he used to listen in at 10 pm. every evening. There was a rumour that Queen Mary had died.

   John Watts also was collecting stores of arms. He brought in 2 Bren guns and Tommy guns, many grenades and ammunition, which he got whilst out on working parties. He brought them in in pieces and buried them.

4. Church. We were allowed to build a small church and her services on Sundays. The Nips brought 2 bottles of wine for Easter Day Communion.

5. Medical. Sickness was not rife and everybody who was really sick was evacuated to Changi, by lorry. I had pink eye and ear trouble.

6. General Treatment, and Work. On the whole we were treated quite well. Our Battery were working with lorries, carrying stores from one place to another. One trip was to Kota Thing, about 20 miles up country, to collect wood from a pineapple factory, and we could get pineapples to bring back.

   Work was not really hard and the guards were quite pleasant to us. One guard used to say "Speedo" or "No Speedo".

   One officer went out with each party to supervise. Another job was to collect cement from the go-downs, where there was also a lot of food, and our people used to bring food back to camp - mostly tomato and Worcester sauces and a few tinned foods. The Guards co-operated and also used to take things for themselves. Eventually somebody was caught - the Nip guard was beaten up by a Nip officer, and it stopped.

7. Entertainment. We were allowed concerts once a week, and lectures were started on a large scale. Also a library was formed

from books people had obtained from houses - there were about 3,000. I worked here as a librarian.

Towards the end of July I got ear trouble again, and as medicine was short at River Valley Camp, on August 4th I was evacuated to Changi by lorry.

Bed bugs and lice made their first appearance at this time.

8. Pay. Officers were paid 35 cents, N.C.O.'s 20 cents and the men 10 cents. per day. Nip orders were not very strictly enforced.

4th August - 6th November 1942 Changi

1. Food. This had considerably improved owing to the fact that pay and a canteen had started and se we got extras. Also gardening began in a very big way, and some greens were ready to be eaten.

About the beginning of September we got some Red Cross supplies, which had come on a repatriation ship. These included milk, cigarettes, bully - in fact everything - and we fed like lords. We still spread it over a long period, and took some up country in November.

2. Accommodation. We were living on charpoys in married quarters.
3. News. This was given out twice a week from a wireless set. It was not very encouraging, as the Germans were at the gates of Alexandria and Stalingrad.
4. Church. Padre Cordingly* had opened a church in a mosque. R.Es and others had built an altar, pulpit, lectern, made a cross and vases out of shell cases. It looked beautiful, just like an ordinary church, with pews.The Sunday evening service (voluntary) was always packed.

In July the Bishop of Singapore had been allowed to hold a confirmation service in this church, which was named St. Georges.

There was an 18 Div. University for History, Geography, English, Economics, etc. There was also a Theological faculty, which I attended - lectures being held about 4 times a week.

The Moslem priest, was very impressed when he paid a visit and said he was so glad it was being used for its proper purpose.

*Down to Bedrock by Eric Cordingly & The Changi Cross by Louise Cordingly published 2013

5. Medical, etc. At the beginning of November about 15,000 had passed through the hospital. There were still a number of deaths some due to Selarang.*

*Selerang Barracks Incident, POWs refused to sign an agreement not to try to escape

6. General Treatment. Fairly good - because we seldom saw the japs. There was, however, a lot of unpleasantness from I.N.A.*
   * Indian National Army formed to help the Japanese.
7. Work. At Changi there was little work under the Nips. There was a hospital wood collecting party - trees were cut down by R.A.S.C., and we took it to the hospital. I went in charge of this quite a lot.
8. Concerts. These were excellent. There were a number of professionals, and amongst other plays they put on "Dover Road" and "Who Killed the Count". On Sunday nights there were classical concerts with a big choir under Padre Foster-Haig. Variety shows were also put on.

This Period was pleasant. I spent some time gardening and one could walk quite a long way and get out of everybody's way.

6-12th November 1942

We were taken by lorry to Singapore station early on the morning of 6th November. The party was made up of 100 officers, 100 O.Rs and 400 hospital personnel, and we were told we were going to build a hospital. The train left at 5 p.m. We were 31 to a cattle truck, and also heavy baggage. It was impossible to stretch one's legs. Took turns to lie down, 2 hrs down, 4 hrs up. Water from the engine to shave in. There were two meals a day, consisting of rice and stew. It was a nightmare journey.

We arrived early on 7th November, Kuala Lumpur at about 2 p.m.; Ipoh that night, and then on through Thailand.

We arrived at Petchburi (Phetchaburi) at about 5 a.m. on 12th November, and Bampong (Ban Pong) at 7 a.m. We did not know where we were going to, but there were many rumours.

Notes from diary, 14th-15th November 1942

Arrived Kanchanaburi in Siam. Hospital a foot under water.

There we were told what we were doing - building a railway to connect Siam to Burma, 200 miles.

17th December 1942 236 B 7.0 LIVERPOOL Y OHMS 35 IMPORTANT HAND DELIVERY- MRS. M HEELAS 102 CAMBRIDGE RD TEDDINGTON MIDDLESEX = OFFICIAL REPORT RECEIVED THAT LIEUT D E N HEELAS ROYAL ARTILLERY IS A PRISONER OF WAR LETTER FOLLOWS SHORTLY = UNERSECRETARY OF STATE FOR WAR

To Mrs Heelas From Monica Millard, Kelstone Lodge Repton, W. Derby

22nd Dec 1942

Dear Mrs Heelas

What good news! We do indeed rejoice with you & how nice that it has come at Xmas time, I have wanted several times to write & ask you whether you had had news but hesitated to do so. Still I had every intention to write for Xmas. You will let us have Douglas's address if you get it won't you, for we should like to write to him too. I am glad Muriel is so happy in her work. She is indeed a busy person & I know how things have to go on in a school! It was a difficult matter in the last war but is 10 times worse this time! Dorothy too has interesting work & must be very happy in it. I am glad that Mr Heelas is well & you too, at least as well as he can be in the circumstances. It is very hard for people like your husband to be without a car & I should have thought that you could have got extra petrol for him, but a car is very expensive to run these days I know; ours has been laid up ever since the autumn of 1940. We are very proud of my nephew, Philip, who is now a Brigadier & has the D.S.O. & the M.C. He is the youngest Brigadier in Libya & has been in it all from the beginning for he was stationed in Egypt before the war. I believe he is known as 'Pip Roberts of the Desert'*, we have heard this from a man who does not know him out there but has heard of him. His younger brother, Jim, who was at Malborogh with Douglas is a P.o.W in Italy, but writes quite cheerily. His letters come through oftener than another nephew who is a P.O.W. in Germany. We are homeless! Our house at Tunbridge Wells has been requisitioned by the Govt, & we have just come back from packing everything up. It was a sad business & a tiring job. Luckily it is to be the Headquarters of the A.T.S. of the S.E.Comand & I think the house will be well looked after.

Please excuse this awful writing as I am writing on my knee by the fire!

Our best wishes to you all & it is nice to think that by next Xmas we may really have our dear ones with us once more! We are so delighted about Douglas & it was so good of you to write & tell us your news.

With love & much rejoicing

*Pip Roberts of the Desert' Philip Bradley Roberts

From THE WAR OFFICE (CAS.P.W.), CURZON STREET HOUSE, CURZON STREET, LONDON, W.1.
Tel Mayfair 9400
29th December, 1942

Madam

In confirmation of War Office telegram dated 17th December, I am directed to state that information has been received that Lieutenant Douglas E.N. Heelas, Royal Artillery, previously reported missing, is now a prisoner of war in Japanese hands.

It is stated that he is interned in "Malaya Camps", and although it is not yet known whether this is a complete address, you are recommended to use it as such in communications to him. Any further information received will, of course, be sent to you immediately.

It would be appreciated if you would be good enough to notify this Department of any information which may come into your possession concerning your son's location, welfare, etc.

General enquires regarding prisoners of war and the treatment to which they are entitled may be made by letter to the above address or in person at the Prisoners of War Enquiry Centre, Curzon Street House, Curzon Street, London, W.1. (open 10 a.m. to 6 p.m. Monday to Friday, 10 a.m. to 1 p.m. Saturdays).

Information regarding the means of communication with Prisoners of War in Japanese occupied territories may be obtained from any General Post Office.

I am,

Madam

Your obedient Servant

G.T.H.Rogers

Letter to Mrs Heelas From L.E. Bingham. Broad Close, Chantry View Road, Guildford.

Jan 30th 1943

Dear Mrs Heelas

I opened your letter to Alec which arrived this morning as he went overseas ten days ago, he was home on final leave when he wrote to Heelas, I don't know where he has gone and I am afraid it will be some time before I know but I will pass on the news when I can begin writing to him.

I am so glad you have had information about your son & that you will hear from him in the course of time.

I wonder if you heard from Major Hamilton who lives in the home above us, as I heard that he & Alec had been talking about your son, who was with Hamilton in France, I think they went to Paris on leave in the early days of the war, Major Hamilton is now wounded out of the army, I will tell him I have heard from you & give him the news.

With kind regards & thank you for writing to Alec & with the wish that Heelas will come safely home.

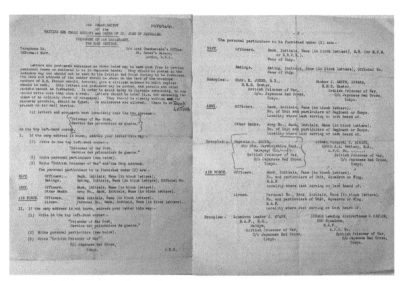

Red Cross Letter Page 1 & 2

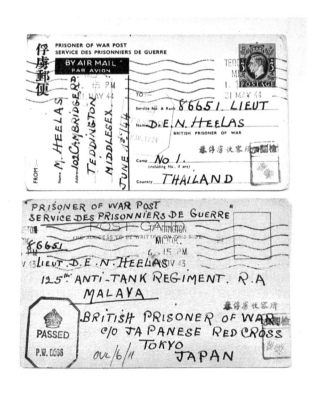

Post Cards To Douglas

Letters to Douglas in Japanese P.O.W camp from Mother
All Letters before the Japanese surrender are written in
capital letters, it was either write in capitals or use a typewriter
insisted by the Japanese, making it easier for their censors.

8th FEB 1943 ADD TO LIEUT D.E.N.HEELAS, 125TH
ANTI-TANK REGIMENT R.A , MALAYAN CAMP,
BRITISH PRISONER OF WAR, C/O JAPANESE RED
CROSS, TOKYO, JAPAN

MY DARLING DOUGLAS

ANOTHER WEEK GONE AND STILL NO LETTER.
I HOPE YOU GET MINE, I AM AFRAID THE POOR
CENSORS MUST GET VERY TIRED READING
THROUGH ALL THE LETTERS, I AM SORRY I HAVEN'T
A TYPE WRITER. WE ARE ALL AS WE WERE WHEN
YOU WENT, A LITTLE OLDER AND BOLDER! MY
CANADIAN NEPHEW HAS BEEN AND DID ME A FEW
JOBS. PUT THE HINGES ON COAL HOUSE DOOR AS
I HAVE A LOT OF COAL PUT IN AND AM AFRAID
OF IT BEING STOLEN. DOROTHY HER FRIEND,
GREYHOUND, D.D, AND LLOYD (AUNT HILDA'S SON
FROM CANADA) WERE HERE TO TEA AND SUPER
ON SATURDAY AND WE DID MAKE A NOISE ALL
TALKING AT ONCE! OUR WIRELESS HAS GONE BUST
TONIGHT. THE FLEX IS BURNT OUT SO STIRLINS
ARE GOING TO MEND IT TOMORROW. MURIEL SENT
ME A BOX OF ONIONS TODAY, THEY WON'T GROW
IN OUR GARDEN. WE STILL HAVE GREENS. IT IS
QUITE NICE PICKING THEM AND THERE ARE HEAPS
IN THE SHOPS. ALSO MUSHROOMS CULTIVATED
ONES. I HAVE HAD ALL THE LETTERS I WROTE UP
TO WHEN YOU GOT TO BOMBAY RETURNED SOME
AIRMAILS WITH THE STAMPS STAMPED BOMBAY
WHICH MURIEL LIKES. THEY RETURNED THE
MONEY, STAMPS 1S3D. BLINKERS RETIRES THIS
MONTH, HE IS 65,. HE IS LOOKING FOR A SMALLER
HOUSE. HE WILL SPEND ALL HIS TIME AT ST PETER'S
I GUESS. YOUR GODMOTHER IS ALRIGHT. I HAVE

HAD ABOUT 48 LETTERS RETURNED THAT I HAVE
WRITTEN TO YOU TELLING YOU THE BITS OF
GOSSIP AND NEWS SO I DON'T KNOW IF YOU KNOW
ANYTHING. MISS HENTSCH DIED. I THINK OF HER
TODAY AS THE PRIMROSE ROOT THEY GAVE YOU
IS IN BLOOM "VERY EARLY" AS IT'S ONLY MARCH.
OLD TATE IS STILL SITTING IN HIS CHAIR! I HAVE
GOT MY CANARIES BACK AND AM GOING TO HAVE
SOME BABY ONES TO SELL AS YOU CAN GET £1 OR
MORE FOR THEM. I WISH I COULD HEAR FROM YOU,
TELL THEM YOU WANT TO WRITE TO YOUR MUM.
I AM SURE THEY WILL LET YOU. WE ARE LOOKING
FORWARD TO SEEING BOSS AT THE END OF THIS
MONTH FOR HER HOLIDAYS AND SHALL DO A LOT
OF GARDENING.

BEST LOVE DEAR BOY YOUR LOVING MOTHER
AND DADDY, HAVE FAITH AND COURAGE.

From Muriel to Douglas

17th Febuary 1943 from Port Regis, At Bryanston School,
Blandford, Dorset

My dear Douglas

I don't seem to have improved yet in writing letters! Everything
here is just the same. I'm still at this job, and haven't been given
the sack yet! I had very nice holidays at home. Everything there
is the same. Mother and I are much improved in health since
Grandpa was put to sleep in December, and our asthma seems to
have gone. The fur evidently affected Ma also, as she is so much
better. It was a pity we didn't know before, and we could have got
rid of the cat before. D.D. still comes and Mrs Howard, and Dar
goes home about twice a week.

Better than nothing. Just to show we are still in the 'pink' as
I hope it leaves you at present. I'll try and be better at writing in
future.

Much love,

Yours ever, Muriel Miss M.Heelas.

26th FEB 1943

MY DARLING DOUGLAS

THERE HAS BEEN NO NEWS FROM YOU YET. IT TAKES A LONG TIME TO WRITE THIS PRINTING BUT THE RED X SAY THE JAPANESE WANT IT OR TYPED. I CAN UNDERSTAND WHY AS PEOPLE WRITE SO INDISTINCTLY AND PERHAPS I DO. WE ARE ALL WELL AND AS YOU LEFT US. THE CHAIR COVERS ARE WEARING OUT, SO I HAVE GOT SOME STUFF TO MAKE OTHERS. WE HAVE BEEN HERE 5 YEARS LAST SEPT YOU WILL REMEMBER US MOVING. I SAW THAT MAID WE HAD TODAY SHE ALWAYS STOPS AND ASKS AFTER YOU. I HAVE PATCHED MY APRON WITH A PIECE OF STUFF THAT WAS YOUR PYJAMA COAT WHEN YOU FIRST WENT TO MARLBROUGH. IT IS AN ENCOURAGEMENT TO WEAR IT INSTEAD OF GETTING MY DRESS IN A MESS! THE MARLBROUGH MAGAZINE HAS COME I WILL KEEP IT SAFE FOR YOU. I SUPPOSE THEY WON'T ALLOW ME TO SEND IT TO YOU. THE SPRING IS BEGINNING AND THE CROCUSES ARE LOVELY ALL DOTTED ABOUT, BUT WE STILL HAVE FIRES ALSO IN THE BEDROOM ON COLD NIGHTS. MURIEL WILL BE HOME FOR HER HOLIDAYS IN FIVE WEEKS AND THEN WE SHALL START ON THE GARDEN, WE HAVE STILL GOT GREENS MR STRINGER PUT IN I CUT SOME NEARLY EVERY DAY. I HAD ANOTHER LETTER FROM YOUR BATMAN'S MOTHER, HE SOUNDS A NICE MAN SHE SAYS HE THINKS A LOT OF YOU, THEY ARE GOOD CHRISTIAN PEOPLE AND IN HIS LAST LETTER HOME SHE QUOTES HE SAID "MOTHER I WALK WITH GOD" NICE? UNCLE HALFORD'S COLIN HAS LEFT HOME, HE CAN'T READ WRITE OR SPELL MUCH, THEY HAD A GOVERNESS FOR HIM. HE'S VERY NICE WEIGHTS 18 STONE AND IS ABOUT 6 FT GONE IN THE NAVY I THINK, AND LLOYD MY NEPHEW FROM

CANADA HAS BEEN IN HOSPITAL, HE'S A CHRISTIAN SCIENTIST! DOROTHY AND HER FRIEND WE CALL GREYHOUND ARE COMING ON SUNDAY. IT HAS TAKEN ME ¾ HR TO WRITE THIS ONE PAGE! SORRY IT'S A POOR LETTER. GOOD BYE DEAR BOY. BESTEST LOVE AND TONS MORE YOUR LOVING MOTHER X

5TH MARCH 1943

MY DARLING DOUGLAS

NO LETTER YET HURRY UP AND WRITE! WE ARE STILL AS WE WERE THE SPRING IS HERE THE TREES IN BLOOM, DOWN CLAREMONT ROAD THE CHERRY TREES ARE IN FULL BLOOM AND MRS MILLER HAS BEEN OVER TO TEA THIS AFTERNOON AND BROUGHT SOME AND I HAVE PUT SOME SPRIGS BY YOUR PHOTOGRAPH ON THE MANTLE PIECE. THE HUNTS ARE IN BUXTON HAVING TREATMENT FOR THEIR RHEUMATISM. PAVITTS KEEP HENS AND SELL EGGS SO WE HAVE HAD SOME AND MRS HARPER LETS US HAVE SOME TOO. THAT IS WHEN WE DON'T GET OUR RATIONS AND WE ONLY HAVE ABOUT TWO A WEEK. MRS MILLERS SON IS IN BOMBAY. I WENT UP TO HAVE DINNER WITH DOROTHY YESTERDAY SHE IS BEING MADE ADJUTANT AND MOLLIE GOURLAY, EX GOLF CHAMPION IS HER COMMANDER. I AM GOING UP ON MONDAY THEY ARE HAVING PROCESSIONS ALL AROUND THE STREETS AND BANDS. GRANPA CAT WAS PUT TO SLEEP BEFORE XMAS AND I HAVEN'T HAD ASTHMA SINCE AND THINK HIS FUR INCREASED IT, AND MURIEL DID NOT HAVE ANY EITHER IN THE HOLIDAYS. I GOT A NICE CHICKEN FROM FOLLETS A BOILER WHICH IS VERY TASTY. BULLEN HASN'T BEEN DURING THE WINTER BUT WE HOPE HE WILL START AGAIN SOON. I GOT YOUR "ALLOTMENT" IN A LUMP SUM LAST WEEK FOR THE SIX MONTHS FROM COX AND KINGS, VERY NICE AND BEING SAVED. BOSS WILL BE BACK IN ABOUT A MONTH. I HAVE NO NEWS. DADDY IS WELL EATS AND

SLEEPS SPLENDIDLY, BUT HE IS RATHER FEEBLE ON HIS LEGS SO HAS NOT BEEN ABLE TO GO OUT MUCH LATELY. DD AND CO ARE WELL, BERNARD IS AWAY AT MAIDENHEAD. I HAVEN'T HEARD ANYTHING OF YOUR GODMOTHER, AM WAITING UNTIL I HEAR FROM YOU BEFORE I WRITE. MRS HOWARD WAS HERE YESTERDAY TO CLEAN UP, SHE LOVES COMING AND WE OF WHAT YOU USED TO DO, EAT BREAD AND BUTTER AND TREACLE FORT!

BESTEST LOVE DEAR BOY, YOUR LOVING MOTHER XX "HAVE COURAGE AND FAITH"

17TH MARCH 1943

MY DARLING DOUGLAS

NO LETTER FROM YOU YET. HURRY UP AND WRITE. I EXPECT YOU HAVE, BUT IT MUST TAKE A LONG TIME FOR THE CENSORS TO READ THROUGH THEM, I WISH I COULD HELP! WE ARE ALL AS WE WERE WHEN YOU LEFT. IT IS DIFFICULT TO KNOW WHAT TO SAY, BOSS WILL BE BACK FOR HER HOLIDAYS ON 6TH APRIL SHE IS SORRY NOT TO BE BACK FOR HER BIRTHDAY, SHE IS LOOKING FORWARD TO DOING THE GARDEN BULLEN HASN'T BEEN FOR ALL THE WINTER BUT WE MUST GET SOME THINGS IN SOON, WE STILL HAVE A FEW GREENS AND SOME SPINACH AND THE CROCUSES ARE LOVELY ALSO THE DAFFODILS ARE NEARLY OUT, I PUT 2 PINK HYACITHS IN A VASE TODAY. MRS HARPER BROUGHT US SOME RHUBARB TODAY. DOROTHY AND HER FRIEND WHO WE CALL GREYHOUND, SHE'S A SKELETON BESIDE DOROTHY (SHE'S A SERGEANT) ARE GOING TO ASK FOR 48 HOURS LEAVE AND COME AND DO SOME GARDENING, I HAVE BEEN CUTTING DOWN DEAD BRANCHES AND SAPLINGS, DADDY IS TOO FEEBLE TO DO ANY GARDENING SO HE SITS AND LOOKS ON, HE IS VERY WELL AND ENJOYS HIS FOOD. I GET A CHICKEN SOMETIMES AND WE HAD SALMON THE OTHER DAY. BLINKERS CAME IN TO SEE US

TODAY HE'S 65 AND HAS RETIRED OF COURSE HE
SENT YOU HIS LOVE. MRS STURGESS CAME TO TEA
YESTERDAY LEFT GERTRUDE GARDENING, SHE IS
VERY CHEERFUL. BLINKERS SAYS ALFRED CHURCH
IS AT THE SAME PLACE AS YOU ARE, MR MILLER'S
SON IS IN BOMBAY. I AM GOING UP TO LONDON
TO DOROTHY'S PLACE TO HAVE TEA WITH HER
ALSO DD TOMORROW. MRS HOWARD WILL BE HERE
TO LOOK AFTER DADDY, IT MEANS GETTING HIS
MEALS READY. WE ARE GOING TO DO A SPOT OF
SPRING CLEANING SOON. TWO HOURS SUMMER
TIME IS STARTING ON 4TH APRI; WHICH WILL BE
NICE TO HAVE LONG EVENINGS. IT IS VERY QUIET
HERE AT NIGHT, OUR WOMAN CISSIE BY NAME BUYS
MEAT FOR DD EACH WEEK FROM A SHOP HERE SHE
CAN'T GET IT IN KINGSTON 13LBS OF IT "DERBY
STEAKS" OLD RACE HORSES, DD PROVIDES HER
FRIENDS UP HER WAY WITH IT AND THEY GIVE OUR
WOMAN 2/-6D FOR GETTING IT. THERE ARE SOME
VERY GOOD FILMS ON JUST NOW I EXPECT BOSS
WILL BE WANTING ME TO GO TO SOMETHING. WE
STILL HAVE A FIRE IN OUR BEDROOM AT NIGHT
ALTHOUGH IT IS NOT VERY COLD DADDY TAKES
SOME TIME TO UNDRESS AND HE LIKES TO SIT PART
TIME AND HAVE A CIG, BUSH SENDS 40 EACH WEEK.
RAZOR BLADES ARE THE ONLY THINGS WE ARE
SHORT OF. BESTEST LOVE DEAR BOY FROM DADDY
AND ME OUR THOUGHTS ARE ALWAYS ON YOU AND
MANY TALKS YOUR EVER LOVING MOTHER

18th APRIL 1943

MY DARLING DOUGLAS

NO LETTER FROM YOU YET HURRY UP & WRITE.
I AM SITTING IN THE GARDEN WRITING OUT SIDE
THE DRAWING ROOM WINDOWS. IT IS A LOVELY DAY
IN FACT THE LAST WEEK HAS BEEN LOVELY BOSS IS
GROVELLING IN THE EARTH UPROOTING WEEDS. I
AM GOING TO DO LIKE WISE WHEN I'VE FINISHED

THIS, WE ARE STILL JUST AS WE WERE WHEN YOU LEFT. I HAD ANOTHER LETTER FROM YOUR BATMANS MOTHER. SHE HAS BEEN ADDRESSING HIS LETTERS WRONG & PUTTING MITCHELL GILBERT. I POINTED OUT HER THEY WOULD LOOK FOR A MAN NAMED GILBERT! IT IS JUST 42 YEARS TOMORROW SINCE WE WERE MARRIED. DADDY IS VERY WELL. BUT RATHER FEEBLE. FORTUNATELY THERE IS AN OLD MAN LIVES OVER THE ROAD. WHO HAS BEEN A NURSE & HE COMES IN & SHAVES & WASHES HIM & I HELP HIM DRESS IN THE AFTERNOON HE CAN JUST TODDLE TO THE PILLAR BOX & WILL TAKE THIS LETTER. WE ARE GOING TO READING ON TUESDAY TO SEE THE PLACE WE SHALL HAVE TAXIS TO & FROM THE STATIONS. IT IS NICE HAVING BOSS HOME BUT SHE RETURNS TO SCHOOL 1st MAY. DOROTHY WAS HOME WITH HER A.T.S. FRIEND FOR THE NIGHT. THEY HAD A BONFIRE & WE MADE SUCH A NOISE ALL LAUGHING & TALKING AT THE SAME TIME! WE HAVE SUCH A NICE WOMAN TO WORK FOR US HAD HER OVER A YEAR. DD IS COMING TOMORROW TO TEA. ALL THE FRUIT TREES ARE IN FULL BLOOM & OUR APPLES CHERRY & PEAR TREES ARE LOVELY. WE ARE DOING A SPOT OF SPRING CLEANING. MRS HOWARD CAME ON WEDNESDAY & BOSS & I HAD A DAY IN LONDON & MET DOROTHY WHO ATE ENOUGH FOR A NAVY! THE AUNTS ARE WELL. I HAD A LETTER FROM AR BEET MORNING. A RICK IN NEXT FIELD HAD CAUGHT FIRE FROM A BONFIRE & THEIR HOUSE WAS IN DANGER WE DO THINK SUCH A LOT ABOUT YOU & WONDER HOW YOU ARE. I DO WISH A LETTER WOULD COME. I EXPECT IT WILL NEXT MONTH. I AM AFRAID THE CENSORS HAVE A TOUGH JOB READING THROUGH ALL THE CORRESPONDENCE. BESTEST LOVE DEAR OLD BOY. YOUR LOVING MOTHER & DADDY & BOSS. XXX

MY DARLING DOUGLAS

STILL NO LETTERS FROM YOU, I THINK MY EYES WILL DROP OUT WITH EXCITEMENT WHEN ONE DOES COME! MURIEL AND I HAVE BEEN IN LONDON SHOPPING IT'S AMAZING WHERE THE PEOPLE COME FROM THAT CONGREGATE THERE AND THE EATING PLACES ARE PACKED OF COURSE THEY ARE THE USUAL EASTER HOLIDAY MAKERS AND WILL DISPERSE SOON. I HAD A TAXI AND TOOK DADDY TO RUSSEL WHITE'S CHURCH FOR "INVALIDS H.C. SERVICE" ON MONDAY, HE HAD NOT BEEN TO CHURCH SINCE DEC 25TH, HE'S VERY WELL BUT FEEBLE AND CAN'T WALK MUCH. DR CAMPS INJECTS HIM EACH WEEK AND HE STAYS IN BED TILL AFTER DINNER. THERE'S A MAN NURSE WHO COMES IN TO SHAVE HIM ETC AND I HELP TO DRESS HIM BUT HE CAN WALK TO THE BOWLING GREEN ABOUT 10 MINS AWAY, FOR HIM 5 MINS FOR ME, ONLY I GO EVERY WHERE ON MY BICYCLE! BOSS RETURNS TO SCHOOL ON FRIDAY, WE SHALL MISS HER SHE IS SO AMUSING. WE HAVE GARDENED IN OUR SPARE TIME SHE'S SET SPUDS, PEAS, SPINACH AND BEANS. BULLEN HAS SO MUCH WORK HE DOESN'T OFTEN COME, WHICH IS NICE AS WE CAN DO AS WE LIKE AND DOROTHY COMES GENERALLY TWICE A WEEK AND MOWS THE LAWN SHE IS ABOUT 16 STONE SO IT WILL HELP HER FIGURE! SHE HAS THREE "PIPS" NOW BLINKERS HAS RETIRED AGE 64, HE'S SPOILT AS HE DOESN'T "BLINK", HE IS COMING TO TEA TOMORROW. ANNIE (CANARY) HAS LAID 2 EGGS SO WE ARE EXPECTING FIVE TO BE LAID. I SHALL SELL THE LITTLE ONES AS THEY ARE SCARCE AND SO FETCH A GOOD PRICE, AS MUCH AS 25/- MRS HARPER OFTEN COMES IN, SHE IS VERY NICE AND WE ALL LIKE HER. HER TWO BOYS HAVE BEEN CONFIRMED AT ST ALBAN'S, BUT SHE DOESN'T CARE FOR THE EXTREME DOCTRINE

THEY PRACTICE AT THE H.C. SERVICE. AS DADDY CAN'T MANAGE TO GET TO ST MARY'S I GO IN THE EVENING AND REPORT TO HIM. WE HAVE "SUN OF MY SOUL" EACH EVENING ON MY HARMONIUM WHEN DADDY IS IN BED AND THINK SPECIALLY OF YOU. I STILL HAVE YOUR CONTRIBUTIONS EACH 6TH OF THE MONTH. I'M SAVING IT FOR A "BUST UP"! I HOPE I SAY ALL YOU WANT TO KNOW, WE ARE AS WE WERE WHEN YOU LEFT AND I'M SITTING BY A NICE FIRE AS IT IS COLDISH. D.D OFTEN COMES OVER ON HER BICYCLE, SHE TAKES HER PARENTS OUT IN THE CAR. GOOD BYE DEAR BOY LOT'S I'D LIKE TO SAY BUT WON'T TILL I HEAR FROM YOU. I MEAN IN ENDING THE LETTERS "LUV" AND SUCH!

BESTEST LOVE AND MORE FROM YOUR LOVING MOTHER AND DADDY

30TH MAY 1943

MY DARLING DOUGLAS

ANOTHER MONTH NEARLY GONE AND NO LETTER OR CARD FROM YOU, I WONDER IF YOU HAVE GOT ANY OF MY LETTERS. I AM AFRAID THEY ARE VERY POOR IT IS DIFFICULT TO KNOW WHAT TO TELL YOU, AS WE ARE IN THE SAME STATE AS WHEN YOU WENT, MY HAIR MAYBE IS GREYER AND DADDY A BIT MORE FEEBLE BUT HE STILL WALKS A LITTLE WAY AND NOW WE HAVE A BATH CHAIR I CAN WHEEL HIM TO THE BUS, MR STRINGER TOOK HIM TO ST MARY'S CHURCH ON SUNDAY WHICH HE MUCH ENJOYED. WE SHALL GO TO THE BOARD MEETING AT THE "BIS" IN A WEEK OR TWO. I MANAGED TO GET 4 TOMATOES TODAY ALSO MRS HARPER BROUGHT 2 EGGS FROM HER HENS AND SOME GOOSEBERRIES. THERE WAS A BAPTIST MINISTER OF TETBURY WHO LODGED WITH ELSI AT AUNT JESSIES AND HE IS COMING TO STAY WITH US FOR A WEEK WHILE HE GOES UP TO LONDON EACH DAY FOR HIS B.D. EXAM. HE IS QUITE CLEVER BUT

HAS BEEN A COAL MINER AND OUGHT TO HAVE ELOCUTION LESSONS, BUT LIKE ALL LITTLE MEN IS QUITE PLEASED WITH HIMSELF! MY SCRAP BOOK (3 OF THEM NOW) IS GETTING FULL UP WITH NEWS AND PICTURES. I HOPE YOU WILL BE INTERESTED, MAY BE YOU WON'T WANT TO HEAR THE TOPIC MENTIONED! BOSS HOPES TO COME HOME FOR A WEEKEND SOON SHE LONGS TO SEE THE THINGS SHE PLANTED, TATES, PEAS, BEANS ARE ALL LOOKING WELL, I'VE PUT IN 2 RIDGE CUCUMBERS AND 2 MARROWS, I WATER THEM EACH NIGHT (OLD TATE IS AS HE WAS SITS IN HIS CHAIR) LUPINS, POPPIES, FOXGLOVES, MARIGOLDS AND SOME ROSES AND OTHER SMALL FLOWERS ARE OUT AUNT BEET SAYS HER GARDEN HAS NEVER LOOKED SO LOVELY, SHE HAS A LOT OF FRUIT SO DOROTHY AND I ARE GOING TO BAG SOME ESPECIALLY CHERRIES. I WONDER IF YOU GET ANY FRUIT, BOSS SAYS YOU WILL LIVE ON PINEAPPLE! I STILL HAVE A TIN OR 2 FOR YOU, I WENT UP TO LONDON ON WEDNESDAY IT'S CRAMMED FULL OF SHOPPERS. MRS HOWARD STILL COMES BUT BULLEN FINDS IT TOO FAR SO DOROTHY AND HER FRIEND MOW THE LAWN AND I TRY TO DO A BIT, IT LOOKS NICE. MRS MITCHEL HAS HEARD THAT HER GILBERT IS OK. BESTEST LOVE DEAR BOY FROM DADDY MESELF YOUR EVER LOVING MOTHER

5TH JUNE 1943.

MY DARLING DOUGLAS.

ANOTHER MONTH HAS STARTED AND STILL NO SOUND FROM YOU. IT ISOVER A YEAR SINCE WE HAD YOUR LAST LETTER AND CABLE, BUT WE ARE

NOT WORRYING BECAUSE YOU TOLD US NOT TO! AND HOPE YOU ARE DOING LIKE WISE, WE ARE JUST AS WE WERE WHEN YOU LEFT "ONLY OLDER AND BOLDER" BULLEN IS HERE TIDYING UP. MURIEL PLANTED TATES, BEANS, PEAS, SPINACH AND I HAVE

PUT IN MARROWS AND RIDGE CUCUMBERS, WE HAVE A VERY GOOD CROP OF PEARS AND APPLES. WE HAVE THE BAPTIST MINISTER STAYING HERE FOR A WEEK HE IS GOING IN FOR AN EXAM IN LONDON. HE IS RATHER PATHETIC AS HE IS SO UNCOUTH AND NO MANNERS, BUT AMBITIOUS AND QUITE CLEVER. I HAVE NICK NAMED HIM "JOHN WILLIE" HE IS QUITE HUMOROUS AGED 34 DADDY LIKES HIM THEY TALK THEOLOGY. DOROTHY AND HER FRIEND "GREYHOUND" CAME AND STAYED WED NIGHT TILL THURS NIGHT WHICH WAS NICE, SHE IS HUGE WEIGHS AT LEAST 16 STONE. I CAN WEAR HER DRESSES SHE CAN'T GET INTO! I DON'T KNOW WHAT TO TELL YOU OR SAY PRINTING THE LETTERS SEEMS TO BE ARTIFICIAL! I HAVE BEEN TO OUR OLD MARKET TOWN BENTALLS ETC TOOK MINE AND BOSSES WATCHES TO BE CLEANED, I LENT HER ONE YOU LEFT BEHIND. I AM KEEPING THE SCRAP BOOKS UP TO DATE, PICTURES AND FUNNY BITS I HAVE 3 OF THEM, I WONDER IF YOU WILL BE INTERESTED IN THEM OR "FED UP"! THE WEATHER IS VERY CHANGEABLE SO HOT SOME DAYS AND THEN IT TURNS COLD. WE STILL HAVE A FIRE IN THE EVENING. DADDY AS I HAVE SAID IN MY LAST LETTERS IS VERY WELL BUT VERY FEBBLE AND LOVES GOING OUT IN THE BATH CHAIR "JOHN WILLIE" TOOK HIM OUT TWICE AND MR STRINGER TAKES HIM SOMETIMES AND TO CHURCH, I GO A LITTLE WAY BUT HE IS QUITE HEAVY. HE DOESN'T GET UP TILL TEA TIME AND PUTS HIS TROUSERS ON BACK TO FRONT IF I LEAVE HIM, BUT HIS MIND IS VERY CLEAR AS A RULE, NOW AND THEN HE GETS MUDDLED HE TELLS PEOPLE YOU WILL BE HOME IN ABOUT TWO MONTHS, RATHER PATHETIC WE AGREE! DD JUST CAME TO TEA. HOPE YOU WILL GET SOME OF MY LETTERS. GOODBYE DEAREST BOY HAVE FAITH AND COURAGE "BEST LOVE" AND MORE YOUR LOVING MOTHER

MY DARLING DOUGLAS

I HOPE YOU GET MY LETTERS I HAVE WRITTEN ABOUT 50 AND NOT ANY HAVE BEEN RETURNED. ALL THOSE I SENT AND AIRMAILS FROM THE MONTH YOU WENT AWAY AND WHEN WERE TOLD YOU WERE MISSING CAME BACK, BUT SINCE WE HEARD YOU WERE A P.O.W AND WE COULD WRITE (PRINT) ONE LETTER A WEEK. WE ARE ALL WELL DADDY JUST FEEBLE, HE GOES IN THE BATH CHAIR MOST DAYS, BUT CAN SHUFFLE TO THE BOWLING GREEN AT THE BACK OF THOSE SHELL MEX HOUSES, AND I FETCH HIM BACK. WE HAVE BEEN HAVING SUCH COLD WEATHER AND A FIRE EACH EVENING. YESTERDAY I WENT UP TO DOROTHY'S PLACE TO TEA, THEY DON'T LACK ANYTHING, WE HAD STRAWBERRIES AND CHERRIES. NEW POTATOES AND TOMATOES ARE PLENTIFUL JUST NOW, OUR GARDEN HAS BEEN LOOKING LOVELY WITH LUPINS, ROSES AND THE FOXGLOVES ARE QUITE A PICTURE SELF SOWN AND ALL OVER THE PLACE. BULLEN WILL BE HERE ON SATURDAY AGAIN. MISS CHENNELS IS COMING TO TEA OF COURSE, OF COURSE EVERYONE ASKS AFTER YOU AND WE ARE SO ANXIOUS TO HEAR. I GOT SOME FISH IN LONDON YESTERDAY FROM A SHOP MY MOTHER AND I USED TO GO TO 50 YEARS AGO! THE AUNTS ARE WELL, DOROTHY, I AND HER ATS FRIEND ARE GOING THERE NEXT WEDNESDAY, THAT IS MY DAY OFF WHEN MRS HOWARD COMES SO WE SHALL GET SOME CHERRIES. WE ARE EXPECTING BOSS HOME FOR A DAY OR 2 SOON, THEY HAVE OVER 50 BOYS NOW, SHE WRITES SUCH AMUSING LETTERS. DAD HAS HER WIRELESS AND HE LOVES THE 10.15 SERVICE, I SEE HIM CHEWING HIS BREAKFAST BUT HE MANAGES TO GET IN ALL THE AMENS, AND ANYTHING HE CAN REPET BETWEEN MOUTHFULS. IT IS NICE FOR HIM BUT MR STRINGER WHEELS HIM TO ST MARYS EACH SUNDAY EVENING, HE DOESN'T

GET UP TILL 4 ISH. THEY HAVEN'T GOT THE PARTS
FOR YOUR COMMANDER AT BENTALLS, BUT A SHOP
IN RICHMOND ROAD HAS ONLY WE DON'T NEED
IT SO WE WILL WAIT TILL YOU RETURN. DADDY
AND I ARE GOING TO READING NEXT WEEK BOARD
MEETING. MY ANNIE IS SITTING ON 5 EGGS AGAIN.

GOOD BYE DARLING BOY. SOON MEET AGAIN,
I HOPE BESTEST LOVE FROM DADDY AND YOUR
LOVING MOTHER

To Mrs Heelas From L.S.Bingham, Broad Close, Chantry View
Road, Guildford

12 July 1943

I am so very glad to know that you have had word direct from
your son after your very long wait, thank you for letting me know
& I shall tell Major Hamilton, also Alec who in all probability is
in this new adventure he was well when we last heard & he was
allowed to give his movements from the time he embarked so I
have been busy following the route on the map.

I hope you hear again if only a few words allowed just to
know he is well.

With best wishes

17TH JULY 1943

THANK YOU AGAIN FOR YOUR P.C. WE ARE
EXPECTING SOMETHING MORE, YOUR BATMAN'S
MOTHER GOT A CARD TOO, SHE'S VERY EXCITED
OVER IT. HE SAID A BIT MORE THAN YOU DID BUT
I EXPECT YOU KEPT TO RULES. HE SOUNDS LIKE A
GOOD RELIGIOUS MAN. HIS IS DATED JUNE 1942,
BUT I WENT TO THE P.O.W. RED X DEPOT AND THEY
SAY JAN 1943 WAS WHEN THEY WERE POSTED. I
EXPECT IT TOOK SOME TIME FOR THEM TO GET
MAIL ARRANGEMENTS GOING. YOUR GODMOTHER
ASKED ME TO LUNCH ON WEDNESDAY, WE HAD
CROQUETTES, SPINACH, NEW POTATOES (SWIMMING
IN BUTTER!) AND STRAWBERRIES D. HAD BROUGHT

FROM SCOTLAND. SHE WAS SO NICE AND OF COURSE IS DOING WORK IN A BOOKSHOP. DADDY IS VERY WELL. WE HAD JOINT ROAST BEEF. NEW "TATES" OUT OF THE GARDEN, PLANTED BY BOSS. TODAY WE ARE GOING UP TO LONDON TO A MEAL, REGENT PALACE TO CELEBRATE YOUR BIRTHDAY. I OFTEN THINK HOW CLEVER I WAS TO SPEND YOUR 21ST WITH YOU. ANNIE'S CANARIES ARE 10 DAYS OLD AND CAN FEED THEMSELVES. I THINK I MUST HAVE TOLD YOU HARRODS CHARGE £4.10S FOR COCK BIRDS SO I HOPE TO SELL MINE! I HAVE 5 OF THEM AND 3 WE THINK ARE COCKS. SHE HAS ALREADY STARTED TO MAKE ANOTHER NEST. I HAVE BEEN TURNING OUT YOUR WARDROBE AND SHAKING OUT YOUR CLOTHES AND PUTTING FRESH MOTH BALL IN THE CUPBOARDS AND DRAWERS, THEY ARE IN GOOD CONDITION. BOSS SLEEPS IN YOUR ROOM IN THE HOLIDAYS. I DON'T LET ANYONE ELSE HAVE IT. IT IS SUNDAY EVENING AND MR STRINGER HAS TAKEN DADDY TO ST MARY'S CHURCH IN THE CHAIR, THEY LEAVE IT OUTSIDE. THE AUNTS ARE VERY WELL THEIR GARDEN I HEAR IS LOVELY AND THEY HAVE HAD A LOT OF FRUIT AND HONEY, I DON'T SEE MUCH OF IT, PERHAPS THEY WILL JOIN US IN LONDON ON THE 26TH. I FORGOT WHAT I TOLD YOU, I WONDER IF YOU GET MY LETTERS, I THINK YOU MUST DO NONE ARE RETURNED. MRS HANCOX CALLED ON FRIDAY SHE SAID BLINKERS WAS LEAVING ST PETERS WE DON'T KNOW ANYTHING MORE. RUSSEL WHITE IS GOING VERY WELL HIS CHURCH BEST ATTENDED AROUND. BULLEN CAME YESTERDAY AND MADE THE GARDEN LOOK VERY NICE. WE'VE A LOT OF PEARS AND APPLES WE SHALL STORE SOME. I WISH I COULD SEND YOU SOME PAPERS. REV ELLIOT WRITES BEAUTIFUL ARTICLES IN S GRAPHIC, FULL OF "HOPE".

BESTEST LOVE DEAR BOY
YOUR LOVING MOTHER AND DADDY

Letters to prisoners and internees in Japanese hands must be limited to 25 words, and must be typed or written in block letters and about family matters only.

11th SEPTEMBER 1943

DARLING DOUGLAS

JUST 25 WORDS TO SAY WE ARE ALL VERY WELL DADDY PLAYS CROQUET IN EVENINGS WITH HARPERS. HAVING DAY OUT TO READING ON TUESDAY!

BESTEST LOVE

MOTHER X

24th SEPTEMBER 1943

DARLING DOUGLAS

WE ARE ALL VERY WELL. GOOD CROPS IN GARDEN & ELSEWHERE. SHOPS etc NO LETTER FROM YOU YET. LONGING TO HEAR & SEND A PARCEL TO YOU.

USUAL ENDING Mother X

1st OCT 1943

DARLING DOUGLAS.

BOSS TYPED ADDRESS ALL WELL. DADDY PLAYS CROQUET. EACH DAY STRINGER WHEELS HIM TO CHURCH EACH SUNDAY. DOROTHY HOME ON SEVEN DAYS. WILL SEND PARCEL WHEN ALLOWED. NO. LETTER YET

USUAL Mother X

11th OCTOBER 1943

DARLING DOUGLAS

ALL VERY WELL CONDITIONS HERE SAME AS WHEN YOU WENT. TOOK DADDY TO LONDON. CELEBRATED 79th BIRTHDAY, TEA AND PICTURES. GUESS WE THOUGHT OF ONE ANOTHER. NO LETTER YET. MOTHER X

NOV. 16th 1943

DARLING DOULAS

STILL NO LETTER. HOPE YOU ARE WELL. ALL WELL HERE. SAME AS YOU LEFT. BOSS HOME FOR WEEKEND DOROTHY FOR SUNDAY NIGHT.

BESTEST LOVE MOTHER X

DEC 8th 1943

DARLING DOUGLAS

NO CARD OR LETTER WE ARE ALL WELL. JUST AS YOU LEFT US TWO YEARS AGO. DOROTHY HERE MONDAY BOSS COMING HOLIDAYS

LOVE MOTHER X, DADDY

To Mrs Heelas From N.K. Anderson. St Catherine, White Post Hill Redhill

23rd Dec 1943

Dear Mrs Heelas

I was not in office on Saturday & was in London all Monday so I only got your letter yesterday.

I am indeed glad that you have had such good news, and that it has come just before Xmas. I am very fond of Douglas & am sorry that I have had so little contact with him since the war began.

If ever you get an address to which letters can be sent do let me know as I should like to write to him,

I don't myself think that my elder son is alive, all that I know of the circumstances seems to make it a very slender hope, naturally his wife clings to it. But my wife and I felt sure at the time that he has gone and nothing that his wife has told us seems to give ground for hoping otherwise. But there is of course the possibility.

With very kind regard to you both.

To Mrs Heelas

27th Dec 1943. Letter from Mr&Mrs J.H.Mitchell, Chez Moi, 8 Avenue Road, Normoss, Nr Blackpool.

It is with great joy I write to say we received a P.Card from our son Gilbert on Xmas day Dec 25th 1943.

He said continuing well but have received no letters yet from you.

Hope you are well and comfortable, Love to all Gilbert.

We do hope you have also got one from Lieut Heelas as well I suppose you have. Hope you are all well in health as so many people are suffering from flu. We would like to know if you have heard anything. We both wish you the compliments of the season and a brighter new year.

Post Card to Douglas. LIEUT D.E.N.HEELAS, 86651, BRITISH PRISONER OF WAR CAMP NO.1. THAILAND

3rd JANUARY. 1944

DARLING DOUGLAS

TWO CARDS RECEIVED DELIGHTED TO HEAR FROM YOU ALL WELL HERE. HAD GOOD XMAS FARE. MURIEL AND DOROTHY TOO.

AUNTS AND GODMOTHER SEND LOVE WITH OURS

Mother AND DADDY

Letter to Mrs Heelas from Joan Carter 'Riversdale',

6th Jan 1944.

I was pleased to hear that you had received a P.C from Douglas, also pleased to see that you had addressed your own P.C, for the last time you wrote you did not, & I had mislaid it somehow. Your news re Douglas was good & most welcome, I know of several wives who's husbands are in Thailand. My husband is in Formosa & has been there since Nov'42. I have up to date received 3 P.C's & one very precious letter (4 pages long). He is well (my last P.C was written July 21st' 43) & is not working, he has received quite a deal of Red X supplies & he mentions boots, food & other clothing, so this was really welcome news. He had not received any word from me, which is really disappointing.

Yes our little girls (she is now 2 years & a month old) is very well, & a real little tinker, & very like her Daddy.

Do let us know if you have further news, & I will do the same.

My best wishes to you & yours, Very Sincerely

Post Card to Douglas

14th JAN. 1944

DARLING DOUGLAS

ALL WELL SAME AS WHEN YOU LEFT. DOROTHY AND D.D. CAME TO TEA TODAY "BLINKERS" YESTERDAY. BIRTHDAY 6th JAN PARTY. RUSSEL WHITE. AND BUNCH'S LOVE Mother X.

24th JAN 1944

DARLING DOUGLAS

GOT YOUR CARD JAN 4th WITH AUNTS NAME, THEY ARE DELIGHTED. ALL WELL HERE. AS WE WHEN YOU LEFT. BOSS BACK AT HER JOB. DOROTHY HERE EVERY WEEK

LOVE Daddy & Mother X.

2nd FEB 1944

DARLING DOUGLAS

ALL WELL HERE AS WE WERE WHEN YOU WENT. AUNTS COMING TO STAY. DOROTHY COMES WEEK ENDS. BOSS WILL COME HALF TERM.

ALL LOVING THOUGHTS Mother X.

17th FEB 1944

DARLING DOUGLAS.

ALL AS USUAL HERE YOU ARE MUCH IN OUR THOUGHTS BOSS COMING NEXT WEEK FOR HALF TERM. DOROTHY SPENDING NEXT LEAVE HERE!

BEST LOVE Mother. & . DADDY

4th March 1944

DARLING DOUGLAS

WE ARE AS WE WERE WHEN YOU WENT. BOSS BEGINS HER HOLIDAY APRIL 4th! DOROTHY IS SPENDING NEXT LEAVE OF 14 DAYS HERE!

BESTEST LOVE Mother AND DADDY

Letter to Mrs Heelas from Edith Statch, Godalming, Surrey

19th March 1944

Thank you very much for your long newsy letter - I want to tell you how glad I am to know you have received a letter from Douglas - of course it's not satisfactory but as you say you knows he's alive, which takes that great worry off your mind, but it's a cruel thing they cannot write a true letter on their own - & to be civil to the dirty little yellow lacks!! - I'ate em! -

This is very funny - the day after I received your letter I had one from a Cousin whose Husband was a Chaplin in Singapore, & taken prisoner 3 yrs ago - & up to now the wife has not known what had happened to him, the only information she could get was that he was missing - !! She has been madly frantic poor girl - his letter is only just a few words, "Love to my darling wife & children" and has taken 1 year to come. So probably came by the same boat as yours. The whole thing is not right.

Trust you did not suffer very badly in last Wednesday's raid - it was bad. Every where I think – I am so grieved to hear the dear Vicar has been so ill again, it must be a great anxiety to you, but try & rest all you can while you have the night nurse, any trouble in the bronchial area is so distressing & weakening, but as that disappears you will find he will soon pick up & get his strength back and the warm sunny weather coming will help him a lot I hope. Please give your husband my love & tell him I often think of our happy days in the district – so with much love to all.

P.S. Please don't labour to answer this

23rd MARCH 44

DARLING DOUGLAS.

THANKS AGAIN FOR TWO CARDS IN JANUARY. NO NEWS SINCE. ALL WELL HERE. BOSS AND DOROTHY COMING HOLIDAYS AND LEAVE. PLANTING GARDEN AND SPRING CLEANING

BESTEST LOVE Mother

18th APR 44

DARLING DOUGLAS

ALL WELL AS YOU LEFT US BUSY IN GARDEN FLOWERS LOVELY GET ORANGES. SOMETIMES. DOROTHY HOME FOR NIGHT YESTERDAY. BOSS HERE. NICE.

LOVE MOTHER X

17th MAY 44

DARLING DOUGLAS

ALL WELL. BUSY GARDENING DOROTHY COMES EACH WEEK. MURIEL BACK AT SCHOOL, AUNTS FLOURISHING. SOLD TWO CANARIES SIX POUNDS!

ALL OUR LOVE DADDY AND MotherX

31st MAY 44

DARLING DOUGLAS

NO NEWS FROM YOU SINCE YOUR TWO CARDS. ALL WELL. DOROTHY COMES EACH SUNDAY BOSS COMING NEXT WEEK HALF TERM. BESTEST LOVE. MOTHER

13th JUNE 44

DARLING DOUGLAS

ALL WELL CHAIR COVERS WASHED AT INTERVALS TO CELEBRATE! TOMATOES. NEW POTATOES AD LIB – BOSS COMING FOR NIGHT NEXT WEEK. DOROTHY COMES. LOVE MotherX

13th JULY 44

DARLING DOUGLAS

ALL WELL. CONDITION AS WHEN YOU WENT. BUSY GARDENING. DOROTHY COMES A DAY EACH WEEK. BOSS COMING FOR HOLIDAYS. HAVE ELEVEN CANARIES! LOVE MotherX

27th JULY 44

DARLING DOUGLAS

YOUR 25th BIRTHDAY ALL OUR LOVING THOUGHTS ARE WITH YOU.

ALL WELL HERE. BOSS COMING FOR HOLIDAYS DOROTHY SPENDING LEAVE HERE.

LOVE MOTHER X

28th SEP 44

DARLING DOUGLAS

ALL AS USUAL. HOPEFUL AND CHEERFUL DOROTH'S MARRIAGE ENDING ETC. HAD POOR SUMMER. AM BOTTLING APPLES, JAM. BOSS BACK SCHOOL DADDY WELL. LOVE MOTHER X

14th OCT 44

DARLING DOUGLAS

DADDY'S 80th BIRTHDAY SUNDAY. HAD CAR FOR SERVICE St PETER'S. DOROTHY AND ME. HE ENJOYED. IT, GOOSE FOR DINNER! LONGING. FOR YOU. BESTEST LOVE MotherX

24th NOV 44

DARLING DOUGLAS

ALL AS USUAL. MET. AR BEET AND JESSIE. BEEN HOLIDAY TEIGNMOUTH. BOSS COMING FOR HOLIDAYS. DOROTHY FOR XMAS. MUCH THINKING OF YOU. LOVE. MOTHERx AND DADDY

12th DEC 44

DARLING DOUGLAS

ALL WELL. AND SERENE. MURIEL AND DOROTHY HOME FOR CHRISTMAS. WE MISS YOU TERRIBLY. AUNTS WELL JESSIE COMING WEDNESDAY. MRS HOWARD COMES. LOVE MOTHERx

30th JAN 45

DARLING DOUGLAS

ALL SERENE. VERY COLD WINTER BOSS AT HER SCHOOL. DOROTHY HERE ON LEAVE. AUNTS WELL. HAD LETTER FROM BROWNING, ENGAGED!

MUCH LOVE MotherX

To Mrs Heelas From H. Lewis. 17 Overbury Avenue, Beckenham, Kent

13th Jan 1945

Dear Mrs Heelas

We are all grieved to hear of the great loss which you and your family have sustained in the passing of your dear husband.

We would like to express our very deep sympathy with you all in your bereavement.

With our kindest remembrances

To Mrs Heelas from The WAR OFFICE, CURZON STREET HOUSE, CURZON STREET, LONDON, W.1.

17th Feb 1945

Madam

I am directed to inform you that representatives of this Department have recently interrogated ex-prisoners of war, lately in Thailand who survived the sinking of a Japanese transport in September last and who have now reached home, for any news they may have of their comrades. From reports obtained from these men the Department is glad to be able to inform you that your son, Lieutenant

D.E.N.Heelas is stated to have been seen alive and well at Bampong, Camp No.1, in June 1944.

It is possible that you may have already received later news by direct correspondence but the report is sent in the hope that it will prove of some reassurance to you.

I am,
Madam
Your obedient Servant
G.T.H.Rogers

To Mrs Heelas from Edith Campbell, 39 Gordon Rd, Kingston. on.Th

28th Mar 1945

Our letters crossed. Thank you very much for your kind one to me. How truly do I understand your loneliness, which as you say, a house full could not alter! It's such an ache & longing for the sweet companionship, only those who go thro' it quite realise. There is much to be thankful for, looking back, & especially for you who have had, & shared so many interests, & still have his children (& y own) to care for. I am so glad you have one Daughter with you, & also a lady, its helpful, in many ways, I find, having my friend, it makes me do things that otherwise I might get slack, I'm not sure if I told you she was bombed out of her home at W'don but is expecting it to be put in order within a month or two, & will then be returning there. I shall miss her very much, & she is not anxious to go, but has her furniture & does not want to part with that. I've already had some other friends, now in Cornwall, asking to come to me, as soon as Peace is declared, which Please God, seems very near now, what a joy when we feel there is an end, in Europe, at least, of this awful carnage & destruction, & our Prisoners of War set free! & no more bombs! I am so sorry you've had another attack of Asthma its such a distressing complaint. I hope you will be free from it for a very long time. Do you think you can come to tea with us, some day in the week following Easter, any day you like except Frid.6th. when I am due at Mrs Eggetts for S.A.M.S. needle work. It will be so nice to see you again I am glad the other Daughter is coming nearer, so she can get home more often, tho' I should think she will be a little sorry to leave Dorset. I must close, my friend is going to post & will take this. Most sincerely do I wish you the deep, time, joy of Easter, it is that faith that makes it possible to carry on. With love & kindest thoughts & best wishes

Letter to Mrs Heelas from Lindsay Dewer, Bishops College, Abingdon, Berks

28th April 1945

I am deeply sorry to hear the sad news of your son. I will remember him in my prayers. I do hope that you will soon receive him back safe and sound. I would be grateful if you would let me have any news of him when it comes. It must be a horribly anxiety for you. I am so sorry.

Letter to Mrs Hellas from Monica Millard, Kelstone Lodge, Repton, West Derby

15th August 1945

I am writing to say that I hope you will now soon have news of dear Douglas, he has not been out of our thoughts for a single day & we are anxious to have news of him. When you do hear will you please let us know something about him. We have always been so specially fond of him.

I hope you & your husband & the rest of the family are well & that your house escaped those terrible bombs. You will see by the above address that we are still in Repton, our house has not yet been de-requisitioned although we expect it any time now. We are shortly going to Tunbridge Wells for a few days to find out what can be done about it. With the servant scarcity now we could not possibly manage it. In the spring we were in Devon & Somerset looking for something but it was quite a fruitless search. I want a small, absolutely modern & easy to run house but I'm afraid everybody wants the same!!

Philip* my nephew was home on leave & he spent a few hours here. It was lovely to see him. Do you know he is a Major General now & has a C.B, D.S.O. & 2 bars, M.C., Croix de Guerre & Legion of Honour. He commanded the 11th Armoured Division since D.Day & his Div was the first to enter Brussels & Antwerp. He is now at Schleswig. He expects his Div to be disbanded soon but will command an Infantry Div. His younger brother , Jim who was at Marlborough with Douglas came back this summer after being a P.o.W. in Italy & then Germany for 3½ years. He has just joined Philip as his liaison officer & my brother (their father) says it is amusing to hear Jim talk to P as 'Sir' & salute P.

* Major-General George Philip Bradley Roberts, better known as 'Pip' Roberts

From Constance M Thomson to Mrs Heelas

20th Aug 45, 8 Egerton Place, SW.3. Your Kind note has come in Thank you. I intended to write tonight. Sunday is a full day for me – I enjoy it, but I don't sit still and write letters! I forget whether I told you that I am responsible for the Book Stall at Holy Trinity, so I am always at morning & evening church & half an hour early to get ready & half an hour at the end till the last straggler goes – and I go to the Incurables for a jaunt in the afternoon – and to bed at night. (I enclose the "Tour in Canada" the spoken lecture was more vital of course. The Incurables were thrilled & one said yesterday "you know I never knew there were clergy who spoke like that. It was like my old Gospel Tent"!

It was delightful to see you all & I was quite overcome with all the food presents. I shall put on stones!

Tell Muriel I would hate her to pretend she enjoyed children's photos if she didn't & of course I wouldn't be offended! I am sorry the real laughing one was not there for you.

I wonder if you will have a P.C. from Douglas.

With love & again many thanks for the years' rations.

Letter to Muriel From P.J.J.Fear .Garsington Rectory, Oxford.

Many thanks for your kind reply. Permit me even thus late, to send my sympathy with you all in the passing of your dear father.

I hope your mother is fairly well & able to keep the home going for you: may she be spared to see the dear boy's return.

You will be in a most interesting neighbourhood at Gorhambury. I have only been there once I think, to enquire about a maid! & so far as I can remember it is ¼ mile, not 4 miles, from St Albans – but I may be mistaken.

How interesting for Dar to go to Ceylon for a short while!

Mind you let me know when you hear from Douglas.

From diary of events written after the war.

15th-22nd November, 1942, Chungkai Camp and Hospital Camp

Bridge Over river Kwai

1. Food. 12oz rice, half a pound veg, dahl, marrow, cucumber melons, brinijals mostly watery. Half an ounce of sugar like tea. Half an ounce of meat, little fat called Ghi; lean and tough. Hot sweet Coffee.

2. Meals. Breakfast, Ground rice porridge - rice and watery stew. Mid-day, Rice and watery stew. Evening meal, Rice and stew with the bit of meat. Rice ball fried. No potatoes, no bread, no milk. Canteens: if you worked you got paid about 1d a day. Bananas: big bunch 1d. Eggs half a penny each. Peanuts, Gula Malacca, Tobacco about one shilling per pound.

3. Weather: 80 degrees. Cold nights in Jan. and Feb.

4. Clothes: G-string, Clompers

5. Description of guards: (a) Koreans (b) Tap Engineers Nicknames: Frog, Bull Frog, Black Prince, Gorilla, Goat, Pig Face, Pudding Face, Old Joe, Jungle Princess, Silver Bullet, Blind Boil, Rocking Horse, Tortoise, Tiger, Basher, Undertaker, Speedo.

6. Work: About 10 hours a day digging out embankment and bridge building.

7. Tools were shovels, chunkels and carriers. No mechanical diggers.

About March 1943

Diphtheria and Evac. to Chung Kai nr Kanchanaburi POW Camp. Worked on Camp work.

22nd September 1943, Chungkai

27th October, 1943 Kanburi (Kanchanaburi)

Speedo on railway. To be finished Oct. 1943. Great ceremony. Golden sleepers. All promised good time.

3rd October 1944 Nong Pladuk, near the start of the Burma Railroad

End of 1943. Went to Nong Pladuk camp located 3 miles from Ban Pong station. Working on railway sidings loading and unloading trucks. Air raids start. 110 killed. Trench digging.

Things get a little better after this for some time.

19th January 1945 Nakom Paton. Parties go to Japan from here, one ship sunk.

24 January 1945 Nong Pladuk.

2nd September 1945 Kan'buri Base

Chapter 6

Japan Surrenders

From diary

14th August 1945

A Korean guard told Sanderson (interpreter) that the war was over. Korean had heard from a Thai.

15th August 1945

Many more rumours from Koreans and Thais.

16th August 1945

More rumours. Thais shouting over the fence etc. Played bridge 8.15 p.m. to 9.45 p.m. Hut commander called to office at 10 p.m. Mashuska (Jap Camp Comdt) stood up and said a major from Jap H.Q. (P.o.W.) wished to speak. He said war was over on 15th; guards would be withdrawn on the following day - not allowed to go out of camp. Mashuska and Major dignified and moved. Col. Swinton (British Camp Comdt) thanked Mashuska for what he had done for Capt. Dower. (Rumour estimates that Capt. Drawer would not have lived much longer.)

Hut commanders returned - everybody came to top of huts and we sang National Anthems of Britain, USA and Holland; it was very moving. Went round friends, discussed things with John Parkinson. At about 11.30 p.m. went to an impromptu concert in a hut, with community singing etc., finished at 1.30 a.m. Talked till 2.15, went to bed and slept from 4.30 a.m. to 6.45.

17th August 1945

Flags hoisted in the morning. Went on camp picquet for one hour. Polished buttons, etc. At 7.30 p.m. thanks giving service - address by Major Wylie - very good; Text: Mathew - "If a man compel three to go with him one mile, go with him twain" on the idea of pulling our weight in world reconstruction.

Feel sorry for some Japs, especially Mashuska and the "busty" Sergt. They are both very dignified. This is a very difficult transition period. The camp is nominally in our hands but Japs supply food and are not allowed to let us out.

9 p.m. Impromptu concert. Went to bed at midnight.

18th August 1945

Fatigues in morning. Col. Swinton paid official visit to the Thai governor of Kanburi. Allowed to walk on aerodrome from 7 - 8.30 p.m. Very pleasant. Talked to Thais and Indians who were very friendly.

19th August 1945

Col. Swinton left for Bangkok; Col. Dean took over command with Comdr. Alexander R.N., starting an information bureau, as there were numbers of rumours in camp.

News service has started: news given out from stage twice a day at 12.45 a.m. and 10 p.m. The camp has had talks to-day with Boon Pong and other merchants for extra supply of food on credit. Plane dropped pamphlets in Thai.

20th August 1945

Col. Thomas who went on 6th party on 15th August to new camp, returned with a medical orderly. They are going to Tarsoa to-morrow to arrange evacuation of the sick. He spoke to us from the stage in the evening and said "Col. Swinton, Australian and Dutch and American Colonels are in a bungalow near P.o.W. H.Q., keeping in touch with Japs and ex P.o.W. camps etc."(They call themselves Allied H.Q., Bangkok, which amuses us.) He described their journey from here:

'They left this camp at 5.45 p.m., left Kanburi station at 12.45 p.m., breakfast at Nong Pladuk; lunch at Nakaron Paton. At a bridge some miles further they had to push trucks over one by one with no handrail and a big drop in the river. They arrived at Bangkok at 2 a.m. on 17th August and were told in sidings that the war was over. They gave three cheers and sang the National

Anthem, and then had to march 9 Kms to a go-down on the docks, and rickshaws took their kit. They were not allowed out - their food is improving.'

We seem to be better off here than in some other camps. People went into Kanburi village.

21st August 1945
Col. Dean and party of 49 officers left to take over O.R's camp at Tamuang; the Japs are being very difficult there. Food is very good - plenty of meat and incudes fried eggs, chicken, pork and pomelo. (Comdr. Alexander R.N. - Camp Comdt.)

22nd August 1945

Built guard-room in morning. Afternoon, the Swiss Consul (Int. Red Cross Representative in Thailand) visited camp. He spoke from the stage and said he had tried for 3½ years to contact camps, but was refused permission by Japs. He did not realise conditions were so bad. (Conditions are very good compared with 2 years ago.)

He gave $25,000 for camp food etc. He was evidently very moved by the bad conditions and impressed at the high spirits of everybody. He had already visited Nakhon Pathom and Tamuang Camps. He took back lists of ex P.O.Ws and said he would radio them to Geneva.

In the evening went into town with J. Bacon - we walked from one end of village to the other and bought one or two things. Went into a cafe and had iced and hot coffee and omelette each - cost $6 for the two. Back in camp by 9.30 p.m.

23rd August 1945

Scraping bricks in the morning for use of new stands in the cookhouse. In afternoon 740 O.Rs came into camp from up-country - they were a Camp 294 km away. They were in a terrible condition of emaciation, suffering from beri-beri, jungle fever and many from dysentery. Their condition was only a little better than some railway sick two years ago. Some of them who had been up-country building the railway said the treatment was much worse now, although food was better.

In the evening I walked on the aerodrome and talked to one of them, and the following are some of the stories.

An Australian, who was believed to have gone a little mental, went out of camp one day and was found four days later wandering about, and was brought back to camp. He was tied up at the guard room like a monkey, and whenever a Jap passed him they beat him. The mud in which he was, was at least two feet deep. After 16 days the Jap camp Cmdt. addressed the camp and said that he had decided not to punish him with death, but warned anybody else that he would shoot them if they escaped. The Australian was left outside the guard room, and after five days was taken to the cemetery, made to dig his grave, and was bayoneted on 14th August.

The daily routine in the camp was - reveille at 5 a.m., and breakfast at 6.30 a.m. Jap guards came through the huts and chased the men out if they were even sitting on the end of their beds at 6.30 - and they would be beaten. They were taken to work on excavating caves in hills, having to do 3 meters a day each. At 2 p.m. food arrived and 10 men at a time were allowed to eat. When they finished another 10 ate etc. They arrived back in camp any time between 8 - 10 p.m. The sick were taken on stretchers to work. They were allowed 30 sick in the camp, and one particular Jap Cpl. used to stand at the end of a hut, make all the sick walk past him, and ask them if they could work on the following day. If they said 'Yes' he said 'OK' If they said 'No' , he would beat them unmercifully, hitting them on the head with the butt of a rifle.

One day all the sick were taken to the guard room and made to stay there 4 hours in 2 ft. of mud. The huts had no beds, and there was a lot of mud to sleep on. It took 36 hours to get there, and they had no food or water on the journey.

Comdr. Alexander, R.N., held a court of enquiry on the spot, sent a full report to Col. Swinton, and as Col. Sagasawa (head of all P.o.Ws in Thailand) is a changed man (i.e. can't do enough for us), something will probably happen. Commander Alexander asked Mashuska to keep in custody the guards who came with the party - he said he could not, but would hand them over to KEMPEI police at which Alexander was satisfied. The O.Rs who had been up country before, said there were usually one or more decent Japs in the camp, but in this one there were none.

24th August 1945

Early this morning another party arrived, about 400, from 299 Km. They were in better condition, but there were many stretcher cases. Heard on the news that relatives in England can write to us not later than the 26th - good show!

Letter to Douglas from Mrs Heelas

24th August 1945. Add to No 86651 Lieutenant D.E.N.Heelas, P.O.W. No 1 Camp, Thailand.

My Darling Douglas

I hope you will get this, how wonderful the war being over, I expect you will not know much about the details so I have kept "The Daily Sketch" for some time for you to read. We are alright here. Only had our bedroom windows blasted out. As Daddy & I slept downstairs – it – did not – matter they are gone back now & your room is being prepared for you & clean. You will probably guess Daddy is not here - he had 3 attacks of bronchitis in 1944 last year & became very feeble & he had a nice Xmas on Monday 25th Dec then on the Wed he was not well - & another attack of Bronchitis & passed on on WEDNESDAY Jan 10th, he was only ill 10 days. I had 2 very nice nurses & Dr Camps did all he could, the end was very peaceful. His body was weak. We had a very quiet funeral at St Peter's, on the Sat, Muriel and Dorothy and we asked DD and Mrs Harper next door neighbour, she had been very kind and Aunt Jessie came she and Boss went to the cemetery and I stayed in the church with Dorothy. Uncle Frank and Maurice came and a lot of clergy and people, and I have lots of letters. Daddy never suffered any pain and he just slept away. Of course he often said he wanted to live to see your return, but it is for the best, he might have been bed ridden & he was able to get dressed each day toddle to the kitchen for meals. I had a man nurse for 2 years from opposite he came each morning to shave him etc.

We are alright here Dorothy is living with me & goes up to London each day, & Boss's school has gone to St Albans, so she can come back each week. We are going all 3 to Bournemouth for a fortnight on Sept 1ˢᵗ and have got the car going so shall drive down. The Aunts are well & we are going to see them on Sunday.

Of course there has been a lot of business over the money!

We are busy getting house & garden ready. I have coloured the kitchen walls & we shall look ever so smart when you come. We are simply longing to hear some news from you. I still have a few canaries & am getting rid of them. I had tea with the Brownings a while ago. Jeffry is in the NAVY. I still ride my bicycle for shopping.

We all send our best – love – Boss & Dorothy – the latter is now Heelas again. Bestest love old boy. Your loving Mother

Letter to Mrs Heelas From Monica Millard, Harewood Hotel, London Road, Tunbridge Wells.

24ᵗʰ Aug 1945

My dear Mrs Heelas

Your letter was sent out to me & reached me here yesterday. Thank you so much for it. I am so sorry that we did not know that you had lost your husband for of course we should have written to you before. You must indeed miss him dreadfully but if he was so frail, I feel sure you would not wish him back & he is far better off now I am sure.

I am so sorry that you have had another attack of your old enemy, bronchitis, but hope you are getting over it all right. I feel with Muriel that she ought to come home & help you, but I can understand how you feel about that. We have come here for a few days to look into things, but for the moment there seems no chance of our house being de-requisitioned & we are without any plans & shall just have to go on at Repton for the present, although we are longing for our own home again. I should really like to sell our house here & have a smaller one but such a thing is not to be found anywhere. We do hope you will soon have news of dear Douglas, we shall be so anxious to hear.

With love from us both, dear Mrs Heelas

Believe me Yours very sincerely

25th August 1945

After the news we heard some stories from other Camps. The new officers' camp at Nakhon Nayok is only about a quarter complete - they are sleeping 12 to a bay; food very bad; latrines have overflowed into drinking water supply. They are evacuating to hotels and houses in Bangkok, starting with 250 to-day.

The 3,000 OR's of 1 Group at Vbon (?) are in very bad condition; a lot of malaria, beri-beri, dysentery etc. Col. Toosey is leaving Bangkok by train to bring them back to-day.

Col. Thomas returned to-day and said that there were no more prisoners up country on this railway. We are to be amongst the last to be evacuated to Bangkok, as authorities say we are best off. It is reported that Thais in Bangkok are starting P.o.W. comforts, such as towels, clothing etc. The Thai Press is organising it, and supplies are being allocated by the Swiss Consul.

This afternoon a fighter plane flew 2 or 3 times over the camp - we all cheered hard, and it gave a victory roll. It is thought it was Fleet Air Arm - it carried a crew of two. The Thais were crowding round on the far side of the aerodrome and were all very excited. We put out the V sign on the aerodrome.

Re Wireless: the wireless was taken from here in Captain Nagoodi's kit! After the finish of the war, the operator went to Nagoodi and asked for 100 batteries. N. asked what for, and the reply was for the wirelesses which we have been working at Chungkai and Kanburi for 3½ years. N. was very surprised and said he supposed we had better have the batteries.

26th August 1945

Major Brodie invited me to his birthday party in the evening. We had iced coffee, fried fish; a salad of lettuce, cucumber, onions etc., fried liver and kidney, pancake with tinned milk and a very good Thai whisky. It was the first time I felt free. The shop was kept by a half German - half Thai. and he spoke those languages and English. In the shop also was a Sakai, the first time I had seen one close to.

The food in the Camp is bad; the rations appear good, but the cooking is bad - it is probably due to lack of staff.

Letters from Douglas Heelas

26th August 1945. This Is NOT AN OFFICIAL ADDRESS, Officers Ex P.O.W. Camp, Kanchanaburee, Thailand

My Darling Mother, Daddy, Boss, Dar, The Aunts at Missenden and D.D. etc

This is an unofficial letter, which may or may not reach you, this is NOT an official address so don't address anything by it.

From a health point of view, I am extremely well. I am longing to hear from you and to know how you all are, as I have had no news from you since July 28th 44. I have received about 40 letters and 19 post-cards from you. I was very sorry to hear about the deaths of Ar J.B and C. Staniland. I have been able to write about 6 or 7 cards to you, I heard from you that you had received at least 2. When we can write officially I propose writing first of all a summary of my doings and then later a full diary. As you have heard we had a very bad time; 3 ½ years too long.

We are now having very good treatment & food and are expecting to move to Bangkok (about 40-50 miles away) very soon. An aeroplane flew very low over our camp yesterday & waved etc.

I have none of the common P.o.W. diseases, but have had diphtheria in Dec 42 very slightly and since then had asthma very slightly on and off & one or two other minor ailments.

Give my love to everybody including my Godmother, Geoffrey Aked-Davies and everybody else. All my love & more longing to see you all.

27th August 1945

In the morning I went to the cemetery to dig a grave. Three died to-day, bringing the total of deaths since the end of the war to 5.

No news owing to the fact that the Kanburi fuel supply to the power station has not come through, and won't be going again for five days. However, a wireless has been obtained from Tamuang.

A party of officers left to-day to take over the O.R's camp at Petchaburi (160 Km away towards Malaya). Two officers arrived from Wacom Ayok via Bangkok. Working hours there were 8.30 to 1 p.m., 3.15 to 7 p.m. One job was to carry bamboo a certain distance, covering 30 Km in a day. There was a lot of beating up etc: the march there (38Km) was awful.

Commander Alexander at lunch time went to meet a British officer and an Australian Sergeant, who were dropped by parachute some days ago, with a transmitter, to report about us. In the afternoon, carried rice from railway.

The Japs in the camp were disarmed this evening. They are confined to their quarters but the officers and senior N.C.Os are allowed to keep 2 revolvers to be worn if they go out of camp on business. The arms are stored in their quarters and not handed over to us, except for 2 revolvers. They are allowed to keep ceremonial swords. It appears to be an unofficial arrangement. (Received 13 letters from Ma dated Feb - August '43. Changed from Tokyo to Thai time.)

28th August 1945

Went to the cemetery again. Captain Newell (the parachutist) appeared in camp to-day and went round. There are discussions going on concerning preparing the aerodrome for landing planes. There is a big Red Cross on the parade ground.

Prices have gone up considerably, a few days ago - eggs now 40c in lieu of 20c., bananas $1 per bunch.

This evening Newall answered a lot of questions from the stage about England. He was also asked whether we smell! He said 'No', but we think he was not telling the truth!

29th August

Went to cemetery again this morning. We are hourly expecting planes to drop supplies here. In the evening there was a very good concert, and about 100 Thais were invited. The set was of all the national flags and the royal crown in the centre. They included playing the Thai National Anthem - quite a good tune. In the interval Cmdr. Alexander made a speech about Thai - British relations etc. and said if it had not been for the inhabitants of Kanburi a lot more of us would have been underground. Everybody shouted for the Governor, who came on looking very smart, and he replied (with an interpreter) about Thai - British relations, and a lot about the peace of the world etc. We all clapped and cheered a lot, and he joined in.

Heard on the wireless to-night that P.o.Ws in Thailand are being flown to Rangoon (some leaving to-day), and also that P.o.Ws have taken over camps from Japs, which is quite true.

30th August 1945

No news this morning owing to bad reception. Went to the cemetery again this morning. Geoffrey Seymour arrived from Bangkok this evening. He is on Allied H.Q. in the Red Cross Department. He said the British Government had authorised the expenditure of $2 million in Thailand on ex P.o.Ws. There are a Brigadier, 2 Colonels, 2 Majors there - they don't seem to know when or where we are going.

31st August 1945

Queen Wilhelmina's birthday. There was a reception given by Dutch officers to British officers; the Governor of Kamburi and Boon Pong were there, also Newall. We had very good drink (for Thai stuff) - too much though. We were received by a Dutch Colonel, and hanging on the wall was a drawing of the Queen drawn by an ex P.o.W. - very good. We then signed our names. They hope to present the drawing and names to the Queen.

We received cigars, cigarettes and soap from some Red Cross organisation to-day. It came over the news to-day that those ex P.o.W. who have already left are on their way from Rangoon - Calcutta, and Mountbatten has said we will be on our way home in a few weeks time. Everybody is getting very bored and impatient to be moving - I suppose a natural reaction.

This evening a Major and two O.Rs came into camp. They were landed at Bangkok from Rangoon to-day by plane - they are living in camp.

1st September 1945

Set out for cemetery 7.45 this morning. We got about half way there when two planes came out of the mist, very low, and looked business-like, so we turned tail and ran back. When I got back to the aerodrome, one plane had already started dropping supplies. It was a two-engined Dakota. Every run in dropped four packages - one could easily see two men at a big door in the side, and after pushing the stuff out, waved to us. I was on the aerodrome itself. As soon as one of the Thais saw what was happening he rushed up to me shook me by the hand and kept on saying 'No. 1'. I should imagine the whole of Kanburi was watching the spectacle - the roads all round were crowded with natives cheering etc - even some of the Japs cheered. It was a very thrilling sight. When the first plane disappeared, the second came in and did likewise - three of the parachutes failing to open, and the boxes burst and scattered everything. I think everything was all undamaged. They even sent an invoice!

At about 10 a.m. two more planes came and I think must have dropped stuff on Tamuang. At 10.30 a.m. a plane flew round the camp very low and dropped messages - they were individual messages from some officers from this camp on their way to Rangoon. One wrote 'We are on our way to Rangoon' - and drew a ladder underneath - the dirty dog! Later on the Thai police brought a lorry with about 10 more packages in it - evidently the second plane which dropped stuff here, mistook a Thai convict camp about 2 km the other side of Tamacan Bridge, and dropped the parcels there. Each parcel usually contained about 2 - 4 gal. tins, wrapped round with sacking and strong rope - the parachutes were made of cotton.

Commander Alexander spoke to us and said he had received a signal from the Army - and realised that after nearly 6 years of war, they still could not send messages!! The message was

"Prepare to move a large number in a short time," - whatever that may mean! He also said that the fit were going to move to Bangkok for evacuation; the light sick were going to Bangkok via Nacom Paton, and the heavy sick to N.Pladuk. to await development. Also he said that about 20 - 30 Indian troops were arriving in camp. We heard on the news that the final surrender takes place to-day in Japan, and that a British brigade will arrive in Bangkok tomorrow.

3 p.m.- just received 100 Players cigarettes - what a treat! At about 6 p.m., when I was on the aerodrome, two Lysander type planes (with fixed undercarriages) came low over the 'drone - one just turned round and made a good landing. After putting his landing light on, the other circled round once and did likewise. Considering there are hundreds of bushes, 4 goal posts, other posts and a number of holes, it was a good effort. There was one pilot in each plane - both American.

Their story was that they left Rangoon at 11a.m., spent a considerable time avoiding storms and running short of petrol, wirelessed Rangoon, who told them to land at Tavoy. They flew over the aerodrome but saw a number of Japs - so they landed on the beach outside the town and refuelled from their spare petrol. When they landed at Kanburi, one had half a gallon and the other four gallons of petrol left. The one with half apologised for not circling the field, but said he had not sufficient petrol to do so. I had just bought some bananas and one of them saw them and asked for one - so I gave him the bunch. We happened to have one drum of aviation petrol, which came into the camp by mistake, so they had that, and then prepared to take off. One got off all right, but the other hit a hole in the ground, broke the landing wheel and damaged the propeller. The pilot was unhurt, but dazed at first. The other circling round evidently saw it, and landed again - picked up the pilot and flew away. It was almost dark by then.

2nd September 1945

At 3.30 a.m. I was woken up and asked if I wanted to go to England or Australia. At 4 a.m. we were told to be on parade in half an hour to move to Bangkok. Eventually 500 of us left Kanburi Station at 5.45 a.m. - 25 to a truck. We arrived at Nong

Pladuk at 8.20. Nacom Paton, where we picked up 250 men from the camp - we arrived at 10. Arrived at a bombed bridge over a widish river about 12. I crossed the river in a small boat, as the bridges looked dangerous, and I am no good at heights. We left there at 4 p.m. and arrived in Bangkok at about 6.15 p.m. We ate fruit - pomelo, banana and papaya, eggs, and drank iced coffee and coconut milk all day long. All the kids and people were cheering us as we entered Bangkok.

The country after Nong Pladuk is uninteresting, and the Bangkok plain is all paddy. We had a big downpour of rain.

We left Bangkok station at 8 p.m. , crossed the river by ferry and went to the race-course transit camp - had a good meal, including chicken. Bangkok is very full of mosquitoes!

3rd September 1945

We organised into parties of 25 for travelling by plane - our serial no. is F/4/D. Wrote my first letter home. This evening I received 5 postcards from Mother dated up to 30/01/45. Had some Thai beer to-night - very good stuff, but $18 a bottle.

This morning occupation troops started to come in. There are a number of Gurkas - from reports, the Japs are terrified, having heard of their reputation. We saw numbers of planes, and one dropped pamphlets in Thai and Japanese. The containers coming down sounded just like bombs.

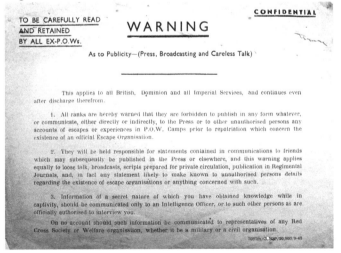

Warning For Ex-P.O.Ws

HINTS ON DIET DURING RECUPERATIVE LEAVE
FOR LIBERATED PRISONERS OF WAR

As a result of the privations you have endured as a prisoner of war, you have probably lost weight, and it is natural to think that the more food you eat the sooner will you recover your lost weight and strength. But you must remember that your physique as well as your weight may be temporarily below par, and this includes your digestive system. Just as you need rest at first and your muscles require gradual retraining, so your digestive system requires rest at first and then retraining in the handling of the sort of foods you normally like to eat.

To get your digestive system back to normal as quickly as possible, a few simple rules that you should follow, especially if you are having trouble with your digestion, are given in the dietetic instructions below. You should show these notes and the following instructions to anyone who is giving you your meals, so that they can understand why you have to be careful about eating for a time, and what they should give you to eat.

(1) **Don't overload your stomach.** Avoid heavy meals, and instead, eat small amounts frequently. Try eating three light meals a day, with three snacks of the biscuits and milk variety —two between meals and one last thing at night.

(2) **Remember that your digestion is weak, and at first give your stomach foods easy to handle.**

Eat: Foods such as milk and milk puddings, eggs, cereals, toast or bread, biscuits, preserves, cake, and fish and tender meat if you can eat these without discomfort.

Avoid at first: Fatty or fried foods, bulky vegetables, raw salads or fruit, highly seasoned dishes, twice-cooked meats, pickles and spices, rich, heavy puddings and pastries, strong tea and coffee.

Beer and other alcoholic drinks are hard on a weak stomach, and you should take these very sparingly, if at all, for the first few days at least.

(3) **Do not hurry your meals.** Chew your food carefully, avoid rush and hurry before and after meals, and take a few minutes rest before and after eating.

(4) **Be sure to take your full allowance of milk.** If you have been given a ration card entitling you to a priority allowance of two pints of milk per day, take the full amount, even if this makes you less able to eat other foods. Milk is one of the most valuable foods there are, and is not hard on a weak stomach.

Your digestive system will get back to normal as your physique improves, and you will be the best judge of this improvement. When your stomach and digestion are back to normal and you find you can eat any food without discomfort, you can forget the above rules and eat anything you like.

THE WAR OFFICE,
A.M.D. 5,
May, 1945.

(B26/342) 50000 8/45 W.O.P. 23469

Hints On Diet During Recuperative Leave

British Red Cross and Order of St. John

WAR ORGANISATION.

It gives us great pleasure to welcome you back.

We should like you to accept these few articles which we hope will be of use to you.

If you require any assistance to get in touch with your relatives or if there is any other way in which we can be of help to you, please do not hesitate to ask one of our Welfare Officers

Good luck and very best wishes from the British Red Cross and Order of St. John in the Middle East.

Red Cross Welcome

My Darling Mother, Daddy, Muriel, Dar, the Aunts at Missenden.

I arrived here yesterday by train from Kanchanaburee about 70 miles away and expect to fly to Rangoon to-morrow or the day after. Thank you so much for all the letters & cards you have written to me. I have had about 50 letters and 19 cards, the last dated 28th July 44. Which I got about 3 months ago.

I think in one of my letters from Shrewsbury House School I said that the greatest day of my life was when we had a fire etc that day has been superseded by Aug 16th 45, when we were told by the Japs in the evening that the war was over. I was sorry to hear about the deaths of Ar J.B. & Staniland; that Dar is a Captain (I shan't salute her); that you have been making money out of canaries; that Blinkers has retired; that Boss and Dar have broadcasted; that Daddy is well, thank him for the three letters he wrote me; All this and more I have got from your letters; when I felt down in the mouth I used to re-read them.

You will probably like to hear my movements etc. These will be short notes and I am writing a full, detailed diary which I shall have finished when I arrive home.

Here goes. By the way I am smoking Players cigarettes (the first for 3 ½ years) which was dropped by air 2 days ago. Here goes again.

We left Stockport on Sun Oct, 26th 1941, arrived in Avonmouth on 27th and embarked on Troopship ORONSAY (orient line; I believe sunk in the war) we sailed to Gourock & left there on Thurs 30th with about 6 other ships & an escort of 6 destroyers & 1 cruiser. On Sunday Nov 2nd we were taken over by an escort of American warships including 1 aircraft carrier, 3 heavy cruisers & 17 destroyers, it amused us as we had come the most dangerous part with such a small escort, sea calm crossing Atlantic.

On Nov 8th early we arrived at Halifax, Nova Scotia & transferred to American troopships; the first time British troops had been carried on American ships. Ours was named J.T.Dickman was about 13,000 tons. We left 2 days later and arrived at Trinidad; I was ships messing officer, it was a clean ship & great fun with the Yanks. We were not allowed ashore &

after refuelling sailed again, by this time we had to wear tropical clothes owing to the heat. We crossed the Equator & had the usual 'crossing the line' ceremony, I got away with it lightly & only got ducked once, thank goodness. Just outside Cape Town we had very bad weather for about 12 hours, I was not ill. We arrived in Cape Town on Dec. 9th after 3 weeks without seeing land.

I went ashore first evening & went to a dance (I didn't dance) organised by the inhabitants for the convoy and in the middle Gen Smuts made a speech, the usual sort of stuff. I was only about a foot away from him. We stayed there 4 days & during that time I sent you a cable; visited Rhodes memorial,; was entertained by some people, one lot of whom said they would write to you. I tried to go up Table Mt but the weather was unfavourable. (Have just been interrupted by a plane dropping pamphlets & the containers sounded like bombs coming down; I thought the war had started again!)

We left C.T. on Dec:13th & just after that our address was changed to Middle East Forces only to be changed back 24 hrs later. We had Christmas on board consisting of Turkey, Christmas pudding etc & on Dec 29th arrived in Bombay. It is a filthy place. (Some pamphlets have just been brought in they are in Thai & lots of pictures, I also hear the first occupation forces have arrived this morning) Sorry to keep going off at a tangent.

On New Years Eve I went to the Taj Mahal Hotel for dinner with some friends, it was bad & expensive. And on Jan 1st 42 we went by train to a place called Ahmednagar about 100 miles away. We stayed here until 23rd, I was messing officer for the Regt & the Regt did training & marches. On the 23rd we went back to Bombay & embarked on the boat "Empress of Asia" It was a filthy boat, food bad, meat & bread, often sour. Off Ceylon we picked up some more boats & on Feb 3rd passed through Sunda Straits. On the 3rd half the convoy turned and entered Batavia. We were told that our destination depended on fighter escort Z (it did not, we never saw any; this is my observation). Early on the 4th we entered Bangka Strait, very narrow channel way & the only one to Singapore from the south. At about 11a.m we were attacked by Jap bombers, our ship slightly damaged no casualties in the convoy. We were expecting more attacks all day but none came till 11.30 5th Feb when we were about 14 miles off Singapore. To cut a long story short we were bombed and set on fire & had to abandon everything, I swam & was picked up and taken to a 2000 ton steamer which landed me safely with 1 shirt, 1 pr shorts, 1 pr. socks & the cigarette case which Dar gave me (since sold to provide me with food, I am sorry). Our equipment & mail went to Java & we were equipped with rifles & sat or stood in a trench being shelled until we surrendered on Feb 15th. I never saw a Jap or fired a shot (anyway I hadn't a rifle!)

On Feb 17th we all had to march to Changi barracks about 15 miles the other side of the island. (I shall pass quickly over PO. life & give it in full later) Most of the damage to our constitutions was done in the 4 months following owing to half starvation, I know what it is like to be hungry & have no money. In April I was sent to Singapore on a working party (not to work myself) but had to come back in Aug owing to trouble in my ear. In Sept there was the "Selarang incident" which briefly was the Japs wanted us to sign promising not to escape, we refused. In Nov I was sent to Thailand 31 officers in a smallish cattle truck, journey lasted 4 days & 5 nights. In the middle of Dec: I got a slight dose of diphtheria & afterwards had to go to work on the railway, not given enough time to rest from the Dip & this brought on a bad attack of asthma which lasted a fortnight, I have slight attacks of asthma since, but not now for nine months, & I think being in better condition it has gone again. I was evacuated to base camp stayed there till Sept, I was messing officer again most of the time & then was evacuated to a place about 40 miles from here (Bangkok) where I stayed till Oct 44. Our camp was badly bombed by our planes (by mistake) in Sept. 93 being killed, I was only 50 yards from a near bomb it was very unpleasant. In Oct 44 I was evacuated to a big hospital camp & stayed till Jan. (I was not really sick but had mild attacks of asthma about once a week (I did not have to stay in bed or anything). In Jan they formed an officers camp at Kancharaburee (I am sorry I will draw a map later): K was the base for the building of the railway where two rivers joined, & stayed there till yesterday. That is a brief account of my doings I have worked on the railway a bit otherwise have done camp jobs such as carrying rice etc.

Now a bit for the end of the war. On Aug:14th a guard (Jap) told our interpreter the war was over & after that many Thais shouted over the fence to us (a thing they never normally do) telling us war over. It was officially given out to us on the 16th at about 10 p.m. (Tokyo Time) we all gathered together & sang Nat. Anthems of England America & Dutch (a thing we had not been allowed to do for 2 ½ years) We then drank tea & went to bed about 2.30 a.m. On the 17th we hoisted the flags. The Thais were very friendly & helped & kept shaking our hands & saying England No 1. They seem to hate the Japs almost as much as we do. On 22nd Aug Int. Red Cross Rep visited us & we sent our names with him for transmission home. That is enough for that.

We are allowed to write one letter per week & it goes by air; I have written one unofficial letter card already, you may or may not have got it. I don't know when we are going home but soon I hope, anyway we leave for Rangoon in the next few days.

As you know when I left home I was going to be ordained, I am not quite sure whether I still want to or not, but I feel I can't decide until I have seen you & talked it over. If I don't I don't think I can do better than stay in the army (if it is possible) I am 26 & don't feel I want to begin from the bottom in a business as I have sort of lost 6 years. Anyway I have not decided & we will discuss this & any other ideas you may have on the subject.

I am longing to hear from you & to know how you all are and what you are doing. I presume you are still at 102 although the lease gave up some time ago. If we stay in India, it is rumoured we may be able to send cloth home, will you please write & tell me what sort you want & anything else such as food or other things that you are short of, I will certainly get some tea (if I can).

I am 3 ½ years out of date & want to know what has been going on, I shall be interested in your scrap books but could you order either every copy of the Daily Telegraph from Feb:10th 1942 - Sept:3rd 45 if possible or else weekly editions of the Times. I feel that there a lot of tit-bits etc one can only get from the press, anyway I leave it to you to do as you think best, remember I have heard nothing for 3 ½ years.

This is the only sheet I am allowed so must stop owing to lack of space. Give my love to my Godmother, DD & everybody else. I am longing to get home.

All my love and more to everybody.

From diary

4th September 1945.
Half of our party went off this morning to the aerodrome. We remained.

5th September 1945.
We left by lorry at 8.30 a.m. for the aerodrome, and arrived about 11. Lady Mountbatten had just arrived and talked to us. With her were Generals and her staff etc. I joined a group who were talking to a Major-General - he was very nice. We were told we could not leave that day. After lunch of eggs and bread I talked to some R.A.F. pilots. We were then given our places for the night, but later were moved to a building where a small staff of medical air evacuation unit were. We slept on mattresses and had our first decent meal of potatoes, peas and tinned sausages.

5th Sept 1945. Bankok Aerodrome
My Darling Mother & Daddy
We are hoping to leave her by air tomorrow for Rangon. This evening I am sleeping on my first mattress for 3 ½ years, and have had my first European meal for 3 ½ years Peas, mashed potatoes, sausage & Thai bread. When I get home I shall not require rice thank you!

We drove in here this morning from a transit camp & we thought we were leaving to-day, but they have postponed it a day.

This morning Lady Louis Mountbatten was here talking to us, she had just arrived & looked very nice with one or two of her staff, she is something to do with the Red X.

We have not received your letter yet, but are told we shall get them soon. I forgot in my first letter to you to say I have written about 6 or 7 postcards to you, you have acknowledged at least 3 and perhaps you got the rest later(this is P.o.W. cards)

159

Just after I wrote on Sept 3rd I got 5 postcards from you dated between Aug 44 & Jan; 30th 45 which I mentioned in my cable. You say in the last that Browning is engaged, I am surprised! How is Geoffery Aked-Davies? I am looking forward to seeing him & his mother & father & sister, I am so glad you have been corresponding with them, they are so nice.

We have all been thrilled today seeing planes land & take off & seeing types we don't know. I saw the first newspaper & magazine to-day I expect you realise we are all very ignorant having had practically no news of anything for 3 ½ years, except secret wireless run by P.O.W. who worked them about once a week, you will be interested to hear about them, they were housed in water-bottles. We hope and expect those who worked them will get a decoration as it was very dangerous work.

It is rather dark now & difficult to see so will stop.

Give my love to everybody including the Russell Whites, Mrs Sturgges, Attfield, Blinkers etc

From diary

6th September 1945

Paraded at 7 a.m., went to one of the hangars, then moved and entered a plane, a Douglas Dakota - 25 seats. We took off at 10 a.m., flew 9-10,000 feet at 180 m.p.h. When crossing the mountains we ran into rainstorms and bumped a bit. Landed at Mingaladon, Burma at 12.30. We were taken in ambulances, after feeding, to a hospital, and then given clothes and other necessities of life. We got a lot of milky drinks and there are plenty of papers etc.

7th September 1945

Particulars of our diseases were taken by Doctor - had x-ray of my chest - nothing wrong.

8th September 1945

Read papers all day. Pictures in the evening.

8th Sept 1945. Saturday. c/o Recovered P.W. Mail Centre,
Bombay, India Command.

My Darling Mother & Daddy

We have still not had anything from home, I wish they would hurry up, we are being made a great fuss of here etc. I went to the cinema last night, but did not like it so came away.

In my last letter to you I mentioned some cheques I cashed as a P.W. The total amount won't exceed £40 to me, but I cashed them at different times when I had no money. In many people's opinion it was better to spend it & die; I am not saying that it was so urgent in my case, but I think it helped to keep up my health & when any epidemic was around I was fit enough to withstand it. Enough for that!

The weather here is rather depressing & it rains a lot, the monsoon is not yet over. We have been done over by the DR a bit to-day, I have had an X ray of my chest taken for asthma, but don't know the result yet, also I visited the dentist & require 1 tooth stopped.

I wrote to the Aunts yesterday & shall not write to anybody but you, until I have had a letter from you & hear all about them. If I can't remember their addresses I shall send the letters to you for forwarding.

To-morrow (Sunday), I am going to talk with the hospital chaplain, & shall probably discuss my future with him. I have just eaten a whole tin of sardines, I was very hungry: Don't think we are not being feed well because we are.

In your letters you mention about corresponding with my batman's mother, Mitchel, I don't know where he is but I believe Singapore. But please DON'T quote me in saying this to her; because I haven't seen him for 3 years & I may well be wrong. I am not getting on very well with my diary of events & shall probably discard it!

Has Dar been demobilised yet? I don't know what you think, but I should like to go away for a holiday, although it will be winter & it would be better to wait till the spring or summer.

I saw in an illustrated paper that a boy I knew @ school has been awarded the V.C. I suppose there will be quite a number of school & RA. Magazines waiting for me at home, keep them till I arrive please in case they get lost.

No more news for now

All my love to everybody

Douglas

From diary

9th September 1945

Went to church in the morning, and to tea with Padre Rice in the afternoon - a very charming man.

10th September 1945

The Doctor would not let me go out as my chest is bad.

11th September 1945

Went into Rangoon and bought cloth etc. Had tea and returned in pouring rain.

11th Sept 1945. Same address,
at Rangoon.

My Darling Mother, Daddy, Boss & Dar.

We are still in this hospital. The DR. says I have got bronchitis & says I ought not to go out, but he lets me! Don't think I am ill, I only weeze a bit at night, but feel very well & eat like a horse. I finished a large tin of sardines during one afternoon at a sitting, as I was hungry. We get issued with 1 bottle of beer a day & brandy or whisky. The other day we were put on to ordinary diet, as opposed to special diet.

This afternoon I went into Rangoon & have bought 10 yards of cloth (green colour) 2 pullovers & a large counterpane which I am bringing to you, as I expect you can make some use of them, I shan't want either pullover as we get issued with them. If I can get any more cloth etc, I shall, it is very cheap about 1/6 a yard.

The letters still have not arrived but there is a rumour that they are in Rangoon being sorted which will take some time as we are all over the place.

I have been working out how much pay etc. I should have & I think by the time I am demobilised (I am in No 26 group) I should have not much less than £1000.

On Sunday afternoon I went to tea with a padre, a very charming man. We talked over some of the difficulties which I mentioned in a previous letter about going into the church. Our discussions were successful & he has persuaded me to go into the church, so unless there are any snages from your end, I shall; but we will discuss it in full later.

Now don't think I have gone all high church because I haven't, but I have been advised by two padre's to go to Mirifield theological college. Their reason is that it is far & away the best training anywhere & they don't turn out duds, when the course is finished. Other colleges in my mind in order of preference are (1) Lincoln (2) Wells.

From what I have read in booklets, it seems that I can get all the fees paid by the state. But I shan't do anything irrevocable until I have seen you. There is a story that all Ex P.o.W.s will leave here within 14 days (I don't suppose I shall be on the first party). It is said to take only 21 days to get home so it looks as if I shall be home very soon. No more to say for now; but plenty when I have heard from you. All my love

Douglas

Leave it to you to do as you think best, remember I have heard nothing for 3 ½ years.

This is the only sheet I am allowed so must stop owing to lack of space. Give my love to my Godmother, DD & everybody else. I am longing to get home.

All my love and more to everybody.

> 12ᵗʰ Sept 1945. Wednesday c/o
> P.O. Box 164, London EC1

My Darling Mother, Boss & Dar

I have just received your first letter, telling me about Daddy. When I left home I always felt I should never see him again, & so it has not come as a shock, in fact I was always expecting to hear in one of your letters as a P.W. that he had died, I realised as time went on, you kept saying Daddy was getting weaker. I am so glad it was such a peaceful end, but of course I should have liked to have seen him & when you wrote on Jan 30th I did not notice that you hadn't mentioned him as you usually did. I gather from this letter of yours that he realised he was dying. But as you say it is for the best, as he would have been bedridden. Anyway he had a good life & am sure enjoyed himself all the time, and I am quite sure he left the world better than when he came into it; which is the main thing. Anyway I hope I shall be able to live up to the high example he set. I am glad in one way for your sake, because it must have meant a tremendous amount of work, & at your age you just can't do it. Anyway we will now look forward to the future. One thing I forbid; you are NOT to travel by bicycle any more, & I don't want any excuses!! And you are to be careful about catching cold etc. Boss & Dar must be firm with you.

I am so glad you have gone to Bournemouth for a rest. What I would like is when I come home is to stay at home for 3 or 4 weeks, I shall have quite a lot of things to see to pay etc clothes & some relatives of my unit whose men folk have died as prisoners I shall have to visit our regt, out of 550, the death toll won't be far short of 150. Then I should like us all to go away for a month, as Boss will probably be home for the holidays & Dar can get leave. I shall insist on paying for it, & shall probably get an extra petrol allowance if the car is registered in my name. Anyway we will talk it over when I arrive. I am hoping I shall be back by about 15th Oct or 20th.

I hope you got my last letter in which I said I am going into the church, unless of course you have any affairs which makes it impossible anyway we will talk it over when I arrive. You can imagine how exited I am to be coming home, it seems to good to be true.

My chest is very much better & the Dr said to-day that I can be discharged any day & think we might go to-morrow to a transit camp from which we go to the boat. I shan't fly again!!

I have just been thinking that you probably have been worried about me, as you have heard such bad reports of condition of P.W.'s under the Nips, but I was never really ill as a P.W. I am longing to hear from you to say that you know I am OK & expect that will come soon.

164

Now, mother, as you are all Boss, Dar & I have got left (as Daddy has gone) I insist that you take the greatest care of yourself. Don't catch cold, don't ride a bicycle. Give my love to the Aunts & everyone. I am just going to write to Lloyds Bank myself.

Letter undated from Cable And Wireless Limited. Postmarked London E.C.4. Postmarked 14th Sept 1945

Electra House,Victoria Embankment,London, W.C.2.
Dear Sir or Madam

It is a great pleasure to me to be able to send you the enclosed copy of a telegram from your relative who is now liberated from the Japanese.

In order to relieve your anxiety at the earliest possible moment this message has been transmitted free of charge by Cable and Wireless Ltd. From the Far East, and by the Post Office, in co-operation with the War Office.

In the same way we shall be happy to send your reply free, if you will write it – using about 12 words in addition to the address – on the enclosed form and hand it in at your local Cable and Wireless Office or any Post Office where telegrams are normally accepted.

Will you please insert on the reply-paid form the address given in the enclosed telegram and sign it with your surname.

With best wishes

I remain, Yours sincerely

Chairman

12th Sept 1945 Telegram 63 Rangoon
Arrived safely at India hope be home soon writing address letters and telegrams to c/o PO Box 164 London EC1 = Douglas Heelas

From diary

12th September 1945
Dance in evening. Had a glass of beer and because of heat I came away. Received first letter from Ma telling me about Daddy.

13th September 1945

In the afternoon went and saw Major Brodie and John Wylie. In the evening went to ENSA show called "A Normandy Story" starring Winifred Shotter - very good.

From Francis Walmesley To Mrs Heelas

13th Sept 45, The Old Cottage, Woking

It was very good of you to let me know the good news so soon. I am ever so glad and I do feel your faith has been rewarded, as you have never given up your hope. I wonder how you will celebrate the great day when Douglas comes home. You will know that his Father is sharing in your joy through you cannot see him. I hope the good news has sent the asthma flying.

I am sending word to Mr Martin & brother Mertyn & asking the Vicar to put a note in the service.

From Douglas

14th Sept 1945 Friday

I have not received any more letters since yours of Aug 24th, and so I have to read that one over & over again. While I am on the subject of letters, when I am next a P.O.W. will you please write on air mail paper as that is better for cigarette papers and a good substitute for "Bronco" !!! I have still got a lot of your letters & all the postcards, but I hope you don't mind me having used some for "Bronco" , the only alternative was a bottle of water & that wasn't a very attractive idea. Anyway I had better get off the subject, as I shall get deeper into the mire!! Bronco of course is lavatory paper.

The day before yesterday I went to a dance here organised by the matron, the hall was well decorated and there was beer & lots of eats, I did not dance and as it was so hot had some beer & came away. Last night I went to an ENSA show called "a Normandy Story" starring Winifred Shotton it was a stage show & very amusing.

I don't of course know what policy you have adopted about entertainment, since Daddy's death, but after thinking it over, I came to the conclusion that from Daddy's point of view it should be a time for rejoicing, but of course it has left a big gap from our point of view, & so have decided that it would be his wish for us to carry on as usual, I should be glad of your views, but I think you will probably agree with mine.

My chest has completely cleared up now & I am as fit as a fiddle, I think it was caused by the change over from Thai to English tobacco as it started when we changed over, but of course the Dr does not agree with that point of view.

I hope you have stopped this bicycle riding, I know the sort of excuses you will make ie (a) I get off when there is a lot of traffic (b) I am very good on it & quite safe etc etc. Well it MUST stop, I hope I have made myself quite clear & I shall hold Boss & Dar responsible to see that it does stop. If it hasn't when I return I shall soon take steps to stop it. I am sorry about these tirades!! NO excuses; No Riding!!

I have seen in the news first lately that, (1) we get demobilised as soon as we are fit and (2) that after a fortnights leave at home, we get thoroughly vetted by DR's. It seems a good idea, we are still in this hospital but expect to go to a transit camp soon, before embarkation.

I have written to Lloyds BK explaining the cheque business & asked them to send me a statement of a/c etc to 102 to await my arrival.

I hope you enjoyed yourself at Bournemouth, I should think it will have done you a lot of good. I am glad you have kept Daily Sketch's for me, will you continue that, as news here is rather scrappy and not too much of it.

I have decided not to write to anybody until I get home & get their addresses from you, one reason is we don't get all that amount of air mail letters & I want them all for writing to you every 2 or 3 days. I haven't been able to buy any tea yet but will probably get the chance if we call in India.

Will you give my love to the Aunts, D.D. my Godmother, the Millards, Aked-Davies, Browning etc & anybody I have left out, Mrs Sturges A H Field Blinkers Russell White.

From Mother to Douglas Addressed to Recovered. P.W.Centre, Bombay, India Command

14th Sept 1945

We were thrilled to the bone when your letter arrived yesterday morning & the telegram soon after giving your address. I hope you got my air mail telling about Daddy passing on last Jan. I went to see Mr Tate yesterday & it made me feel thankful that Daddy had gone with no pain & in peace, as he is still in bed & is always in pain & can't move & has been like that for nearly 3 years – he was so delighted to hear of you. Everyone enquires about you, people I don't know when I'm in Norbiton shops & ask. We are sorry that Dorothy had arranged to go to Ceylon as secretary to her Colonel out in connection with the Army Welfare work which she is now working at in the War office & she flies there next week. We can get her off after 6 months she says or she signed on for a year. Her 'marriage' is all finished, they never lived together, I think her reasoning must have "stopped" her so it has been annulled, which means she is D. Heelas again. Muriel is leaving her job to live with me, so there will be 3 of us, of course we miss Daddy terribly and am afraid you will too, but he got so feeble 'it is better' than he should have stayed to be bed ridden. Miss Chennels comes to see us and DD is a faithful friend has to cycle over & comes 2 or 3 times a week when she can she came yesterday & is coming again tonight. She was so pleased you began your letter & included her. I have a sweet little woman an Eastender, bombed out of London & has been 4 years last month came first after you went. She's nothing to look at but she is so kind & thoughtful & was sweet with Daddy, didn't mind what we asked her to do. I think she loves us, she wept with me when your letter came, & said I don't want to go case master Douglas might come & I have to answer the door to him, she comes from 8 to 11.30 and Mrs Howard still comes on Wed. The girls have been getting the house ready cleaning up for you. The kitchen walls distempered! & Boss has done your bedroom, black leading the grate, & done all the paint work. We had our bedroom windows blown out by the flying bombs. I hope you look well, you will find me a bit older, whitish hair, I am in my 72nd year, but still can ride my bicycle, & we have the car going for you, so you can go all over & see your friends.

From Dorothy to Douglas

14th Sept 1945

We are absolutely thrilled to hear you are safe and well after all this time, and are longing to see you again. We had only 3 cards from you, one about each Xmas, & last Feb we heard this the Red Cross that two survivors from a torpedoed ship had seen you in Bampong in June 44.

I am very disappointed that I may not meet you for a few months, as before the war was over I had asked to go to Ceylon for a bit, and it has now come through and I am going for six months, leaving here next week by air. There might be a slight chance of seeing you in India. Just in case, my final address over there is c/o Lt Col Noonau, H.Q. SEAC (D.S.R.), and I shall be in Kandy. I am now a Junior Commander in the ATS & have been a staff officer at the War Office.

Mother is really very well except for her asthma, & even this has gone since we heard from you. The car is out & going beautifully, & you will be given extra petrol for 600 miles as well as our ration of 6 gallons a month, so mind you apply for it.

All our friends are terribly exited over you, Mrs Sturges, Mrs Chenells, Millands, Aunts, Godmother, Percy Fear (who has written 3 times in the last 2 weeks to ask after news of you!) etc.

Boss looks just the same & behaves even younger than ever. I have got a motor bicycle which I am now trying to sell, unless you would like to have it. It goes quite well, but I think the car will be best for you. I've dusted everything in your cupboard ready for you, & Boss is spring cleaning your room. We have never been so excited in our lives before!

I'm not married anymore now & have changed my name back again, I'll tell you all about it when I see you which I hope won't be long. I am very sorry now about Ceylon, but can't get out of it now. With all my love & longing to see you again. Dar

From diary

14th September 1945

Played bridge in the evening.

15th September

This afternoon Lord Louis Mountbatten visited the hospital and spoke to us about ships to take us home; a general summary of the big events of the war, and the steps he was taking to see that ex-Jap guards would be dealt with. He was dressed in ordinary green slacks and tunic with 4 complete rows of ribbons and looked very handsome, tall and red-faced. He has a terrific personality and was very amusing. He ended on the theme that Japan was well and truly beaten on the land, sea and air, and that it was not just scientific devices that did it.

Later in the afternoon went to see a Padre West about ordination, who held a sort of retreat, although silence was not kept. Stayed the night and came back to hospital on September 16th in the evening. Also met a Padre Hodgson.

To Douglas From Mother

15th Sept 1945

I have had another cable with a different address from that I sent a letter yesterday, so I had better send another in case you don't get it. We can't get over you coming home, it seems too good to be true after all these difficult years. We had a fair amount of bombing around here and our bedroom windows out. We got an inside shelter in the drawing room as Boss was so scared, but Daddy was wonderful and when he was in bed never bothered, said God would take care of him. I used to get under the bed or the dinning table! I hope you got my letter about Daddy. I am afraid you will miss him, and he was always saying "I want to live to see my boy", but he never suffered any pain, which he so much dreaded, so I am counting that and many other blessings and I feel he is at peace in that now. I am glad your health has not been too bad, but I fear you have had great mental torture, even if not bodily however it is all over now, and you are young and can begin afresh. Dorothy is sorry she is going to Ceylon, but can't get out of it now, but will come back as soon as she can. Boss will be home to take care of you & we shall soon get you right & feed you up. The girls are so kind & thoughtful take too much care of me really! & they were wonderful during the sad time in Jan. Mr Russel White I'm sorry to say is leaving Twickenham for Tonbridge. They have a baby girl a few weeks old which is a great excitement to them after 3 boys, the youngest 9.

There is another vicar at St Peters, Mr Smith found it too hard work, I think. I've been round to tell a lot of the people you are coming back soon Bush & Pavell are delighted & so are all & I rang up Blinkers & Mrs Sturgess & rang up your Godmother we went to tea a few weeks ago, she is very well but so difficult to understand, I'm a bit deaf, so make that an excuse for her to repeat!

We are getting ready for you bed made clean sheets flags out! I have been sleeping in the study as I had to turn out of the dinning room where I slept on account of Daddy's illness- & I am here still writing you this letter – Cissie (our woman) brings my breakfast at 8.30 & she is looking forward to taking you yours up to you in bed! The car goes well - & we are just off to do some shopping & see Aunt Nelly, we went to London yesterday to get Dorothys tropical kit. You are allowed enough petrol for 600 miles so you will be able to drive here & there - & we've 2 spare wheels! The car was a job at first wouldn't go up hill,- & Boss had to get out & push

From Douglas

16th Sept 1945 Sunday 8 p.m.
(Posted on 17th). Rangoon

I have not had any more letters from you, since the first one & still live in hopes. Yesterday afternoon Lord Louis Mountbatten came to the hospital to talk to us, he told us the rough details of ships & when they were arriving, he reeled them all off without any notes; he then gave us a very rough outline of the course of the war & in more detail of the campaign in Burma; then he told us what orders he had given to bring ex Jap P.o.W. guards to justice & finally said that it was not just the Atomic bomb that beat Japan, but that they were thoroughly beaten on land, sea & in the air. He is tall handsome, a red face & has four complete rows of medal ribbons. He gave me the impression of being a terrific personality and was also very amusing. There was no ceremony we were sitting in a concert hall & were told not to get up when he arrived or departed, in fact when he came to get up on a box, he was so ordinary I didn't think it could be him. I think it is very nice of him to go round all the P.o.W.'s because he must be very busy.

After he had left I went (by previous arrangement) to the house of the Bishop of Rangoon to meet a Padre who is traveling round concerning ordination candidates & he gave me addresses etc. for when I get home. Among the things we discussed, he said, (1) He thought I should have to get matric & for that purpose advised me to get a parson to allow me to stay in his house to study for matric for 6 months. He suggested that the parson be fairly high church & a bachelor, NOT one who took in people in the normal course of events, he suggested all these things in view of what I told him about myself & my still rather doubtfulness as to whether I am suited for the church (I will elucidate this when I see you) I think the above is a good idea & I shall make it a condition that it is a country parish. He said I must go to the right man & is writing to somebody in London about me. (2) He said he thought I should not like Mirfield & advised against it, so I think I shall take his advice. (3) He gave me details of interviews & connections in London etc. He was very nice, named West & he is writing to you. I am going to write to somebody in London to send me forms etc. to 102 to await my arrival.

After the talk with him we had a sort of retreat, we didn't keep silent because I said I couldn't!! & I also said I couldn't concentrate much but he realised that (You see most of us are rather upset mentally & I think it will need rest to get right again, for instance any sudden bang I jump out of my skin; please don't think you are going to get a lunatic son back, I haven't reached that stage!! but I find it hard to concentrate on anything as yet, probably due to the excitement of being free again, we then had two short services & addresses I stayed the night & to-day we went to H.C. at 7.30 a.m two more addresses this morning & one this aft. Last night we sat & exchanged experiences. When I came away I thanked him very much & said I only took some of it in, which he quite understood. I hope I am not boring you with all this. I do want you to realise that I shan't do anything irrevocable until I have seen & discussed it all with you. Enough on that subject.

We are standing by at very short notice to move off to the ship. I don't think I ordered copies of "The Marlburian" to be sent to me, if not would you please write to the publishers & ask for back numbers which I have missed if its possible, you will find the address in a back number of "The M" which are in the cupboard of my room. I think I have seen copies up to the end of 1940 but you will see which are the latest. I saw in a back number of the Telegraph that Mr Miller's son has died, very sad.

I suppose Boss will soon be going back to school after holidays. Is Dar going to stay in the army? I should think she must be a very efficient officer by now & what a high rank, I feel very small fry, is she a major yet? Have you given up riding a bicycle yet? 'Beware' if you haven't!!!

I hear you've all gone 'Labour' now, from what I have heard & read it looks as though it will be a good govt. Longing to hear from you again, your first letter is getting quite worn out from being read. Give my love to the Aunts & all else who deserve it, DD. Does!!

From Rev Frank H West Chaplin Eastern Forces ,c/o ACG 12th Army S.E.A.C to Mrs Heelas

16th Sept 1945.

As I have seen quite a lot of your son during the last day or two, I thought you might like a report on him, as it were from a third party.

Many families at home must be worrying about the effect of 3 ½ years captivity on their men folk.

Your son seems to have come through very well. Physically he seems quite fit, and good food and a long sea voyage should thoroughly reinvigorate him.

He is very cheerful and mentally active, but of course the scarcity of books in the camp and the continuous tension makes it difficult for the men to concentrate on one subject for long. But you will find his manner quite normal. So you need have no fears that a boy broken in health and spirit is coming home to you.

In a few months he should be quite readjusted to normal conditions. He is thinking of ordination – so I had him round here for a short retreat for Ordinals. I have given him all the advice I could as to his best procedure.

I thought he was an extremely nice boy. I hope you'll have him back in a few weeks.

From John Pennelli, South Dene, Kingston Hill, Surrey to Mrs Heelas

16th Sept 1945

Just a line to congratulate you on the good news regarding Douglas.

I do hope that he arrives home safe & sound.

It is surely wonderful how God answers prayer.

I am pleased to tell you that Mrs Church's son is also on his way home from the camp in Singapore. I am so glad for the poor old soul has been terribly worried about him.

I trust that you are keeping well also the family.

Doris & I send you our kind love for the good news. In Christ Jesus our Blessed Redeemer & friend

From Muriel to Douglas

16th Sept 1945

We are delighted to hear from you again. We got another long letter from you this morning dated 3rd Sept I do hope you are well on your way home by now.

Life has gone on much the same here since you went, except for Daddy. It was far better for him that he went, he got so feeble, and could hardly walk at all. I think Mother realised this too, as she was very sensible.

I wonder if you have heard of Doodle-bugs* yet. We came down to having a table shelter in the drawing room & Dar & I used to sleep in same. We had quite fun, although it was very frightening at times. Do you remember us popping in & out of the cellar?! (Dar has got 'La Boheme' going on the gramophone!)

We've had your battery wireless mended, & it goes beautifully. I've been sleeping in you bedroom since you went. Mine got too full off mess! But I got mine ready for residence yesterday, so yours is ready for you.

Our school has moved to St Albans, so I keep coming home!

Chet bought a little Austin sports car, so we come back in that.

I keep giving notice, but they won't let me leave. Anyway I am arranging now to go about three times a week this term, so I can stay at home & entertain you & Ma. Ma is very well, except for asthma sometimes. D.D. still comes. We had "hand on heart" yesterday to book her for your arrival! She sends her love.

Did you see any Siamese cats? We haven't any cats now. Grandpa was put to sleep two years ago, as he got too ancient.

Well buck up and come home. Heaps of gardening for you to do!!

Much love your loving Muriel

*Jet engined missile V-1 also known as the buzz bomb, first landed in East End London 13th June 1944 killing seven people. Over the following four months they claimed the lives of 6,000 people and left 18,000 injured.

From Jessica, Vancouver BC, Canada, to Mabel (Mrs Heelas)

16th Sept 1945

I have been thinking of you such a lot wondering if you have heard anything of Douglas. Surely he is on his way home now. Do let me know.

We hear you are all having a bad time now in England although the strains of war is over, the tiredness must be dreadful, especially when everything seems to be just as bad or worse with the food situation. We are all wondering what the Labour Gov. is going to do about it. I fancy they will have more bad headaches before they get things settled.

We are getting more rationing especially meat. I hope it does you some good but I say all the meat is going to the continent.

I am a hopeless person to do anything. All my time is occupied with trying to keep the house fairly clean & cook. There are no servants about, I have a girl who comes (when she feels like it) for 3 or 4 hours every two weeks.

From M Millard, Kelstone Lodge, Repton, W.Derby to Mrs Heelas

17th Sept 1945

You can't think how relieved we were to get your card this morning & to know that your Douglas is on his way home, you must indeed be exited about it. I am so glad that he is well but no doubt he must have changed somewhat after all he has been through, poor fellow.

There are several boys in this village who are on their way home from there. It is sad for Dorothy that she will just miss him perhaps they might meet on her way out somewhere?

I hope you are well again. Thanks so much for letting us know about D. We rejoice with you.

From P.H.F, Garsinton Rectory. Oxford. To Mrs Heelas

17th Sept 1945

Many thanks for P.C.

I rejoice with you that Doug is safe.

Deo gratias!

I have just phoned & told your relations here & they are delighted!

What a reunion it will be! & how difficult for him to take up again.

From diary

17th September 1945

At 2 p.m. I went by lorry to a camp, No. 5, at FARHU, about 15 miles out of Rangoon. Am sleeping in a large marquee on a ground sheet. It rains cats and dogs. They have an ENSA van which broadcasts over loud speakers. Food only fair.

18thy September 1945

Told in the morning I am in charge of a draft of 50 men - had to make out nominal rolls (27 copies).

From Robert Sly, 'Carola', Southfield Road, Chislehurst, Kent. To Mrs Heelas

18th Sept 45

I was so glad to get your letter & to hear the good news about Douglas. I do hope he will be home soon & fit & well. What the poor chap must have suffered all these years, yes & how you must have suffered too may it be all over now soon, & forgotten in time.

I am being well look after by 2 dear people living opposite, they have been & are more than neighbours – "they have heaven sent" dears & cannot do too much for me but for them I do not know what would have become of me. I hope you are quite well again after your nasty attack of asthma, too bad you having to suffer so much. Take care of yourself, the weather is so treacherous these days no two days alike, & nasty winds, & the temperature so variable. I shall be glad to hear still better news of Douglas. Give him kind remembrances & best wishes for his future may good luck be always with him.

From Aunt B to Douglas, B.Young, Bloomfield Cottage, Great Missenden, Bucks

18th Sept 1945

We were thrilled at receiving your letter this morning. Of course we knew all about your letter & cables home, but is nice to see your very own hand writing! It is wonderful to think you are on the way home & having decent - living - I expect you will see a difference in most of us. Jessie & I are 4 years older & much greyer, but your Mother has had rather a lot of Asthma this winter & is much thinner than she used to be - but I expect your coming will buck her up. Muriel looks a picture of health & in good spirits. There's nothing like living in the country to keep one fit. Poor old Dorothy looks tiered, she has been working very hard living at home & going to her job in London every day, we think the trips and Ceylon will be good for her. Well, this brings much love from Jessie and your loving old (over 80) Aunt B

From Mother to Douglas

18th Sept 1945

It was wonderful getting the epitome of your doings, 1st part of the boat till you got to Bombay you described in a letter, a lovely one I nearly know by heart – as it – was the last - & you told of the people. In March 1942 we had a letter from the war office that you were missing, which was a great shock they warned us you might be alive somewhere. Then in Dec 1942 about 10pm a telegram came by a special messenger (Kings messenger) & neither Daddy or I could read it, we were so frightened what it might be, so the man did - & we just leaped above with joy! Today we got your 1st PC saying you were in safe hands written 6th Sept & we have got 4 airmails & the long letter so we are well up. We only got the one about the bank yesterday & will go on Thursday, as we are meeting Aunt Jessie for tea. We use the car again now have been up to London most of today shopping etc for Dorothy, in preparation to her leaving for Ceylon next week. We shall miss her very much, but it will be good for her. The Aunts rang up to say they had a letter from you they are thrilled with it. Send one to your Godmother if you can. We have kept the Daily Sketch for some time & lots of cuttings 3 big books. So I think we shall have enough back news for you. By now you will have heard about Daddy I'll tell you more detail, during 43 & 44 he got much weaker & for 2 years could not shave or bath himself, starting about the end of 42, I tried to do it but it wasn't a success & I remembered a man over the way said he was trained as a nurse retired aged 80! So I asked him to take on & he did not want payment he said, he was quite good and after a few months (I used to give him a present of 10/- a month) he wanted pay, eventually I gave him 25/- a week & he wanted more (he is

Welsh!). So as Daddy had got quite weak I had a nurse for the morning & I managed to undress him etc & until Jan this year we got on alright, he was up for dinner, I got 2 chickens from Louth - & he came in the kitchen & we gave each other little gifts, as before & talked of you, that was Monday 25th on the Wed he got a chill and bronchitis came on again he'd had it twice the previous year & he just lasted till 10th of Jan & slept most of the time, the doctor tried everything, we had oxygen administered every hour for 15 min night & day for 3 days, relays of nurses came through the night 6 hrs at a time, & then the Dr came through the snow late at night to inject – heart - stimulants & other things and he passed on, 3 o'clock on 10th Jan Wed. We had the coffin taken to the mortuary Paine's & I asked Russell White to assist Eric Smith at the funeral on Saturday at 10 a.m. It was a distressing time & we felt we could not bear to follow behind the hearse, so I rang up Paine & said we'd go in the car first. I asked DD to come also Mrs Narper next door who had been so kind & Aunt Jessie came - & we sat in front – lots of people (Parsons etc were there) we had no music we couldn't bear much, it was a terrific ordeal as you can imagine, & we wanted you. Eric Smith – gave a very nice little talk & said the funeral was arranged as the family wished it, quite unorthodox I know & spoke nicely of Daddy. I've got all the news paper accounts for you. Boss, DD, Ar Jessie went to the cemetery, I stayed in the church with Dorothy. Frank & Muriel came & came on here after for a cup of tea. I had a lot of letters of sympathy etc & nearly all mentioned you. I've not touched Daddy's papers etc - thought you could go through them with me & burn any we think. I'll not go into the money part it is rather long, we went to see the lawyer in Reading, Boss & I. He's ever so kind & helpful. Also the Bank manager here who let us have some for Death duties, but we are all right for £.s.d & I mean you have a good holiday & think of a good plan as you suggest to go somewhere away. Boss & I'd love it in the car.

Hope you won't mind me writing alone, Daddy. But it will be a little preparation for a talk on details you may wish to know the end was quite peaceful.

I feel I want to write to you every day! Thank you for your last in which you say you have bought 10 yrds of green material and a bed spread both will be useful, all things like that are terribly dear here and also require coupons which you haven't got. Bob Abraham died & Mrs wore bright green, I did wear dark blue, really I believe it originated with the pagans, & it doesn't alter one's feelings. You say you think you will be ordained, & wish to go to Mirfield theo – college although you won't be high church, my dear you may go with evangelical ideas, you'll come out a "Mirfield Father" its quite a school for anglo catholics & stepping stone for R.C's! how ever there is plenty of time to talk it over & probe into the real teaching they give, I want you to do as you think best. I should like Russel Whites opinion as well as I think its is worth a lot. Mrs Howard is here working today & sends her love, she's over 70 & is wonderful, she used to be so good to Daddy. I used to go to London or out for a change on the day she came until last year he seemed to miss me, so did not often go. All the people in the shops we deal at are so pleased to hear of you, in Follets this morning all 3 assistants gathered round me to hear about you and offered me stuff for plum pudding (under the counter) that means if you don't know, the shop keepers have things that are scarce under the counter for regular customers & their favourites, I'm in the "back room" at some shops & get marvellous fish. I call myself his "best girl"! of course they all got to know Daddy & he often went in shops & asked to sit down & was friendly. We still trade with Bush, one of the brothers is ill, T.B I think, they are elated over you & remember you calling 'Bush bicket-pease' you will get a welcome home from everyone, I hope you are better, I too have been having bronchial asthma, I am sorry you should have it, Muriel is so much better & scarcely ever has an attack, I think it's the cat going, fur is her down fall! Mrs Little the "char" we had here once brought a chicken for us to celebrate you being found, & we will have another when you come, it's very kind of her, her husband is back after 4 years in a German camp & was wounded in his ankle which is difficult to get well. D & I happened to be in London on V Day & it was amazing to see the people all dancing in the streets & siting on the kerbs eating, mothers & new born babies, bottles of milk & men selling flags etc, at an enormous price & noises of all kinds. I'd like to have joined but D was in the dumps all because her girl friend had given her the "cold shoulder" so she wouldn't play, no buses or taxis could drive & we walked miles to Waterloo. Boss went up to Buckingham Palace with her pal "Chet" you saw her at Dover once, & saw the Royal family & the yelling crowds & cheering etc, & got home about midnight, it was a thrilling time, like as when you heard the Japs had surrendered then again we all went mad & put out our flags. I remember & have your letter from Shrewsbury House saying the school fire was the "time of your life" I've kept all the letters you've written to me, Shrewsbury House, Marlborough & since you went to be a soldier. Mrs Millard wrote congrats. I wonder if sponges are dear with you if not get yourself one, they are 2 & £3 & one close £1 and very few shops have them. We have made some jam blackcurrant, plum, raspberry, Boss got the fruit at her school farm & we picked blackberries at Oxshot woods & I made it into jam. The car goes well & you will get enough petrol for 600 miles, it has been "done up" & looks quite nice. I sold some earrings of Ar J.B's for £15 & spent that on it & a bit more of my own, I've saved your £3 a month for a "rainy day" so it will be lovely to go away for a change, I've only had one week in 4 years! Except of course to Tetbury to see to poor Ar J B but that was a sad time. Daddy & I stayed there & her mind went & she thought she was staying with us, but she was so well she was only in bed for 3 days & slept away. I went to her, daddy wasn't up to it, & we'd only been home for a week after a fortnight with her, that was about April 1942, she died age 80.We are amused when you were in the jungle you wrote in ink, now you are in civilisation you use pencil! Well dear boy! We hope to see you very soon our eyes & ears are all agog for news. I haven't heard if Mrs Mitchell has had news of her son I wrote a card to ask. We will call at Coxs Lloyds Bank when we go up by car to meet Aunt Jessie tomorrow in London.

Goodbye bestest love, your loving mother, also the other friends love, XXXX

To Mrs Heelas From Muriel Staniland, The Abbey House, Lauth, Lincolnshire

19th Sept 1945

My dear Mrs Heelas

I am more than glad for you all in that Douglas is safe. He must have been in the same camp as my nephew Peter as we have heard from him from Rangoon, on his way to Bombay. He too has escaped any tropical deceases and seems in good spirts. I do hope that christ inevitably the Japs will be brought to retribution for their crimes, but I fear nothing will make any impression on them, as they are more like animals than human beings & I think the world would have been better if we had merely wiped them out. I hope this is not too unchristian as I suppose there must be some divine reason for their existence.

Poor Douglas, I am afraid it will be a shock to find his Father gone, but I hope, knowing how frail he was he may have been more or less prepared for it. Peter got 75 letters and post from us, but his mothers last card from him came last Christmas Day when she was here & it was six months old.

I am glad Muriel is going to be with you as you could not manage alone, especially if you are going to let rooms. I think it is a good idea, as it is so difficult to get accommodation anywhere & with all those old rooms you might have had them requisitioned. Dorothy ought to have a good time in Ceylon. She is lucky to have struck such a good job. I'm sorry for the account of your health I had hoped you got over your asthma. Geoff has some stuff that he uses directly he gets it coming on & it stops it. It is the only thing he has found that relieves him.

My love to you all & great joy for your news.

From Douglas

19th Sept 1945

My Darling Mother Boss, & Dar & the Aunts

We left hospital about three days ago and now in a transit camp. Tomorrow early in the morning we are leaving to go on the boat, I know the name of it, but there are still censorship regulations & I don't know if I am allowed to tell you so I won't, but I am certain to get an opportunity on the way of telling you.

I have got 50 men to look after, so I shall be quite busy. We have been issued with quite a lot of clothes & necessities. I shall try & get some tea & other things if we are allowed ashore in Ceylon, but I don't know if we can; I hope so!

I think it will be quite a nice boat trip & Lord Louis M has given orders that they are only to be filled to 2/3 capacity as he says we have been crowded up too much & he wants us to have a comfortable journey: very nice of him. On the same boat will be my Colonel Col Dean who is extremely nice & we get on very well together.

I have had no more letters from you since the one you wrote on Aug 24th, but still thats something & we should be home soon.

I don't know when I shall be able to write to you again so don't expect to much, but I will write at the first opportunity. I am just going to have dinner (7.15 p.m.) so will stop as I have no more to say.

Longing to see you all. No more riding the bicycle I hope.

Chapter 7

Boat back to England

From diary

19th September 1945

In the afternoon, fitted out with kit and given our haversack rations. Very busy rushing about.

20th September 1945

Got up at 4.30 a.m. - moved by truck at 6 a.m. to docks, then by landing barge to ship, which was lying out. It is a Pacific Steam Navigation Company boat, H.M.T. ORDUNA - cabins hold 30 officers. I am on a top bunk of 3 - it is very hot in the cabins.

Food is very good, nice lounge and plenty of deck space. I think it will be a nice voyage. A lot of work all day running about in conversation with the draft, but it is something to do. About 12 noon we moved about 10 miles down river and anchored. Very hot in the cabin at night.

21st September 1945

Sailed at noon - they say only 18" Clearance over bar, draft of ship is only 2' less than Queen Mary, tonnage is 15,000 odd. Soon out of sight of land.

22nd September 1945

Slept on deck last night - it started raining about 5.30 a.m., so moved down. A lot of work to-day, pay etc. Vaccinated and T.A.B. this afternoon.

From Emily Thomas, Warren Point, Gloucester Road, Kingston Hill, Surrey to Mrs Heelas

22nd Sept 1945

Thank you for your nice letter, we are glad you think the white heather brought you luck.

We were so pleased when we read in the 'Comet' that Douglas was safe.

We had a letter from Charles a week or two ago, he said he had been very ill for over two months with Amebic dysentery Intestinal colic and Impetgo and that when he was brought back down the line he had little wish to live, his nerves were all to pieces.

After a visit from the Padre to whom we wrote asking for news and receiving the cable from us he felt much happier and says his one aim in life is to avoid hospitals, he has spent 4 ½ months out of 11 in them.

This morning he wrote saying he is in the Province of Bihar India Command.

It was nice seeing you and Dorothy at the Flower Show quite like old times.

We all send our love and wish Dorothy a good voyage.

Letter to Mother from Douglas, H.M.T. ORDUNA. Somewhere in Bay of Bengal

23rd Sept 1945. 9.AM.

My Darling Mother, Boss & Dar & the Aunts

There is now no censorship so I can tell you all. We came here early on Thursday morning & got on board from a boat which brought us from the shore. At about 1 p.m. We started down the Irawaddy for about 10 miles & anchored, & on Friday we sailed at 12 noon, I gather we had to wait for the tide.

It is a nice boat about 30 years old 1500 tons. The food is good & the boat is not too crowded. I slept in my cabin the first night, but found it too hot so now sleep on top deck under the stars. I feel the sea air will do us a bit of good, so I stay in the air as much as possible. The sea has been very calm up to now, although there is quite an up & down motion of the ship & some people have had to miss a few meals although not ill, but I am unaffected. It is so nice at night not having to bother about black – out, as we did on the way out.

There is a cinema on board, although they can only accommodate about 300 a night, but we shall all see the films; there are plenty of books, games etc. We had a church service at 7 a.m. This morning & there are two more to-day.

The sort of routine is; get up at day light about 6 a.m. Breakfast at 8, ships in section at 10a.m. Which I have to attend as I am in charge of a draft of men, it is rather nice as it gives one something to do. A cup of tea & biscuits at 11 a.m. Lunch at 12, then I sleep on the deck until about 3, tea at 4; then a salt water shower (also one when I get up in the morning) dinner at 6 p.m. Then either sit on the open deck or last night played bridge, about 10 p.m. I take my blanket on the deck & go to bed.

We are due at Colombo about midday on Tuesday the 25th & I am hoping we should be allowed to go ashore. There is a rumour that we shall be going to Liverpool & the trip should take about 25 days. It is rather a slow ship, only goes about 12 knots an hr. I don't know if its my imagination, but the sea seems to get a bit choppy, which will be very pleasant (I hope!!)

We have a wireless out fit, with microphones all over the ship, so wherever you are you can hear, they turn on the news & they play gramophone records through it about twice a day. There is no more to say now so will start again later. A bit more – Yesterday aft, we were inoculated against Typhoid & vaccinated. I have been vaccinated about 4 times now since a P.W. That was one thing the Nips gave us, we had inoculations against cholera, dysentery, plague & typhoid about every 3 months, although our doctors didn't think much of the stuff.

We are on a Pacific Steam Navigation Co. boat which in normal times does the S.America trip.

6.30 p.m. Monday. We are due in at Colombo at dawn to-morrow, I don't yet know whether we shall be allowed ashore. It is very windy & we are rolling a bit but the weather is lovely although it has been very hot this afternoon. We should see the shores of Ceylon before dark. I must stop now as they are closing the mail bags. I shall try & cable at Colombo if I can. You won't hear from me again for a least 11 days as our next port is Port

Said. I expect you can get news of the movements of the ship. No more news.

All my love
Douglas
No more riding bicycles!! Just going to play bridge.

From Mother to Douglas

24th Sept 1945 Monday

Thank you for your latter & cards, about 5 in all, & today we got almost the first you wrote on Sept 5th saying you were in Rangoon. I hope you are feeling better & less hungry. We've read a bit of the awful times the men had in Jap hands. I went to Cox's bank with your message they want to know the name of the man who had the cheque which was lost, they were very nice, & said they'd do their best for your interest. I see you have got the news about Daddy as in the last card you crossed out Rev, don't be too sad about it, you did not see him, when he became so weak he was always cheerful & it is best as it is, only it would have been nice if you were here to see him. Dorothy has to go off today on her way to Ceylon flying there & hopes to see you on route! She will only stay there 6 months & less if I want her back, she can get compassionate leave, as she's due out of the army now. Boss will see to me I seem a nuisance, however you will be home & want me. We met Jessie in London, she is 'Girl Guide' so neatly dressed up, looked so nice. There's a lot of work for you to do here in the house & gardening, we can't get work people I am lucky having a morning woman & she's so nice & kind & comes about twice a week. I haven't been to well, not actually ill, I've been through a lot & after 44 years together the separation is a bit difficult to get used to. She only charges a very little & taking care for Daddy.

LATER. Just come back from seeing Dorothy off in the coach for Swindon & found 3 letters from you on the mat, one written 12th,14th,16th all most interesting, but we are mad to see you! Am glad you are not surprised about Daddy. But let me tell you, taking care of him kept me young & fit, & I had a special job which wanted me, & so no one else "See" I went to JELLY when the job finished & my boy if you debar me from riding the bicycle I shall go to "rags" & be old, it's better to take one risk being killed which is 1 in a 1000, & I'm no fool I don't want to be maimed any more than you want me to be, I've ridden for the last 5 years & never as much as a scratch on me, & I thoroughly enjoy it, & getting my basket full of vegetables & remember I used to ride it miles before we had a car, & it has sort of grown on me, & 2nd nature to ride, so no NONSENSE ABOUT DEPRIVING ME OF MY ONE PLEASURE!

I expect by now you will have got more letters from me & hear of Aked-Davies from what Mrs said poor Geoffery was so worried as to what was the right thing for him to do, about joining up or going on with his studies, that he took the matter in his own hands & I am afraid he put himself to sleep, in the papers it said 'sudden death'. I've kept all the correspondence for you & a letter from Geoffery, he wrote, after we heard you were a P.o.W they are living nr Worthing, I am writing to tell her about you. She got me a tin of Himrod asthma stuff once. I'm a bit off Mrs Altfield she never came to see daddy lately, I used to ask her & there was always a long pause & she never took any notice when he died. I saw her at the flower show & she was all dressed up 'like lamb' & she's guilt Mutton! Miss Chennells, Mr Miller, Blinkers & DD have been faithful friends coming. I believe Bishop of Rangoon & Bryan Greens Parson friend of Boss's brother in law, he married his sister, I don't think from what I know it is necessary that you rush into ordination unless you feel you are 'cut out' to Preach & teach the Gospel. However you will be able to talk it over as you say & R White & others will advise & you can speak your thoughts & ideas & wishes. The lease on this house ran out but the owners never said anything & neither did we, & as we couldn't get anywhere else or so cheap we are staying on & see what you think. I have left all Daddy's desk as it was for you to sort out, what need not be kept. There's his watch for you. He did not actually know he was dying as he was in comatose condition most of the time & Dr Camps gave injections to make his breathing easy, he said when he was well he hoped to live to see you again.

Bestest love your motherXX

From Diary

24th September 1945

O.R's pay day.

25th September 1945

Officers paid £4. Land sighted at dawn. Sailed into Colombo harbour about 12 noon. Taken ashore by landing craft at 2.15 p.m. - with a band of Indian Pipers on shore playing. Taken by lorry to officers' club, had lunch, then taken by a F.A.N.Y. to the barracks where I sent a telegram home, changed £3 into Ceylon currency, and got a pair of rubber shoes. Then I went and bought tea, a fountain pen and one or two odds and ends. The F.A.N.Y. said the cloth was too expensive. Had tea at a club, and arrived back on ship at 6 p.m. An excellent reception was provided for us. At 12.30 a.m. saw some news reels of victory, and other things of war effort. Went to bed on deck at 1.30 a.m. Ship took on stores all night - oil, water, vegetables etc.

26th September 1945

Sailed at 1 p.m. All the ships in the harbour sounded their whistles and waved etc. They also sent a message - "Bon Voyage - Good Luck". We sent messages of thanks to the shore. All the Ceylon dockers were on strike, so the Army and Navy personnel were manning the supply ships etc. Retarded clocks 60 minutes.

From Douglas to Mother

26th Sept 1945. H.M.T Orduna, Indian Ocean

We arrived at Colombo yesterday about 12.30 p.m and we were allowed to go ashore. We were taken by landing barges & got ashore at about 2.30 p.m. (Boats can't tie up to the quay so they have to anchor out.) On the quay there was an Indian band which played us ashore; we were then taken by lorry to officers club & had lunch. After that I was taken by a 'Fanny' to a barracks just near, where I sent the telegram to you & changed some money. We then went & bought some tea, which I am bringing home; and we went to by some cloth, but she said it was too expensive

& wouldn't let me buy any, she thought I could get it cheaper at Port Said. The cloth we saw was about 30/- a yard. Anyway I only had £3, so it wouldn't go far, so I bought myself a fountain pen, which I am writing this with. We then went back to the club, where she left me. I then went out again myself & bought some odds & ends that I wanted, had tea & was taken back to the boat at 6 p.m., when everybody had to be back. They were very good to us & had everything we wanted clothes, rest rooms, showers, baths, bands playing all afternoon.

Colombo is the cleanest eastern city I have met, much nicer than Bombay or Rangoon; Bangkok is a nice place too, but millions of mosquitoes. We then had dinner on the ship & an ENSA crowd came aboard & gave two 1½ hr performances, I did not go. They also had some news reels brought on which we had not seen ie, Victory day in Europe & one or two other war scenes; everybody saw these, they had to have 5 performances 40 mins each & I couldn't go till 12.30 a.m.

We had to stay on board this morning & we sailed at 1 p.m. As we were going out of the harbour, all ships blew their sirens to us & made a terrific noise, they also sent a message "Bon Voyage, Good Luck" we sent a message back to the military Governor thanking him for hospitality etc, I think everybody enjoyed themselves.

Rumour has it, that we are not going to Port Said but to Port Suez, I hope not as there is nothing there. The sea was a bit choppy last night but flat as a millpond again to-day. I will continue this letter when there is something more to say.

Sunday 30th Sep

There is nothing new the sea is quite choppy to-day. To-morrow we should enter the Gulf of Aden. Every night now we are putting the clocks back. I hear that we shall call in at Port Suez for clothes & then on to P. Said for water & oil, so shall probably get ashore there.

Letter to Mrs Heelas from Russell White, St Stephen's Vicarage, East Twickenham

Yes, I rejoice with you about Douglas's safety. It must have been just overwhelming for you when first you heard. I expect he will need a little fattening up when he makes your hospitable home.

Now about Ordination, I am sure that it would be wise for Douglas to wait until he has collected his thoughts and ideas before he actually takes any definite steps. There are certain steps of procedure which now have to be taken before a candidate goes forward. I need not worry about them, but I will talk to Douglas when he returns. I shall not be very far away, 45 miles, and there are fast trains to Tonbridge from Waterloo Junction. Further I shall be in London each week for C.M.S. Committees and could meet him then. I do not know my new telephone number at the moment, but The Vicarage, Tonbridge, Kent will find me. I hope that Douglas will not decide to go to Mirfield. The tendency there is to turn everyone out in the same mould and often to cramp personality and style – NO, we must arrange something different if he decides to proceed.

Mary Elizabeth is now over the nine pounds, which is almost four pound advance on her lowest weight, and this in less than three months. So like all the ladies, she is starting to throw her weight about early! What a scandal!

We move about Oct 23rd. Later on I hope you will be able to come to see us. It takes about 1 ¾ hours by road.

To Mrs Heelas From THE WAR OFFICE, CURZON STREET HOUSE, CURZON STREET, LONDON, W.1.

27th September, 1945

Madam,

I am directed to inform you with pleasure that official information has been received that your son, Lieutenant D.E.N.Heelas, Royal Artillery,

Previously a prisoner of war in Japanese hands, has been recovered and is now with the Allied Forces.

The repatriation of recovered prisoners of war is being given highest priority, but it will be appreciated that some time must elapse before they reach the United Kingdom.

Information of a general character regarding these recovered prisoners, including their movements before they reach home, will be given from time to time on the wireless and will be published in the press.

I am, Madam, Your obedient Servant, A.S.Weston

From Mother to Douglas

27th Sept 45

We (Boss & I) are all in a whirl having just got your wire from Colombo. You will just miss Dorothy who is going to look for you en route for Ceylon, & she started by air on Tuesday. Can scarcely believe the news & are getting the house ready only I'm afraid its still so untidy, same old 'junk' & more! You must let us know when you are discharged as we can fetch you in the car. There seem to be various centres where you go, one is at Missenden. I expect you will be fairly thinner. I've lost 5 stone since 39 so we shall look alike! Your friends will be delighted to see you. I've telephoned to some & written to others, we have lots of newspapers for you to read & keep you quiet!

The woman "Cissy" by name is longing to take your breakfast up to you in bed. I've had my brought for about 3 years & don't get up till 10.30, sometimes later, idle I am! "Yah"! I went on my bicycle yesterday & enjoyed it too, shopping!! It is pretty cold here already so we have a fire & as coal is rationed I've bought some logs. You must go to some funny plays, we went to two which made us laugh & laugh!

I've had a nice letter from Russell White & I'm sure his advice about ordination will be best, also heard from Rev West in Rangoon & am writing back, he said you are a nice boy (extremely nice!). But anyway you will want a good long rest, to collect yourself, as the isolation in Siam from the world must have been awful mentally, before you decide what you will do, & there's heaps of work for you to do here, & in the garden, & you will want to go & see your friends there will be the car for you &

you get enough petrol for 600 miles. I hope you will enjoy the sea trips which will do you no end of good.

Your loving Mother XXX

Letter to Mrs Heelas from Edith Densham, Boscombe, Hants

27th Sept 45

Thank God dear old Douglas is safe. It was sweet of you to let me know, as he has been in my prayers night & morning all through this terrible time. Our Colin is in Bangalore on his way home, safe & well as we heard this week. My brother & sister in law have had a very very anxious time, but it is only a little waiting time now, & we are all so thankful. Colin was doing office work, so mother hopes he was under a kind Jap, but it was weary work waiting for news & I think 2 years silence. He wrote in March & then silence until this week.

They lost their eldest who left 6 little children, but the other four boys are all well & safe. A second little niece lost her husband after 4 ½ years absence, & saw him for 2 hours at Liverpool on his way home. He contracted Infantile Paralysis at Naples. The rest of the 19 serving are safe – nephews & in laws.

I am sorry to say my sister has not been well. They were badly blasted when the bomb fell in 'Clarence Road', & were out of their house for 9 weeks - Then returned, & were blasted again, but are in good order now, & when I saw them last May my sister had a slight stroke after a nervous breakdown, & it has affected her mentality. Sylvia is still with them but I expect to join my brother & sister, when her husband is demobilised next year. Audrey & her husband are moving to St Matthias Nr Tulse Hill next week from Somerset. She has two little girls. I have been here for 3 ½ years, & am almost one of the family, but will be glad to have a home of my own & my own things, when the time comes – Boscombe suits me & I find plenty to do, as one can always lend a hand, owing to maid shortage. We only have a morning woman & often 10 or 12 in the house. Quite a small but charming guest house. Only 2 minutes from the cliff & fairly large gardens.

I have kept in touch with you through St Peter's magazine, & was very very sorry for all your trouble with our dear old Vicar.

He was so sweet to me, when I was laid up & used to cheer me up through the weary pain. You will love to have your boy home again, but it's a sad home coming for him without his father's presence.

I am sorry I did not see you at Southbourne but later on we will be able to meet. I hope the Bronchial trouble is better.

Letter to Mrs Heelas from Mrs Aked-Davies. Cromwell Lodge, 30 West Avenue, West Worthing

27th Sept 45

I have been thinking so much about you lately, on waking up this morning as usual my eyes fell on photographs of Geoffery & from thence my thoughts went to Douglas I had just decided to write to you today to enquire whether any news had come through, when at that very minute the post did arrive with your letter!

We do indeed rejoice with you at the glad tidings. I have always felt that Douglas would come back to you safe & sound because all along you were full of faith & never lost hope.

I think it amazingly kind & thoughtful of you to send on his actual letter. I hope you do not mind my keeping it until the weekend when my husband & Beryl will be here. They would be so interested to see it. I feel so touched that in his very first letter Douglas should go out of his way to remember Geoffery & to say he is looking forward to seeing him – I know how genuinely grieved he will be when he hears of our loss. Geoffery was always so fond of Douglas. Always wanted to travel back together as you know they used to go off in such high spirits at Paddington that it made up for having to part with them.

I am afraid Douglas also does not know about his fathers death. I do hope he hears before he comes home so that it will not be quite such a shock to him.

I expect with care & good food he will soon pick up again.

We shall love you to come over to see us. At present my husband & Beryl come down every Saturday & go back early Monday mornings.

I am still doing my Army Welfare work & one of my jobs had been issuing this "Leave" petrol, so I have come across a great many ex P.o.W.s & I think they appreciate this petrol more than anything.

How splendid your junior Commander going off to Ceylon. You must be very proud of your family, just as they are of you carrying on so bravely all this time.

Please give our love to Douglas as soon as possible. What a meeting you will have.

Letter from Dorothy at Hotel Carlton, Karachi to Douglas Addressed to Lieut. D.E.N.HEELAS, R.A. Recovered P.O.W.Center (ex POW No.1. Camp, Thailand) RANGOON, then forwarded to P.O.Box.164. London E.C. England

27th Sept 45

Darling Dug

I'm writing this just in case it reaches you somewhere. We got here yesterday by air & were leaving for Colombo this morning – but were left behind & hope to go tomorrow & from there to Kandy – address HQ SEAC, c/o DSR & my name is now Heelas again.

So if you get the chance could you cable or get in touch with me somehow there – I'm sure I'd be allowed to get somewhere to meet you & if you go home by sea you'll perhaps go to Colombo.

Lots of Love Da

My rank is J Comd D Heelas A.T.S.

To Mable (Mrs Heelas) From Edith, Canterbury House, 6 Gordon Rd, Sevenoaks, Kent.

28th Sept 1945

My dear Mabel

Your welcome letter did indeed fill me with joy & it is wonderful news to hear dear Douglas is safe, & on his way home to you. I've always felt this would happen eventually, but what a lot of suspense & longing you must have endured all these years!

I was just in London for the day when your letter came & I rushed to telephone Violet the good news, she was so delighted, & will be writing to you. Did you know there is a new baby there, another little girl, such a dear little thing! Caroline is very happy with her baby sister. Ian is on his way home from South America, where he went on business for his friend. It is so glorious to think that long awful war is over at last. I'm very busy flat – hunting (or even a room or two), for Mollie & myself would do. I still live in a boarding house, & it is being given up in a month or two. London seems full of foreigners, & Hampstead is just a Colony of Austrian Jews.

I guess Dorothy will enjoy her visit to Ceylon, & do hope she manages to meet Douglas on the way. Do you expect him soon? You will be busy making happy preps for him, & how he must be looking forward to seeing you all again.

He must have had a dreadful life in the hands of the brutal Japs, & what thrilling adventures, he will have to tell you all about it. We shall hope to see him, & you must both come & pay us a visit as soon as you can.

We think he is the dearest boy, God bless him, & he will soon be home.

Much love from Edith

From Mary Thompson, Dillingburgh Rd, Eastbourne. To Mrs Heelas

30th Set 1945

What a lovely surprise we had when your letter arrived! It was good of you to let us know about Douglas being safe. What a tremendous amount of suffering some of the men have gone through. He is the second we have heard is safe. The other is one who was out there when the war started. He sent his wife & youngest son to Australia.

It is good that Douglas has taken the passing of his father so well, but he is sure to feel it when he gets home. It was unfortunate Dorothy having to go to Ceylon. Did you envy her going by plane I wonder?

Our eldest nephew's son, David was a P.o.W. in Germany for just over a year. There was great rejoicing when he got home, now he is back in U.S., where it seems likely he will become an

American citizen & marry. We saw him in June when he was 21, such a nice boy.

From Mrs Aked-Davies, Cromwell Lodge, 30 West Avenue, West Worthing. To Mrs Heelas

30th Sept 1945

I am returning your precious letter herewith. My husband & Beryl have so enjoyed it & join with me in thanking you most warmly for your kindness in letting us see it. The next excitement will be when Douglas actually gets home. You must be counting the days.

We should very much like to give him a little present to welcome him home & would be most grateful for your help in this matter. I don't know whether you could make any suggestions, or do you think it would be better to wait until he gets back & ask him himself. We thought of a wrist watch, but of course he may still have his own. It is such a glorious afternoon we are actually sitting out in the garden.

From Faith Watson. 42 Latchmere Road, Kingston-on-Thames, to Mrs Heelas

1st Oct 1945

What wonderfully good news I know how thankful you must be especially that Douglas is in fairly good health. What terrible experiences some P.W have had both under the Germans & Japs, especially the latter. It is right that the world should know about the evil Japs tho' very terrible for the relatives of the suffering & of the dead who have been tortured & murdered. I too am looking forward to seeing him & you & Dorothy too if she can come. Give me a few days notice of a day when she too is free. Not a Monday, nor Thursday when I go to doctor. I hope you keep fairly well. Behind the scenes life isn't exactly easy for either of us. I long to get away to a hot dry climate!!

Dear Douglas. How happy he was when (the first time I met him) he told me that he had passed his certificate. What job will he want?

1st Oct 1945

We've had another letter from you dated 19th Sept & yet you have only received my one dated Aug 24th its disappointing if you don't get all I've written I have sent quite a lot. I am hoping by now you have, its hard to believe you are really coming home. We are getting the house ready as fast as we can. We don't want it to look too shabby & untidy for you! All our friends are so delighted the news is in the Comet & St Peters magazine - & I've had lots of congratulatory letters – also one from Rev West – Rangoon – which I have thanked him for – he says he likes you! We wondered if you would like the aunts here – or wait – till - & go & see them by car. Aunt Beet is not too keen on leaving her house – she's nearly 81 (next Feb) not very well - & fat! We have begged D.D to arrange for a good feast – for us. Muriel & I motored down to Broadstairs on Sat – two nights - & came back yesterday Sunday. Uppers wanted her to arrange for some things from the old school Port Regis to be sent to St Albans where they are now – so he gave us the petrol – it was a lovely day & we enjoyed it & called on Gertrude Easton, my old school friend on our way back – as we almost passed her house.

We have heard from Dorothy she had got to Cairo on her way to Ceylon by air, wishes she was home!

Ar Jessie has typed out the long description you wrote of voyage out, its most interesting.The house is full of newspaper 'Times'& Sketches I've tried to keep them in dates & I've got some books with newspaper cuttings in it, it will take months to tell & hear all! Mrs Howard still comes each Wed – she's anxious to make your bed for you so we shall let her, I've had suet given me under the counter for a plum pudding 'under the counter' means the stuff is scarce - & only sold to specials – its not on show – I'm 'under the counter' in many shops!

(Muriel) I've asked Ma to ask you to buy any sweets you can lay your hands on! She thinks its greedy, so I have to write it myself! So if you can at any Ports, DO!! Aren't I greedy? But we only get ¾ lb a month. Bosses!

I have a very nice woman who comes each morning from 8 till 12 & cleans up – she's nothing to look at an Eastender bombed out – but is so kind to us. We sat with one another when your first letter came! I've had her nearly 4 years & Daddy loved her she was so kind to him didn't mind what she did for him – I call her my "house keeper" because the lawyer said if I had one, we could get a rebate off the death duties - & she does do my shopping often. Boss is trying to get the lawn mown but the machine isn't too keen, wants sharpening. Bullen doesn't come – finds it too hard. We are all older, & old! I seem to have a lot to say too much really. I hope you are alright & the asthma not too bad, I have had to get a spray thing to keep mine in abeyance – Goodbye dear boy. We are longing for "the day" Bestest love from both Your loving Mother. Let us know where you will be dismissed.

2nd Oct 45

Every day brings you nearer & we Boss & I more excited & getting cleared up & ready as quickly as we can! We had about 5 letters from you the last as you were preparing to go on board, I am glad you have got some clothes given although all those you left are still where they were in your room & I managed to keep the moths from eating them up! I have your letter in which you wished me to give Jeffrey & Mrs Aked-Davies your love & mention how nice they were. I promised when we corresponded about Geoffery's death I would let her know when you came & she had written such a kind letter & Dr & Mrs A.D would like to give you a wrist watch as a welcome, so I have written to accept it for you & suggested you should be presented personally with it, you can go & take me & Boss in the car it's only about 50 miles.

Dorothy has got to Ceylon & all her letters wishes she was at home again, if she doesn't settle we must get her back again. I expect she will end by weeping on the Colonel's shoulder! I guessed she'd be homesick. I'm sorry for her, I told her that if she went she'd wish she hadn't, & if she didn't go she'd wish she had, so it's better to go!

I hope you have got some of my letters as I have written quite a lot, & told you a bit of what has happened since you went I think I've asked you if you would like the Aunts to greet you here or we go & see them. Any how D D is bagged & we hope to be able to fetch you by car from some where. If you have any pal you want a bed for on the way back, he can have one here. You mention your Col. I see he is in the P.C. Photograph of the officers which is on the drawing room mantle piece. Must stop for post

Bestest loving Mother XX & Boss

She goes to her school for the day 3 times a week, at St Albans. The Aked-Davies's live at Worthing, he goes up daily to his job in Harley St

3rd Oct 1945 Wednesday

My Darling Douglas

Just a last minute scrawl to tell you how we are longing to see you & touch you!

Boss & I are on "silent" by the telephone & door to await any news.

My woman' housekeeper we call her, hopes you'll have your breakfast in bed so she can bring it, she's a funny looking person, so don't be alarmed, age 50! Mr Sturges came in last night he's been most nights to hear news & to bring his paper which always has a map of your boats doings & where . He's going to help decorate the house with flags!

Bestest love & I'm so excited, your motherXX

Look out for the white flag at the station.

If you have a pal who wants a bed we can do it, & theres one seat in the car.

From Douglas

3rd Oct 45. Thursday H.M.T. Orduna

Yesterday morning at dawn we passed through the "Gates of Hell" (and it is too) i.e. the entrance to the Red Sea. The shade heat yesterday afternoon was 92 F, but I gather that is cool for the Red Sea. We have passed numbers of islands mostly uninhabited of reddish colour & some which have been volcanoes. We have also passed many ships going both ways & lots of them have sent us good luck messages. We are expecting to reach Suez Saturday night or Sunday morning. I am busy writing letters to different people. Slept on deck last night with only a sheet over me it was very warm even then.

From Aked-Davies to Mrs Heelas

4th Oct 45, Orme Gardens, Louth, Lincolnshire
How I rejoice with you, I'm so very thankful Douglas is really on his way, I had wondered about him now that the Japanese prisoners are getting home. I suppose it won't be very long now till you really get him, how exited you will be. Its sad that Dorothy has had to go off before he gets back. I do hope she will like Ceylon when she gets used to it.

Thank you very much for sending the dye, which I have given to Mr. Evans. If Muriel is still with you please tell her I have sent off the new lines: Papers & certificates to the address at St Albans also Miss Chatham's ?????. I have been decorating this morning, Leslie Swingler, son of our church warden who has a living near Spalding is preaching. Marcus isn't out of the merchant navy yet. You will see our parish news in the magazine.

From Mother to Douglas

5th Oct 1945
Thank you very much for your letter with the name of the boat, we have read of it's movements & can see you are due in Liverpool next Sat week, & will be at Euston, we will meet you there in the car. I expect we will get a wire saying the time, & day, writing this seems as if it can't be true & is only a 'castle'! Dorothy will be sorry she is not here, she sounds by her letters homesick & I should never be surprised she takes steps to get back. I am afraid you will have missed each other as she went by Colombo & Ceylon, she was going to look out for you. Boss and I are still striving to get cleared & clean up for you, the grass has grown so long she is cutting it by hand. I'm afraid the mowing machine needs sharpening, its difficult & impossible to get anything done in the way of work & repairs there's heaps for you to do. Boss & I were wondering what to do to give you a welcome, so we have decided on a good feed if I can get it together from "under the counter"

it will be something towards the times you have starved & had unsavoury rice! I am glad you are having a nice sea trip, as you say the air will do you good, sounds lovely to sleep under the stars as you put it, but it would kill me off! You don't seem or sound or write as if you have had any of my letters yet, & your last letter is dated Sept 23rd but I expect you will get them at Colombo. We stayed on in this house after the 6 years lease ran out, we never said anything & neither did the agents, & it is 8 years since we came. We couldn't get a cheaper one, its very comfortable & Daddy liked it here, the only draw back is it's a long way to walk to the bus, at least for me, but I can go on my bicycle as easy as "pie", you see I hate walking, you see for all those years we had no car. So I am still going to ride it, if I want to, so there! I must have my freedom, free speech and free to do as I like, as Churchill would have it!

Mr Stringer came in last evening he is very delighted about you coming. I have had lots of telephone messages of congratulations & letters, poor Mr Miller rang up. I told him I hadn't let him know as I knew he would see it in the paper, on account of his sorrow, & he said he guessed why, as I'd always promised I'd let him know, he has been very nice coming over to see Daddy. I value those friends who did, & feel they are real as it is a long way. I'm disappointed in Mrs Allfield she never came for years, I continually asked her she's one who likes to be in the "lime light" & is very big at St Peters functions, dressed up like a "lamb"! I am very well except I get asthma so much & always in the morning very stuffed up. I stay in bed until about 11.30 & write letters, which I am doing this now. Miss Watson has retired from typing school in pain with arthritis. We have no cat only a few canaries which I am trying to get ride of as I can't be bothered to look after them, & they make such a mess with the seed & attract mice, but I must keep Dick & Annie the old ones.

Goodbye dear boy we are so looking forward to your coming. Bestest love from us both

6th October 1945

Entered the Gulf of Suez at 9.15 a.m. Arrived at Port Suez 10 p.m. Had a concert this evening performed by ex P.o.Ws. Changed their money into sterling.

From Douglas to Mother

6th Oct 45

We are due at Port Suez this evening & as the mail box will close soon, I am finishing this off. I have written letters to the following addresses to you for forwarding

    Mr & Mrs Millard

    Jeffrey Browning

    Desmond Lang (Bp of Woolwick's Son)

    My Godmother

    Geoffery Aked-Davies

I have written many other letters including one to Russell White Cornwall (Marlboro') & some other friends from school. I thought it was a good opportunity as I don't want to spend my time at home writing letters. I had Blinkers & Mrs Sturges on my list, but I am fed up with writing so they will have to go without!! We are due to pass Mt Sinai in an hour or two. I will give you my probable future movements. Arr.Suez to-night, we shall probably be given kit to-morrow leave there Mon morn the 8th (Daddy's birthday) 10 hours through the canal arrive Port Said Mon evening, oil & water, leave Tues evening the 9th; 6 days to Gibraltar the 15th, 4 days on the 19th arrive home. All I know for certain of the above is 10 hrs Suez to P.Said; 10 days P.Said - home, weather permitting; the rest is conjecture. I expect you will be given instructions as to when we arrive, you can always ring up the shipping company if necessary. I shall presume you will meet me in London, but don't bother. I will try & let you know when I land & what time I expect to arrive in London. I believe we go to a camp at Port of disembarkation for some hours to get railway warrant etc. I assuming this will be my last letter to you; although I might be able to send one at P.Said if I can I will. The lunch bell is ringing. Just had lunch, the bridge has just reported that Mt Sinia is visible on the starboard (right) side. I suppose I have seen lots of hills which look like any other & everybody's opinion differs so I am afraid Moses will have to come down, before we know which is which.

I am hoping to get a letter or something from you at Suez as have had nothing except the one at Rangoon, it must be difficult to distribute them as we are always moving around.

Give my love to the Aunts.

From Mother to Douglas

7th Oct 1945 Sunday

We are nearly made with excitement now! & have found the name of your boat in the papers, & where it is. So I expect you will have got my letters in a batch. Its simply lovely having yours & you write such interesting ones, it's a marvel how you do it, after being shut up so long without, & remembering the dates. If the strike is over I guess you'll go to Liverpool if not to Southampton, but we shall get a cable from you I expect to say where you'll be & we shall meet you in the car, so look out for us.

We are just going to St Peters Harvest service & shall come out before the sermon & go to the cemetery & put a few flowers on the grave It has not been made up yet or the curb put back, we shall have to have an inscription put on, that's the sort of thing you can attend to. I wanted you badly often to arrange things. Now even Boss is feed up with the up take & a good adviser also Dorothy.

Bestest love dear boy

From Douglas to Mother

7th Oct 1945. H.M.T Orduna, Suez

I have just received two cables dated one I can't tell date & other 28th & two letters 25th & 27th Sept. I will let you ride your bicycle again. I am very grieved about Geoffery Aked-D. I don't quite understand what you say about him, but I will hear when I arrive.

We arrived here last night about 10. We arrive at Liverpool on the 19th weather permitting, but suggest you meet me in London or wait for me at home.

We have received our clothes this morning they are lovely. This is an extra letter & mail is just going. Not stopping at Port Said I am sorry to have missed Dar. Keep fit & cheerful.

From Diary

7th October 1945

Went ashore by landing craft at 8.45 a.m. Dutch boat from Rangoon with ex P.o.Ws tied up, having left a day after us. Taken by train for about 15 mins. to clothing store, where we were fitted, and another shed with refreshments - canteen with tables and chairs, etc. Went back by train to quay and saw some German P.o.W. - they looked fit and well clothed.

Went back on board, received two cables and four letters, and wrote home. Heard about death of Geoffery - am very upset. This evening entertained by John Trevor, who acted one man part from Merchant of Venice, then had a B.B.C. pianist, whom we would not let stop. These two were excellent, and it was the best entertainment since being freed. The men had an ENSA show.

8th October 1945

Went ashore at 9.15 a.m. to a place for P.o.Ws. Sent a cable to Mother and Dar - had some refreshments and went back on board. At 2.30 p.m. we sailed across the bay to the entrance of the canal, and anchored. At 6.30 p.m. we sailed - could not see much of the canal because it was dark.

8th Oct 1945. Monday H.M.T. Orduna

My Darling Mother & Boss

They have reopened the mail box.

We sail at 2 p.m. this afternoon. The undated letter I wrote was yesterday. I had just received your letters & read very quickly thro' as we had to post them but having read carefully I understand about Geoffery Aked-Davies, it has come as a great blow to me. I have always considered that he was my best friend & there is

205

nobody else who comes up to his standard. I suppose the main course was over work. I am just going to write to Mrs Aked and shall address it to 46 Rose Walk West Worthing. I think this used to be the Worthing address & if its returned to you perhaps you will forward it on. I am sending you & Dar a cable. We are due to arrive Liverpool on the 19th, how long before we start for home I don't know.

To Douglas from Mother

8th Oct 1945

Thank you very much for your last letter which we got on Sat 6th, you do write interesting stuff & Boss & I love reading them. I guess by now you are well on the way. I do hope the weather is fine & sea kind & not toss you about too much! It strikes me you are all having the time of your lives with attention & fuss on board, well you deserve all you get after all these years of stress. Boss and I went to St Peter's Harvest service yesterday. The friends made such a fuss of us, shaking hands, we had quite a small crowd round, & such enquires about you, all so delighted to hear the news. Mrs Sturgess all togged up, white gloves etc, & me in my bare hands! & Mrs Allfield also togged up looked very nice, & I went for her for not coming over to see Daddy & she said how sorry she was & had no real excuse, except indolence, so I forgave her & she's coming to see you. I said I could provide a bath chair & you could give her a ride round, & tip her out as of yore! Its quite fun remembering all the funny days of the past, there was Miss Salter who always sat next to Daddy at the school treat teas, & teased each other & used to fill her plate over flowing with food! We had a nice service, simple a bit slow but quite a good sermon & congregation. Then Boss & I went to the cemetery with flowers. Martin & Walmsley (Blinkers) are giving up being Church wardens, I can't think who they'll get, but there are a lot of new people since our day. Boss is mad to have 3 chickens to lay us an egg each day, so we are going to try to get a little house to put them in, we can get the chickens laying at say 25/- each, in the old days about 12/-. Everything seems double price, & we've only had one egg in 10 weeks from the shop. I've sent to Louth for a couple of fowls for a feast when you arrive, we've got oranges & apples & nuts from our own trees & Folletts let me have suet (under the counter) for a plum pudding, it is rationed now, so scarce, but really we have plenty of food of one sort or the other, meat is the worst, our allowance is ½ lb a week which means 3 chops! You get double rations.

Dorothy hasn't got to her destination yet & is in Karachi, has been waiting there for 10 days for a plane on, the one she left here in put some of the passengers off there as the weather was bad & they had to lighten the load to take extra petrol & fly high. Poor girl is home sick, & is going to try and get back, she says she'll swim home! She'd better come by sea I don't like the sound of the aeroplanes, & I fancy you don't by what you say. I'm glad you are having this wonderful sea trip it will set you up for the winter. I'd like it only I'm a bad sailor! Dr Camps has gone away for a month to his house in Sark, he has been coming to see me twice a week, but I'm well now since you are coming home, of course Daddy gone & you away did mean a lot of stress, as he calls it. I only have asthma at times, funny I had it when you went away, remember Mrs Sturgess helped you buy your undies, I couldn't get out! But I shall meet you. I'm hoping we shall hear when & if you come in to Euston. There's a strike on in Liverpool so you may go to Southampton, Boss has gone to do a spot of work at her school today, & I've strict orders not to go on my bicycle & it's a lovely day! Good bye dear boy we are counting the days, hours & minutes till you come.

From Diary

9th October 1945

Woke up to find us still in the Canal, not very interesting. Saw some date palms. Tied up at Port Said at 8.30 a.m. It looks a nice place with trees on both sides of the road. Passed a ship with American troops - no enthusiasm on either side. Also passed a ship with British and African troops - great excitement on both sides. Sailed at 11 a.m. - a bit choppy outside.

10th October 1945

Very high wind and a big swell - quite a number did not appear at meals. Calmed down towards the evening. Wore battle dress for dinner.

From Douglas

10th Oct 1945 Telegram from Suez

Suez received cables and letters missed Dorothy grieved Aked-Davies arrive Liverpool nineteenth.

To Douglas from Mother

10th Oct 1945

We just got your wire sent from Suez saying you will be in Liverpool on the 19th, somehow I fancy that is a mistake as the newspapers give out your boat is due on Sat or Sunday next 13th or 14th. So I've sent a message to the PO to have the date queried. I can't wait, for you for so long as that! I see you have got my letters by mentioning Dorothy & Asked-Davies. This morning David Bingham phoned up to say he'd heard from you & is so delighted, gave me his telephone No. for you to ring him up. Major Hamilton has a flat above them I think, & they were speaking of you & next day your letter arrived. Boss has gone to her school to-day & I'm still in bed, expecting Mrs Harvard any minute to make your bed! The last we heard from Dorothy she was in Karachi waiting for a plane & about 80 others, the weather was not too good. I don't think her job is very urgent, its war office N..2 in connection with entertaining the troops. Boss & I went to DD's tea yesterday, they do seem to live in a turmoil, getting the tea was quite a scrum! We were to get the aviary they had for the rabbits of mine. I've heard from your bat & also wife, they have heard from Gilbert that he is on his way back, you may come across him, also Mrs Carter & think he is a Captain from Sunderland. He remembers you & sends congratulations. I guess you will have a 'roundup' of all your pals! Desmond Laing is married some time ago. I have sent for the Marlboro's from 42 but they haven't arrived yet, also I saw advertised a book of the men on active service & their boys 80 got it (Marlborough). Boss & I are still getting ready for you & when ever you come we shan't be finished! The gutters on roof are being cleaned out now, I told the house agents you were coming & they must be done as they haven't been cleaned for 2 years, you see we're all so work up, people at liberty, & those there are & always seem to be striking for more money & less work or something or other. Must stop & get up & do a spot more work.

Bestest love old boy
Your loving Mother XXX

To Douglas from Mother

11ᵗʰ Oct 1945 Postmarked Undelivered for reason stated
return to sender

In bed 10.30 AM. & just getting up!

I got your very interesting letter yesterday, & also one from Dorothy XXXXXXXXXXI've crossed this out incase the censor wouldn't like it! I have kept all her letters like yours full of a very interesting journey. I rang up your S.S.Co & they confirmed what you said due in Liverpool on 19ᵗʰ & Muriel & I are so looking forward to meeting you in London. She's going to clean up the car & we've saved the petrol for October. We've left a lot of apples cox's on the tree for you to pick. I've readdressed the letters for you, but did not send Aked-Davies as I thought it might be hurtful to the family. I hope that is what you wish, as when wrote you did not know he was gone, I sent her one of yours in which you spoke nicely of him, & they were very touched, & wish to give you a present. Davis Bingham rang up & gave his telephone number & will you ring him up. Desmond Laig is married! I've sent the letter to the Bishop's house. I think I won't write more as I've really written all there is to write unless I start long stoves! I'm glad you didn't buy cloth at 30/- a yard!

Bestest Love, your loving Mother XXX.

We are so excited can scarcely believe its true hurrah!

To Mrs Heelas from Catherine Thorpe, Kingston Hill, Surrey

11th Oct 1945

We all rejoice with you in your good news. I knew you never gave up hope of your Douglas's return & how right you were. I think the mother always knows. We too had good news. My sister is in England after 5 years under the heal of the Germans in Holland, & her boy is safe after being in a prison camp all that time in Germany. So we have had a wonderful reunion - her other boy escaped from Java joined the Australian Navy & was transferred to the English. He & his sister who is in the R.H.M.C. contacted their mother in Holland on V.Day so it was a memorable day for her - almost too much happiness all at once after the black years.

Maybe you would bring Douglas to see us. His experiences must have been terrible & he probably will be glad to forget them as soon as he can.

From Muriel to Douglas

12th Oct 1945

We are thrilled that you are so near. We MUST meet you in London, so do let us know by what train. Our telephone number is Molesey 506 - in case you have forgotten! This is really to explain the letter situation. We were told we could write one letter after the Jap war was over, in case it would reach you - hence the letter of Aug 26th. After that we had to wait till we heard from you - which we did on 13th Sept. Since then Ma has written dozens, & even Dar & I & the aunts. Evidently, from your letter at Suez you haven't got a good many of these earlier ones. I expect they just missed you in Rangoon.

Dar left England for Ceylon the same day that you got to Ceylon - Sept 25th - She has arrived there, & seems to be having a good time.

We are very busy getting tidy for you. The more Ma tidies inside drawers the worse the outside of the room becomes!!

Dar & I have been trying to stop Ma riding her bicycle for ages, but she won't have in! Now we have the car going again, there isn't much need.

Longing for you to be back. We shall not move far next Friday, as we shall be all agog & ready to meet you. I hope you will get this at Liverpool.

Much love your loving Muriel

From Douglas to Mother

14th Oct 1945. Sunday 3 p.m. G.M.T. H.M.T.
Orduna Mediteranean

We are staying down at Gibraltar to pick up mail and perhaps drop some too, we are due there at 9 a.m. to-morrow morning. I am expecting lots of letters from you. When I got on board finally at Suez there were some letters.1 from Boss: 1 from Dar: 1 from Ar Beet & two from you. I have only had 5 letters from since I have been free & I am hoping for the back ones to-morrow.

We are having lovely weather & yesterday & this morning could see the African coast, this evening we should be able to see Spain. The other day we saw Malta & Sicily at the same time. I am still sleeping on deck at nights, but I am afraid to-night will have to be the last; to-morrow we change into winter clothes.

Thank Boss for doing my room I am sorry to turn her out, & am very glad you won't be at school all the time. I see you have booked D.D. When am I going to see the Aunts? I suggest we go over by car on Tuesday or Wednesday 22nd or 23rd week when Boss is at home.

On looking through your letters I notice I have had none addressed to Bombay, they are all Box 164. I am afraid when you see me you will think I am a fraud, it's not me who needs feeding up it's you folks & I have brought a 9/6d box of sweets & some chocolate for you, so don't bother about me, I look & feel fitter than ever; I must say this trip has done us good & we are being fed very well indeed. I am sorry to hear Russell White is leaving.

From what I gather I go straight from Liverpool home, whether it will be 20th or 21st I don't know provided of course we are not held up by fog or seas. We are due in some time on the 19th. I will if possible send you a telegram as to what time the train arrives in London & shall look out for you there if I don't see you I will telephone to see if you are meeting me there or not.

211

14th Oct 1945

Time for you is getting very near, & we shall soon get you back. Boss & I are very excited & still getting ready! We shall meet you at Euston, Boss is cleaning the car up & we shall have a flag on it. I hear it is like a football "scrum" at the stations & women fainting & children screaming. So I guess we'll be there early to get our place, I'll bring a white flag so you will see us quickly.

I've managed to get a Pheasant we've never had one in this house! Also a rabbit from Louth at our old grocer there, & I've laid in a stock of cider so we shall feed you up alright.

I expect this the final edition there may be a late extra! Your Godmother rang up to say she'd had a letter from you seemed quite excited, she never noticed I'd readdressed it! She speaks so scotch & indistinctly I can't grasp what she says & I made the wrong answers, so had to own up I was deaf, which I am a bit. We hear from Dorothy she seems to have settled down & having a good time in her way, going out with officers, I've given her lots of warnings & jaws to be careful, I'd like to see her properly married & I don't think she will be silly again. She says there is rumour the H.Q. of her department, may be moving to where you were, I've got all her letters for you to read. I have so much for you to read you'll never get through it & it will take ages to tell and hear all what has happened in 4 years. Muriel is mowing the lawn for the last time this season. She's a splendid worker inside & out & loves gardening. She will go all day to her school tomorrow & on Wednesday, & we shall sit by the telephone on Thursday to hear when you are coming or maybe we shall get a wire, we've got the petrol in car all ready. We watch movements of the boats & see yours is due on the 18th. I shall ring up ships Co on Wed & see if there's any alteration in the date, so good bye old boy.

Bestest love your loving mother XX thanks so much for your letters.

From Diary

19th October 1945

Soon after daybreak we took pilot on board. Whilst going up the Mersey Spitfire flew very low round the ship - the pilot waving. Ship docked about 11.30 a.m.. All the ships in the river blew their whistles as a greeting. Lord Mayor, Port Admiral, representatives of Army and Air Force made speeches through microphones on the landing stage - with a band playing. Crowds watched the ship dock - relatives waving and shouting to each other.

Disembarkation started about 12.30 p.m.

From Douglas 4.15 Liverpool OHMS.

19th Oct 1945

Arrived safely see you soon

To Douglas From Dorothy Telegram from Peradeniys, Ceylon 20th Oct 1945

Congratulations Douglas return love, Dorothy

Douglas married Jean continued in the army through the 1950s spending sometime in Germany

PART 2

Dorothy

Dorothy

Let me introduce Dorothy. She was born in 1911, and from 1924 to 1930 went to St Mary's Hall boarding school at Kemptown in Brighton, Sussex. She did well, with credits in English, Arithmetic, German and Music. Dorothy was a larger-than-life character as you will attain from reading her letters. I was so enamoured with her after I first read the letters I felt she was my personal friend, and I am sure that you will feel the same.

After Dorothy finished school she went to St James's Secretarial College, Grosvenor Place London S.W.1. There she once again did very well and got over 90% Diploma in Shorthand, Typewriting and Bookkeeping, Dorothy passed the Royal Society of Arts Examination for Shorthand, managing an impressive 120 words per minute!.

Between 1932 to 1939 Dorothy was Secretary to the Headmistress of Tiffin County School for girls in Kingston-on-Thames, Surrey. With the war coming she joined the Auxiliary Territorial Service, going from Private, Corporal then Sergeant (clerk).

In August 1941 Dorothy married and became Mrs Newson, but she realised her mistake and the marriage was later annulled.

In Febuary 1945 she served as A.T.S. Staff Officer in the War Office, London. With the war finally over she signed up for a year of volunteering with A.T.S. Staff Officer in the South East Asia Command, so these letters start as she was about to leave England for her big adventure of travelling to Ceylon and then to Singapore. She was hoping to see her brother Douglas before she left England, after he had been held in a Japanese prison camp, but he hadn't returned by the time she left.

DOROTHY. M. HEELAS
Born 1911

Education & Qualifications:
St Mary's Hall, Kemptown, Brighton, Sussex, (Boarding School).

Passed General Schools Examination of the University of London, with credit in English, Arithmetic, German and Music.

1930-1931 St James's Secretarial College, Grosvenor Place, London, S.W.1.

Awarded College Diploma for Shorthand, Typewriting and Bookkeeping – and Shield for over 90% in Diploma examinations.

Passed Royal Society of Arts Examination for Shorthand (120 words per minute).

Experience:
1932-1939 Secretary to the Headmistress of Tiffin County School for girls, Kingston-on-Thames, Surrey, (500 girls)

1938-1947 Served in the Auxiliary Territorial Service -

1939-1941 In the ranks – Private, Corporal, Sergeant (Clerk).

1942-1947 As an officer – Subaltern, Captain and Major.

Studied for four months 1944/45 at A.T.S. Staff College and passed The Course, j.s.c.

Served as A.T.S. Staff Officer –

Feb 1945 – Aug 1945. War Office, London.

Sept 1945 – July 1946. South East Asia Command, Ceylon and Singapore.

Aug 1946 – Sept 1946. War Office, London.

Oct 1946 – Oct 1947. Central Mediterranean Forces, Italy.

1948- 1950 Various temporary positions in London, including work for a publishing house, export and import firm (D.J.Fowler), consulting engineer, and the B.B.C.

Secretary to Oliver Messel – artist and theatrical designer – in London.

In New Zeland – two months housekeeping on farms, and six months waitressing in hotels. No clerical position taken as period of stay was limited at that time.

1953-1954 Returned to England for one year.

1954 13th October – Arrived in Australia.

19th October – Started as shorthand typist with the Snowy Mountains Hydro-Electric Authority, up to Grade 111 position as secretary to the Chief Civil Engineer.

1960 Returned to England 29th June 1960 From Sydney to Marseilles on the 'Caledonien'

Chapter 8

Journey to Karachi

Letter from Dorothy on her way from Chippenham to serve in Singapore.

25th Sept 45. Earl(Duke) of Lausdoune's Country Seat,
Chippenham.

I do hope you got back alright. We drove down here thro'
Marborough & Reading – stopped 20 mins for tea in a cinema
café at Reading. Got here about 8 & am sharing a room with a
FANY- who is very nice. We are going tomorrow about 5.45am
& have just been told all about the aircraft etc.

Very nice Navy man & a nice Lt Col. Must go.

26th Sept 45. Malta.

We landed here for lunch & leave again at 3.15. We started at 5.45
a.m! & I got a nice seat - one on its own. I'll go into more details
of all that later - as I am not feeling too good at the moment! For
the last hour in the air it was very rough & although I wasn't ill - I
couldn't move from my seat.

Practically everyone felt bad & one man was – so there. We
have two lavatories, very convenient - & when it wasn't rough it
was lovely. We came over Southampton & the Isle of Wight –
France - Sicily & the Mediterranean.

The other girl is very nice & there is also a nice WVS woman.

I hope you are all Okey-dokey – be careful.

I wish I was at home with you.

It is very hot here - & I've taken off my coat.

We are just going to see if we can see a bit of Malta

27th Sept 45. sent from Carlton Hotel, Karachi, India (Pakistan)

We arrived here yesterday evening & were going on to Colombo at 9.30 this morning - but have just been told that some of us are not going yet - including us three women. There were only 6 of the 18 staying here - the rest of them stayed in a Camp at the Airport - two who stayed here are going, & the other man is left with us. He is a civilian - belongs to the Borneo Rubber Com and is quite the nicest of them all. He has just gone to the airport to see what's happening. It is about 10 miles from here & we came by a sort of taxi.

We three share a bedroom here - which has its own bathroom & WC - hundreds of blackies everywhere!

I'll enclose pictures of the aeroplane & hotel!* There are 18 of us travelling - 8 civilians - a queer looking lot - they are to do with opening up rubber coys & transport etc in Singapore & other places. It's very hot here - but a good breeze & lots of fans everywhere. When I get to Kandy I'll write a better description of the journey. I keep thinking of how soon I can get back & whether its better by sea or air!

There are heaps of queer birds making noises outside in the trees - but I haven't seen any yet.

At this moment I am writing this in the lounge & there are three barefoot blackies polishing the floor all around me.

I wonder whether you have heard from Dug (Douglas) again. I'm going to try & see him if he hasn't left yet.

I feel quite alright in the plane now. The pilot told us that we ran into an electrical storm (very unusual at this time of year) just before Malta & that was why it was so bumpy. I discovered that everyone felt ill after it - not only me! & one man was.

Ma's bed-jacket is being knitted in the plane all over the world!

Ma, don't bother with those corsets if you haven't already - as I don't think I shall need them.

We are all wearing tropical kit now. I bought a very nice real leather bag with a zip at Cairo - a largish one, which holds lots of things - very cheap - Not a hand bag..

All the servants wear white coats & trousers & sashes & turbans & sort of bedroom slippers. Just outside our room there is the hotel laundry all in the open air - washing things in a pool of water & looking at us dressing!

We drove all through the back parts of Karachi to get to the hotel & saw lots of natives & their houses - awful poor looking - some women all veiled. In one island in the middle of the road, about 6 men just sat talking.

I could write for hours - but it would take so long.

Boss - the WC at Shaibah Airport was a sort of large bucket, & you shovelled sand in! Otherwise they all have had plugs.

The food in this hotel is lovely. Last night we had tomato soup (cream on top), fried fish, roast beef, potatoes (with butter on) & carrots, then fresh fruit salad & cream (with banana in it!) & coffee.

This morning we had delicious porridge, then sort of lots of bits of meat & potatoes (all beautifully mashed) - tasted rather like kidney, & toast & butter & marmalade.

We were woken this morning by a blackie (Actually they are all brownies!) with tea on a tray.

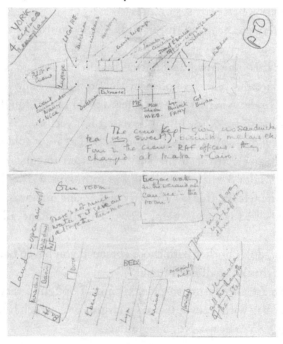

Plan of Aeroplane and Hotel

28th Sept 45. Karachi.

We are still here waiting for a plane. Apparently the reason we got chucked off the other was that they were expecting bad weather, would have to fly high & take more petrol & fewer passengers - & we, I suppose were the least important.

It is awfully boring here – as there is nothing much to see in the place - & anyway we can't go about alone much.

Ma would love the birds here - they sing all day long outside & heaps of little ones fly in & out of this hotel lounge, as there are so many open doors & sort of lattice work above.

Lots of open carts are in the streets drawn by camels (one hump) & people go about a lot in gharries, a sort of taxi with a horse! I haven't been on one yet.

We pulled up here last night with a French Lieut. Colonel. He is Chief of Staff to General Le Clerc in Kandy & he also got left behind by a plane yesterday. We had dinner here with him last night - but he's an effort to talk to as he does not speak much English.

There are heaps of people staying here – all English – but no one has spoken to us – I suppose three females together is too much!

There are all man servants here - we are called with tea at about 8.00 in the morning by one of them, who then takes & cleans our shoes. They also do out the rooms & make the beds (which only has one sheet no blankets).

It has not been terribly hot anywhere yet, there is always seems to be a good breeze. The afternoons are the hottest.

We all went to bed & slept after lunch yesterday & tea arrived at 4.30, so we didn't come down till dinner.

But I'm longing to leave here & get to Kandy - then I can start making plans to get home again!

I'm sorry I haven't been able to buy any stamps for Boss yet – but I'll get some in Ceylon – when we arrive.

I had my first banana for breakfast this morning - it was lovely!

I am wearing my vest!

I am longing to hear from you – it seems ages since I went - I wondered whether you know when Douglas is arriving. I wrote to him in Rangoon yesterday - just in case he might get it.

It was rather funny about my fountain pen, after all that bother trying to fill it on Monday. We were told before leaving England, to empty all pens – as if we had to fly very high they would leak! After all my trouble.

We were given a talk before leaving England about flying & were issued with oxygen masks and life saving jackets in case we had to land in the sea and were taught about the dingy etc.

The place were we stayed at Chippenham (a mile out) was lovely rather like Boss's hole - with a drive 4 miles long – huge pillars & pictures all over the place – owned by the Lausdownes. It was run by the R.A.F. Transport Command. The airport where we flew from was Lyneham - about 9 miles away, towards Swindon.

How is the lavatory? Is it stippled with gold and green yet?!

Ma - don't bother to send my cigarette case - it isn't worth it, if you haven't, as I hope to come home as soon as I decently can!

You would like the other girl I am with, her name is Lyn Burbeck & she comes from Aberystwyth (Welsh!) – but is very nice. She is quite large, no make up, & very natural – she is 25, her sister is in Kandy, so she is very lucky.

30th Sept 45, Still in Karachi

How are you both? (Not that I can get an answer) It's awful having no letters at all from home, & we are still waiting to leave here.

Yesterday afternoon we went and sat in the hotel gardens and sunbathed. The weather here is lovely, quite hot (90 o in the sun) with a nice cool breeze. Then we had tea in our room & then went shopping about 6. We got a gharry to take us into the shopping centre, & the driver made the horse gallop & race another gharry. We were terrified as it felt as if it would overturn! The drivers are awfully amusing - they all either talk or sing to themselves as they go along.

I noticed that one chemist - a small one, with a stall like a kiosk, not a proper shop - had some asthma stuff advertised – so I asked about Himrod* & he had some. So I have bought 2 tins of it. We have palled up here with a V.A.D who is waiting for a plane to England, & she has promised to take a tin home for me & will send it to you from England so I hope you will get it soon. She comes from Didcot.

When I get to Kandy I'll send the other tin & Boss's sandals.

I also sent you a food parcel yesterday – you give the shop a list of things to send & they do it for you, & I'm afraid it will take 6 weeks to arrive. There was not much choice of things to send so I have ordered, 1 lb tea!!, 1 lb butter, 1 lb tinned pineapple, ¼ lb cherries(cooking things), 1 lb cube sugar, ½ lb mixed fruit (sultanas etc) and ¼ lb jellies. We are only allowed to send 4 ½ + ½ lb for the packing = 5 lb.

I'll send another one later & will go to another shop & try to get a better variety of things.

It is now 11am & we are soon going to the Karachi Boat Club to bath & sunbath. There is an English church here which I should quite like to have gone to - but we were too late getting up this morning but may go tonight.

It is awfully funny having a male servant for our bedrooms. He calls us, cleans our shoes, makes our beds etc. If we want anything washed, we give it him in the morning & it is brought back at tea time, beautifully washed & ironed, charges about 10d for a coat & skirt (tropical kit). Our servant has a sweet face & is always smiling.

I am sorry to bother you with my business – but could you please either see ring up or write to C & C & tell them that I am not going to insure my motor bicycle after all – say how sorry I am to have been so slack not answering their letters & ask how much they want me to pay. It is the state Assurance Co done through C & C. Thank you! (It is all in my other name)

All the P.O.W. who go home by air go through Karachi, so just in case I have given them Douglas's name & told them to let me know if he arrives. I think he has probably already left by sea by now, though.

The trees here are lovely, some a little like willows only not quite, with flowers all over rather like nasturtiums.

I haven't written to anybody else but you yet – except I sent a card to the aunts from Cairo. I will try & write to them today.

I do hope you haven't got asthma again - mind you don't, & I hope the Himrod will come soon – it only cost 3 rupees 12 annas which is about 4s/6d. There are 16 annas in a rupee and 13 rupees 6 annas to £1.

It is now 12 o'clock & Eberlie & the V.A.D. have just come back from the Air Booking Center. The man says there are now 80 people waiting to get to Ceylon and there is no hope for us for another 5 days.

An ATS Senior Commander has just arrived, but I don't know her.

* Himrod for temporary relief of bronchial asthma

1ˢᵗ Oct 45, Still in Karachi

Still here - & feed up with it!

I didn't go out yesterday morning & in the afternoon we three & the VAD went by gharry to the Karachi Boat Club - which is sort of just at the opening of the sea - but looks more like the river. It is sea water. We sunbathed on the side - lots of other English there – they were very brown. The water was lovely & warm – Boss would have loved it. We got back here at 7 & did nothing again.

An ATS Senior Commander has arrived – she left London last Thursday & is going to Madras. She also is now waiting for a plane.

The newspapers here are hopeless & give all news of things happening in India and hardly mention any of our news. I wonder if it would be expensive to send me the Overseas Daily Mail every week from a shop? Could you find out sometime please?

I hope your health is well ...... Be good & do as Boss tells you!!

It is now 2 o'clock & it is funny to think that this time last week we were having something (or nothing) to eat in Marshall & Snelgroves. I wish I was with you both now.

Our time here is 6 hours ahead of you so while I am writing this you are still a bed!

It's awful not knowing what you are doing & how you are – I'm longing to get to Ceylon to get your letters.

It is most amusing to see the laundry being done outside our window. It is done mostly by men & a few women. They have a large square sort of stone tank with soapy water in it in which the things go, then all around there are wooden planks on which they beat the clothes up & down for ages. They seem to turn out very clean!

There do not seem to be any cats & few dogs about. There are a lot of cows that are allowed to stray anywhere they like, & they roam all over the town & in peoples gardens. I think they are meant to be sacred. They are like our cows, but have a hump on their shoulders.

2 Oct 45

Still here.

Yesterday morning I went with the Sen Commander the VAD & a WAAF Officer to the Air Booking Centre, where I drew out some money – as mine had all gone! Eberlie & Lyn went shopping first & we were to meet in the town. However we were about 1 ½ hrs late for them, & they had gone, & they met two men who Eberlie had worked with in England. So they went out with them all the rest of the day & probably will each day until the men go at the weekend.

I find it rather a relief – as Eberlie is so keen on the menfolk & it has made her very excited!

I spent all yesterday afternoon in my room with the VAD, who came & had tea up there with me.

I wonder if Boss has got her own bathing dress?! As I didn't think mine was holey – but yesterday I found the piece between the legs full of holes – I couldn't buy any green wool, so I have had to patch it with Khaki material & then darn over with khaki wool – but it shouldn't show at all!

I am going in the town with the VAD this morning & this afternoon she & I are going to bathe & sunbathe at the Boat Club.

I'm absolutely sick of being here.

I wonder what has happened about Boss's job. I am sorry to have seemed so selfish over coming away but hang on & I'll be home soon! If I have to swim!

I can quite see why Ar Jessie used to treat underlings as dogs – as they all do here more or less.

Yesterday afternoon in my room our servant (bearer) came with another one & told me he was leaving here & he'd brought the new one to introduce him – we are sorry as ours was so nice. Anyway I saw him later & gave him a tip & shook hands & thanked him for looking after us - & he was so pleased!

I have written to you every day since I left England & I do hope you've got all the letters.

I wrote a letter to the Aunts the other day.

Has Douglas come yet?

Chapter 9

Ceylon

From Dorothy to Ma and Boss (? & Dug?)

5th Oct 45, From RAF Station, Koggala, Ceylon
I have done a lot since I was last able to write to you.

Last Thursday we were told that two new Sunderland Flying boats were being flown from Karachi to this place and that we could go on one of them. They were new planes being delivered for use here & were operational ones, not really intended for passengers.

On Wed. morning we went by truck at 6am(!) to a place called Karagi Creek, a sort of large harbour for flying boats, about 40 mins by road from the hotel. There were 6 dutchmen, one Frenchman & us three in the truck, no seats, we sat on our luggage & along an awful road! During a monsoon some time ago, the road had been washed away in three places & we just drove on the side, sort of wasteland.

The hotel apparently never provide early breakfasts for people, and so we had only had tea at 5am, & when we got to the RAF place they gave us breakfast in their mess, fried bacon, toast, marmalade etc. We walked down a sort of pier into a dinghy (motorboat) & were taken over to the plane, only about 5 mins in the boat.

In our plane there were the three of us, one Dutchman and the Frenchman. The former spoke English well, but the Frenchman hardly any.

We were put in what they call the ward room about the size of the of the back kitchen - with bunks on each side with lilos on them. We played bridge & read & slept & the crew cooked us a hot lunch (stew from tins & peaches & tea) all spread on the table. There were 6 in the crew.

We took off at 8am. In the afternoon the pilot asked if anyone was interested in flying the plane, so I said yes first, & Lyn & I went up a sort of hatchway into the pilots part. It was rather frightening at first - nothing between you & the sky, & the sea 10,000 ft below.

I sat in the pilots seat (it was dual control) & he told me how to do it, & I flew the thing for about 10 mins! Neither of the others did. We were all very thrilled as the crew all had a bet on that we would beat a Catalina Flying boat that had started 3/4hr before us - and about 4 in the afternoon we saw it - while I was in the pilots seat & we got quite near it & passed it & waved to the men in it!

8.30 p.m. KANDY

I arrived here at 7.0 tonight – but I'll continue my tale where I left off. (I hope you are interested in all this!)

We landed on a large lake (just near the sea coast) at Koggala (Ko-ge-la) at 6.0pm & were taken to the RAF Officers Mess there & told they would put us on the train for Colombo at 5.30am on the next morning. We had two rooms - one for two & one for one (which I had - which wasn't so nice) in a little house on our own - overlooking the lake.

We went to the mess for dinner & sat with three men Officers there - who were very nice & friendly. They were leaving for Singapore that night - one of them was an old boy, head of the Indian Red Cross & welfare - had been for over 20 years. He knew Dr Cox (His name was Jolly). We sat outside after dinner, it was a lovely evening, every where was full of little lights flying about, sort of firefly beetle things & a noise all the night of crickets & frogs. It was very hot there, sort of wet hot - & heaps of horrid insects!!

All the RAF Officers were very friendly & said we had much better not go by train but try and wrangle an aeroplane or truck to Kandy the next day. Apparently, if people arrived from Singapore wanting to go to Kandy they were taken by plane, & we might have got in one. So next morning (Thurs, yesterday) we didn't go by train at 5.30 a.m. (train to Colombo takes 4 ½ hrs & then another from there to Kandy taking 3 ½ hrs!) We went & saw the Movements officer who said a truck had come from Kandy & was returning at 2 p.m. & we could go on it. Then at 1.30 we had a message to say we couldn't go, we didn't know why. So Elizabeth (Ebeulie) & I laid down & Lyn went to see what she could do. She never came back until 4 p.m. to say a flying jeep had just come in & was leaving to Kandy at once & could only take one, & she was going. So she went straight away.

I don't know whether you are interested in all these details or not - but I'll continue in case! Anyway I'm in Kandy now, & I will finish how I got here (by jeep) in my letter tomorrow - as I am going to bed now.

I do hope you are all okey-dokey – I'm longing for tomorrow in case there are some letters waiting for me from you.

7th Oct 45. HQ SACSEA, (D.S.R)
I'll continue telling how I got here before I say anything about this place. (I shall be thinking about you seeing Douglas this week or next, as, as soon as I got here my Col remembered about him & rang up someone who knew things straight away, & they investigated and told me he had sailed from Rangoon on the 20th September, & passed through Colombo on 26th - so I just missed him. If he had been a little later I was told I could go to Colombo & try & see him).

On Thursday last, after Lyn had left on the plane, Eberlie & I went & bathed with four RAF Officers at Koggala. The coast is simply lovely - sand, palm trees & blue sea with lots of surf. The waves are large that is not good to bath right in the sea, & the RAF had dropped 2 depth charges to make a sort of pool which is part of the sea too!

On Friday morning we were thinking we'd have to go by train after all - & then the man said there was a jeep there, waiting to take a Brigadier to Kandy, who was supposed to have arrived from Singapore three days before. As he never came, we were allowed to come in the jeep all the way here (Kandy). We started at 1.30 p.m. & got here at 7.0 (about 80 miles to Colombo, & 60 miles from Colombo to here). We had a black West African driver, who was very nice! It was a lovely drive - all along the coast to Colombo. The road seemed to pass through villages the whole way - hundreds of natives, & masses of children. The men

& women all wear long skirts - different colours - & shirts, none of them wear shoes. We went through Colombo - a large place on the sea & then climbed up all the way, rather like roads in Switzerland. Kandy is about 1,700 ft high & there are hills all round. I think the highest is about 7,000 ft. It is much cooler here & there didn't seem to be any insects, thank goodness.

We arrived here at 7.0 p.m. & after asking different people, I was sent to the WRNS officers mess for the night - & Eberlie went 4 miles out of Kandy – as she works for a different HQ (ALFSEA!)

A WRNS officer was awfully nice to me & gave me a room - & I'm to stay living here now. There are about 40 WRNS, 11 WAAFS, 5 ATS & a few FANY's in this mess. We all have separate rooms - called bashas. The walls are made from sort of plaited bamboo. The place is built round a large courtyard, with earth in it & plants have just been planted. They all seem very free & easy and wear civilian clothes off duty.

Yesterday morning I went down to the HQ - about ¾ mile away - which is in the Botanical Gardens - so there are lovely trees & plants everywhere. It is a large camp - huts everywhere - all different offices. Lord Louis Mountbatten hangs out there too. They have named all the different paths & roads like London. My hut is in Ludgate Hill, & there is Piccadilly Circus, Camden Hill, Regent St etc etc !*

I am in a hut with Lt Col Noonan (the man I knew) & two other Majors, who seem quite nice. They have soldier clerks (white) & one typist, a WREN.

There is one ATS officer living in this mess who I was at Bagshot with & I saw her yesterday evening for the first time. She was delighted to see me & has been very kind. I sat in her room while she was dressing to go out to a party & she suddenly said would I like to go to, as she knew they were a girl short. She ironed my dress for me (Boss's white one) & I togged up in it & the blue velvet belt Ma made & they said I looked alright!

We went by truck into Kandy to the officers Club, where they had booked a long table for dinner & quite a large Dance floor. There were heaps of people there - mostly in evening dress. There were 13 in our party - 7 men & 6 girls & everyone danced with everyone & we ate in between dances - I enjoyed it very much. I sat next to a man (a Lt Col) who asked me to go for a drive with him today, & I'm waiting for him now - but I don't know whether he'll turn up! He used to play Rugger for England & has played at Twickenham & the St Mary's ground in Kingston Lane.

I haven't had any letters from you yet – but I saw in a paper that lots of mail had been held up by bad weather in the last 2 weeks – so I'm hoping to get some very soon. The address on this letter is the right one now.

Boss – I have written to Vivian today – Apparently it is very grand to know any tea planters out here - !

How's your health Ma? That VAD left Karachi last Thursday or Friday & she has taken a tin of Himrod for you.

I don't quite know when I can send Boss's sandals – I shall have to find out things like that soon. I sent you off another food parcel before I left Karachi - as we can't send any from Ceylon. Usual things - butter, sugar, fruit, pineapple, sugared almonds, cherries.

At the party last night, I met several other ATS I knew – two from the Staff College, another I knew at the Transit Camp. Apparently the Chief ATS out here is one called Esmie Lawrance, who was at Bagshot too & was awfully nice.

Yesterday morning I was taken to see the ATS officer in charge of the other rank ATS here (about 40 of them). She lives about 2 miles out – up a hill & has 4 other ATS officers living there too. I'm awfully glad I don't have to stay there, as it is so out of the way.

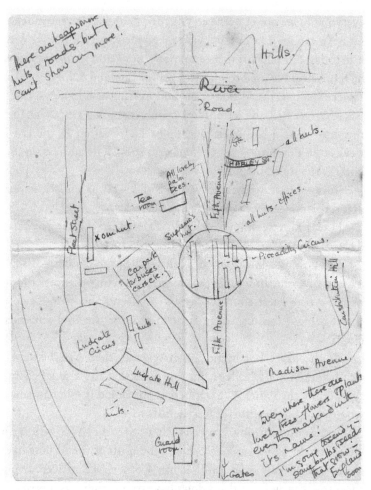

Plan of Camp

8th Oct 45. H.Q., S.A.C.S.E.A, (c/o D.S.R)
I got my first letter from you today dated 1st October & one you redirected from Violet Johnstone, I'm afraid all your other letters have gone astray somewhere - as you didn't put DSR on & also because I should have said SACSEA & not SEAC – I am hoping they will turn up however – as I want to know how, why & where etc you went to Broadstairs! I am glad you went too. Please note above address as being correct now.

I quite like it here, it's not nearly so hot as Koggala and not as hot as Karachi, although the temperature today is over 80°F !

They all say this is unusual & it is usually much cooler. Anyway at nights we have sheets & a blanket.

My Lt Colonel is sweet he scrounged a typewriter before I came for me - as he knew I liked one! He keeps to himself though off duty, and says he doesn't go out. My present ambition is to go out with him! But I don't suppose it will come off!

I want to get this off quickly because of the address - so I'll start another letter this evening & tell you more news.

I wish my trunk would come – but I'm afraid it won't for at least another month. Some have been here for two months without theirs. I'm going to have lunch tomorrow with Esmie Lawrance - the Senior Commander ATS here. I knew her very well as she was at Bagshot too and is very nice.

I'm looking forward to distempering the hall etc! & stippling the lav !

Must go and eat now (6.30 p.m.)

I've got to try & wash & set my own hair tonight - apparently there is no one to do it!

8th Oct 45. HQ. SACSEA, (c/o DSR)

I have just washed my hair & tried to set it! It is pouring with rain now & lightening hard. Apparently a monsoon of sorts is due - but it doesn't rain all day & night - only sometimes. There is a bad drought here so it is a good thing.

I had a nice letter from Violet today – she wants me to go for a short holiday with her to Calais – which I should have done if possible. She is coming out of the army soon and may go to Canada & help someone run a sort of roadhouse hotel there.

Just as I finished writing to you yesterday, at lunch time - that man did turn up to take me out! In a jeep with an Indian soldier driver. The man's name is Lt Colonel Fry - & he is a solicitor to the Liverpool Corporation quite high up, I think. Anyway he is a bird* & is very nice. We went & had lunch at the Queens - a big hotel in Kandy 4 miles from here - then we went for a drive for 25 miles - up into the hills. We had to keep putting the hood up & down as it kept raining, then stopping. He sat at the back & I was in front with the driver. I wore my blue dress (25/- Bentalls one) & he had spats & shirt. The road was zig zag all the way up &

in the end he drove, as the Indian didn't seem good. Apparently they are allowed to hire these jeeps on their days off - but have to take a driver. We went very high - through a tea planters estate (!) & two or three villages & stopped at the top of a mountain & could see miles round. It is like a mixture of Switzerland & Scotland - lovely hills - they are all about 4,000 to 5,000 ft high.

Then we went half way down again where there was a waterfall & a large pool & intended to bathe - but I wasn't keen (I was rather worried how to undress) & he wasn't keen much & went to sleep for about 1 1/2 hrs, & I meditated!! Then we went down into the same village where there is a rest house - sort of road house cum hotel, & met that girl Pat Style (who took me out on Sat) with another man - a Lieut Col too & we sat out on the verandah & talked until it got quite dark. They are both solicitors & talked about different cases they'd had - very interesting. All the time there was lots of thunder & lightening - which was lovely in the hills.

Then we had dinner on the verandah with oil lamps - soup, hard boiled eggs on toast, chicken, & jam pancakes. Then he drove me back about 10 p.m. I enjoyed it very much.

When I was walking to my office in the gardens today, an officer came up & spoke to me, & it was Freddy Jacques. He used to be the fiancé of that Miss Edwards at the Transit Camp & she broke it off & married a man in the Air Force. She has been to our house, a very pretty girl, a Sgt Major. His parents never approved as they are Jews. He was so nice & funnily enough he turned out to be the Field Cashier here - the person I have to see about my pay. We didn't mention Miss Edwards. He used to sing & play the violin well & we used to do a lot of it in the Sgts Mess.

My Colonel Noonan (I call him Eric from now on! Tho' not to his face – altho' he calls me Dorothy!) went & had lunch today with the Supremo. They call him that - Lord Louis Mountbatten. I want to see him badly, but haven't yet. I made a mistake about my office, it is in Fleet Street – further down Ludgate Hill! Lord Louis's office is just off Piccadilly Circus!

I should love the Daily Sketch Overseas Edition please – that means you haven't got all my letters yet – as I did suggest having something like that in a letter from Karachi. Thank you.

I think I shall like it here - & Eric says I can go home when I like - he will arrange it. Unfortunately - the HQ may be moving soon to where Douglas was captured – Eric says he hopes to take me too - but it is a question of not much accommodation there - & I may have to go to Colombo to the Radio Station first for a bit, I don't want to do that, as I like working for Eric!

I haven't done any work yet! except some typing. We control a lot of Army Newspapers & the Editor a Colonel Frank Owen (who used to be Editor of the Evening Standard) is also writing a book on the war (The Fall of Singapore, The Campaign in Burma, 1946). I typed some chapters of it for him today.

I am enclosing some stamps for Boss today, I hope they arrive safely - as they cost quite a lot!!! Let me know if there are any others she wants. I have written to Viv!

I don't think I shall be able to send that Turkish Delight to you - as we can't send food by post. So I may have to eat it myself! Sorry. Also I'm not sure when , or how I can send Boss's sandals – it is very difficult to send parcels home – but I'll find out more sometime.

I have bought Ma an Indian note case for all her money!

We all have Ceylonese boys to wait on us here, for our rooms & in the mess. They all look about 14 & wear white vests and long white skirts - no shoes. The ones who wait table wear white coats.

The WRNS all look so nice here - they wear white dresses & hats, with their blue ranks on their shoulders. The Navy Officers wear white skirts and hats and socks.

I can never wear any corsets in the daytime here as we wear socks a good thing I'm so thin!!

* ' bird' handsome

9th Oct 45. H.Q. SACSEA

I'm like Dug - I still haven't any letters from you, except that one dated 1st October. I'm still hoping they'll turn up sometime – if they get returned to you – please send them all back to me – as I don't know what you are doing all this time. I'm sitting in my room now sewing! I bought some sort of muslin today & have made a curtain for my window - as all the blackies can see me dressing!

I went to lunch with Esmie Lawrence today – the senior A.T.S. here - she was very nice to me - afterwards I went to Kandy to the Officers shop, where I have bought some khaki drill of 3 shirts & two pairs of slacks. They have got a Sgt tailor there who is making them for me - I've got nothing much to wear at present, except those two mosquito shirts - which are rather hot. Those bush shirts I got in London are no use at all. The tailor here measured me, & I am going to be fitted on Friday. He is good they say - & he makes all Lord Louis Mountbatten's things - I saw one of his coats being made. I also bought a khaki beret - which we are allowed to wear - & I look very good in it! much better than those large bush hats.

I went into a few shops to get an evening dress made - but haven't done it yet. I am going to have lunch on Friday with Sheila Drake (a Bagshot friend) & I shall get her to go with me & choose.

We are supposed to wear long sleeves & skirts or slacks in the evenings because of mosquitos, altho' people don't always seem to - so I shall have a dress with long sleeves made.

It's funny buying things without coupons! but nearly all cotton materials are rationed now, & I shall have to buy linen or silk.

We all get a drink ration every allotted to us every month here, 1 bottle of brandy, 1 of whisky, 4 wines & 8 of beer!! The whisky & brandy cost 5 rupees each, about 7s 6d! I don't want mine as I don't like it, but I shall give my Colonel some, & Viv if he wants it, & the man who took me out. He said he was going to ring me up sometime but hasn't yet.

I do wish my trunk would come. I am very short of night gear, I've only got one pair of pyjamas - too thick & a petticoat.

We have large trucks with seats to take us to work every day here, 2 leave in the morning & bring us back & when one wants to go anywhere like Kandy, you hitch hike in these, or jeeps or anything military. I came back from Kandy in a police (military) car today.

In the mornings I usually walk - it only takes about ¼ hour & in the evenings I walk back with my Eric! I wish he'd ask me out with him - but he never seems to go anywhere as far as I can tell. Everyone likes him who knows him - he is so kind to everyone, especially those under him.

Buck up & write 1000s of letters to my proper address soon - & tell me everything from when I left all over again - in case I never get the others!

Old Dug will be home this week or next I suppose it will be exciting, & I'm longing to see him again.

I don't know whether he got any newspapers dropped on his camp - but my branch here was responsible for dropping 100's on POW camps. I have just been reading the files about it.

10th Oct 45. H.Q., SACSEA, (DSR)

No letters yet - but I'm still hoping. Nothing has happened to me since yesterday & I'm rather fed up doing nothing in the evenings. I usually talk to a few girls & then come & sit in my room & write to you. Pat Style (the ATS who took me out to the party) has asked me out to another next Monday. I'm hoping that Vivian might ask me to go & see him, and if so I shall try & go next Sunday.

Pat & I & another ATS officer called Susan Kitching, went into Kandy for lunch today. They both came especially to help me buy some stuff for a dress. We had a meal at a restaurant first - two eggs each and masses of fried bacon!!

Then we went to a shop & choose some very pretty stuff for me (no coupons!), sort of linen'y' with little flowers all over it - you'd like it. I got 6 yds, then we went to the tailor - who is sweet & we choose a pattern & he measured me - & I'm going to be fitted on Saturday! We don't have to wear long sleeves in the evenings now - it has been changed.

Funny, the officer (FANY) I had supper here with tonight lives at Hampton Court (not in the Palace) but in a house somewhere near.

I'm glad you are getting your £4 safely. Why don't you use it for Cissie? Then you'd feel justified!!

I see a boat has just arrived in Southampton with POWs - I wonder whether Dug was on it - I do hope so.

I'm still very keen on my Colonel, but I'm afraid it's no good yet! He doesn't seem at all interested!! I suppose that is why I like him.

Eating in the mess here is rather like a hotel. Quite a large room, with about 12 tables for four each - & hundreds of Ceylonese boys to wait on us - with one older man as the head one.

How's your health? Do your teeth have to come down at Boss much?!

11th Oct 45. H.Q., S.A.C.S.E.A., (c/o D.S.R.)
I got another letter today thank goodness! It might have been your first one – I am not sure, but was dated 29th September and told me all about you going to Broadstairs. I am glad you went and enjoyed yourselves - what a dirty old dog Sir Milsom is - I can't think how Boss dared to stand up to it!

Thank you for sending off the parcel - I don't know whether it will ever get here! Apparently if you had only put D.S.R. on the letters and left SEAC, as it was everything would be alright. I hope you get my letter to-morrow or Saturday telling you about the address.

Of course everything I want seems to be in my trunk! I should love to have my black velvet dress here - and now all the dock people seem to be on strike in Liverpool, it may make a difference to my luggage! On the other hand I may never be asked out again.

I am writing this in the office - my Eric has gone to the Canteen to have his tea. The other Major is away in Colombo for a few days, so Eric and I take turns to go for tea so that the telephone is not left. Sickening, as I'd like to go with him.

Its just been pouring with rain again. It rains every night, starting about 8 and simply pouring - just like the worst rain we have ever had in England, only going on and on.

All the Navy officers look so nice here, and yet rather funny - as they wear white shorts, shirts, socks and shoes. They look like little boys dressed up to go out.

Has D.D. been visiting regularly, if not, why not? And she must NOT have her hair cut while I am away, unless she lets Boss do it. I'll delegate this job to Boss only!

There really is nothing more to say at the moment, so I will close hoping this finds you in the pink – no F.C.

14th Oct 45. HQ SACSEA, (DSR)

I got back this evening to find a letter from you dated 6th Oct - it was lovely getting one. I wrote to you yesterday saying someone was going home and would post some Turkish Delight for you in England - but she couldn't get it in her luggage, so it hasn't gone sorry!

I had quite a nice day today after all! I had breakfast about 8.45 a.m. & directly after, one of the WRNS officers asked me if I'd like to go with them on a picnic as they had a spare seat unexpectedly - & I'd have to be ready in 5 mins. I also had to move my bedroom upstairs before I went, so I washed and shoved everything in suitcases - my "boy" was helping(!) and left him to cart them all up here which he did after I'd gone. I see he has helped himself to 20 Craven A cigs too!! But I shan't say anything as we are warned to keep everything locked up.

I went in my blue dress - cotton one - & sandals, & we had a sort of truck thing!! There were 3 WRNS officers & me & two men, a Lt Col & a Maj. & we left here about 9.45 and drove to a place called Nuwara Eliya (Newa-railia) which is 6,200ft high in the mountains, & is where everyone goes on leave & days off etc. It is 48 miles from here, & a wonderful drive just like Switzerland, zig zag roads with precipices etc! We had an Indian soldier driver who wasn't very good indeed. We stopped for coffee at a rest house on the way up. Every 15 miles about all over Ceylon there are rest houses - sort of hotels - run by the Government, who put Cingalese in to manage them. We got to the top about 1.30 & went & sat by a huge lake & had our lunch - which they'd brought. Two cold chickens & salad, hard boiled eggs, bananas, tinned peaches & tinned cream, beer and orangeade, very nice.

It's a largish place - with a golf course, one huge hotel - the Grand - which we went into afterwards for a wash & brush up.

The trees there are lovely - we picked mimosa, & gorse & arum lilies (which grew wild in a field). It was quite cold & we had to wear our coats.

We left about 4 p.m. & came down to the rest house again – thro' lots of cloud as it had started to rain. We had tea 2 eggs boiled, each & bread & butter & jam (guava jelly) & bananas. I had to pan out all the tea!

Then came down & got back here about 7.30, had dinner, & I've just arranged my room. It is so much nicer than down stairs.

We passed heaps of tea plantations in the drive - some of them very high up - saw lots of native women picking the leaves. They wear large baskets fastened to their backs. In Neware Elija where it is cold - they nearly all wear brown blankets - sewn to make a hood over their heads.

I'm sorry about DD's dog - I hope it will soon decide to get better - or other wise, so she can come again. I hope Douglas's first night home will supersede the dog's needs!

I'm glad you heard from Mrs Rodgers – I always liked her, but she was so taken in by June & Chairman Mould. I believe the Co has gone to Africa – so will you write to J Comd Marjore Fletcher at the Transit Camp & ask her to send the hymn book – she knows I wanted it - & she is the only original officer left there now. Do it soon otherwise they'll forget.

I haven't heard from Viv yet, but hope I shall - as I'd love to visit a tea estate. It is not far from where I went today - if you look at the map.

I think it is going to be a job sending Boss's sandals, as I have to get an export licence, & then they'll take 2 months to reach you - so I propose to keep them & bring them back with me. She won't really want them until next summer. The shoes are much more expensive than Karachi - so I'm glad I bought some there.

Must stop & go to bed. We put the clocks back an hour tonight.

16th Oct 45. H.Q., SACSEA, D.S.R.
I have just got two more letters, one dated 27th Sept and one you wrote on 8th Oct - also one you forwarded from Greyhound.

I was thrilled yesterday as I had a telegram from Douglas, and he is landing at Liverpool on 19[th,] - although by the time you get this you will have seen him. He sent the telegram to me addressed to Colombo, and I got it safely. He says "Suez. Sorry to have missed arrive Liverpool nineteenth much love Douglas Heelas".

I went out to a dance last night at ALFSEA(!!), which stands for Allied Land Forces, South East Asia. It is all sort of part of this H.Q., but the camp is about 5 miles the other side of Kandy. We went in a truck about 7.30, I wore that pink satiny evening dress. The dance wasn't bad, but I was rather bored! I talked to the same man the whole evening and danced with him, he was a Major and quite interesting. He had lost two fingers in Africa and also couldn't use the other hand much as he had a bullet in his arm. We got on alright, as his wife lives in Weybridge, and he is in the Buffs* and was at Canterbury and knew the Aldridges, and he also knew Christopher Staniland. I wasn't sorry when the evening was over, I think I'm too old for these things, as they just bore me, unless I get someone really wonderful to talk to!

I nearly sent you a telegram to say when Douglas will arrive, but I'm sure he will be able to send you one himself. I shall think of you all with your grand supper in the dinning room.

When I come home, I shall come by sea - as they always send us back like that, and anyway I think I'd rather. I suppose I should get over being seasick, if I ever was!

Killing about Gwen and her stockings! I like your letters - only they are rather short and now and again I'd like some longer ones please - written on ordinary airmail paper. I had one from you like that and it was just as quick getting here. When they are addressed properly (!) they only take 6 or 7 days to get here.

Talking about the Indians that I told you about in Karachi, and your remarks on how uneducated they are. I happened to see these figures yesterday.

Men who are literate-19%

Women who are literate-5% !

Yesterday, Lord and Lady Louis Mountbatten came to lunch in our mess. They had a long table down the middle - beautifully set, with mats and bowls of flowers, and we sat at small tables round as usual. We had grapefruit, roast meat and two veg. and plum tart. Then afterwards we all went into the anteroom, and some of us were taken up to be introduced, and I was one. I shook hands with both of them, and he asked how long I'd been here and I said 10 days, and that was all. They were very nice and friendly.

6.00 p.m I have just got back to the mess and the girl who was in my room before me left this typewriter which she has borrowed from someone and not yet given back, so I am using it.

It is simply pouring with rain and has been all day. I went into Kandy for lunch with Pat Style. We went to a restaurant and had two fried eggs and bacon and toast and coffee, and I am ashamed to say I had it all over again!

Then we went to the tailor and I tried on the dress he is making for me, he had practically finished it, only had to do the belt, and it fits beautifully, and I really look nice in it. Its just a sort of cotton material little blue red and mauve flowers all over it, and the neck is sweet.

He is going to make me a blue sash to match the blue flowers. Then we went to the officers shop where I got some sandals, very cheap ones, but quite nice. I've got so friendly with the woman who serves in it, that she has asked me to tea in her bungalow. She is Australian, large and fat, and her husband has some Government job here. She doesn't get on with some people, but I've managed her rather well – I can when I like!

I have bought you two more tins of Himrod to-day, and I think I'll try and send them to you one day.

It is a pity Boss can't come and get some clothes made out here – they do it so beautifully. Would you like me to have one made by your measurements?!

* Royal East Kent Regiment, Canterbury.

17th Oct 45

By the time you get this I expect Douglas will be at home, I do wish I was there to help welcome him. Tell him to eat an extra helping of everything for me!

Ma, you were wrong about clapping your hands for anything, you just shout "Boy", and one comes running. They are any age, and sometimes an oldish man of about 70 will come in answer to Boy! The ones we have to wait on us in our mess and as servants for our rooms are very young, about 16 or 18. Some of them are sweet. One boy looks after about 3 of us, and as there are about 70 people living here, there are quite a lot. They love airing their little bit of English, and going along the corridors where they all stand about you have to say good morning, afternoon etc., not once but every time you pass!

I am getting on with your bed jacket. I had finished the pattern on both sleeves and then found I wouldn't have enough wool to make them long enough, so I had to undo them and start again, making them narrower. They were much too wide before anyway.

I am under the counter in a shop here, and got a very nice cigarette lighter to-day for 2 rupees 50 cents (about 4/6).

It is sickening, as my Eric had said a long time ago that he would take me to Colombo to see our Radio Station when he next went there. He is going on Friday with our General, and I can't go as I'm the only officer left in our office, as the other Major has gone to Calcutta to see about our newspapers. Our department run a newspaper and magazine ("SEAC" and "PHOENIX"), which is done from Calcutta. The broadcasting studios and transmitting stations are just outside Colombo. I expect when Douglas heard the wireless in Siam he was listening to our station, Radio SEAC. The editor of our newspaper is Lt. Col. Frank Owen, who is former editor of the Evening Standard – quite a big pot. I have done several bits of typing lately for him, for a book he is writing about the Burma campaign.

This morning all the corridors here were covered with masses of horrid flying things. Apparently they are flying ants and came in great hordes in the rain, and shed their wings, and it was their wings lying there. They were all swept up in great heaps. It has been pouring with rain all day to-day.

Thank you – don't bother to send me Boss's bathing dress. I have patched mine with kharki material, and then darned over that with khaki wool – it looks rather good in green! Anyway I remember that Boss's was full of moth holes in exactly the same place!

I don't know when we shall bathe again – but I suppose there will be some at Singapore.

They are going to start to move things soon, and are taking away all our chests of drawers on Saturday.

You will have to write reams to me after Douglas has arrived, and tell me every word he says!

We all have mosquito nets over our beds here every night, actually I'm quite glad to have one, as it keeps out any other insects there might be.

Did my photographs ever come? After all that fuss about them, I didn't need them at all. We have to have a pass here with a photograph on it, but we have to have our photograph taken in the camp by the proper Army people, and hold up a board in front of us showing our name and rank. I have had mine taken, but have not got it yet.

I told Esme Lawrance, the chief AT here that the Holding Unit didn't know anything about what we needed here, and she is writing to London giving instructions for any more people that might come out. I've met someone else here who was? treated badly by that Quartermaster – she couldn't stick her, and also had to fight to get her kit in time.

Please give my love to the Aunts, D.D. Mrs Harper, Cissie etc.

You say that you lost my address and had to ask Captain Lack – well if he gave you H.Q. SEAC only, and didn't mention the D.S.R. part he deserves to be hung! As he knows perfectly well that that is essential.

Our General is called Kimmins a relation of Boss's Anthony, I think.

We have a nice little ironing room here, with an electric iron.

19th Oct 45

I have had no more letters from you yet, and hope you are all alright. I am thinking of Douglas getting off his boat today and sending you a telegram to meet him.

We had an awful storm here the night before last – wind and rain. The wind was a 95 miles an hour gale, and yesterday morning there were three huge palm trees down right across the main road, and everything had to go round until they were removed.

I haven't done anything or been anywhere since last Monday, and am very bored. There is no work to do, so I am writing this in the office. This is a lovely typewriter, Boss, an American Noiseless Underwood, and has lovely signs - **** $$$$

One of the officers who belongs to this department (he travels round most of the time) has just arrived back from Bangkok, and Singapore. He is in the office with me now, a Squadron Leader Gerry Fitzgerald. Apparently he used to be on the London stage, and most people seem to be on the London stage, and most people seem to have heard of him, but I haven't. He is very nice and quite amusing. He is typing to his wife, and I am typing to you!

It strikes me that you have been having much better weather than us! We have had nothing but rain for four or five days – but to-day is alright at present – lovely sun.

I'm glad you've stippled the lav. Did you do some green and some gold, as I think that would look very nice. I'm looking forward to doing the hall when I return.

I've given up hope of my Eric! he's just very nice and that's all, he never seems to go out anywhere.

It is sickening – I shan't be able to take any photographs here, as my camera is in my trunk. I did pack badly, as there are heaps of things I should like out of it, and apparently they take two or three months at least to come.

I am going to send you 2lbs of tea to-morrow, and I shall also send 2lb to D.D. for Christmas, and I might send the Aunts some. They've got a special scheme here for sending it off for us, and to-morrow is the last day we can do it, and they don't think we shall be able to send any from Singapore.

Later on, I will write to Karachi and have another food parcel sent to you, as I have the address of the shop there. You should get the 2 parcels I sent you round about Christmas time.

One of the WRNS officers here – a vary nice one – lives in Kent, and we have discovered that we both know an A.T.S. officer very well. Her name is Anne Burke, and she was at the Transit Camp with me for a long time. It seems she lives near the WRNS officer, and their families know each other very well. So we are going to write Anne a joint letter one day.

I sent you a magazine and two newspapers the other day. They are what we produce – not here but in Calcutta, and we are their boss. The magazine, Phoenix, is rather interesting to keep, as it shows the first P of Ws. Released in Bangkok.

Mind you write and tell me ALL Douglas's news soon - I am longing to hear all about him.

The man, (Squadron Leader Gerry) Fitzgerald, says he has had lots of talks with prisoners in the Rangoon hospital. He was also present at the surrender in Singapore, and managed to get the blotting paper which the Japs used for their signature, for a souvenir.

I hope you've got all the flags out - and the chickens have arrived from Louth. I am glad you are going to keep chickens.

20th Oct 45.

I got a letter from you to-day dated 12th October – lovely, and this evening I got one from Boss, dated 1st – as she had forgotten the D.S.R. part like you had.

What AWFUL photographs those are of me – thank goodness I don't have to have one of them on my pass! I haven't got the one they took here yet, but I know that they refuse to give us any extra ones to keep, so you won't see it till I come home.

This morning was the last morning that we could send tea away from here. They do all the sending, 2 lb. to each address we give, and it should take about 8 weeks to arrive. I just went on the loose over it and sent nine lots – I thought it would be a good idea, I hope you think so too. Each one cost me about 5/-, but as it may be the last ones we can send I made hay! I could think of heaps of other people to whom I should like to have sent it, and it was difficult to stop at the nine – I hope you agree with my list, and any of them you see you might tell them to expect it in about 8 weeks.

I sent three to you lot, one addressed to Ma, one to Boss and one to Dug! I thought I'd better keep you well stocked up in case the rationing goes on for longer than what we've got. Actually I know an address in Karachi, and one in Durban where I can get things sent to you if ever you are short of anything – so let me

246

know at once if ever you are. The others I sent to; The Aunts, D.D., Miss Mead, Mrs Howard, Cissie, Dr Cramps. Good???!!!

It's now 8.15 p.m. and I am just going to get ready to go to the local cinema to see GRACIE FIELDS! She was coming to give one show only on Thursday, but couldn't get here because of the weather and there were no planes flying, that performance was all for other ranks. Now she has arrived to-day and is giving two performances, and we have been allowed to go to the second one at 9.30 p.m. I am going with four other girls from here. They drew for the tickets, and of course I didn't get one – but Patricia Style did, and she was already going out with someone somewhere else, so she gave me hers.

22nd October 6.00 pm I haven't had time to finish this before- & will now have to write it (not type), as the girl next door isn't well & is lying down.

I went to see Gracie on Sat. She was very good, most amusing. Her husband Monty Banks introduced everything, a little fat man, quite funny. There were also two girls who sang, a man who sang beautifully called Lunce Fairfax (Desert Song, Ol Man River etc) and a girl who played the accordion. The Cinema was packed, men standing in the aisles too.

Just before I went I had a telephone call from Colombo from that girl Susan Kitching (whose room I now have). She is now going home by sea & is waiting for a ship. She wanted to know if I could go & see her yesterday, Sunday, so I said I would. There is a special train here called the 'SEAC' special which goes to Colombo at 8.15 in the morning & starts back at 6.30 in the evenings just for all troops & you don't have to pay the fare - but have to get your ticket two days before. Of course I hadn't one - but everyone said I could go & risk getting in a row. Actually it didn't matter – I explained things to the soldier who collected them. I palled up with a Major on the train- rather an awful one though- dull. At about 9.15 a.m. we went into the dining car & had four eggs & bacon each! (That is the thing to do!). Susan met me in Colombo at 11.15 & we then walked along the sea front to the Galle Face Hotel – a huge one, with gardens right down on to the beach. There we had two long lime juice drinks & a Colonel came up who we knew & asked us to join him & his friends (two Brigadiers & a Colonel). They weren't bad – but we didn't want to stay with them all day – as they wanted! So at 12.30 p.m. we went & bathed in the swimming pool belonging to the hotel – the sea is not safe there. Then we went in & had lunch – lovely – soup, curried eggs, roast beef & veg & pear tart. Then we wandered round town & a tout asked us if we'd like to see some jewellery etc – so we followed him down an awful little back street & into a funny shop – more a house – where we sat round a table & the man brought out boxes of rings, etc – about six other blackies looking on. There was an English sailor there too. They had lovely stones in the things – a lot of them are found in Ceylon & so are quite cheap. One was a lovely yellow sapphire – for 100 rupees (£7.10). I didn't buy anything – but Susan got some topaz earrings for her Mum.

Then we went into a shop where they were making shoes with crepe soles – lovely ones & I shall go back there & buy some next week. Does Boss like brown suede, or ordinary brown leather with crepe soles – or shall I get her some more sandals? Let me know. Would Dug like any? If so, what size I don't think they'd have any to suit Ma. But let me know – as I don't suppose we can get things so cheap in Singapore.

Then we went into the back parts of a shop where they were making bookends – elephants – bowls etc – all very cheap. I didn't buy anything – but I'm going back before I leave Ceylon. Then we bought some bananas (!) & went in the officers' Club - & then she saw me off in the train.

Everyone palls up on the train - & I went & had dinner with a Lt Col, a Lieut & a FANY who were sitting in my little compartment.

We had four eggs each & bacon again & then I had two more!! The Lieut's father used to be foreign editor of the Daily Mail & he lives in Dulwich.

I enjoyed my day very much- & next Sunday I shall go to Colombo on my own – if nothing better comes along.

I've had two more letters to day – Ma's dated 17 Oct & Boss's dated 14th – pretty good. I'm going thro' all your last letters in my next one - & will answer all queries – as I haven't time now & also this will get too heavy for air. I managed to send down a parcel to Colombo to day – which Susan is taking with her to post – in it is two tins of Himrod, two packets of chocolate & the Turkish Delight!

Haven't you got that other Himrod yet? You should have by now.

I'm going out to dinner tonight with a Major Falkland Cary – a nice man – I'll tell you how & why in my next.

I am going to Singapore by SEA, and also home BY SEA!!

22ⁿᵈ Oct 45

I spent yesterday in Colombo with Susan Kitching, the girl who is on her way home. She is going by sea by the Athalone Castle (or something like that) and says she will post these things for you in England – some Turkish Delight, two tins of Himrod, and some chocolate. So I hope they reach you safely – you won't get them for about four weeks.

23ʳᵈ Oct 45

It's now 10.15 a.m. and I've got nothing to do, and my Eric is at a meeting, so I shall write to you. I'll tell you about last night first. At tea time yesterday a Major sat at my table who I knew (he had gone on that picnic with us the other week), and we talked. He is keen on drawing and designing clothes, and had designed a dress for Patricia, so I asked him yesterday if he would draw me one to make me look thin – so he said would I go out to dinner with him last night and we'd discuss the dress! So I did – I wore that pink silk dress (I don't really look that nice in plain material I think). We went to the officers' club called the Follies – just tables all round and very nice food. He was most amusing and I quite enjoyed it – he drew several sketches of dresses etc. and is going to draw me one to "slim" me. He is quite clever I think, as he works for Airborne Operations. He has to go Delhi to-day for a month – but it was nice to go out again.

I'm going to answer things from your letters now-

1. Don't get rid of all the petticoat patterns – as they are still the nicest ones to wear, and I shall need lots when I return home!

2. Killing about Geneste – I wonder if she'll believe in her Ma's spooks! I quite agree with you about telling Colin we know what he's done.

3. Thank you for my pay sheet – I've written to the bank before about putting my proper rank on the envelope – but they acknowledged the letter and then took no more notice – so I left it.

4. I'm glad you are allowed to ride your bicycle by Dug, I don't mind you riding it provided all the rest of the world stays at home and leaves the roads empty, as its always the other people that are dangerous.

5. I'm glad about the chair covers – hope they'll look nice.

6. What a fool Dorothy Little is – she only wants to get married for the sake of it – she'll probably go to the dogs one day.

7. You've got the wrong end of the stick about Violet Johnston – its not Calcutta she might go to, but Canada. I'm sorry for her parents too – but I don't think she and her mother ever hit it off. Greyhound told me in her letter that she had tried to ring you up two or three times but couldn't get through. I have only written to her once since I've been here.

8. Boss's letter (dated 15 Oct) – made me laugh a lot!

9. The alphabet on my address (H.Q., S.A.C.S.E.A. (D.S.R.) stands for :-
Headquarters,
Supreme Allied Commander,
South East Asia.
(Director of Service Relations)
which you can write out in full every time if you prefer!

10. I'll look out for over printed stamps if poss – only in the Army everything is OHMS and no one seems to use them.

11. My health is very good, thanks. Only I'm worried about my figure, as I eat very hearty – especially heavy on bananas which is one fruit that is fattening.

12. I don't want to fly any more either - now I've done it once. I am going by sea to Singapore, and early in the new year I am coming home by sea. This Department is closing down altogether quite soon in the new year, and then I shall return. So you had better start tidying soon.

13. A. I don't know what to do about Viv. I have written to him again – on the 19th – and hope I might hear. It's a bit difficult to get there I believe, as its about 12 miles from the nearest station – and they have now stopped all 'recreational transport' here, ready for the move. I wonder if he has left Ceylon, or gone to another estate. Couldn't you find out from his relations?

14. Everything here now is 'Getting ready for the move'. They have taken away the chests of drawers from our rooms, and to-day they have started taking away the cupboards and tables out of the offices. The people don't start going for another three weeks, and then we go in bits and pieces.

I shall probably not move until the beginning of December. I do hope they have a big boat that won't roll too much!

I quite like it here now – but I really haven't enough work to do.

I like typing for Lt Col Frank Owen. He was in here all yesterday, and I was typing from the proofs of a book that he is writing on the Burma War. He is very large, full of humour, and shouts not talks, especially down the telephone.

I didn't get the letter you sent to Karachi, so I'm glad it wasn't a good one.

15. I have got three coconuts for you! But don't quite know yet how I shall send them!

16. AS SOON AS I hear whether you want me to get you any more shoes, and or Dug, I am going to apply for an export licence from Colombo, which is quite easy, and I shall then pack them up and send them, with coconuts. If you don't want any more, I'll send the sandals. They don't seem to have strap shoes at all, but either laces or sort of no laces, but not court either, sort of ones you get into without either – I suppose there must be elastic somewhere. Can you understand? (I can't!)

It is now 11.30 a.m. We've got a Mr Norman Collins, who is the Director of General Forces programme of the B.B.C. representatives for India and Ceylon. They are mucking me up in the office – in and out, wanting transport, which I can't get, wanting me to fix up to get them to see Generals etc! They are going to see General Slim at 12, and the Supremo this afternoon. Lord Louis is always called 'Supremo' here.

I am sending you off copies of our magazine every week – called Phoenix – as it is quite interesting, and very easy to send.

I hope you get those food parcels before Christmas – let me know when they come.

I am going to write to Brandy – and I'll tick her off about the address – as she knows it quite well!

Nothing more to say – it's a lovely day to-day but very hot.

We go & have tea every day in a canteen & our offices in the grounds. It is a large static building, used to be something to do with the gardens. It is run by local European inhabitants – very nice – just tea & cakes.

24th Oct 45

I wonder how you all are with our Dug at home. Has he got his chair back, which has been so carefully preserved in my room?

I went to Kandy at lunch today and had bacon and eggs (2) twice! I really shall have to stop eating so much! I bought these pink envelopes – all I could get.

I did heaps of typing today for that Frank Owen. Yesterday he said how very quick I was & a marvellous typist & where had I learned etc! and I really have ideas now of trying to get a job where he is after the war. He is sure to edit some good paper in London, as he is very high up in the newspaper world (late editor of the Evening Standard) He is very quick himself & has a wonderful brain & I think it would be a good job for me if I could get it. I shan't say anything to him yet. In one of the magazines I've sent to you, he has written an article.

He has just been away for a week to Batavia with General Slim & while he's in Kandy he lives with Lord Louis. He goes back to SEAC Newspaper HQ, Calcutta on Saturday, but in December they are all moving too Singapore with us, so I might a chance to mention the job then. He's a very hearty - hale fellow well met (or whatever that saying is!). Anyway if I offer him a cig, I throw it to him across the room, sort of thing!!

I've made myself a pair of knickers! From some white muslim I bought for curtains. I cut them out by just laying mine on top of the stuff & cutting round – they came out far to big & I've taken darts in all over the place – they are a killing shape, but quite wearable!

I had a very nice letter from Chet, & I shall answer it soon. Please tell her I will certainly get her some sandals. There is a rumour that you might have to give up coupons for them if we send them home – so I still haven't decided whether to send them, or keep them until I come & try & get them thro' the customs. (Hope this letter isn't censored!) What do you think?

I have written to the Planters' Association in Kandy today to ask about Viv – as I've had no answer to my second letter to him.

Boss – I'm sure you'd like to hear about our lavs! There are about eight of them – wooden seats with lids – very clean – but no plugs - & you can't see the bottom, or where anything goes! So I asked & was told they are at least 60 feet deep and (this is what I was told!) – they put an animals carcass down there & the maggots go on it, & they continue to feed after they've finished the animal on what we give them! Isn't it a filthy idea – they say it's the cleanest & healthiest way of any - & there is certainly never any smell!!!

In hotels & restaurants & places like that – they have normal plugs. I had a rat in my wardrobe last night - so I made my boy (called Gunnei!) come and turn out all the shelves for me this evening. He told me he had found a rat on top of the wardrobe this morning & had put it out of the window. He won't kill things as he is a Buddhist.

There are lots of little animals in the gardens just like squirrels & they are tree rats. There are also peacocks there - I saw one yesterday – lovely colours.

They called for the type writer in my room to day.

Ma you needn't worry about the Indian's being ill treated - I don't think they are now – not beaten or anything like that. People just speak to them sharply, like to naughty children, they do try to 'DO' us so in the way of money - & they are so ignorant - otherwise they are just like children. Here they are much more educated & cleaner & don't beg so much in the streets. I think they are all Chinese people in Singapore.

They have changed our working hours here now, as the clock has been put back an hour – We work from 8 a.m. to 12.30 pm. &

2-5 p.m. Needless to say, I never get there till about 8.30 or 8.45 a.m. – Eric doesn't mind when we arrive! I always take 4 bananas with me to eat during the morning – hence my tummy!

If you ever think of what I'm doing – we are 5 hours ahead of you.

25th Oct 45.

I'm very thrilled as I've just had a very nice letter from Douglas, dated 14th Oct, and posted I suppose in Gibraltar. Thank you Dug, very much for it. I am so glad you are well, mind you rule the roost at home and make them do exactly as you want! I shall write to you one day. I'm sorry I beat you in rank, but I expect you'd have been much higher by now if you hadn't been a POW.

I've just had a letter from Boss dated 3rd October, which has made me laugh a lot!

The answer to her problem at the end $(\frac{3}{4} + \frac{1}{4} = \frac{1}{8} - \frac{5}{8}$ what is $\frac{1}{2}\% = \,!)$ is:- $\frac{9}{10} + \frac{3}{7} - \frac{6}{9} = \frac{21}{24}$ - & see if you can do that on your typewriter – same size?!

I wrote to the Buchannaus the other day, & couldn't think of a question for him for ages & I put, How long each day does an elephant work and why?

The answer is 4 hours only, but I've forgotten the reason! I was told it is a good reason, so if he replies I shall have to find out again.

How nice Douglas's writing is now, I hardly recognised the envelope.

A man came up to me after tea today & said he was sure he'd seen me before somewhere! We discovered he was at the men's Staff College when I was at Bagshot, & we went to a dance there. But he still thinks he's seen me somewhere else too. He is a very nice man so I hope I'll meet him again – a Major. He picked up the enclosed feather for me, which is from one of the small birds here. I haven't seen any yet, they say there are heaps – paraquets(?) etc.

We are all busy getting ready for the move- there are large packing crates outside all our huts & our tables & chairs are gradually being put in them. The Advance Party go at the end of this month, & I go in the middle of November in the first Sea party.

I agree with Dug, I don't really want to fly again, I am glad I have once and that's enough! Anyway it's very boring, it should be lovely over snow mountains.

I sent our "boy" out for some bananas today and he's brought me 12 lovely large ones which I'm gobbing now!

The money here is Rupees & cents- 13 rupees to the pound, which is about 1/6d each. But really they only buy about 1/- worth each. There are 100 cents to the rupee. In Singapore we have dollars - one being about 2/6d.

27th Oct 45

I had a nice letter from Ma yesterday dated 19th, all agog cos of our Dug coming back. I'm longing now to hear when and how you met him and how things went off generally. For goodness sake don't get the house too tidy, or you won't know your way about in the dark!

That Col Owen (who's book I have been helping to type) asked me out to go out to dinner with him yesterday - and then he had to put it off at the last minute, as he had to muck about with a film called Burma Victory, for the Supremo. So he has asked me to go on Sunday night, and I shall. I think he is only doing it to sort of thank me for doing his typing, and also because I let him have my beer ration. I am going to try to get in a word about a job after the war.

I'm sorry about Esme's dog, and hope D.D.'s is better now. Have you got the chickens yet? I'm all for them and will help to cope when I come back. I was thrilled with the letter I had from Douglas the other day (but I think I told you that one!)

D.D. has never written to me yet - so next time she comes she is to be sat down with a pen and paper and MADE to write - and it must be readable too, and not stuff about the weather - I want good Kingston Hill gossip!

A lovely peacock has just gone outside my office window – but it won't put it's tail out.

When I met Esme Lawrence the other day (our chief AT here) she asked me for how long I signed on, and I had to say I hadn't and she said I should and would send me the form. Like a silly I did sign on for a year (the least time) and returned it to her. Then I found out from the others, that you don't really have to sign anything, but can stay under a Gentleman's agreement, for just as long as you are needed in your job. So I have written to ask her if she will cancel my signing, and that I am quite willing to stay as long as Eric wants me, but that when I go home, I don't want to have to be in the A.T.S. in England for some more months, and I explained that Muriel had left her job because of me, and that she wanted to go back and I wanted to be at home for a bit etc. I have not had a reply from her, but Eric says he will take the matter up for me if she won't do it. So I think I'll be alright. I should be back quite early next year - BY SEA!!

Thank you for thinking of Christmas presents – but Please don't bother to send me any, as it is so difficult to pack up things, and they take months to get here – so wait till I come back, and then I'll ask for all the things I should have had! I am not sending you any either – I'm sorry, but really it is so difficult to send parcels. On the other hand I might send the cocoanuts and a few bits and pieces, if I can. Anyway you will have the food parcels round about Christmas time.

28th Oct 45

I'm so glad you got the hymn book from the Transit Camp. I know that Mrs. Waterfield very well. She was my platoon officer at OCTU (typewriters – gone – I've left it to the WRNS clerk – as it was hers anyway!) and was also at Egham with me. I got a better result than her at Egham! I think the CO must have gone to Africa – she was due to go at the beginning of October – so I haven't bothered to write her.

The Air Force officer in my office is leaving for UK next Wednesday - to be demobbed - he is very excited. Has Boss ever heard of him - he used to be on the stage, singer & comedian - Jerry Fitzgerald. I had to pretend I had - but I hadn't - but everybody else has!

Sunday – 10.30 a.m.

I didn't have a chance to finish this yesterday. I went to the local pictures last night (first time for over a year!) & saw a new film - 'Burma Victory' & another English one called 'For You Alone'. The Burma one, is the one Frank Owen had to go to America & advise about a few months ago - & he & Eric & the Supremo spent all Friday & Saturday cutting about till it suited them. I believe it is to be shown in London - so you should try & see it - it's very good.

There is a WRNS officer here called Pitts Tucker, so I asked her yesterday if she was - & she is a cousin of Peggy's. She says she often used to stay there, but not so much now as "Uncle Walter is so difficult" Actually, she looks & is, rather bad tempered herself! She is coming home soon.

I have bought a jar of Peach jam, made in the Gardens. I hope it will keep to bring home - will it?

Thank you very much about my motor bicycle – I enclose a cheque for it – with a tip of 4/- for you!!

Sometime ago, I asked Miss Jackson, the NAAFI manageress of the Transit Camp, to get me another fountain pen like mine - & I was going to give it to Ma – but if Dug hasn't one perhaps he'd like it. Anyway, I wrote to her the other day & said if she could get it, would she send it to you & you'd pay 9/2d for it! They are very good indeed – mine works beautifully – so will you please & I'll repay you if, and when it comes.

I have just eaten a whole grapefruit in my room! I am going for a walk with a WAAF this afternoon, & out with Frank Owen this evening – I hope.

I haven't got the newspapers yet – but expect they'll arrive soon. Hasn't that Himrod came yet? The girl's name was Dorothy Stagg & she lived at 23--? Avenue, Didcot. She should have got home about 9 or 10 October & posted it to you. I gave her the money & some stamps & a note for you.

30ᵗʰ Oct 45.

I can't remember when I got my last letter! I haven't had one from you for two or three days - the last one was where you were waiting to hear when Douglas was arriving - so I'm longing for the next when he has.

I was going to Colombo for the day on Sunday - but Col. Owen asked me to go out to dinner with him on Sunday night at 6.30, which was much nicer, so I didn't go to Colombo. I mucked about in my room on Sunday morning, and went for a bicycle ride with another girl in the afternoon – a WAAF officer, who has only been out here for three days.

There are five official bicycles in our mess, which we can use when we like. We didn't go anywhere special - and had to walk quite a lot, as it is so hilly. Then we had tea in the local officers' club. We really live at a place called Peradeniya, and are about 4 miles outside Kandy.

Col. Owen came for me in a taxi about 7. I wore that blue and mauve flowered dress - last year Bentalls 32/6 one! We went first to the Suisse Hotel in Kandy, where he stays - and had a drink there - AND MY ERIC TOO! Then Col.O. and I went into Kandy to a Chinese restaurant, and had some Chinese food, and ate with chopsticks! He is so nice and interesting to talk to. He knows all sorts of people personally - including our Winston. He has offered me a job! Definitely he says - as he seems to think my work is wonderful! He is going to be a big bug on the Daily Mail when he goes back so I think it would be rather nice - don't you? It happened when we were talking with Eric - and he was saying how silly I was to sign on for a year without asking him first, and he would have stopped me doing it. He says of course I can go back early next year, and he is going to get me out of having signed on. Then I mentioned I needed to get a job when I got home, and Col. O. immediately said "I'll give you one with me". So I clinched it! I hope! He drove me back after dinner and I got back about 11.30. I enjoyed it very much. I am writing this in the office now (it is 11.30 am) and he is opposite me writing some more stuff for his book etc. I did heaps of typing for him yesterday. He goes back to Calcutta on Thursday unfortunately. He lives in a flat in Westminster and has an American wife. When we go to Singapore – he, and all the newspaper staff are moving there too from Calcutta, so it should be rather fun.

The other officer in here Sq.Ldr. Fitzgerald is going home to-morrow to be demobbed, and another of our liaison officers has just arrived back from Singapore, Bangkok and Rangoon - he is Sq.Ldr. Mc Kinnon. All the officers in our mess had invitations to a dance at the Air Force Headquarters here last night - about 6 miles the other side of Kandy, and some of us thought we'd go. So this Mc Kinnon who only came into the office yesterday, found out I was going and said he'd like to too - so I asked him to dinner first. I wore my new evening dress and looked quite nice. He's not bad - but such a bore! And he can't dance for toffee - but he's really not bad, I suppose. I had to stick with him most of the evening - except one dance which I had with someone else, who could dance. The food was lovely - chicken, pork, trifles, jellies and coconut ice. He's very tall and not bad looking - he was a pilot in Coastal Command. NOW – isn't it funny – he asked where I lived and I asked him, and he lives in Aberdeen – so of course I asked the usual question about Douglas Thompson – and he is a relation of theirs and knows the family quite well. His mother was a first cousin of Sir Fredrick Thomson. You might tell Lady T. when you write to her next. He has a wife and two kids of 2 and 15 months who live up there somewhere.

(It was awful just now, while I was writing this, he came up to speak to me and kept looking at what I had just written - but I don't think he could read it! Anyway he has just gone out of the office.)

While we were getting ready to go out yesterday evening - about 6 o'clock, suddenly, wherever there was light, crowds and crowds of flying white ants appeared - in our rooms - downstairs and everywhere. You couldn't walk for going into them. I turned out the light in my room quickly, and started to get ready in the dark, as I couldn't stick them. They were there for about ½ an hour - and just as suddenly they were all dead or dying on the ground, having first shed their wings. I was talking to someone who knows about them - and she says they live in their hills quite normally, and now and then at certain times, probably something to do with breeding, they all come out like that, and swarm all over the place in great crowds, and then shed their wings and

259

die, and one or two 'Queen' ants live on - or something like that! They are horrid while they last. Then the boys all get brooms and sweep up great piles of them and their wings.

I had yesterday afternoon off and went into Kandy with another girl, a Junior Commander in the A.T.S. who has been here for 6 months. My Eric asked me to buy him some pyjamas for him from the officers' shop - some poplin ones. His last words were that I wasn't to buy any with flowers on! We got a lift into Kandy, and went to the Officers' shop, where I am 'under the counter'! I bought a torch some hankies (although I don't really need them!) – and she said she hadn't any pyjamas left, and didn't expect they'd have any more. There were lots of people in the shop. Then suddenly just before we left, she hoicked something out of a drawer, thrust them under my arm, and told me to put them away quick before anyone saw - and they were one pair of pyjamas she had left. Jolly nice of her, and Eric was very pleased with them. She is having some nice sheets in soon, and I shall buy a few pairs – they are very cheap, and quite nice ones (better than those I got at home) – so they will come in useful.

Leslie Henson is coming to Kandy to give a show tonight, and I have got a ticket for it – some of the other officers are going from our mess.

While we were in Kandy yesterday, the other girl, Margaret, took me into one of the big European shops there. There are three of them, Millers, Whiteways and Cargills. We went into Cargills, as she knows the manager there. She met him sometime ago, when she joined the local dramatic society to which he belonged. Anyway he was a very nice man - has lived in Ceylon for 20 years - but is a bachelor - quite a bird. And he said they were shutting the shop in 10 minutes and would we go back and have tea with him in his flat – so we did. It is over the shop, and a lovely flat - all the rooms sort of run into one another and have hundreds of windows in them. We had tea, with fresh milk - and sardine sandwiches - very nice. We never get fresh milk here - it is always tinned. I asked him if he knew Viv, but he didn't.

I had a letter from the Planter's Association about Viv, and he has moved but not very far, I don't think. He is now at an estate in Opanike, and I have written to him there now. ......

If you are fed up with initials, you can put my address as I've put it to-day if you like! It will change soon, but I'll let you know what and when later. Probably it will be about the middle of November.

It breaks my heart here to go into shops and see things like, Lux, Parker fountain pens, joints of meat, ham, tins of fruit of all kinds, jam, sweets, chocolate etc., no rationing and no queues! But it is impossible to send things like that. I am going to order another food parcel for you in a few days, when I get to a post office, from a firm in Durban. I have a list of things that they will send, all sorts of clothes, stockings, etc. - but I shall send the food part.

Can't think of anything more to say. Longing to hear from you.

31st Oct 45. H.Q.,S.A.C.(Kandy), S.E.A.C.(c/o DSR) For a change you can now address my letters differently - in fact you have to - as it's official! as at the top - this is because part of the HQ has moved to Singapore. My address will be different there – but I'll tell you when!

That Sq Ldr MacKinnan I told you of – went to a school in Edinburgh – Loretto (Boss'll know it) & then he left & went to come for Matric at Maiden Early!! & so knows the bis very well.

I drew a ticket to go & see Leslie Henson on Tuesday night (last night). First, another ATS here called Helen Stewart asked me if I'd go & have dinner with her & her friend at the local officer's club (called the Victory Club - (they are all Naafis really – very well run)). So I did and her friend is a Lieut in the Intelligence Corps & is a Dane - such a nice man, & a lovely accent. Then we hitch hiked - to Kandy to Trinity Hall (I think it's part of the University) - which was packed. Supremo was there in the front row, Leslie Henson was sweet - very funny, & also there were Nan Kenway and Douglas Young (They broadcast a lot). & she played the piano beautifully - also a girl who sang called Helen Hill. They were all very good. Then we hitched back in an American lorry.

It's awful - we are so waited on here! - our boys are always here when we come back at lunch, again after tea, and after (+before) dinner. You can't open your own door - they do, - put the light on! & then I think of you lot, cooking, washing up etc! I am sorry. Altho' I really rather enjoy a bit of house work!

I have been to the pictures this evening & saw Blythe Spirit with a WRNS officer – a very nice one who lives in Ikley & teaches Geography in a school in peace time. I asked her if she knew Rachel Veinan, & she does – she is in Colombo, so I am going to write & ask her to meet me. This WRNS says Rachel married a nice man but he was an R.C & she knows things were a little difficult. I have just been sitting in the WRNS' (Clare Hamilton) room & we ate a grapefruit each, peanuts & lime juice (only it was mandarin orange juice!)

The photograph they took for my pass here is jolly good - & I'm going to try & get one to send you. I don't know if they'll let me yet.

That ATS, Helen Stewart, comes from Dumfries & has met Greyhounds father. She says he's awfully rude! & a bit peculiar. I haven't written to G.H. at all – only once since I left England. That man took me out to dinner last week – the one who designs dresses (Lt Col Falkland Carey) rang me up & asked me to 11's (elevenses) in his office s'morning – so I went & he has designed me some dresses! I shall have one of them made (short) as it looks quite good. I've had no letters since the one dated 19th yet – but hope there'll be something tomorrow.

2nd Nov 45. HQ SACSEA (Kandy), SEAC (DSR)
Thank you for your letters dated 22nd & 25th Oct, I was so depressed because I got the last yesterday, & you said you'd told me all about Dug's return etc, & I hadn't had it! Anyway I got it today, and am so pleased to hear he got back alright.

How sickening about the car. I wonder if Mr Pond would come & really see to it. His number, in case, is Ealing 6111.

Please address my letters from now on as above and ON and after 6th November when you write put HQ, SACSEA (Singapore) SEAC (DSR) – in fact you probably won't get this in time to write to Kandy anymore. I am going from here with the First Sea party, and leave on about 14 November. It takes about 6 days by boat. I've had to go to two meetings in the Camp to represent my Department about the move – as it is a terrific affair, as we are taking all the furniture etc. too – meaning lots of special trains & ships.

I've been very rash today! I drew some money from Freddy (Miss Edwards' ex young man) today & went into Kandy with Patricia at lunch time. We both bought a small tin trunk each – or rather a tin suit case – as we must have something tin in Singapore & my trunk hasn't come yet.

Then we went & bought some materials! I will send you little bits of them in my next letter – I can't in this as we can't put anything in.

I'm glad that Douglas seems so well & that the aunts came etc. I am very angry that you have not got that Himrod – as I gave her about 2/- worth of stamps & also 9d to post it with. Could you write to the Post Office & see if they will give her the letter – it can't be a big place. She is Miss Dorothy STAGG 23, ?? DIDCOT, Berks.

The girl with two more tins, left Colombo by boat last week, & should be home in about 18 days.

I'm sure I ask lots of questions in my letters – but I don't always get the answers – so will you look through & see please!

There is probably going to be a general strike on in Ceylon soon - at the moment all the banks have struck! Viv has never answered my letter – isn't it funny?

I've learn't something about Eric today from another girl who is an R.C. She says she's seen him at mass, & he acts as an acolyte there! He is obviously Irish.

It has been terribly hot & sticky here the last few days & is now, so I shan't write a long letter. I asked my 'boy' to get me a few bananas today - & he's bought 3 dozen! I don't know how I shall eat them all.

I am sorry about Uppas & the school. I do hope he'll find some decent masters soon. Wouldn't An Jessie go & help a bit? I should have but Mrs Stouges Gertrude in the head it I'd been you!! Can't do with her at all. The aunts haven't written to me ONCE yet – how about ticking them off! DON'T forget the SINGAPORE address next time you write.

4th Nov 45. H.Q., SACSEA (DSR), (Singapore), S.E.A.C.
Pink – day dress

Thin pink & yellow – evening – it's really very pretty

White – with flowers – blouse for my khaki slacks

I've had a very nice day today – I wasn't going to do anything, & then at breakfast a WRNS officer asked if I'd like to go on a picnic with her & some others & they would start at 10.30. So I did – I wore the dress that belonged to Ma. There was this girl (Clare Hamilton – who comes from Ilkley – I told you about her the other day) & a friend of hers – an American Colonel – about 50-ish, but very nice – and another WRNS called Rebecca James (who has lovely curls) & an American Sgt who drove – a very nice man. They had the most gorgeous car - American – held five people easy! & was so smooth you couldn't feel it moving! We drove through Kandy & right up the hills to a place called Elkadawa (Elk-a-dewer!) 21 miles away & 4,000 ft up, awful hair pin bends and precipices on the sides! When we were quite high there were a lot of people on one of the bends & we got out, & a bus full of people (all natives) had gone over the edge & fallen 50 ft & broken in half. It had happened yesterday - 3 killed & 16 injured. They are not at all good drivers. We never go in native buses, it isn't done.

About 2 miles from the top we turned such a sharp corner we had to back to get into it & we were in a tea plantation - we went on up - left the car where the road ended walked 50 yds up again & there was a lovely lake. No one else was there - as it was sort of private being in the tea estate - & they do allow Service people to go there. First we all had some coffee, then we bathed & tried to teach the Sgt to swim. Then we lay out, then we had lunch - tin tongue, sardines, bread and butter, two eggs each, tin peaches, bananas, lime juice etc. Then we lay out, then bathed again & then dressed & went for a bit of a walk up a hill – hills were all round, most lovely views. I have got quite sunburnt – face & top half!

Every now & again the clouds came down over us, but mostly the sun was lovely.

We left there about 5.30, drove down to just outside Kandy to the Military Hospital & called to see one of the officers there.

When we came out the Sgt said the car wouldn't go! So he telephoned the American place, who sent someone in a jeep to mend it, & also another car to bring us back!

Does Cissie take up Dug's breakfast? What things did he bring back with him that he had bought in Rangoon?

I went shopping again with Patricia yesterday & went to have a dress made at our tailors. Then we got a taxi back – for a change – as we usually hitch hike. You would have laughed – the taxi was quite an old four seater - & had to be pushed by someone else before it would go, & then the man drove straight into a garage to get some petrol as he said he hadn't any! And we had got it to save time as we were late!

On Friday night I had to stay late to finish some typing for Frank Owen & then it started to pour with rain. So at 7 Eric telephoned for a car – which came in the end & when we went out to it, the driver had disappeared! So after sitting in it for 20 mins I suggested we walk. So we did & he carried the tin trunk I had just bought. Its quite a small one – but I need something tin in Singapore, & my trunk hadn't come yet. I enclose some patterns of the stuff I bought.

We are having to start taking mepachaine pills now, the stuff against malaria, because of Singapore. I think they make everyone go yellow!

I am going down to Colombo one day this week to buy some shoes, & sandals for Chet – they are much cheaper there than here.

I am sorry about Ma's F.C. Do be careful with her - & she is NOT to go out if its cold or raining!

I think we are sailing for Singapore on the 15th.

I'll write more tomorrow by typewriter – it is very tiring by hand to say enough.

7th Nov 45.

I have had no letters since the one dated 25th October – but it is something to do with the weather this end, as no one has had any for a few days. I had a very nice time yesterday – Tuesday. I got the day off and went to Colombo. There is a Major Howes who is another of our 'liaison' officers and travels about, and he arrived back here from Singapore on Monday – and he was going to Delhi for a few days last night by air, so he also went down to Colombo yesterday in the train with me – and I spent the day with him, as he didn't leave till 10 last night.

The train left here at 08.15 hours, and about 9 a.m. we went into the dining car and had breakfast, two eggs and bacon. We arrived at Colombo at about 11.30 a.m., went by transport to the Air Bookings Office where he got his ticket, and then went to the Galle Face Hotel to leave his luggage. It is a lovely hotel (I think I've told you about it before) right on the edge of the sea – only its own wall between it and the beach. Then we took a taxi to visit Radio SEAC – our broadcasting station out here. They are in a large, lovely private house – and have offices and broadcasting studios. We were shown all round – even into the control room and saw the man broadcasting. The head man there, the Station Director, is a Major MacNabb, who is simply sweet! Then about 12.45 p.m. he and Major Howes and me all went to the Galle Face and had lunch. Then McNabb drove us into town and left us and we went shopping all afternoon. It is much nicer shopping with a man, as they don't 'Do' you quite so much! I bought some very nice sandals for Chet – they are the same shape as Boss's only a bit more money, as I got hers in Karachi where everything is cheaper. I also bought myself a nice B.B. from a European shop – Cargills. We went into Whiteaways there too. I have also bought you two more tins of Himrod! There is another WRNS officer in our mess going home by sea who is going to take another tin for me, also my hot water bottle, and also a pot of peach jam, if she can get them in – so you should get all these in about a month, I hope.

To finish yesterday – we had tea in the Grand Oriental Hotel, which is just near the harbour – then we mouched a bit more, and he took me to the station and saw me off in the train about 6.30. I also bought myself some shoes – at least I am having them made for me (!) which costs just the same – brown suede with crepe soles, oxford shoes. This was in a funny little back street in a room – not a proper shop – and I had to sit on a chair with only three legs. We went to another small place where there were making book- ends with elephants, bowls etc., They all sit round cross legged doing it. The only person who could speak English there was a small boy aged 8, who was simply sweet – it was funny seeing all the grown up natives going to ask him about the prices etc. when white people go there. He was a very intelligent little boy.

One filthy habit ALL the natives have here is chewing betel nuts, which are red, and then spitting out the muck all over the road. The result is the road covered with red marks, and their teeth and tongues are also red.

11.30 a.m. – Three letters have just been brought in to me – one from Dug dated 25 Oct, one from Ma dated 31ˢᵗ Oct. and one from Ar.Beat dated 28 Oct., so I've just stopped this to have a good read! It is nice getting them. Have you done anything about trying to get that Himrod from that girl – I can't understand her not sending it to you, unless she didn't get back safely. Funny about Boss and my shoes – she can take her pick. You can also have my coat, and anything else you want! I am glad we've got chickens!

I wonder how much they offered for my mo-bike – I really should like to sell it, I think. I really ought to get £10 to £15 for it – I don't think I'd accept less than about £9. But if you can sell it for me – please do, and perhaps you could put the money in my post office book for me, and keep £1 for yourself.

I am worried now because you are still ill – what are you going to do about it? You must NOT ever get cold - for goodness sake have a coat made of cotton, wool and fur!

Will you tell Douglas that I have asked about his photograph and I am going up to see some Film Unit people here about it this afternoon. (I may finish this later).

I am "under the counter" here with heaps of people!

(a) at the officers shop the large fat woman who thinks I'm so nice, and different from the usual run of officers.

(b) with our head 'boy' (he's a man really) in the mess, who knows I like bananas, and every evening at dinner hands me a parcel of them to take away with me.

(c) with the boy at the bar - who gave me two extra bottles of beer last month.

(d) with the manager of Cargills – a big European shop here. Another girl introduced me to him, and he got out the shop van the other day to drive me back here!

I give all my beer to Frank Owen – at least he buys it from me – as that is all he drinks, and I don't want it.

I found out Rachel Vernon's married name from some WRNS officers who know her here. She is stationed at Colombo, and they say she is very nice, and most attractive. I think her husband has had to go to the Middle East or somewhere. I wrote her yesterday and suggested we should meet next Sunday – but now I'm not sure whether I want to, as that Major MacNabb may be coming up to Kandy, and I don't want to miss him!

Coming back in the train from Colombo last night I met some very interesting people – they were seven Army nurses - AIMNS. They used to be at hospital in Kandy - then were sent hurriedly by air to Singapore on 4th Sept. They saw the surrender ceremony there, and had to work in the hospital there immediately after the Japs had gone. They said everywhere was filthy, and full of bugs etc. They had also been flown to work for the prisoners of war etc. in Java, Sumatra, Bangkok etc., and had lived in all sorts of queer conditions, with no water, no lavs etc. They were just returning to the hospital in Kandy, as they had finished their work with P.O.W's.

Please don't bother to send me anything for Christmas – just send me a few extra letters! I am afraid I am not sending you anything either, as it really is too difficult. You will have to wait until I get back for presents.

I leave for Singapore with the 1st Sea party, sometime next week – I think we are going on a big boat called the Devonshire, and it takes about five days. I have got to have my luggage ready by this Friday.

I haven't heard from Viv at all – do you think he has gone away for leave, or perhaps doesn't want to see me? I can't make it out at all. I believe it is an awful train journey there from here, and don't want to risk going and finding him not there – and now we can't get any transport to take us anywhere as it has all been sent on to Singapore. I might try and see from the Planters

Association whether he is on the telephone and ring him up. I'll do that to-day if I can, and let you know what happened.

3 o'clock.

I didn't have time to go to the Planters' place to-day, but I have just been to see the Film Unit people here about Douglas' photograph which he says was taken. Can he give me more details; i.e. the exact day on which it was taken, and, if possible, by whom – it might be Army, Navy or Air Force photographers, or by the Public Relations people of Indian Army. Can he give me ANY idea of who took it, and the date, and I might be able to trace it.

You MUST go through my letters and see if I ask any questions, and answer them please!! I know I ask lots of them, then forget what I've asked, and if you don't reply to them – well anything might happen!

Tell Douglas I'll accept his pact about not writing to each other – but I insist on having some letters from Boss sometimes, as they make me laugh – and of course longer and longer ones from Ma!

I do hope my Uppers has got some masters now, I feel rather sorry for him.

Love to Cissie, Mrs Howard, Mrs Harper, DD – Last because she hasn't written to me yet!

9th Nov 45.

Please give my love to Chet & say I'll write one day – anyway I've got her sandals which is the chief thing!

I had Boss's letter today, which she wrote to me at Karachi – on 9 Oct. Not bad! Thank you

I am leaving here on Tuesday next. We go to Colombo by train & embark on the boat there. I'm hoping it's a large one & that the sea will be calm! I think it takes about five days to get to Singapore.

Did I say I have sent you another parcel by a girl who is leaving by sea on Monday, 12th. It should take her about 18 days to get home, & then she'll post it to you. I've put my hot water bottle in - & do use it, so it doesn't perish – a pot of peach jam, made from fresh fruit from the Botanical Gardens, & a tin of Himrod.

I have asked my Eric to dinner in the mess here on Monday night - & he is coming! I didn't think I could manage him alone - as he doesn't talk much, so Patricia Style & a Lt Col friend of hers are joining us. There is a little room next to the mess with glass partitions - for special parties etc, & we are using that. They always make it look nice with mats & flowers etc!

A girl has asked me to go out to a party tomorrow in the Officers Club - dinner & dance - three men & three of us. She is in the WAAFs – a very nice girl.

I have got my new dresses – an evening & a day. The evening has long sleeves. They are quite nice.

I've had a very nice letter from Rachel Vernon (now Kemball) – which I enclose. I'm not going to Colombo to meet her as it isn't worth it just for that – so I shall wait till she gets to Singapore.

The rats are getting awful in our mess. One ran out of my wardrobe last night when I opened the door. Also Patricia who lives next to me, left her beret on her table last night and when she woke up this morning there was a large hole in the middle of it. They eat buttons off people's things too. Her "boy" Perera, was rather amused, she showed him her hat (he can't speak much English) & he looked about for a minute & then said "b...... mouse!" Patricia told him he was naughty & mustn't say things like that!

I went into Kandy & have found out Viv's telephone number, & I'm going to ring him up tomorrow morning!

What do you think of my proposed job on the Daily Mail after I come home?

8th Nov 1945 To Dorothy from Rachel
Please excuse a very hurried & scruffy note. I was so glad to hear from you – of course I hadn't forgotten you. I went to your home once & you had a Siamese cat which impressed me very much.

Will you be coming down to Colombo anyway on Sunday? Because I am on watch from 13.00 till 20.00 but if you are here I could meet you for tea (I could sneak out quite easily for an hour or so & could take you to our canteen in Navy Office) I should very much like to see you before you go & it seems the only chance. My office no. is 2236 & I shall be there from 1 o'clock onwards. I'm sorry things are so complicated & hope you won't think it isn't worth it.

I do envy you going to S'pore – my husband is there & I hope to join the W.V.S. & follow out in about a month's time. I'm in the throws of getting out of the Wrens now!

I hope the plan suggested will suit you.

11th Nov45. 6 p.m. In my room

(otherwise called cabin or basha)

I've just had tea & come back from a long walk! We have been about five miles altogether. I went with another girl a FANY officer. She lives at Hampton Court somewhere - quite com: but a nice. The sort who has holidays in Youth Hostels & holiday camps at home! We went about 2 miles along the road - the opposite way to Kandy & then turned off up a lot of steps cut in the rock - about 150 of them. At the top is the Temple of the Rocks. It's a sort of cave cut out of a huge rock & inside there is a large Buddha figure - made of plaster & coloured, lying on a couch of stone. The walls are all paintings of saints etc. The Buddha was carved two thousand and thirty four years ago, which is BC. Rather wonderful. There was a priest there who could talk English & explained. He had his head shaved & wore a bright orange sari & shorts. We had to take off our shoes to go in (socks on!)

(By the way there is a thunderstorm on now, lots of lightning & thunder, but no rain - yet).

Of course lots of small kids followed us up – they always do – hoping to get some money.

(Rains just started - pouring!)

We had to pass a black dog on the way up which scared us as it barked at us. I'll tell you why we were scared later on! – next letter!

Then we walked back here & have just had tea. A girl called Helen Stewart has asked me to have dinner here tonight with her & two men friends, & then go & see George & Margret at the local cinema – by the Dramatic Society of ALFSEA (!). They are another Headquarters under SACSEA - & have a huge camp about 5 miles the other side of Kandy. Stands for Allied Forces,

S.E.Asia. You know I love amateur dramatics! But its better than nothing.

This morning Helen & I went into Kandy to church – St Paul's the English Church there. We hitch hiked (the only way to get about) I got in the front of a huge lorry, & she got in a jeep. The church was full of people – lots of troops – all kinds & some English civilians – a few sort of Eurasians (they call them burghers) & a few better class Singhalese. Near us there were three small Singhalese children – all with white muslin blouses & red sarongs (long skirts), they were about 8,9 & 10 years – they all (that class) talk English all the time & go to a good school. The boys wear shorts & shoes – which shows they are up on the ordinary folk. The service was quite nice – sermon not bad, parson sweet! Rather like Peter Green style & like him to look at. We had O Valiant Hearts (to the time of Abide with Me – which was a pity – as I love the other), O God our help & at the end Once to every man & nation, comes the moment to decide – which was very appropriate as the parson had been talking of the atomic bomb – but no one knew the tune. The choir sang our anthem – very well indeed. (Nothing was slow, which was good). The choir boys were all natives & some white men & some black. Red cassocks & surplices. We had a gun go off at 11 & Admiral Sir Douglas Pennant read the lesson. It was a lovely Church – quite large (big as Norbiton without galleries) & so light & airy.

Afterwards we went & waited for a lift & got one in a lovely car, with an Admiral in front & two Major Generals. I thought I knew one of the later as Major General Kimmins who is Assistant Chief of Staff here - & who is my Eric's boss once removed! (Maj. Gen. Kimmins – Brigadier Wandell – Eric.) (Patricia Style works as his Staff Captain.) So I plucked up my courage & said my sister taught & was where his brother's kid went to school- & he knew all about Port Regis & was very interested - & the Admiral (I don't know his name) said his wife's sister is a land girl at Gorhambury!

It is funny out to see the people washing their cars & bullocks in streams! The animals love it.

I saw today a sort of young waterfall – with two men washing themselves under it, & another man washing his cow at the same time! Another funny thing is that they all walk along the sleepers of the railway line – if they want to go to the next place! We are quite near a level crossing & you look along the line & see people coming & going for miles all along it!

Tomorrow is my last day at the office - & I'm going to ask for the afternoon off to go shopping. I leave here Tuesday for Colombo, & think we go straight on the ship – which sails on Thursday, & get to Singapore in about five days. So you may not here from me very regularly for a week – as I don't suppose we shall be able to post anything from the boat.

Write a lot, & often – thank you. Hows Ma's health?

I hope Boss got my letter to say Viv is in England.

13th Nov 45. 4 p.m.

I am still here in Kandy, although we were supposed to have started this morning for Singapore. I got up at 6.30 this morning, and we were all told about 7a.m. that the move had been postponed until Thursday morning at 11 a.m. - so we go then. Apparently the ship is still in dry dock having a hole mended! I don't know how I'm going to manage my luggage – as we are supposed to have not more than we can carry ourselves. At present I have my big blue suitcase, the canvas one Greyhound gave me, my haversack, a shopping basket (!) my greatcoat, two macs and that summer coat. I shall have to try and re-arrange things. What has stumped me is a mosquito net and three sheets and pillow cases which we also have to take. My small tin box and ATS kit bag have already gone. Don't be alarmed by the shopping basket – it is a native affair and quite different from Kingston Hill-ites!

It was a lovely morning – I had four letters – the first for about five days. Two from Ma dated 5th November, one from Dug with the hidden treasure in it, and one from Mrs Harper. Will you thank her very much for hers, and say I'll write to her one day from Singapore. Douglas' letter is too much for the one reading I've given it so far! and it made me laugh quite a lot. Why on earth didn't he hide something really worth getting – I don't know whether my brain will take in all his directions for only 5 rupees! But you never know – I might be able to go and dig!

Thank him very much for the letter – I shall go over it again tonight and try and pick out the sense!

Everyone in the office was very jealous, as none of them got any letters to-day. The mail situation has not been good lately because of the weather and aeroplanes not being able to fly.

I had a nice time last night – my Eric came to dinner. I togged up in one of my new dresses, it's quite a short one, pink and brown sort of muddy stripes and I really look quite nice I think. Patricia Style and a friend of hers called John (Lt Col Carew Jones) came too, as I thought Eric might be bored with me alone. We sat in the anti-room first and had some sherry which I'd got - then about 8 we went in and had dinner in our mess. I had asked to have the little room there, which is sort of partitioned off from the large room, with glass. It had all been beautifully laid with mats and a nice bowl of flowers, and we had a head 'boy' and two others to wait on us. We had thick soup, roast beef and Yorkshire, and cabbage and roast potatoes, and then a sort of trifle, and coffee. We also had a bottle of wine. (Actually we always have three courses like that every night - and it was only the usual meal).

Then we went back and talked and they stayed until midnight. We talked about all sorts of things and Eric was very interesting. He won't talk much about what he does in America, except that he is in films and produces and acts. He must be quite high up I think. He knows Greta Garbo, Bing Crosby, and my Herbert Marshall quite well. I didn't ask about any more! We went to see them both off at the gate, and left quite a lot of drink bottles on the table in the ante-room, and also a tin of Patricia's cigarettes. When we got back after about 10 minutes, the cigs had gone, and one of the bottles had had a lot of drink taken out of it. So we asked one of the guards (They are Royal Marine Military Police – who guard our gates) what had happened, and he said he thought his pal had taken the cigarettes. And he had, and had them in their sort of guard room - wasn't it a cheek? We had to report it to the "Quarters" Officer to-day, who is going to have a row with them about that and the drink. What's the good of having guards who pinch things themselves.

The officer who looks after the whole mess (Quarters officer) is a WRS - very nice and capable. She used to have a very good job before the war looking after the staff etc. in Claridges hotel.

Albert, our little black office boy brought me in a pawpaw today - it is a sort of melon or cantaloupe. So I shall eat it tonight.

We have all had to start taking mepachrine pills now, for anti-malarial precautions, ready for Singapore. Apparently after a few weeks of taking them you turn quite yellow - but not forever!

There was a nasty accident here yesterday. I went into Kandy in the morning shopping for sheets etc, met Patricia for lunch, went shopping again and then waited outside the officers club for a lift back to the office here. While I was waiting a jeep passed me with an Army officer driving, a WRNS officer next to him (one I know quite well who lives in our mess) and a Naval officer sitting behind. I got a lift in a Military Police truck quite soon afterwards - and when we had gone about two miles we saw crowds of natives all looking at an accident, and I saw one native on the ground all twitching. I couldn't see any more much because of the people, and then the ambulance came up. Apparently the jeep had had to swerve to try and avoid the native woman and had gone into the ditch. The woman has since died which is rather awful. The driver had a compound fracture and severed a nerve in his arm, the naval man had his ribs broken, and the WRNS is only cut and got shock. It is a very dangerous road from here to Kandy, as although it is fairly wide, the sides are not 'made up' at all, and sort of slope downwards, and of course there are always swarms of natives about, just lounging along - lots of little native houses and shops all the way along.

I said in my last I'd say something about the black dog we were frightened of the other day! We were only afraid of being bitten, because if you are they rush you off to hospital and give you 24 rabies injections – all in your tummy! There was a mad dog here in the gardens last Friday, and the guards were out with guns trying to shoot it. It bit one man and he had to go to hospital. I didn't see it at all.

I'm very worried about this beastly signing on business – I can't remember whether I told you about it. But I saw our chief AT, Esme Lawrence when I first came, she asked me whether I had signed on for a year, and I hadn't and she sent me the form. Instead of saying anything to Eric or anyone, I stupidly just signed it and sent it to her. She has sent it on and the authorities in India have now approved it – which means I am stuck in the A.T.S. until next September (not necessarily out here all that time). I wrote to her and Eric also rang up for me to try and get me out of it, as I have since found out I need never have done it, but just stayed on a 'gentleman's agreement, and when I came home, just be discharged. Eric keeps saying why did I do it without asking him, and it makes me sick to think I did it. Anyway Esme says I had better leave it for the moment, and as soon as I want to go home, quite early next year, I must start agitating to get it changed on compassionate grounds – one being your health and the other being Boss having left her job for me, and now wants to return to it. So I shall have to wait a bit and see what happens. I don't want to be in the A.T.S., after I get back, for about five months – it would be awful, and anyway I want to get that job in the Daily Mail, and Frank Owen goes back about next January.

I love all your letters, but still no-one answers any of my questions, or comments on my suggestions etc!! Has Ma ever got any of that Himrod yet? If not, has she written to that girl in Didcot? I don't agree with her being ill at all, and she is not to do it again, see?!

Please give Canon Anderson my love next time – and all the others there if you see them. How nice being given a watch by Mrs Aked Davis. I am still considering whether to buy one (a wristwatch) here or not, but I don't think I shall. The cheapest are about 90 chips (chips are short for rupees!), and 100 chips is £7 10s, so that they are really quite dear.

5.30 pm. (back at the mess)

I've just got back & found another nice letter from Ma, dated 29 October & am glad to hear you have got the Himrod.

I hope the chickens are laying well now.

They are doing repairs or something to the Electric works in Kandy tonight - & so all our lights have been turned off until 6 tomorrow evening. We have all been given one candle each!

Although we were going to start today – we were only going to get the ship at Colombo & not sail until Thursday. Now we aren't starting until Thursday morning & sail at midnight – so it really is much better.

Must stop & read all your letters again.

I have sent off a few more magazines & have also addressed a cocoanut – but I don't know if I can get that posted yet!

Chapter 10

To Singapore

18th Nov 45. M.V. Devonshire. (Motor Vessel) Here I am in a ship & feeling quite well, thank you! I'll tell you my doings from when I left Kandy. There were about 14 of us women officers in the First Sea Echelon, & we left our mess at 10 a.m. on Thursday morning. We were taken by truck to Kandy station, where there was a special train in a siding for us. There were heaps of male officers, & other ranks etc - about 700 altogether (another party of 700 had left the day before too). We left at 11 a.m. - had sandwiches & bananas in the train & got to Colombo about 2.30 p.m.. The train went right down onto the docks, & there we sat for about 1 hr. A van with tea came along - but I didn't have any as it was sweet. Then we all had to get out & go on to a kind of jetty - we nearly all got a 'boy' to help carry our cases - although we had been told only to have enough so that we could carry on our own. I had my blue suitcase, the canvas one, & I made a hold all of my mackintosh cape, to hold my coats & mosquito net & sheets.

We had to go past a table & give our names & were allotted a cabin. The man asked me if I'd like one to myself - wasn't I lucky? As heaps of the other women officers are sharing 2,3 & some 4 in a cabin.

Then we got in a sort of landing barge & stood in it, & were taken right to the other end of the harbour, where this boat was - about 20 mins? drive? Sail? or wot? Then we all got off on a flat sort of raft & had to climb about 30 steps up to the ship. I was very lucky as a Major near me took two of my cases for me.

Someone showed us where to go to our respective cabins & I found mine okey dokey. It really is a lovely one, 1st class in peace time (this is a Bibby Line ship) - I am about one deck above sea level (or perhaps two - I don't know).

There is a bedside light & another one, a shelf just over my bed for my books & a fan with hot or cold air.

We had a very good dinner at 7.00 p.m. then went along the decks a bit and went to bed early. It was lovely to see the sunset on the harbour - which had lots of ships in - & then to see them all lit up when it was dark. We sailed about 7.30 a.m. the next morning. I feel very sorry for all the men officers, as all the women on board have been given the cabins. There are quite a lot of WRNS ATS, WAAFs, FANYs & civilians - Colonels and Majors, and below they have to sleep on the deck on the ground. The troops also on another deck, lower down. All the women officers and men of Colonel and above have their meals in 1st Class Dining Saloon, the Lt Cols have theirs there - only before us - & the Majors & below & or women have theirs in the 2nd Class room. The food is very good indeed - always soup, meat & pudding & coffee for lunch & dinner. Porridge, tea or coffee & bacon & eggs (or something like that) toast & marmalade for breakfast - & tea & bread & butter for tea. There are no alcoholic drinks on board at all - but morning & evening we can buy glasses of lemon squash or tomato juice with ice. Some of the officers in a 2nd class cabin have got bugs - heaps of them. The ship's officers are very upset & are doing their best - & they are now having to sleep without mattresses & have been fumigated etc. Apparently on the last trip they were used by Indian officers - whose habits are not too good! I am really very lucky in having a nice cabin to myself.

Two WRNS are ill - seasick - but the sea is very calm. There is always a very slight roll, & I'm not keen on actually walking down the stairs! But I feel quite all right. On Friday night it got a bit rough & I was playing a game with dice in the lounge, & I suddenly said I wanted to go to bed - & went! But I felt quit all right after a few minutes lying down. Another WRNS officer, who is worse than me - came to see me & said she felt wonderful - & on her way back to her cabin - she was sick!

We do nothing all day - mostly sunbath - I am very brown - especially face and arms! Boss would love it - & I wish she could be here too – not Ma as she'd not enjoy it !! We have to wear uniform in the mornings & evenings - but can change in the afternoons & I put on my bathing dress, my blue dress over it, find a patch in the sun & then disrobe! It is quite crowded every where & difficult to get nice positions!

We had a morning service this morning, which I went to - there was an RC one at 10 & an interdenominational one at 11 on deck - quite a lot of people. An ATS private played the piano - very well indeed - at a good pace & followed the singing well. We had about five well known hymns, 2 lessons & few prayers & a sermon - quite good but much too long - about ½ hr. It was taken by a lay reader - who was a private! He had red hair & was very much in earnest, rather the "Have you been saved" type.

They have loud speakers all over the ship & give out announcements over it & in the middle of the sermon they switched these on to give out the times of the meals for the troops! I felt so sorry for the preacher - he had to stop until it was over. One of the Lt Cols was very angry & went & complained afterwards.

I am quite pally with one civilian - she's about 36 & has been over here for 2 years doing cipher work etc - all secret - to do with the men who were parachuted 'behind the lines' in Burma. She is very nice & is very keen on singing & acting etc - & is going to help on the last night with a singsong. So last night we thought we'd go & play & sing & we went into one of the lounges - where they were all men - reading, playing bridge etc, & of course daren't do it. So we went outside & a Major there said of course we should play if we wanted to! & he came & a few other officers & I played out these song books, Lily of laguna etc - (I wished I had more - only two books with me - the rest are in my trunk). Then a Lt Col came who could play by ear - fairly well - & we sang some more.

All the waiters and stewards are Indians.

We are all having to take mepachuine – which makes people turn yellow in time! I haven't started to go yet. It is against malaria – one pill a day.

I shall post the sleeves of your bed jacket when I get to Singapore. I am just finishing them - & it is very difficult as there is not enough wool to make them quite long enough. Also I had to undo the collar & use that too. If I were you I wouldn't have one, but just a ribbon around the neck, as collars do get in the way. I shall post them separately by airmail, so they should get to you as soon as a letter.

Those sketches you said you'd sent never arrived.

I do hope you are alright – especially Ma's health. Do be careful - & never go to Mrs Sturges again – I can't do with that Gertrude.

I have shown Dug's "treasure" plan to Patricia's friend John - & he will be stationed at Changi - & when I have worked out exactly what Dug says - in English! He is going to help me find the treasure - just to see if it is there!

21ˢᵗ Nov 45. 4.30pm M.V. Devonshire, Straits of Malacca
The sea is still like a mill pond! We can see land in the distance each side now, & a man has lent me his field glasses. I am in my cabin writing this & keep looking out of the porthole to see a few ships pass & the hills of Sumatra & Malay. All the afternoon I sunbathed on deck in a deckchair - I am very brown now. It seems awful to think you are all shivering with cold & fogs, & we are so warm - too warm sometimes! I do hope you have got a nice lot of coal in - & mind you keep burning logs.

There is one man on board - he's about 60 - wears white trousers, a long white coat and a beard. He is an RC & I think he's a priest, a Frenchman. He sat at our table last night at dinner & he and I talked hard all the time. He talked English quite well. He has lived in Siam for 45 years & in 1934 came to England to try & raise money to build a school for boys, & then went back & built it. When he was in England he went to see a parson 'near Wimbledon' & got so excited when I told him about Daddy as he was sure it must have been him – for no reason at all! I'm sure it wasn't, as he got to know the parson through a person called Norwood who also ran a school for girls in Siam – I'm sure Daddy didn't know him. He was so nice & friendly & told me a lady in Colombo had asked him if she could plait his beard & he let her! When he was in England he used to go & see the King and Queen of Siam - who lived in Surrey, & they helped a lot with his school. He had to leave it when the Japs came, & he's very sad, as part of it has been bombed by the Americans - & he has got to start getting money for a new one all over again. He knows Ban-

Pang well, & was very interested in Douglas. The school was the College of the Assumption Bangkok.

Boss & DD will be very interested to hear that the lavs here have plugs & when you shut the door the light goes on, & a fan starts to give more air! We are due in at Singapore tomorrow morning & disembark at 9.30 am. We had a bad rainstorm for about ½ hr this morning – but the sea stayed calm!

Last night there was a singsong for the other ranks & heaps of us officers went & joined in, I enjoyed it very much & sang - Lily Laguna, Land of Hope and Glory etc. Two men sang alone - lovely voices. A Captain played beautifully - all by ear. There is a WAAF officer on board who plays awfully well – lots of things Boss knows – Clare de Lue & a Chopin Etude etc. I'm 'soil' amongst them!!

I'm getting like Ma asking for things now. They had tapioca for lunch & I asked the waiter for some cheese & he brought me a bit all covered up! & told me no one was to see. A girl at another table asked & didn't get any! I also got two helpings of bacon & eggs at breakfast! I think I go down rather well with native servants as I treat them like human beings & smile!

There is a FANY who lived in our mess & who is on board & her name is HELLIS – so we think we must have originated from the same monkey. Her mother is Swiss & she has lived in Switzerland a lot – somewhere near the French border – but knows all our parts well.

The Entertainments Major asked me to collect 12 women for tonight for a Quiz & a spelling bee & after asking masses of people I have got them for him. I'm not going myself! They are also having another singsong first.

I am longing to see if there are any letters for me in Singapore.

I do hope you are all okey-dokey – I'm longing to see you all again & shall start agitating to come home early next year! Then we'll go for a motor tour in Switzerland!

There is another ATS officer on board who has only just come out from England. Her name is May & she's quite 3 times as fat as me - rolls of it! She has very pretty curly hair & such a nice face & doesn't seem to mind her size at all & is very amusing.

Lots of Officers have met that awful Quartermaster who wouldn't let me have my kit - & they all agree that she is a female dog! The fat AT had the same trouble as nothing fitted her either.

22nd Nov 45. 3.0 p.m.(I think!) HQ SACSEA (DSR), (SINGAPORE), SEAC

I have just got to the end of my journey & am writing this on the balcony of our bungalow & trying to keep cool! We got to just outside the harbour about 9.30 am yesterday morning - all my luggage was packed & everyone ready to get off - & then we were told we had to stay on board another night. It was a lovely day and I sunbathed on deck in the afternoon, & after tea I was asked to play bridge for the first time. I did enjoy it – with a Colonel & Lt Col women nurses & a civilian woman. They couldn't play for money as I hadn't any! I spent rather a lot in Kandy and can't draw any more until December, so I have now borrowed some to get on with.

This morning we had breakfast at 7.15 am & moved in right up to the quayside & went off the boat in shifts - we got off at 10.30, got into a truck & were driven here. Everyone seems very thrilled with everything - I'm not sure yet until I know whether I have got to sleep with 4 others or have a room to myself! (I'll explain that one later)

We are just outside the town in a road off Orange Grove Rd (in case Dug knows it). There is a large block of flats standing high up called Ardmore Flats, & all the women other ranks are there, WRNS, ATS etc. Then all round are lots of bungalows - they aren't really as there are upstairs rooms very large, & we have about 12 of these houses for the women officers. The chief WRNS officer (Madeline Piendergast - who is sweet) has been here for some weeks trying to get things ready for us - but there are still heaps of things wanted. Apparently the Chinese looted everything after the Japs had gone - even wash basins & electric light fittings. She has put all the ATS together - so I shall have Patricia Style & another one I know, Helen Stewart - only they haven't come yet, & at the moment I am the only AT here. Our bungalow has a huge entrance hall, which will be a sitting room, & upstairs two large rooms & one small one - with two bathrooms adjoining & lavs. There is one ATS officer belonging to the British Military Administration who seems to have arrived and she has put her luggage in the single room, but Madeline says she meant the senior of us to have it, & thinks that is me, so I am hoping it is. We have no furniture much yet - beds, mattresses & sheets & there is a large fitted in cupboard & a few chairs - that's all at present! The servants are sort of Chinese-Malay - we have a Chinese boy for ourselves, his name is Wee Wung! It is terribly hot & I have just had a lovely cold bath & am much cooler.

HQ SACSEA are all working in the Cathay Building - a huge block of offices built just before the war - I shall probably go there tomorrow - we shall have to be taken & fetched there as it is in Singapore town.

We have our meals together in another bungalow - all tables for four, very nice & airy & very good food. Waited on by Chinese cum Malay. For dinner today we had a piece of fried steak, mashed pots & marrow - which was all cut up small with sauce on - you should try that way, it was lovely. Then blancmange & dried apricots, fresh bread, butter, cheese & coffee.

It is rather wonderful to think that only three months ago the Japs were all over the place - some of their signs are still about the town.

One man on the boat who was quite nice – very amusing was called Donald Speers - he is a Capt RAMC – but is not a doctor. He says he is a horse! doctor! His parents live at 37 Combe Rd Norbiton & he lives in Norwood.

5.30 p.m.

I've never been so hot, just dripping! I learnt at tea that we aren't meant to have more than 3 in the room (& that not for long) & at present only two. So I've moved three beds & mattresses out of my room & its much better. I shall share with Patricia, who is flying & should be here tomorrow. She & I get on well together.

We have got no furniture in the room yet, & apparently we have to go & pinch it from empty houses around - which I hate doing alone - but I shall have to try & get a chest of drawers, the fitted cupboard, wardrobe, one side & shelves the other.

I have come into the office this morning & there are only two letters for me – one from Violet & one from Marcia Haines - most disappointing – but I think there must be some from you somewhere coming & I hope to get them soon.

Yesterday morning I went round a few empty bungalows with 3 others to "pick up" anything useful! but didn't get anything. It's a shame the way furniture has been broken up - by the Japs & Chinese. In one bungalow there was a lovely sofa & two large chairs - all the material cut off & the stuffing pulled out - cupboards with doors broken off and shelves missing - tables with no legs etc.

When I got back to my bungalow someone had been & pinched a wardrobe from the empty room next to mine - so I was furious as I wanted it - & asked the boy who had taken it - so he said No1 Bungalow next door. So I got four sailors, described the wardrobe & told them to go and bring it back - & they did and struggled up the stairs with it - only for me to find it wasn't the original one at all - but a much better one! So I am laying low & saying nowt! Yesterday afternoon another girl & I (Harry - who is a WAAF (real name Harris)) got a lift in a jeep into Singapore to the Cathay Building (where I am now) - where the HQ is. It is a huge skyscraper - 12 floors - & was built as flats (not offices) before the war. Everything is a mess at the moment - 100's of coolies hammering everywhere, packing cases, furniture etc all arriving from Kandy.

My Eric doesn't arrive till tomorrow (I'll do my usual drawings in my next letter!).

Patricia Style arrived yesterday afternoon by air & is sharing my room - so it's nicer having her. We have scrounged two tables now & the room isn't too bad. We are getting proper chests of drawers on 30th, the ones we had in Kandy.

I do hope you are all well - & not to cold. It is very hot here – but apparently the day we arrived was one of the hottest they had - & it is not so bad now.

Violet says her youngest brother, Sam, is in Singapore – but doesn't know I am. So I shall try & find out where he is.

Write lots!

25th Nov 45. 11.30 a.m.

I had a letter from Ma yesterday dated 30 Oct which somebody brought on from Kandy – I had some dated later than that before I left. I do hope Ma's health is okey-dokey now. We are getting on fairly all right - we have a third in our room - but I don't mind much as she is very nice & I knew her well in London. She was the Adjutant at the Holding Unit in Raduer Place, when I was at the Transit Camp.

I met a Major in the Australian Army at the office the other day - & again yesterday & he took me out last night - we ate & then went to the pictures. Not bad. He is very interesting as he is a paratrooper & used to drop behind the Jap lines & has fought in Africa, Greece, Italy & New Guinea. His father was a clergyman in Manchester & he went to Worksop - then he became an engineer & then came out to Malaya & ran a rubber plantation - then went to Australia & sheep farms there. I'm only telling you all this as I know you are interested in my goings on - not that I'm interested in him especially! He goes back to Australia next week.

My Eric is arriving by air tomorrow. I shall go to the office properly tomorrow - although we can't do any work yet - no files or stationary have come.

The officers Club is quite near our mess, & there is a swimming pool there & this morning I went with two girls & swam at 7.30 am! before breakfast. It was lovely & quite empty.

I'm not at all pleased to hear in Marcia Haines' letter yesterday that a J/C Lane is coming out here soon. She was a great friend of Lille Myer's (My old Col's creature) & used to share a flat with her - & before that she lived in the Transit Camp & was most objectionable. Excuse the writing but I'm on my balcony writing on a large sort of China vase cum pot affair!!

My small tin box came today, & all things inside have got wet & stained, some other girls have too, I suppose the sea water got in the hold of the ship. Anyway nothing is very bad & I have hung it all out to air. My nicest bit of material is OK! I enclose a pattern in case I didn't & Boss's & Chet's sandals are alright too.

10 mins gap

That Major has just been round to ask me to lunch in their mess as they are having curry - so I shall go. Curry is very rare out her because of the rice shortage.

I'll try & tell you more about Singapore when I've explored it. I believe the shoes here are 30 dollars a pair (dollar = 2/-4d) & the materials are very expensive. They hope the prices will come down soon. A bottle of ink is 7 dollars! = 14/-! Could you please keep the aunts posted about me & give them my love occasionally – as I hardly ever write to anyone except you lot - & then my brain is done! How are the chickens? Why not rise to six & then you might get an egg now & again!

25ᵗʰ Nov 3.15 p.m. Too Boss
I am only writing this to show off the typewriter, which is a simply lovely one to use, and looks nice too. I have already written a letter home this morning, and so there is nothing to say! I have been to lunch in the mess of the Major from Australia I told you about, and we had a lovely curry, and now I am using this typewriter for fun.

How is your school getting on? I do hope you have got some more decent masters by now, and that poor old Uppers is feeling better about things. I intend to come back quite soon next year, and shall agitate that you need to get back to your job – so tell Uppers not to give up hope about having you again.

How are the chickens that you and Douglas nurse?!

I shall try and get you some nice shoes one day, when I have some money – they cost about $30 I believe. (That sentence was written purely to show off the $ (dollar) sign) !!

I know I haven't written to Chet, but please give her my love and tell her not to give up hope, as she may get a letter one day. Anyway I have got her sandals, and I cleaned both your pairs to-day, to keep them nice – I hope!

Can't think of anything more to say. Time you wrote again.

28ᵗʰ Nov 45.
I am writing this in the office & about 4 small Chinese girls are in & out, talking at the tops of their voices, & picking up all the cigarette ends they can find! They have black hair, plaited & put

in a large bun behind & they wear black trousers & blue coats. All the women wear the same style, some in light colours.

On Monday night I went out with that Major again - he has a motorcycle & we go on that. He is a very good driver & goes quite slowly. We went to the pictures, after dinner in his mess, then after that we went and had steak, chips and two fried eggs in a club! On Sunday night we went to see Changi - I couldn't see much in the dark - but I saw the prison. I stayed in last night & gossiped with another girl & tonight I'm going out again with the Major to a new Officers Club which is opening. It is in this building- Cathay - downstairs and is run by NAAFI. It is a huge room with a dance floor, tables all round & a band platform - all modern. We go down there during working hours for 11's and tea, & at tea time the band play Hawaiian guitars etc! There are tables all round.

The Major leaves for Australia on Friday.

I haven't been round the shops yet - as I have no money until December.

It's awfully interesting driving round at night - as in all the side streets & on the sides of the main roads too there are 100's of little stalls - all brightly lit up with electric light & Chinese selling things. The taxis here are funny too - some of them are just pulled by a man like I showed you in Ceylon & some are pulled by bicycles & hold two people.

My Eric has arrived & yesterday he took me out to take the minutes of a meeting at the Pavilion Cinema. He & two other officers & me went by car & met there about 12 men - all (except one English civilian) were sort of half casts or Chinese & they were the representatives of all the big Cinema Coms, M.G.M., Warner Bros etc. from America. It was all to do with releasing the Army Cinemas back to them for commercial use again. It was very amusing - as some of them are rather difficult & they all talked at one. The Chinese owners of the cinema were there too. I managed the minutes alright.

I went to the WRNS canteen last night & bought some starch, soap flakes – milk chocolate & a tin of grapefruit. It seems such a pity I can't send it to you.

Everyone is slowly going rather yellow now! I am - it is due to the Mepachine pills against malaria.

I still haven't had any letters since I have been here – except one dated 30 Oct – so am longing to hear how you all are. Give my love to anyone necessary.

3rd Dec 45.

It's lovely I had two letters from Ma last Friday, & 5 more on Saturday – the latest being dated 18 November – so the mail seems better now. I've also had one from Dug, An Beat & Greyhound. I do hope Ma is quite alright now – for goodness sake don't get ill again. I am sorry about the questions – I am quite satisfied now that I have all the answers! Let me know when you get the food parcels (2) tea (3) and two parcels I sent by girls going home. I have 2 more tins of Himrod in stock here & shan't buy anymore.

What a nuisance the bank are – they were quite alright before I went away. Anyway I will write to them & explain. I am also going to ask them to send me £20 from my money to a Bank here – as I feel I should like to have a little in reserve. Of course you can send that grey coat to Mabel Jackson. I think it's a very good idea – as it is awful stuff & not warm enough for you. I'm sorry I haven't sent the pink sleeves yet. One is done & the other only 20 rows off & I will send them in two envelopes by airmail. I have had to undo the collar to make the sleeves long enough, & even now I don't think they are. So perhaps Boss could knit a frill to go on the end of some wool!

I quite agree with Ma's parliamentary views & think she'd have done well. Parliament would never be able to rise once she started!

I don't think you need be frightened that I shan't want to come home - I know I shall! I quite like going out with people, but I get very bored when they are not interesting. My Australian Major (Charles Wolfe) has sailed for Australia today to be demobbed & start his sheep farming again. I shall miss going out with him, as he was so interesting & had traveled a lot.

I'll tell you my latest doings now. I went with 7 other girls to a dance in a private Naval Officers mess on Friday. They had a lovely large bungalow - with a huge verandah for dancing. There were 8 Navy officers & two Air Force & a very nice Captain in the Royal Mail Steam Packet. He was such a fine looking man, about 50 - with a beard and I told him about Uncle Napier & he knew all about the earth quake & how the three were killed & knew their names. I danced with him several times & the whole of the rest of the evening I danced with a Navy Lt, who was very nice - also called Charles - & I am going out with him again next Thursday to the Officers Club with 4 others.

On Saturday evening a WRNS officer asked me to join her party & go to the new officers Club at Changi - the HQ of ALFSEA (Allied Land Forces etc). The transport (a 3-ton lorry!) was 1 ½ hrs late fetching us as they lost the way, & so we didn't arrive until 10.15 p.m! Changi is about 15 miles away. The dance was in a huge bungalow - which used to be an officers mess in peace-time. There were about 12 in our lot – all very nice – from Major up to Brigadier! I danced with a Lt Col once during the evening - I had already talked to him on the boat - & he knows Reading well! He has asked me out next Thursday & I have got to get myself out of that now to go out with the other. I wish you were here to ring up for me!

I'll continue my doings in my next!

Thank you for my chicken!

3rd Dec 45. (Later on in that day) 8.30 p.m. I sent one letter to you this afternoon & am finishing my "doings" up to date in this one! I went out on Sunday evening with Charles Wolfe (Australian Major) & a Major in the Royal Marines & we went to the pictures after dinner in the mess. They were very grateful to me as I gave them all my beer ration (which I don't drink). Afterwards Charles & I went to see the "New World" in a jeep which was very interesting - only we were rather late going & most of it was beginning to shut. There are lots of places here, Great World, Happy World, New World etc, they are large sort of parks, entered thro' a gate, & inside there are heaps of outside cafes, dance places, cinemas, theatres, stalls & booths to buy things at (Boss – rather like the Tivoli in Copenhagen), everywhere brightly lit up. The largest dance hall we went in to & had a few dances - all for nothing - as that was the one where anyone can go & dance with Chinese girls for payment - sort of hostesses - very well behaved & managed. They call it taxi-dancing! There were quite a lot of English officers & ORs there.

Charles arranged to & settle himself on his boat today & then help me buy some shoes this afternoon - but he came to my office this morning at 10 to say they were sailing at 4., so he's gone. I haven't done anything tonight – I've just had dinner in the mess with Patricia & a Lt Col friend of hers.

This afternoon Patricia & I went in her General's car to get some money from the Field Cashier in Raffles Place. Neither of us have dared to go shopping yet, as we had no money before!

Boss would love the port here hundreds of ships & docks in the harbour. It really is a wonderful sight.

I'm going through your letters now picking out bits to answer! I'm glad Dug has my sponge - as the one you gave me to bring out here is lovely & quite large enough for me.

I think I'm just a little thinner – my tummy is not nearly so large – which is a good thing as I can never wear any sort of corsets – even in the evenings – as it is much too hot.

I'm sorry Viv's "done the dirty" – thank you for letting me know what happened – as I did my best to get hold of him here. You needn't worry – I never swear or cuss! The worst is "my hat".

I am glad to hear about the eggs – makes it worth while keeping them.

I'm jolly glad Boss met Mr Orr & boasted about me – mind you pile it all on with him & his co-boasters! What's Germany compared with the first women in Singapore!!

The third girl in our room – Betty Haine – has gone to Changi now, & we are saving the bed for a WRNS officer called Pat Wolesey – who is coming this week with the 2nd Sea party from Kandy. I did tell you about her once – she is what they call "Quarters" officer & will look after our bungalows, meals, & deal with the Chinese "boys" etc. She used to be over the domestic staff at the Mayfair & Claridge's Hotels in London.

I have got you a nice Japanese fan ready for you to wave next summer! I do hope you agree to me not sending any Christmas presents. I am going to try & collect a nice lot of things to bring home instead. I sent you a Xmas card today – we were only allowed one each of that sort - & it is a very grand one!

We have a Chinese woman who comes to our bungalow every morning to do our washing & ironing. Four of us share one - they are called "amahs" She's sweet quite small, wears black wide trousers & a sort of pyjama white coat with a high neck. All the amahs wear the same. She can talk a little English.

Every night after dusk there is always quite a noise going on in the animal world - I suppose they are mostly sort of crickets & there are bullfrogs which make a noise like a car horn. But the insect & rat world are not nearly so bad here as in Kandy. We never seem to have anything in our bungalows at all.

We have no hot water yet - but it never matters - as it is so hot it is nice to wash in cold water. I have a cold shower everyday about 6pm.

I don't seem to have told you much about Singapore yet – I will after I have been shopping there. The difficulty doing that is transport – it means hitch hiking mostly.

Write lots more – I love your letters.

6th Dec 45.

I have had another letter from Ma & one from Boss dated 20 Nov – Thank you. You asked what hat I wear – well I have a khaki beret – but nearly always carry it & don't wear one at all – it doesn't seem to matter. I'm glad the parcel came – a girl took it back in a ship & posted it from home. I'm glad Ma is better – do be careful.

I have quite a lot (7) sheets to bring home – good ones – so don't buy any.

I stayed in on Tuesday night - & washed my hair. Last night I was duty officer at the Admore flats – where all the other ranks (WRNS, ATS, WAAFs) live – which meant checking them in & seeing everything was alright.

I am going out tonight with that Naval Lieut I met last week, Charles Strubin and 4 others are coming too. We shall go to the Tanglin Officers Club.

I am going shopping at lunch time today to try & get some shoes – they wear out very quickly here.

My Eric has started going out, but not with me, with a WRNS officer who I know well. She's very nice, I don't mind a bit as I am quite off him! Which is rather a relief!

The view from my window in the office is rather nice at least it isn't a window but a balcony with all glass doors. There are lots of hills in the distance – heaps of trees & houses near to, & on one side, the sea.

Patricia & I went down to the officers' shop yesterday & I have bought some lovely coloured wool – violet – to make you a cardigan. It is 4 ply Patons Baldwin – but unfortunately only 8 ozs were left – so I bought the grey.

Frank Owen hasn't arrived here yet from Calcutta, where he is now finishing off the publishing of SEAC newspaper there. It is now going to be printed from here.

Patricia has asked me to join her & John on Christmas Day at the Phoenix Officers' Club – which is the Café at the bottom of this building – a lovely room – dance floor & band - & they are getting a party together of 24 people altogether.

Can't think of anything more. How's my 'leg' ?!

7th Dec 45.

I've just had two letters from Ma dated 27 & 28 Nov – so they've been quite quick. I am so glad you got the food parcels & I'm sorry there are no more on the way at present, except tea. We were not allowed to send any from Ceylon & can't from here – but I shall really make an effort & write to a place in Durban to send some. Its just a question of how to send the money that has stopped me so far – but I really will find out. I wasn't sure whether you liked brown sugar – I'm glad you do.

I enclose a few pictures of Singapore etc. (written on backs of). Could you please keep these & those from Ceylon for my album, as I haven't got my camera yet.*

I have hardly any work to do in the office, which isn't nice – but when Frank Owen comes I expect to have more.

I went out last night with another girl & two Naval officers. Her partners name is Teddey & he is a nephew of that Air Marshal, 2nd in Comd to Eisenhower - a very nice man. Mine was called Charles Stubin - also nice & dances very well. He is taller than I am, fair & not bad looking. I am going out with him again next week & sometime he is going to take me round the harbour by boat. After the dance at the club & dinner there, we went back to their mess & had more food! & talked to them & some other officers & I didn't get back until 1.30 am!

I wore my new evening dress, sort of red green & yellow – with long sleeves.

We wear civilian clothes whenever we like off duty. I bought some cheap white stuff the other day & went with Patricia to a Chinese tailor – where she arranged for an evening dress to be done, & I asked him to make me a blouse with my stuff. We worked out a pattern & did some measurements etc, then asked his charge & he said 18 dollars! (2/4d a dollar) = £2 approx. So I took the stuff away and shall get it done at the officers' shop, where they have proper prices.

The shoes in the shops are Lovely – practically all with crepe soles – but I shall buy gradually & collect things to bring home. I don't think I can get Ma a dress made – as there is no woollen material anywhere – all silks, georgette etc – some of it is lovely stuff.

I enclose a card I had from An Beat yesterday – typical!

You needn't worry – your letters aren't a bit dull & I am interested in every little bit. How sad Mr Bush dying. Funny having Geoffrey Staniland – how long will he stay?

I am sorry to say we have got rats in our bedrooms here, they come out at nights from the roof & this morning one officer's buttons had been eaten.

I haven't done much about Dug's treasure yet. As a matter of fact his instructions are so intricate that it is difficult to get the sense from the senseless!! I have shown it to someone who works at Changi & he says he thinks the Jap aerodrome was built over the spot & it is now littered with broken planes etc.

Did you get my letter telling of a Squadron Ldr Mackinnon who is a cousin of Douglas Thompson? As I've had no remarks on that! He is not in an office now, but works for the War Crimes Commission. He is a dreadful bore.

Where I work! Cathay Cinema is in front and the entrance to the flats is round the other side on high ground, I am five floors round the lefthand side of this picture.

In between these two buildings leads to Raffles Place - a large square with shops where we usually go and shop.

I hope you are all okey-dokey & not too cold. We have had a lot of rain lately! I am afraid I have been going gay lately! On Thursday last I went to the Tanglin Officers Club with 3 others. On Friday I stayed in - on Saturday I went to the Club again with Charles Stubin who is a naval Lieut - not bad - lives at Maidenhead! Yesterday another girl invited me to a picnic organised by a Chief Commander in the WAC(I) ATS for Europeans in India). She was a nice little thing - very amusing we went in a nice car, her, me, my friend & another girl - a nurse & three Naval Lieuts. We drove to Changi & then to a Royal Marine Camp called H.M.S. Landawell. There we went on a sort of jetty and climbed on to a L.C.R. (Landing Craft Rocket). It is a ship just off the secret list & all the deck is covered with hundreds of rockets - 1,000 of them. They are let off in 36's to help troops landing on beaches. The Lieut in charge took us round & it was most interesting. Then we all went into the "wardroom" and talked and heaps more Lieuts arrived from all the other rocket ships. At I pm. the other three girls & 4 men went in dinghies round a sort of point of land, and I went in the car with the rest of the men. I wouldn't risk being ill! Actually we did "the dirty" on the others, as instead of going straight away, we stayed on board and ate our lunch, all tinned stuff - & we were two hours late meeting the others! They had to stay in the swimming pool to wait for us, as it was raining by then.

We found a nice bungalow by the pool - right on the sea & just walked in & made ourselves at home, & gave the others their lunch. It belonged to a General who was out. The swimming pool is the sea - but has nets all round because of sharks.

Then we went back to the ship - the car broke down half way & we were towed by a lorry. We had tea on board, sat & had supper, & then most of us went to their picture house. It was packed with Navy & Marines & when us girls walked in - everyone shouted and cheered as it was unknown for girls to be there! We saw a Diana Durbin film, very good, then we went back on board & talked again - then drove back & got in about 12. The Navy are awfully nice men - so friendly & hospitable. Sorry this is so dull - I'll write more this afternoon.

10th Dec 45. (Later in the day!)

I got a letter from Mother today dated 22 November - which is one behind some of the others I've had.

At last I have done something more about a food parcel & have ordered one from Delhi. I shall endeavour to do this regularly every fortnight or so. I've asked for 1lb tea, 1lb sugar (brown if poss), 1lb butter, & 1lb jelly crystals. What do you like to have? Other things are honey, jam, marmalade, sultanas, raisins etc. Mixed peal, currants, sweets, dried fruit, honey. I have asked about tinned fruit & will send that next time. I am collecting a few tins of grapefruit, peaches etc, to bring home.

I went into the town at lunch time today, got a lift in a jeep & another lift back in a jeep. I bought a pair of sandals with crepe soles, sort of natural coloured leather.

One thing I didn't tell you until it was over - when I was out in a jeep one day with that Australian Major - he let me drive it - it went beautifully - & then we got stopped in a Military Police Trap & they took my name as I haven't a Military driving licence! Nothing more happened until Saturday, when my Eric got the report on me & was told to take what action he thought fit! (which of course mean't nothing, thank goodness). The policeman had put down that the major had said he was "learning me to drive"! I shan't do that again.

I think I'm going to a party tomorrow in Johore, in the Sultan's Palace! With the Navy people I met yesterday. I'll write better tomorrow!

11th Dec 45.

I'm sorry I write such rotten small letters - but as soon as the second typewriter arrives from Kandy, I'll be able to type some longer ones.

I went out to dinner last night with that Naval Lieut, I call him Charles11 - we went to his mess, which is a very nice bungalow, they call it H.M.S. Round the Bend! & have amusing drawings one of them was done all round the walls - elephants, rabbits etc. We had a nice meal – about 4 other Naval officers there too. We had lovely soup, roast pork & roast potatoes - the first time I'd had fresh food for ages. All the stuff we have is tinned or dehydrated - except for the fruit, pineapples, melons, Oranges, bananas. I expect we shall get fresh stuff later on. We all take Vitamin tablets as well as mepachrine. I think a hot climate must suit me, as I always feel so well here, & haven't had anything like prickly heat or dengue (ask Dug) etc.(touch wood!)

Charles 11 has two watches & he has lent me one for as long as I am here which is very nice – thank you for your offer of one when I come back. I don't really want to part – sell mine, as it is about the only 21 birthday present I have left! But I'll think it over!

Nearly all the 'coolies' who work in this building (Cathay) are women - clean windows, dust & sweep etc, & they wear sort of blue pyjama suits & funny hats. I can't draw them at all!! When I went down to lunch today about 12 of them were sitting on their haunches in the corridor having their dinner (they bring it each morning in baskets). They had a bowl of rice & about 6 other dishes in the middle, & all picked out of them with chopsticks!

I'm quite friendly with a WAAF officer called Harris here - & this morning we hitch hiked into town where she had to deliver a letter – then we called on Charles 11 & a friend of hers in the Navy & went to a hotel & had some coffee! I am going to spend the whole of Thursday afternoon shopping properly & hope to get some nice things.

How did Dug get on at Oxford?

I hope you are all okey-dokey and not too cold, I'm so hot!

13th Dec 45.

I got two letters from Ma yesterday – one dated 23rd & one 30 November. I am glad Ma is better. I'm sorry I did the map wrong – can't think why, as we came down the coast by Sumatra & I saw it through field glasses. I find it very difficult to remember what I've told you in other letters – so I shall keep an account of my doings & tick them off!

Did I tell you that Violet Johnston's youngest brother Sam is out here – I am trying to find out where he is – which is difficult as I don't know what he is in – I've written & asked Violet too. Then this morning a WRNS officer told me she had met a girl last night who said she knew him & that he knew I was here &

was trying to contact me! So I'm hoping to find him out thro' this girl! I remember him well at Wimbledon - he must be about 26 or 27 now – he used to design aeroplanes in Portsmouth before he joined up.

On Tuesday I went out to a sort of party with the naval people we went out with last Sunday. There were 7 girls & 7 men – all Naval officers – dressed in their white evening dress – looked so nice. We wore short ones. We went to their mess – a huge bungalow. Before we went Pip another girl & I (who went from our mess) had a good dinner. When we got there we were given little sort of savouries etc & talked - & then we were given serviettes on our laps & platefuls of turkey, tongue & salad & then peaches & ice cream! I managed it quite well!

We didn't do anything much except talk, dance a bit to the gramophone. I played the piano a bit, not at all well as I had no music & it was a rotten piano. Another man, a Lieut also played badly I thought! He was very tall & good looking & he is John Rouson who does those cartoons "Boy meets Girl" in the Sunday Despatch. He & that one called Dick are two who work directly under the Admiralty & go round discovering mines & torpedoes etc, & finding out new sorts - sort of spies - & do a lot of under sea diving - very interesting to talk to. They are two of only 32 survivors from the job which had 500 men at the beginning of the war - all the others blown up while at work. They've both got rows of medals.

Last night I stayed in & washed my hair!

It's very amusing here to see along the sides of the roads heaps of small stands with people selling fruit, cigarettes (mostly black market ones stolen or sold, by the services). Also there are lots cooking food - some of those are sort of 'travelling' ones carried on a man's back (a cooker one side food other side) - then he squats down has a little charcoal fire in a tin & cooks things like bits of meat on the end of a stick - holds them over the fire & keeps pouring bits of fat on. The other side thing is a box containing all the food etc, & two weeny stools which the customers go up & squat on. As they go about they ring a bell.

I am going to have lunch here today & then go shopping with Charles - its so much better having a man - they don't diddle you quite so much.

The amahs who wash our clothes every day iron with charcoal irons, I expect you know what they are like.

We are making plans for Christmas now. Patricia & John have booked a table for 30 at the Phoenix Officers Club (the café under this building) for Xmas Eve dinner & dance. We have bought 3 boxes of crackers for it – awful price 66 dollars each box - & they are Tom Smiths so are probably 6 years old & no good! (I didn't pay!)

Yesterday afternoon when I got back at 5.30 I went swimming at the Club with another girl - which was very nice as it was especially hot yesterday. It seems so funny to read about you having ice, snow, fog etc.

I have bought your pink jackets sleeves & collar here today - finished - & will try & send them by air today. I'm getting on fine with the violet one – front right side is finished – can't think what sort of shape it will turn out –but I'm doing a highish neck, I've only used 1 ½ oz for right front – so I may have enough for the whole thing with just a panel of grey down the back – do you agree to that?

I've just heard that our clerk couldn't send you that coconut – they wouldn't accept anymore to post – I'm sorry.

I'll certainly write something to Mrs Stringer – I'm glad she's had her op' at last.

17th Dec 45.

I enclose some Japanese money – which is worthless now.*

I got two letters from Ma on Saturday – the latest dated 2nd December, thank you. I also got one from Hildegard & Mrs Buchanan (Cardiff) Hildergard seems to be coming here definitely as a F.A.N.Y.

Last Friday evening Patricia, John (her friend), me & Charles (the Naval Lieut) had dinner in our mess & then went to a private picture show at the Pavilion Cinema - my Eric asked us to go. It was a preview of a picture which will be put on for the troops & is something to do with our Department as all the films for the troops come under us. We went above the larger cinema into a very small one - only about 15 people there - so it was rather nice - a very good picture called 29 Acacia Avenue with Gordon Harker. Afterwards we went back to Charles mess & talked - & Patricia's John did a lot of conjuring tricks - awfully good - & then found he had missed the last ferry bus back to Changi - so we got a truck & took him back - Patricia & I didn't get home until 3.30 am!

I didn't go out on Saturday, & had a feast of tinned peaches & cream in my room with another girl, Helen Stewart

Yesterday morning (Sunday) it poured with rain & stopped about 11 & I went bathing with Charles at the Club - then had dinner in his mess. In the afternoon we just sat & sat & knitted your thing & had dinner at the Phoenix Club - I was so hungry we had two dinners!!

The atmosphere here is very damp - & everything feels damp - & all our shoes & things get green mildew on if they are left even for two days.

Did I tell you I went shopping last Thursday - & went bust on some material for an evening dress for Christmas - it is black georgette (!) & some black silk for a petticoat. I am going to have it with no sleeves & a little coatee. I also got a lovely evening bag – all white furry – (probably rabbit!) - it wasn't very expensive - & Charles insisted on giving it to me! So I took it. Next month I'm going to start buying shoes. Tell DD I shall probably buy her some to bring home. What size does she take?

All the materials here are real silks, georgette, crepe de chine etc - lovely stuff - do you want me to bring any of any sort home? It is really only useful for undies & none of us are "that sort"! I had letters this morning from Greyhound & Miss Chennels.

We have got a chest of drawers each in our rooms now - & Patricia & I are still only two in our room, which is nice.

Jap banknotes

18ᵗʰ Dec 45. 3.30 pm

Typical- Miss Chennels says Jean was going to India – but her papers got mixed up & another girl was sent instead!!!

Meow!

I always find it very difficult to start a letter if I haven't any to thank for - so that's a good start!! I'm afraid all my letters sound as though I'm very gay here, & I must say I do enjoy going out - but I'm sure a few months will be enough.

We always get lots of invitations to go on different ships etc here, & some of us put our names down to go on one yesterday called the Aulania to a sherry party at 6.30. A naval lorry called for us at 6.00 (8 of us 4 WRNS 3 WAAFS & me) & we drove for miles to the Naval Base right in the north of the island. We drove right up to the ship which was in the docks & went up a gangway

& had to salute the quarter deck or something - I just copied everyone else! It was a lovely ship - all White - used to be Cunard White Star, (it's now a 'repair' ship. We went in uniform.) all decorated with flags, music playing & about 60 naval officers all in their white mess kit. There was lovely food – snacks & sherry etc. & we all talked a lot. I went down the stairs (companion way!) with two others to the cloakroom & I slipped and fell - but only got a bruise on my b-m! About 8.00 p.m. 3 of us were asked by 4 of the officers to go to Johore over the causeway to an Officers Club there - just what I've always longed to do. So we all got in a nice car & drove there - about ¼ hr - had a lovely dinner in the Club & danced & they drove us back about 12.30 a.m. I palled up with a Naval Dentist from Chester such a nice man - the best of the bunch! All the naval dentists are called "Toothy". I do hope you are all keeping warm - don't let Ma catch another cold. Its very hot here this afternoon - the sun is streaming in our window. I have written to the Forwarding Officer at Liverpool to ask what ship my trunk is on.

19th Dec 45.

I have just got a letter from Ma dated 11 December & all your Xmas cards & Chet's letter. Thank you all so much. Please thank my 'Him' for his (or her?) card quite the best & Ma's & I love the animal one too. The record I made I put in a cardboard hat box near my dressing table in my room. It was full of other records too & mine was near the top - be careful taking it out as it is rather large. It has to have special needles - they are either with the record or on my table in a paper packet. To make it go properly put the speed on fast. Also, after using the record - please wipe it over with a piece of soft rag & oil (bicycle oil or something similar) as it is special stuff.

I think I must have had all your letters now – except some between 2 & 11 December which will probably come soon. It is funny tho' I haven't had one newspaper from you, so I shouldn't bother with them.

All the natives here love gold teeth (for BOSS!) & sometimes have a whole mouthful of them!

That naval Lieut Charles is half Swiss (name Stubin) & knows Switzerland well - all our places. That girl, I know Ebeilie, who I came out with, lives in a bungalow now - I've got to like her much better. She has heard that her trunk has arrived in Colombo & as mine was with hers, I'm hoping mine is there too.

We are having dinner & dance at the Phoenix Club (the one under the Cathay) tonight - Patricia & John, Charles & me & Harry (a WAAF officer - Harris - very nice) & Ted (who is Tedde's nephew). Lord Louis is also having a party too, so it should be rather fun. I still might manage to send Boss's & Cht's sandals with a Duty Free label parcel – but I can't get down to finding out about it! I hope you will all have a nice Xmas – I shall be thinking of you & wish I was there too – Patricia & I often look at the time & then work out what our respective families would be doing – we are 7 ½ hrs ahead of you – so you work it out too! Not bad your last letter only took 8 days to get here.

22nd Dec 45.

I have been down the town this morning & sent you a telegram - it is an E.F.M. one & you have to choose their phases by numbers - so it might be rather peculiar wording! I went in Genearal K??? car with Patricia – as she works for him & is able to borrow it sometimes. We have got a third girl in our room now – but we asked her to come as we are very friendly with her & we all go out a lot together – she is a WAAF called Arlette Harris (Harry is her nickname).

I bought myself a pair of crepe shoes yesterday, brown leather with crepe soles. There is a new thing out here now for sending parcels home. We take the things to the W.V.S. in the G.P.O. & they do all the packing & sending – so Boss's & Chet's sandals will definitely go next week - & will probably take 2 months to arrive!

Please thank Douglas very much for his letter about Changi etc. I showed it to a man who works there & he seemed to know the places. It is very difficult for me to get there - except at night to a dance or something - because of the transport - but I shall try & go there one day to find Dug's tracks & treasure. I couldn't

304

possibly walk there like he did! over 15 miles. He would enjoy seeing all the Jap prisoners working there.

I have sent a very interesting Phoenix magazine home – full of pictures of Singapore & I enclose a few more I got today.

I am storing up a lot of tinned stuff to bring home, fruit etc, I've also got a tin of lambs tongue - is that any good? I think I can get some ox tongue too.

It is terribly damp here & if we don't wipe our shoes & clothes & suitcases etc, at least every 2 days they go all green with mildew. Also the rats are awful - get in our chest of drawers - they've eaten 3 buttons off my blue cotton dress. We put some poison down & it has been taken.

24th Dec 45. 10 a.m. – Christmas Eve
Our second typewriter has just come, but hasn't travelled too well and is tied up with string, and it sticks now and again - which will account for all mistakes.

It's funny to think this is Christmas Eve - the sun is shining and it is very hot. When we woke up this morning we tried to pretend how cold it was and that there was snow outside, but it didn't really work!

I got a letter from Ma on Saturday dated 7 December, but I'd had one before dated 11th December, which is the latest date I've had one.

We have got a big party on tonight at the Phoenix Club here - 30 of us altogether, organised by Patricia, which should be quite nice. We have got a long table for dinner, and there will be dancing afterwards.

Tomorrow morning I am hoping to go to church at 7.30 hours if I can get transport, with Patricia, and again at 10.30. We shall go to St.Andrews Cathedral. We are having a Christmas lunch in our mess and have been allowed to invite one guest each, so Harry and I are joining up and inviting her friend Ted (nephew of Tedder) and my friend Charles - both naval officers from H.M.S."Round the Bend" (as they call their bungalow). In the evening Harry and I are going to their mess to have another Christmas dinner! I am afraid my figure is going to suffer.

I think it will be a good thing if Dug stays in the Army for a bit and looks round. After all, the pay is very good, and couldn't he ask to be posted near home on compassionate grounds.

Charles has given me a necklace for Christmas because I lost mine at their party a few weeks ago. It is sort of black and silverfish thing with a sort of native priest done in silver on it and has a thin silver chain - it is Siamese work – there are a lot of things made like it, cig. cases, ash trays etc. So I thought I had better give him something in return - although I haven't got much money left till January when I can draw my next pay. So I've composed one of my usual poems and enclose a copy for you! ala Hiawatha.* The case I got really was second hand, but holds 32 cigarettes quite easily, and was cheap!

I went to sleep the whole of yesterday morning on our balcony, with another girl, had lunch in the mess and then went back for more sleep and knitting etc. in the afternoon, and washed my hair. It was rather nice. I went to the pictures in the evening and saw a thing called "Sailors Three" with Claude Hulbert in it – quite funny.

I am glad that Yolande is going to do stop-gap in Boss's job and that she'll be able to go back there. I think the whole of this H.Q. will be closing in April, so I should definitely be coming then - if not before.

I wrote to Mrs Stringer in hospital the other day – quite a nice one!

I shall like to hear what you've all given each other for Christmas - I am sorry you won't have anything from me – but I am going to try and collect some nice things to bring home with me.

Would Ma like me to get her any counterpanes? They are very cheap and quite nice material, and are made rather like the ones Ma used to make, only the patterns of flowers are printed on the material and not appliquéd. Let me know. I've got some nice hand towels.

We haven't any hot water yet in our bungalows and it is rather hard to keep clean in cold all the time! There are a lot of bathrooms in the Cathay Building here, Eric has one leading from his office, with hot water, so one lunch time I shall bring my things and have one here. I always have a shower every day (cold!), as I find it easier than getting into a cold bath. Actually it is a lovely feeling having a shower when ONE is hot!

Could someone sometime look in the big brown trunk in my cupboard and just have a look and see if my skates are alright and not rusty. Are the moths making hay? Also Boss might give my accordion an airing now and again. Why not have Dug learn the cello? And we could go round as a quartette!

I have given our four male clerks a bottle of beer and 10 cigarettes each for Christmas - out of my ration - as I have plenty. I have given Cynthia, our WREN, three bottles of beer and 10 cigs, as she had all her ration of beer stolen from her bungalow, and she always gives it to her boyfriend. The thieving round here is awful, and anyone can go into the bungalows any time, and they are often empty - the doors are open and are never shut or locked. Several people have had their electric irons taken. We had two being sent here from Kandy for our use, and the crate was broken open on the way and they were both gone.

I do hope you will all have a happy Christmas and enjoy Aunt Nellies – and SEE THAT MA DOES NOT GET F.C.

*Feeling that I'd like to give you
Something small and something useful
Something you could always carry
Carry in your trouser pocket
Or your shirt or mess kit jacket,
I bethought me go my money
Lack of money, not abundance
Feeling shameful, very shameful
That I'd spend it on my own clothes
Not on giving things to others
Things that would be worth the buying,
Gifts that cost a lot of money
Worthy of the one who gets them.
Thinking thus I wandered idly
Wandered over Singapore Town
Looking, seeking, never finding,
Hourly getting more anxious,

Anxious lest I fail to find some
Present that would give you pleasure.
Walking, running, ever faster
Down to Raffles Place and High Street
Back along the North Bridge Road, till
There I stopped and looked and entered
Entered there a shop whose window
Looked inviting, full of presents,
Prices suiting even my purse.
Bargaining with Chinese salesmen
Trying hard to beat their charges
Down to normal saner levels.
Eventually a cigarette case
Old and second hand and tatty
Covered over with stains and mildew
Drew my eye as being cheapest
Cheapest but the best in value
For the merger sum I offered.
Knowing this was what you needed
Just for use in South East Asia
Having stored your silver good one.
So I bought and here present it
With my very kindest wishes.

By the way the cigarettes are not intended for your use, but
should be handed back to me, when you have seen how many it
holds which should be quite enough for you to smoke in any day.

26th Dec 45. 1.30 p.m. In my room after lunch.
I do hope your Christmas is going alright - I'll tell you what I've
been doing. On Xmas Eve Patricia & John had arranged a party
at the Phoenix Club for 30 of us - all very nice people including
a lot of ATS officers I know well from Changi. She stayed behind
to decorate the table with crackers etc & I came back here & put
a sheet over the table downstairs of our bungalow – got flowers
from the hedge - lovely sort of fuchias(?) & glasses & drinks etc.
We had to get ready in a hurry - I wore my new black dress which
I am not too pleased with. It is beautifully made - but he lost my
drawing & did it entirely another pattern & it is too low behind

so I have to be pinned a bit. Actually I think it looks quite nice - but when I went to have a fitting I was horrified he had gone & muddled my pattern with Patricia's & made it with no back at all, & just a strap round the neck!

So I made him alter the whole thing to have proper arm holes. Anyway all the guests arrived by about 7.30 p.m.& we had sherry etc & then went to the Phoenix in several cars. We had a long table at the end of the room - & there were flowers - orchids - for all the girls. They are very plentiful here & when we go out with anyone - it is always "done" to give us a spray!

The dinner was good hors d'oeuvre, soup, pork & veg & ice cream, & we danced a lot & after it was over some of us went in the kitchen & had sausage & fried potatoes!

There is a gas strike on in Singapore now! & cooking is most difficult - they had a lot of sort of braziers in the kitchen there.

I met that man Harry Fry (the solicitor from Liverpool) who took me out first in Kandy - & he has asked me to go to ALFSEA at Changi to a dance on Saturday.

Yesterday morning Harry (the WAAF) Pip (a WAC(1) - ATS who live in India) & I went to church. We hitch hiked in a lorry which drove us up to the door, & the driver, a Captain - thought it a good idea & came in too. It was funny to see cars, trucks & lorries all parked outside the Cathedral. We got there about 10.15 (service at 10.30) & had to queue to get in the doors. The place was already packed full of people standing all round the sides. The man took us & put us in the choir stalls to wait & he then fetched some kneeling stools & we sat between the choir & altar - & gradually that all filled up too - people sitting on the pulpit steps & the extra clergy seats. It is a lovely Cathedral, very light & airy - lovely stained glass windows - the lights of which all reflected on the white pillars. It doesn't seem too high - two candles & white lilies on the altar - but no other decorations. It was a very nice service O Come, Hark the Herald, & While Shepherds watched - one lesson - & usual prayers & a sermon by the Bishop of Colombo - who had been asked to come by the Archbishop of Canterbury - quite a good sermon - he is exactly like a cross between Dr Camps & Christopher Bunch! The Bishop of Singapore helped. The choir was a mixture of Chinese

& Malayan girls - English, black & Chinese men - all with white surplices.

Lord Louis Mountbatten and his WRNS daughter were there in the front row and I had a very good view of them.

We hitched back on another lorry & at 12.30 p.m. Harry's friend Ted & Charles (who live in the same mess) came to lunch in our mess. We had a table for 4. They had decorated our mess beautifully with red leaves, balloons, silver tinsel etc, & a sort of tree meant to be a Xmas tree (there are no firs here). We had turkey & pork & veg, (soup first) plum pudding & sauce, apples, nuts & sort of savouries & we all sang etc, & finished about 2.30 p.m.. Then we all went to sleep on our balcony. Ted & Charles went about 6. Harry & I went to our mess for supper - cold ham & veg & tinned pears - then at 9 Ted & Charles came back & Harry & Ted went to a party with an Admiral & Charles & I started to walk to the Tanglin Club to dance. It was very dark on the road & I fell in the ditch! No water but rather muddy - so we came back I washed & so we didn't go - but talked on the balcony till the others came back about 12 p.m.

This morning I have been to sleep on the balcony & have just had a good meal.

Are you bored with all this - or do you like hearing all the details!!

We have just seen a lovely bird sitting on our fence - blue back, long yellow beak, dark head & white front – What is it?! An Beat should know.

2.30 p.m. must go now - Harry & I are going up to HMS 'Round the Bend' that naval mess - to help decorate for their party to night.

We have got yesterday, today, & New Years Day as holidays.

I got a letter from Ma yesterday dated 5 Dec – thank you – also the Surrey Comet of Oct 5th! First paper I've had.

27th Dec 45. 4.30 p.m. in Office
I haven't had any letters from you for a few days but several Christmas cards from the chickens! The one that arrived this morning was pretty good - from Leg - he can certainly draw the

best and has the best feathers. I got one from Horn yesterday - thank you very much - everybody is tickled with them.

Yesterday afternoon Harry and I went up to that naval mess - H.M.S. Round the Bend to help them do the decorations - as only one of them, Ted, was able to get off that afternoon, and we had a whole holiday. It was rather fun, we picked lovely yellow and red flowers from the hedge in the garden, and heaps of quite large red and green speckled leaves. There is nothing like them in England, but they looked lovely in vases (tins disguised). First of all we hung large flags all along the front of the bungalow, which is a huge verandah the whole length of the place. Then I put pieces of string round the pillars and intertwined ferns and red leaves in between all the sort of balustrades. We started decorating at 3 p.m. and didn't finish until 6.45 p.m.. We then got taken home and changed awful quick and got back about 7.45 p.m. with three other girls from our mess, in evening dress. It was a very nice dance - a Dutch band of about 6 and lovely buffet food - there were about 24 people altogether.

Their bungalow was some sort of Japanese officers mess - and in the garden there is the remains of a Jap tank, and an overturned car, and there are heaps of sort of slit trenches dug.

I am sorry the bank are so stupid still. I wrote to them about my name about 10 days ago, so they should be alright by now.

The Major in my office Major Cronin, has a lovely radiogram in his mess with about 300 good records, overtures, sonatas etc. all high class stuff played by the best orchestras, and on Sunday five of us are going there to have a sort of recital. He does quite a lot of it for small parties of people. I typed his catalogue out for him, and we are going to choose what we want to hear.

Must go & catch my bus at 5 p.m..

31st Dec 45

I haven't had any letters from you for a week, but I believe a lot of mail came yesterday, so I'm hoping. I keep on having chicken Christmas cards which cheer me up, and I am composing a suitable reply for onward transmission to the hens! I had a letter from Greyhound too – I'm afraid I hardly ever write to her.

I have just sent a letter to a firm in South Africa asking them to send you a parcel of food etc.

1 lb castor sugar (or brown if possible)

½ lb icing sugar

½ candied peel

1lb currants

1lb slab of chocolate

I hope it won't be too long in arriving. I have heard from the man in Delhi that he has sent that one I ordered, and I shall write him again and have them sent regularly.

Last Saturday night I went over to Changi to a dance in the officers' club there with Harry Fry, that Lieut.Colonel I went out with in Kandy. He fetched me in a car at about 7.45 p.m. and we got to Changi at 8.30 p.m. and had a buffet super and danced etc. The floor and band weren't too good unfortunately, so he is coming over here to the Phoenix one day next week. He drove me back about 12.30 a.m.

Yesterday, Sunday, I washed my hair and lazed all the morning and afternoon. In the evening the Major from my office Paddy Cronin (very Irish and very old maidish but very nice!) came to dinner in our mess with me and Harry (the WAAF) and her friend Tedder, and afterwards we went to Paddy's room in his mess and listened to his radiogram until about 11 p.m. Very nice. He lives in a lovely bungalow about 10 minutes away from us by car. He has a wonderful selection of records – all good ones – I made a catalogue for him of them all a little while ago. He has a very nice room – long and narrow with windows along one side, and nice furniture.

I enclose a copy of the program of things which we chose*(So Boss can see my musical tastes). Harry (the WAAF) plays the piano and has reached exactly the same stage as me – she passed the Final exam too, but she knows much more about music than I do – she knows things like Boss does! She can't remember things on the piano any more than I can without the music, thank goodness!

I forgot to tell Boss the other day that when we saw that picture privately called 29 Acacia Avenue, it was written by Sydney and Muriel Box, and I think she is Viv's sister.

I am sorry I can't send anything for Ma's birthday, but really it is difficult to do that. Once again I don't think I shall send the shoes by the W.V.S. as it is more than likely they will never reach you, as we have to get a declaration form from the customs and put on the outside of the parcel what is in it, and they are sure to get stolen.

If ever you feel like sending me a cable I shall be very pleased to get it! I don't know how much they are your end, but they are very cheap here and quite quick. I am going to send one for Ma's birthday – we do it from Cable and Wireless Ltd (your one is in the Strand). It would be nice if you did sometime, as I would know how you all were within a day or two instead of waiting for letters which seem to take some time nowadays.

We have got another holiday tomorrow being New Years Day

I'm getting on fine with your violet cardigan, and have finished both the fronts and have started the sleeves next. I have ideas of embroidering coloured flowers all over it in different coloured wools – do you agree? I think Boss may have to finish off the final bits of neck etc. as I can't manage that without a pattern. I wonder if your pink jacket has arrived yet.

It has been extra hot here the last few days, but usually quite a nice breeze too. Do let me know where Christopher Bunch is as I would like to see him.

Theres nothing more to say at the moment. I'm longing to hear from you again.

*1. Overture, Finlandia, Sibelius,

2. Violin Concerto, 'E' Minor, Mendelson,

3. Violin, La Capricienne, Elgar & Melodie, Tchaikovsky,

4. Violin, Le Coq D'or, Rimsky Korsakov & Air for the G String, Bach,

5. Piano Concerto, No 1. in B Flat Minor, Tchaikovsky

INTERVAL

6. Overture, Fingal's Cave, Mendelssohn

7. Piano, Ecossaises, Chopin & Waltz 'E' Flat Major, Chopin

8. Piano, One Fine Day, Bach & Sonata in 'G' Major, Scarlatti

9. Piano, Nutcracker, Tchaikovsky

10. Tales from the Vienna Woods, Strauss

11. Piano Concerto, No.2, Beethoven

First of all - many happy returns of the day to Ma – I do hope you will give her a nice birthday and everything she wants (within reason!) and I'll present my present when I come back – soon I hope.

I'm so hot at the moment its difficult to type, as everything is so sticky, and it is thundering and raining a bit too.

I had a very nice day yesterday. Slept on my balcony all the morning, and about 12.30 went up to HMS Round the Bend, that naval mess, to lunch. They had a piano there, which they'd hired for a week, and I took my few pieces of music and we all played and sang until lunch at 1.30. At least I played and they sang - five naval officers, all very nice. One of them could play a bit too, and he and I played things like Lily of Laguna etc. together, me at the top and he at the bottom. One of them had a banjo too, and played it quite well.

We had the most lovely lunch - curry and I had two enormous helpings - then fresh fruit salad. Afterwards we all sunbathed in their garden – I wore a pair of white shorts and white shirt belonging to one of them, as my dress was so hot. One of them took photographs, which I hope to be able to send you sometime.

In the evening two of them, Charles and Ted came to dinner with Harry (WAAF) and me in our mess, and afterwards we changed and went to the Atomic Club, which is a new club, just opened, run by a Hungarian. They have a lovely place with sort of open verandahs all round, a good dance floor and band. We are not allowed to eat any cooked meals outside our messes, so we had some crab salad - and I drank lemon squash all the evening. They had other drinks! We got back about 12.30 a.m.

The day before, on New Years Eve, about four of us went to the Phoenix Club where they had dinner and dance and got back at 1 a.m. quite nice.

Doesn't it sound awful, all this social life? I do hope you are interested in all my activities - anyway I shall have had so much of it when I return I shall be content to stay at home at night, I should think.

I have just been rung up by a girl called Betty Crawford, who is a WAAF in Supremo's office, and arranges all his social life, and she has asked me to go to dinner at Government House tomorrow - it's really a sort of Command to go - so it will be rather nice. I do wish I had my black velvet evening dress here, as I feel so comfy in it, and the black one I've had made, he made entirely the wrong pattern, as I told you, and I have to be pinned up underneath which is rather uncomfortable. I'll write and tell you all about it on Friday. I think everyone gets asked to these "dos" sooner or later.

I wonder if you have had any bananas yet - I see a ship has arrived in England with some. The shops and stalls here are full of them, but I never buy them now as they are so fattening. I am a bit worried about my figure again - either I 'm getting fatter or my clothes are shrinking!

I suppose its partly not wearing any corset things – but it is impossible to wear anything in this heat – although I do usually in the evenings.

I wonder how you got on at Christmas – I thought about you a lot, and kept adding up the time when you would be doing certain things – most times it came to the times when you would be making fresh brew!

Frank Owen hasn't arrived here yet from Calcutta, and no one knows where he is, which is rather funny, as all the big wigs keep asking for him. They say he is touring round Burma in a jeep!

Everyone here goes round saying one expression now - we use it all day long, about everything, it is GOOD-O!

Do let me know Christopher Bunch's address – I'd love to get in touch with him and get invited to his island. I think I know which it is, but am not sure.

Please give my love to D.D., the aunts, Mrs. Howard, Harper, Cissie etc. I haven't written to anyone but you for ages – but will one day.

I'm sorry my letters are so dull now, but hope to liven them up one day!

3rd Jan 46. 9.45 a.m.

My darling Ma, Boss, Dug, Wop, Nip, Leg, Horn and Hun

I went to the Phoenix Club last night with two naval officers I met on that boat I once went on, the Aulania. It wasn't bad - one of them was quite interesting, he is an entomologist and is out here doing things to mosquitoes. He used to be on the convoys going to Russia. We went in a truck which was rather difficult to get in and out of, and I hurt my big toe getting out, broke the nail right down - but its not very bad now.

I'm dreading tonight going to Supremo's to dinner - it means I have got to be pleasant for a whole evening, awful fag!

I can't think of anything more to say at this early hour.

4th Jan 46.

Its lovely, I've had four letters to-day from Ma – two were dated 19th and 21st December, and two others dated 27th December – only 8 days ago. I have just had all the newspapers you sent - Sketches from October 11 to 19th and the Times for that week too. I can't think why they take so long and letters don't. Still it is very interesting to read all the news as we get so out of touch with all the small things that are happening in England.

I'm rather upset to hear about Boss definitely leaving – is it really necessary, as I'm quite sure to be home in the spring. I feel awful about it.

The name of Lady Thomson's relation is Squadron Leader Mckinnon, whose wife and two kids live in Scotland. Actually he is awfully "wet" and a bore, and he has now left our branch and is working for the war Crimes Commission. He is very tall and thin and quite nice looking. He used to fly in Costal Command.

I must tell you about last night now, when I went to dine at Government House. (You can brag about this to all the Kingston Hill'ites as much as you like, as it is really something worth talking about!)

INTERVAL – there is a terrific thunderstorm on at the moment and Boss would be terrified! Pouring with rain.

There were four of us women invited, me and Harry (WAAF) a FANY called Pamela Hempsted, who is very nice, and a civilian girl who works in one of the branches, sort of civil servant. Supremo's car called for us at our bungalow punctually at 8 o'clock, and we were ready, (Harry and I). We then called for the other two at their bungalows and were then driven to Government house, which isn't very far from us, in some lovely grounds - like Richmond Park, all grass and trees. Two of the A.D.Cs were on the steps to greet us and took us into a sort of drawing room on the first floor. The house is simply enormous, and he lives in one wing and has a sort of flat with just four rooms - a living room, dining room, bedroom and spare room. It was very nicely furnished and there were photographs on the walls of Bertie, Betty, Lillibet and Margaret Rose, all signed! We were given cocktails and after about five minutes he came in and we were introduced to him. When we arrived one of the A.D.Cs asked us our names, and remembered them after that for all the introductions etc. Some other people came then - a civilian man called Sir Harold MacMichael, who apparently is a very big bug in the Colonial Office, and his A.D.C. who is a Captain. There was also a Major invited, who works in the transport section of SACSEA. The two A.D.Cs are Captain Brockman, R.N., and Wing Commander St John, both awfully nice and so friendly - also a Major Papps, who did all the introducing and telling us where to sit etc.

We all sat round and talked for about 10 minutes - Supremo talked quit a lot and told us how fed up he was with all the trouble in Java - he was most interesting about it all and discussed it quite freely. Then we all got up and went into dinner. I was very thrilled as I was put on his right, and Harry was on his left, places of honour.

This is an awful typewriter – it got damaged coming from Kandy and is tied up with string, but still jumps!

We talked very friendlily at dinner - I told him about Douglas and his hidden treasure and that Daddy was a Parson - that was because we discussed the service on Christmas Day at the Cathedral when the Bishop of Colombo preached. Supremo says he has an argument to start with him, as in his sermon said that all women should be treated like mothers and sisters, and he says if that happened the world would come to an end with no population!

317

THEN - what do you think happened? (Turn over and see - ½)

SOMETHING came in the room and walked right through it - A SIAMESE CAT!

So of course that started me off on them, and he has two of them, they were flown out from Siam for him, and he has five real Siamese kittens, born last week. I did want to see them, but didn't like to ask.

FOOD - we started with very nice soup, then a piece of fried fish with lovely sauce, then roast beef, Yorkshire, and real boiled potatoes (which we don't often get, we mostly get them mashed, dehydrated) and peas, then real pineapple or bananas or apples. I had a slice of pineapple. Everything was beautifully served. Polished table with sort of tiles for mats with mottoes on 'In Honour Bound', or something like that, with the Royal Coat of Arms. We had proper desert plates and finger bowls. We drank lemon squash (at least lime - real limes) and coffee and port.

There is a show on in Singapore for three weeks of the London Ballet, and I thought I'd improve my education by going to see it - so Harry and I put our names down for tickets, and of course drew two for yesterday, and so couldn't go as we were going to Supremo. So during dinner he asked if we'd seen it and I said no, and that we were going that night as we'd drawn tickets! So he was very upset, and told his A.D.C. to remember to ring up and see that we got tickets for another night! So I hope he'll remember.

After dinner we all went down to a huge sort of ballroom where there were about 50 chairs one end and the screen the other, and had a picture show. (Actually my department had to arrange to supply the picture as we deal with films and he always gets them from us.) There were about 20 other ranks and servants at the back, and we all sat in the front row. The two other girls were put one each side of Supremo, and I sat one end next to Sir Harold MacMichael - who was very bored with the picture and said it was too complicated for him! He also told me he hated Ballet and could see nothing in it at all. He was quite a nice old boy, and is, apparently, extremely important out here,

First we saw a news reel which was very good - all about the trials in Germany - excellent pictures of Goering, Hess etc. I do hope you've seen it too. Then a Mickey Mouse - very good and then the big picture called Road to Utopia with Bing Crosby and Bob Hope - and it was rotten. Actually I went to sleep practically the whole time, and Harry did too! It was meant to be funny, but wasn't. I don't think Supremo liked it much either.

That was over about 11.15 and we went into one of the 'state' drawing rooms downstairs for drinks. It was a huge room, lovely furniture, and large portraits of George V and Mary etc., On one of the tables there was a lovely box with an inscription on it that was given to Supremo by the Prince of Wales on one of his hunting expeditions, with a picture on top of them all actually doing the hunting etc.

Quite a lot of big bugs of SACSEA came for drinks - they live in a bungalow in the grounds of Government House - Major Gen. Kimmins, Air Marshal Gibbs (who I talked to) and a few others. There was whisky and lime squash to drink, all of us women had lime. Then about 11.45 we were told our car was ready, so we went and Supremo came to the steps to see us off and shook hands, and I thanked him for having me.

I really enjoyed myself very much. I wore my new black georgette dress, and think I looked alright.

I found out where Christopher Bunch is stationed and have written to him. He is at H.M.S. Landswell, where I spent one Sunday on a rocket ship, it is near Changi. I have never discovered Violet's brother yet – my only hope is that she will answer my letter sometime and tell me whether he is still here.

I am so glad the tea has arrived safely – and that the Dr. is pleased with his.

Did Boss ever get those foreign stamps I sent? I hope the other sleeve will arrive – if it doesn't you'll have to cut one arm off!

I am glad you all enjoyed Christmas at Aunt Nellie's – I quite agree with you about the drinking to those absent.

I wrote to my bank about a month ago and asked them to cable £30 to the Mercantile Bank in Singapore, and they've never done it yet – so if you feel you can, could you possibly ring them up and tell them I want the money at once if they haven't done it by then. I wrote them a long letter and ticked them off about my name – so they shouldn't be in a muddle about me now. They are Messers. Glyn Mills (Holts Branch), Whitehall. I wrote them on 10th December – and the money should have got here by now.

P.S. After dinner we went to his bathroom, thro' his bedroom - & I put my coatee on his bath towel! The lavatory is on a sort of throne! Steps up to it!

7th Jan46. H.Q. S.A.C.S.E.A.,(Singapore),
S.E.A.C., (Service Relations Division)

Thank you Boss very much for your letter dated 23rd December, which cheered me up no end as regards leaving her job – although I hope she'll be able to go back one day if she wants to. I had a letter from Hildegard Francis this morning – she has arrived in Calcutta, and thinks she may be coming here sometime – so I have given her my address.

Please don't forget to bring my weighing machine back from Port Regis sometime – as I don't want to lose it.

Also please don't sell my motor bicycle - as I think it will be useful to me when I come back. Someone might have it out and give it a clean sometime please - as I did clean Boss's car for her!

I haven't done anything since I wrote last. I went up to the Tanglin officers Club and danced after dinner on Saturday with Charles (the Naval Lieut.). It is rather nice as we are only about 3 minutes walk away from the club and we can just go in and sit and dance when we want - no money needed.

It is very difficult to go to places far afield as it is so hard to get transport. Yesterday, Sunday, I washed my hair and sewed and knitted all morning – slept all afternoon, and was duty officer all the evening in the Ardmore Flats where all the other ranks live, WRNS, ATS, WAAFs. It only means sitting there all the evening and checking them in at the times they should come, and seeing there are no males lurking round after 10.30 p.m.. There is also a Royal Marine sentry on guard all night.

I can't make up my mind (as usual!) whether or not to have my hair cut shorter. It has got quite long again and is still quite curly at the ends - but it is so hot on my neck. On the other hand, if I have it cut I can't roll it up round a ribbon which I do sometimes. Lots of girls here who have dead straight hair at home find it sort of curls a bit here and looks rather nice - because of the damp climate I suppose.

I had a letter from D.D. on Saturday, and also one from Phyllis Smith who sent you all her love, (Boss must explain to Ma who she is - she came over for the day once). Her fiancée who was a prisoner in Hong Kong has arrived home in England and she is being married on 19th, and then he has to go back to Japan, and she hopes to follow sometime. Her mother is going to Canada to stay with Tubby (her sister Frances – who I was very friendly with at school).

That Junior Commander Lane (friend of Myer, that creature who had ?T.B.?) has arrived out here, and is not liked by anyone, funnily enough - even those who didn't know her before. (I suppose I could be had for libel over that!) but her manner is so sort of unpleasant. Actually I don't think she can help it, she was born abrupt. I have been very pleasant to her but don't go out of my way to meet her. Apparently she asked the head WRS officer if she could come into our bungalow, but I said I'd walk out if she did (!) so she has been put in another one. I don't mean to be nasty about her, but she just isn't my style.

I am sorry to hear about Mrs Pettit, and also sorry that it has scared Mr Davis - although I should think he is very strong.

3.15 p.m. There's nothing much more to say. I have just had a letter from Marjorie Fletcher - only original officer left at the Transit Camp. She says the C.O. is coming back from Africa at the end of January. She has been there a month to see her Mum.

Please don't stop sending the comets and Sketches as I still read them all though, even though they arrive about two months late. I have only had one Comet so far - but quite a lot of Sketches and Overseas Sketches too. Please send the Comet every week if you can be bothered.

I am glad you like the Phoenix Magazine - we think it is rather good too. Unfortunately it is closing down on 16th Febuary.

I do hope Ma had a good birthday - I thought of her and wished her the usual. I sent a cable so I hoped it arrived on the right day.

                                                    11ᵗʰ Jan 46.

I had one letter from Ma the other day dated 15ᵗʰ December
– thank you - but the mails are very bad again and we've had
nothing for three days. I'm so glad you got that parcel safely with
the hot-bottle, jam etc., and that the jam was good.

I wrote to Christopher Bunch the other day, and he rang me
up and arranged to come and see me yesterday morning for a
few minutes after a meeting he had to come into Singapore for.
He arrived about 11 a.m. and I took him down to the restaurant
to have tea and biscuits. He is awfully nice, and seems to have
changed quite a lot, is thinner and exactly like Alice. He was a bit
shy - but we talked quite well about everything, and he asked me
to go out with him next Friday to the Tanglin Officers' Club. He
is also going to bring with him a man who was his great friend
at school, and who is working out here with the B.M.A. (British
Military Administration - sort of all Army people who manage
the civilian affairs until the Government starts operating again).
He is a chartered accountant.

We go down to our restaurant in the basement here regularly
twice every day! tea and biscuits in the mornings, and tea, ice
cream and tinned fruit (pears or peaches), and biscuits in the
afternoons! Sometimes I go with Paddy Cronin the other major
in my office, but usually Patricia and Harry (Girl) call for me and
we go down together.

Last night my (her Boss) Eric's mess gave a party - he lives in
the S.E.A.C. Newspaper mess - the staff who print and write all
the stuff for the paper - they come under us. They have a lovely
bungalow, only about five minutes away from where I live - so I
walked there with two WRNS officers who had also been asked.
We went about 7.30 and talked and drank and had buffet supper
- which was lovely! They had lots of pineapples which looked
whole - but they had been hollowed out and a lid made, and were
filled with fruit salad. There were sardines on fried bread and
lovely cheese things, salad and sandwiches. Then at about 9 p.m.
we all went into the garden and saw a film called "The Way to the
Stars" about the R.A.F. an awfully good film, which Dug would
like. Of course I forgot to take my glasses, so I sat in the front row
at the end next to Admiral Sir Douglas Pennant, who was very

nice and friendly. It is his wife's sister's friend who was a land girl at Gorhambury (where Muriel works) and I asked him her name last night, and of course I can't remember it now – it might have been Harding.

I wore a new dress last night – went and fetched it from the tailor yesterday afternoon. It is short – that one with checks, sort of pink and mauvy and it looks very nice – it will be most useful at home. I also bought myself some white sandals with crepe soles – I know it sounds awful, but white shoes out here look very nice and everybody wears them.

I went to the Phoenix Club (it is the restaurant here really) on Wednesday night with Lt.Col.Fry - it was quite nice. Everyone goes here, one always sees faces - never get away from the same people, but I suppose it doesn't really matter. Patricia and John were at another table, and Harry and Ted at another one.

The A.T.S. Senior Commander who had our single room in our bungalow has now moved to another one, and we have got a W.R.N.S. First Officer (Major) in now, temporarily. She is very nice indeed and has a lovely job. For two years she has been sort of secretary to the head of a Naval Intelligence branch and travels about with him all over the world - Australia, Java, Ceylon, India, and has just come from Hong Kong, which she says is a lovely place. She doesn't seem to know anyone here, so we are taking her out to night. Eight of us are having dinner in our mess and then going on to the Atomic Club to dance.

It was very funny when we got back about 6 last night, Harry and I decided out tummies were enormous (you know mine is!). She is much smaller and thinner than me, so she and Patricia and I lay on the floor and started doing exercises, but we laughed so much I don't think they'll do much good.

There is an awful bout of thieving going on in our bungalows at the moment - natives get in in the night and take things out of the bedrooms while the people are asleep - a horrid feeling. In the bungalow next to ours the other night one of the girls woke up to see a man just coming in to the rooms so she yelled out and he disappeared. They have got extra Marine guards now, who walk round all night.

I am miserable as I have lost my beret. I left it in the mess at lunch time yesterday and it has just disappeared, and it was marked with my name. They are absolutely unobtainable here, and I wondered whether one of you could please buy me one and send it out in a good envelope, by air, as they are very light. Just an ordinary khaki beret size 7 ¼ or 7 ½ - preferably 7 and a quarter. You can get them from anywhere that sells army clothes. My felt hat is so hot and I have nothing else. Also I have no ATS badge to go on it now, so if you could you get one of those too - not a brass one, but a dark coloured one which officers wear.

I do hope the other sleeve to your bed jacket has arrived by now – I don't know what Boss can do if it doesn't. She'd better undo the collar and make the other sleeve narrower and try and make two that way – as the sleeve is a very wide one – or isn't it?

I had a nice letter from D.D. the other day – please thank her very much and say I'll answer it one day – although I think she might put up with reading mine to you!

Christopher says his Ma and Pa will probably move to Tonbridge too, to be near Margaret.

I have sent to Delhi for another parcel for you - Sultanas, sugar, jam, tinned fruit.

The first one should arrive about 10th February and the next about 7 March. I'm afraid, although I've written the letter to Durban for some stuff, I haven't yet managed to get the Postal order to go in it but will do so as soon as I can.

If any of you want to use any of my haversacks or dispatch cases (!) you have my permission! I have managed to pinch a nice brown leather dispatch case here, which I use every day to carry my knitting and books about in.

Must stop, as I have a slight bit of work to do!

While I'm writing this you are all in bed asleep and it is 2.30 a.m.

12th Jan 46.

I sent you a letter yesterday asking you to buy me a beret - well if it isn't too late, please don't bother as I found mine. It was on my bed when I got back last night, - so someone must have picked it up and put it there for me. If you have already bought it, please send it just the same, as mine is really rather small, and I can sell it and use the new one.

It IS a small world! Last night eight of use had dinner in our mess - Patricia, Harry, me, that nice First Officer WRNS (Clare Blanchard) who is in our bungalow - and Charles, Ted, John and another Naval Lieut. (Can you cope with all these names??!! - don't bother with them.) Then we went in two cars to the Atomic Club to sit and dance. It is a nice place not too crowded. There were three naval Lieuts sitting together by the side of the dance floor, and I was sure one of them was Riley Carr - but wasn't certain for some time. We kept on looking at each other. In the end, after I had seen some of his mannerisms I was sure it was him and went and spoke - and it was! We had a long talk and he asked after you all. I think he is going to Borneo on Tuesday, but is coming to have tea with me here this morning.

The funniest part is, that he knew I had come out to Ceylon – because he came out to India or somewhere in an L.S.T. ship - and the first officer in it was Keith Harper! They got talking together about places etc. and mentioned Teddington, and Riley said how he knew me there and so they found out - isn't it funny.

Riley has gone very grey at the sides of his hair and seems smaller, and somehow rather deteriorated in a way - yet he was very nice, and sent his love to D.D.

I'm in a muck (soil) about your violet cardigan. I have done one sleeve and half the other, and I think I shall just have two ounces left for the whole back - so I shall have to put grey wool in somewhere - but I don't know how, as if I do it in stripes, you have to keep the mauve wool going across the grey at the back (can you understand?!) and I can't see how it would save much. Couldn't you please send me some ideas. The pattern is 6 plain two purl all the way - and I'm going to embroider coloured flowers all over it! Do let me know how to do the back.

There is an awful mixture of population in Singapore, Indians, Malays, Chinese etc. It was funny yesterday, I saw a tall Indian with a black beard and moustache, wearing only a shirt, nursing a little baby, and fondling it - it looked most peculiar! All the natives have a funny form of squatting too - Dug would know that and can demonstrate for you!

We are gradually getting more things for our bungalows now - we each have a chest of drawers and a wardrobe for hanging things in. Downstairs we have got a sort of sitting room with some easy chairs and tables. We are going to make some curtains one day.

I wonder if Dug has quite decided about the Army yet, and if so when he has to join his regiment again. When I come back he must jolly well get a lot of leave, compassionate if necessary! and I hope you will all meet me in London. I expect we land either at Liverpool or Southampton. I know this is a bit soon to talk about it, but I really can't think of anything to say! I wrote a long letter yesterday, and have only written this to tell you about Riley. You might tell Mrs Harper about Keith.

14th Jan 46.

I've had six letters today - the first for about a week. Two from Ma dated 29th and 31st December – one from Miss Mead, one from Mr & Mrs. Cissie, one from Hildegard and one from Archie Dunlop (which I'll explain later). Thank you also for the cuttings about Singapore and Dorothy Aitken. Its quite right about Singapore - everything is terribly expensive and they make money out of us right and left. Harry and a friend went into a restaurant yesterday and had two lemon squashes and it cost them just over 2 dollars, which is about 4/-8d!

About Archie Dunlop - do you remember Eve Dunlop, that Sgt. From the Transit Camp with grey hair and blue eyes? She and her husband used to have an orange plantation in South America, and both came to England to join up. I knew him quite well at the Transit Camp - he often used to come there when he was on a course learning Japanese in London. He was in the Intelligence Corps, and came out to this part of the world two years ago. I had a letter from an officer at the T.Camp the other day and she gave me his address - Port Dickson, a little way up the coast. So I wrote to him, and have just had a reply to say he is now out of the Army and has got a rubber estate and is a civilian again. Eve is trying to get out here to join him, but can't get a permit yet. He says he is coming in to Singapore soon and will ring me up - and we are going to meet - and also Freddie Jaque (Miss Edward's late fiancée - who is the Field Cashier here).

Riley Carr came here to lunch with me here to-day. He wanted to go out with me on Saturday, but I said I couldn't. He has changed so much, hair all going grey, and I think he is rather fond of the drink. I feel sorry for him he seems so depressed about life - but he is not nearly so nice as he used to be, and I am very glad he is going to Borneo to-morrow.

Please thank Cissie for her nice letter and say I'll answer it one day. I had a long one from Miss Mead, all about cooking and keeping chickens and teaching the boys at Bedford School. She has some of the staff from there P.G-ing and one of them for one term was Mary Scrutton - who was teaching the Classical Sixth (brains!) but who left and is secretary to Professor Gilbert Murramy. Mr Scruton went to lunch one day and referred to me as Miss Watson's highly qualified and capable secretary!

I went with three others to listen to Paddy Cronin's radiogram last night - very nice and peaceful. I chose all the records. That song "Ich muss…" is simply lovely, do see if you can buy the record for our grammy.

Yesterday morning I went with Harry (the WAAF) and Charles to the 'Lido'. It is really the Singapore Swimming Club in peace time, and is simply lovely. We have ferry buses that go twice a day on Sundays from our bungalows for anyone who wants. We left at 10 a.m. and got there about 10.30. It is the other side of Kallang airfield and takes some time to get round there, although when there it is quite near the harbour. It is an enormous pool with sea water and you can bathe in the sea too, only in a netted in part because of sharks. We stayed in the pool – very clean and the biggest I have ever seen. There were heaps of people there (all services), all ranks. I saw an Air Vice Marshal and Colonel in the water and heaps of privates etc. Jolly good thing – they all seem so happy too. It is so big it didn't matter being a lot of people. The dressing rooms were very nice too. There are tables and chairs all round and we had tea and biscuits and ice creams. We came back to lunch at 12.30 p.m.. Apparently there is also a large ballroom there which they are going to open up. I went to lunch at HMS

Round the Bend that naval mess and afterwards we all sunbathed in the garden and I got quite brown.

You'd be amused at the names of the shops here, which are written in English and Chinese- Chop Ching Yong - Lee Lee – etc. - I can't remember more!

They have brought out a new rule here now that officers are not allowed to take any bottles of drink with them into the Officers clubs at night. The Clubs supply a certain amount instead. It is quite a good thing - as some of them do drink far too much - but it makes it much more expensive. Also they are going to start having a curfew from 1 a.m. to 5 a.m., which I think is also a good thing, as I know some parties go on very late indeed (not those I go to!)

I am so glad the chickens are laying well - what a treat to have eggs. We only get them here about once a week. We had some chicken at the Phoenix Club on Saturday night, which was very good.

Miss Mead had got her tea and seemed pleased with it. Do you think I could ask her to leave that table-cloth to me in her will?!

Please do tell Ar Beat and Ar Jessie I am sorry I haven't written to them for so long but will one day. I'm sorry they have been ill. I just can't bring myself to write any letters at all except to you - and I've got so many I ought to write.

Dr Camps hasn't written yet - but I am definitely expecting one from him - written legibly so I can read it, not in prescription writing!

18th Jan 46.

I had a very nice letter to-day from Mrs. Howard – beautifully written and expressed. Please thank her for it, and say I'll answer it one day.

I also had a letter from the M.F.O. in Liverpool saying my luggage left England on 29th September. So I have written to one of the officers at Radio SEAC in Colombo and asked him to try and trace it for me.

Last night I went to the Great World - one of those sort of fair arrangements. It was very amusing. There were heaps of stalls selling shoes, materials, cosmetics, knick-knacks (!) toys etc. I bought a pair of cheap sandals, and also a lovely little white fluffy dog - all fur! Boss would love it. I have named it Louis!

It is now 4.30 p.m. and two Surrey Comets have just arrived – thank you. I don't know what dates they are yet as I shan't open them till I get back tonight. I am going out with Christopher Bunch to-night. I hope he'll do some talking!

Did I ever tell you about all the transport in Singapore - there are quite a lot of cars used as taxis by the locals - all different sizes and makes, English and American, and all in the most dilapidated condition - some are quite as bad as Edward and Boss's A-S*. Quite often they break down and have to be pushed. The buses aren't much better - and have streams of oil smoke coming from the back. We never go in them - as they are crowded with natives.

I just can't think of one thing to say – my mind is a complete blank – and Eric and Paddy and Bobby Howes (the other Major in our office) are all sitting round talking – so I'll shut up, although it is awful waste of paper. This typewriter is awful – keeps sticking.

*Austin Standard

21st Jan 46. 11.30 a.m.

I had a letter from Ma this morning, dated 10th January, thank you. Didn't you ever get that cable I sent for your birthday?

I've got RINGWORM!!! Not really - but I went to see the M.O. this morning (a Naval doctor) about my hands. They are all peeling everywhere and itch terribly and are a bit swollen in the fingers. He says it is quite common out here and is a form of ringworm - but not the catching sort. He has given me some ointment to put on and I have to go back next Saturday. Sickening. But it's the first thing I have had wrong with me since I've been out here.

I had Saturday afternoon off and mouched round the town – bought a sponge as mine is so full of soap now and I haven't got Ma to wash it for me. Anyway there is no hot water and no soda. Sponges are quite plentiful and cheap, so I'll bring a few home.

Yesterday I went to the Lido (Singapore swimming club) by myself as no one else could come. We have a bus which takes anyone who wants. I had a lovely bathe and then sat by the sea and sunbathed. I went to get ready at 11.30 a.m. and met Patricia and John, who had come there especially to get hold of me to take me out on a picnic as they had a car for the day. They had a tin of lamb's tongues and we bought biscuits and bananas, and went off. The driver was sweet - Indian - with a black beard & whiskers & bobbed hair - & kept laughing. He is called Whiskers - even officially. We went north of the island, had lunch near the coast, then crossed over to Johore & went for a long drive onto the mainland - through villages and rubber estates. The hills in the distance were lovely. Then we came back & marched in Johore village - & came back for tea about 5.

I had a nice letter from Mrs. Harper this morning - please thank her & say I'll try & reply sometime.

Killing Boss having a job – I haven't heard from her yet - so am looking forwards to hearing about it.

23rd Jan 46

There's nothing much to say. Hildergard came here to tea yesterday. She's just the same - quite nice. She drives a van and gives out tea and cakes etc. to the men arriving on the docks from ships. She is coming up to dinner in our mess one night.

I stayed in last Monday night and wrote a lot of letters- one to Watty, one to Miss Ghey, one to Cissie and Mr. Cissy one to Hazel Dalgleish and a card to Boss and a card to Joyce Townsend. Do you remember meeting her in Bentalls just before I left, and I promised to send her a card. She was at Surbiton High School with me.

The Chinese women who work here still come in every day and take all the cigarette ends out of the ashtrays. There is one special one who comes into our office every morning - such a funny looking little thing. She has her hair in a huge bun behind, but I think she is only about 12 or 13. She always tries to make me give her a proper cigarette too - she goes to my tin and opens it and then looks at me. I give her one about once a week. They pick them up all over the streets to, then some stalls in the back streets have all the ends and make them into new cigarettes and re-sell them again! We never buy any outside, but get ours from the Naafi.

My hands are still a bit of a soil! I am supposed to put some awful greasy stuff on night and morning, but I can't do it in the mornings as it makes them one mass of grease. It was very funny on Monday night, I put it on last thing and put some sort of glove bags I made out of some old silk knickers - then I couldn't touch anything and so Patricia and Harry had to take off my shoes, put me in bed and tuck my net in - and we got the giggles over it - very silly, but quite funny at the time. I have to see the doctor again on Saturday. They are peeling all over now, but don't itch so much.

I washed my hair at lunch time to-day – started at 1.15 p.m. and it was quite dry by 2 p.m. – shows how hot the sun is here. I see from the papers you have got a "freeze up". I do hope you are not too cold.

Ma had better sit in front of the drawing room fire and not move, so that she doesn't get F.C.

That black georgette dress I had made dropped all round and trailed on the ground – I think it must be from hanging up all the time – so I have had it shortened and also had the back made much higher and it is quite nice now.

Frank Owen has arrived back and is very nice.

Must stop, got some work to do.

25th Jan 46.

I got a letter from Ma to-day dated 14th Jan, and one from Boss dated 10th. Thanks. I'm interested to hear about Boss's job – I didn't know she was working for Bernie – jolly good pay. Have you got a cat now – Ma mentions it licking the butter etc. and I haven't heard of it before. If so, what sort?

I am awfully pleased, as Boss's and Chet's sandals are at last on their way home. I have addressed Chet's to you as well. One of the clerks in our office is going home by sea, starting on about 3rd Febuary. He will take about 3 weeks to get back, and it will probably take a little time after that for him to get all his luggage

– but he has taken them for me in two parcels all ready to post, and is going to register them – so I hope they will reach you safely.

My hands are still in a bit of a soil - they are peeling all over and are very stiff and itch something awful. I went to the doctor again this morning and he has given me some different stuff to put on.

I was very interested in Dorothy Little's wedding – what a muck up her life sounds.

My Eric is going to England next week, and will arrive there on 4th Feb. so I am going to ask him to take Ma's brooch and post it, and also a letter to you.

Tell D.D. I'll give her a new light for her bicycle for her 21st birthday!!

Must stop I've just been given a bit of work to do – I'll reply more to Boss's remarks on my work in my next letter!

28th Jan 46.

Eric is flying to England in the next few days and has promised to take this small parcel for me. I can't ask him to bring anything bigger as he is only allowed to take a little luggage. He is supposed to be leaving here on Wednesday, and will arrive in the U.K. about 4th February - but at the moment the R.A.F. are striking everywhere and there are no planes going - so I don't know whether he will get away. I have told him to give the parcel to Brandy to post.

They are only two small brooches for you - one of Kandyean silver and the other is Chinese lacquer. I am sorry there is nothing for Dug or Boss - but I haven't managed to get many presents yet – and Boss's sandals are on their way.

I shan't write more – as I shall write another letter and post it to-day, which you will probably get first.

30th Jan 46.

We are having great excitements here at the moment, as there is a general strike on. Yesterday morning, the stewards (boys who cook and wait at table) told our Quarters Officer that they all had to go on strike although they didn't want to. Our amah told us that she had been warned that she mustn't do any work for us. She was awfully good, and did all yesterdays washing quickly and it was finished by lunch time. When we came back yesterday evening, she had washed the rest of it and hung it on a line on our balcony, so that it looked as though we had done it. She is so nice - I wish we could get her to come to us at home - she sews and cooks and washes and is a sweet person. She loves us too, as we are very nice to her. They managed lunch in our mess very well (and dinner last night and breakfast to-day). They have everything on a serving table and we help ourselves. Some of the WRNS petty officers and a few of the officers help serve and wash up, and they have a few British O.Rs to help in the kitchen too. We are all going to take it in turns to help behind the scenes - I am doing my bit at dinner on Friday.

All the shops are shut - no taxis or rickshaws on the roads - large groups of natives all lounging about with nothing to do. Half of them don't want to strike but daren't not. Apparently its something to do with some people who were arrested in December, and its all sort of political too. I don't know how long it will go on for. We made our own beds and swept our room yesterday too - and our offices were not cleaned this morning. Its really rather fun if it doesn't go on too long.

I shall be delighted for Douglas to have my Sam Browne* - the only thing is that I lent the cross shoulder bit to Lt Col Pedrick-Harvey one day, as he had to go somewhere smart and hadn't one and it matched his belt. But I have written to him - about four days ago and asked for it back, and told him to send it directly to Douglas. If it doesn't come in a few weeks, ring up Brandy and ask her if she knows his telephone number at Mill Hill, and ring him up for it.

Yesterday morning I went down to the Officers' shop with Patricia and was waiting in a queue to pay my bill, when I saw a girl in W.V.S. uniform, and I recognised her as Rachel Vernon (now Kemball). She is very pretty, and hasn't changed much since I saw her when she was 7! She was very pleased to see me - and is going to get posted to Penang where her husband is stationed. She says Audrie has been on a hospital Ship for sometime, but is now home again. Clare is much better and is living with an aunt.

If you think of it, you might ring up Mrs. Vernon and tell her how we've met. Her father is still going strong.

Eric has started for England this morning. He is flying to Colombo to-day, spending a day there, and hopes to reach England on about the 4th February. He has taken a small parcel from me and is going to give it to Brandy to post to you. I am afraid there is nothing much in it - two brooches for Ma, and a chicken each for the children. I have bought two lovely chicken ornaments too, which I shall bring home with me. Paddy Cronin, the Major in our office, has given me a lovely little lacquer bowl. I darn his socks for him and get him a little drink now and again.

The WRNS officer has gone out of the single room in our bungalow now - the one that leads into our bedroom, and we hope we have at last got it for ourselves - although one ATS officer keeps harping on having it. Anyway Patricia has moved into it, and we have made her bed into a settee and covered it with a counterpane. We have bought some pale green material and made curtains for the windows, and I scrounged some cushions from the office, and we have covered those in a dark reddish colour, and the room really looks very nice now. I was given the choice of going into the single room - but when it came to the point, I didn't want to move in. I sleep under two corner windows and prefer to be in the larger room as it is more airy.

When I got up on Sunday morning, I went to my cupboard to do my hair, picked up my brush and suddenly saw a dead rat lying on the shelf. I was so startled that I threw the brush right on the rat and ran to Harry! After breakfast the boy removed it, and washed out the shelf for me, and I washed my brush thoroughly. I gave him three cigarettes for it.

Going home the other day we saw an amusing sight. There were lots of people sitting at tables outside their homes in the main road, having a good meal, and all around them were easels – about 20 of them - with the most lovely wreaths on them. Apparently it was a funeral feast, and goes on for several days!

All the officers clubs and cinemas are shut - and so we have to eat in our own messes now until the strike ends.

*army belt

I had quite a lot of Daily Sketches and Surrey Comet on Saturday, all for dates in November – which is very nice thank you. This morning I had a very nice letter from Ar.Jessie Young – typewritten very well.

The strike is over at the moment – it only lasted two days and everything has gone back to normal. Apparently they are expecting it might break out again this week, and that it only stopped last week-end for the New Year celebrations. All the Marine guards in our camp are armed. Febuary 2nd is the New Year for the Chinese – all the shops were shut and they wander all over the place dressed in their best – and have all the flags out etc. All day long they set off fireworks and crackers – they make such a din, but you can't see much from them!

The whole of yesterday night and the night before it simply poured with rain the whole time – apparently it is quite unusual for it to rain for such a long time. The roads were all flooded in spite of the ditches. Everywhere round here there are monsoon ditches all along the sides of every road – so that the rain can get away easily when it does come.

Everyone is in a bit of a scared at the moment, as there are several cases of infantile paralysis amongst the troops and the natives. We have to gargle salt and water twice a day – our bungalows, every room, are sprayed twice a day and we are not allowed to bathe in swimming pools. I hope it won't get any worse.

If you have the energy and time, could you please make me some more name tapes and send them out in an envelope. I want to mark all the towels and sheets etc. I have bought – and I haven't any left.

I wrote to Mrs. Harper yesterday

We are locked in our office this morning! When I arrived the outer door was locked and the key wasn't on the ring with the ones belonging to the inner doors. It had been handed in as usual on Saturday night to the reception desk, and now it seems to be lost. We have managed to get in through another door in my room, which opens out into another department, and the locksmith is now trying to get the proper one open.

My Eric should be landing in England about to-day, if he has got on alright from Colombo – so you will be getting the parcel soon. It makes you seem so much nearer doing it that way.

I had the afternoon off on Friday and went shopping in the town. I went down in a taxi with Patricia and then we went on our own, which is so much easier. I found a loverly shop called Tang in River Valley Road – which sells practically everything. I went very rash and bought a lovely tablecloth for Ma with six serviettes to match. It is Irish linen, sent to China and embroidered with various shades of blue – all Chinese scenes. It really is very nice and worth the money. I am trying to collect a few things gradually for bringing home with me. I also bought two pairs of chopsticks in a box – they were very cheap – so when I come back we'll have a go at them!

If Ma will send me the size of her shoes and draw outlines of her feet on a piece of paper and send to me, I could get her a pair of shoes made from nice black leather, with either leather or crepe soles. I should do that if I were you, as they make them very nicely and are not too expensive. I shall buy Boss some, blind. What about Dug? What size does he take?

You needn't think I won't like home food when I come home. We nearly always live on tinned stuff still here. I am longing for a nice bit of meat – any sort – roasted, with fresh boiled potatoes and cabbage, cooked by my Ma! Also some nice fresh apples.

My hands are a bit better and are bits of peeling skin everywhere (Boss would love it!) – the doctor says they will take some time to clear up and I have to put stuff on them three times a day. Several other people have had it too. What is worse is that I have had lots of horrid places on my face and under my arms – again the doctor says it is a form of ringworm. But they have practically gone now, thank goodness.

I haven't been doing anything extra special lately. I went up to dinner in Round the Bend (the naval mess) the other day with another girl, and afterwards we all sat and sang songs with one of them playing the banjo. I have been going out with several different people lately, but its no good telling you different names etc!

We nearly always go to one of the officers clubs and have dinner and dance. On Friday I went to one of our private film shows – which I now arrange, as one of the majors in our office has gone home on release (Major Howes) – and he used to do it. It is rather fun inviting a few people to come- General Kimmins – and a few others who Eric likes to have asked. I went with Patricia and John and we saw a film called At Dead of Night – it was terribly good and very frightening. It was all about people having dreams and premonitions of things happening, and then seeing the things happen. Charles (that naval Lieut. Who I go out with sometimes) has had some lovely postcards from his parents, who are staying in Arosa now – it makes me feel quite homesick for the snow. They are both Swiss so got permission to go specially. Lets go to Switzerland again next year – I'm sure we could.

I spent Saturday evening in, and went to bed at 10 o'clock which was lovely! Yesterday I stayed in all day and knitted and read and sewed and wrote letters – it was pouring with rain the whole day. Harry was in too, so we had good gossips. Patricia has gone to stay in Kuala Lumpur for a few days – I hope to go there one day before I come home too. You travel up by train though the night, and have sleeping bunks.

Frank Owen hardly ever comes into the office now – he is writing a proper book on the Burma War and does it all in his own room in his mess. But I mean to get out of him a definite idea of a job on the Daily Mail before he goes home. He is due back fairly soon. I haven't got my trunk yet – but the ship is 'alongside' and is being unloaded now, so I may get it any day. I'm simply longing to have it!

Harry is as fond of food as I am – and we often at night have little picnics in our room of biscuits and sardines, or lambs tongues, and tinned fruit! I won't get any more of the tongues – but they really are nice indeed. Would you like some tinned Spam????!!! I don't seem any fatter yet – in fact I think I'm thinner – anyway in the tummy line. I have just had that white evening dress of Boss's cleaned and hope to wear it again – as it was rather dirty. Unfortunately all that nice sort of pattern on it has disappeared with the cleaning – I am sorry – but it still looks quite nice.

I think my job here finishes sometime in April – so I shan't be long now. I am looking forwards to coming home very much – but I'm very glad I took the plunge and came here.

I can't think of anything more to say – my letter from Ma was dated 19th Jan, so I am looking forwards to the next. I wonder if you could possibly buy me a bit of ribbon, or material or velvet etc. the colour as on enclosed bit. It goes with one of my evening dresses and this is so old and ragged that I can't wear it – it is for my waist. I should like it a bit wider, so perhaps you could get a very thin bit of material and make it into a belt. If its too much fag, don't bother – but ribbon is very scarce here. Don't really bother to buy any, on second thoughts, just send it if you have any handy.

7th Feb 46.

I got a letter from Ma yesterday dated 28th Jan – not bad, and I got one from Watty this morning – rather pathetic, isn't it. I was disappointed as it was Ma's writing on the outside, and only her letter when I got into it!

I still go out with Charles quite a lot - he dances very nicely and is very nice - but he is much younger than me - only 24! But I quite enjoy going out with him. The other officers in his mess are also very nice - I'll list them to you in case you are interested: I have no top dog at present unfortunately! May meet one some day!

1. Lieut.Tedder - who is very friendly with Harry the Waaf. Smallish and very fair hair.
2. Lieut.Commander ?? "Len" I don't know his other name! He is quite nice but a bit "wet"!
3. Lieut.Worrall "Wogs" – who is small and dark and amusing. His father is a big bug in some shipping firm.
4. Lieut.Dickson "Dickie" – smallish and slight and much older than the rest – about 40. He plays the banjo very well.
5. Lieut. Whiting "Whitey" – who is 6ft.3" and very dark. His father is Commodore (or whatever they call it) of all the Southern Railway Cross Channel boats. He lives in Southampton. He sometimes goes out with me and other girl and Charles and we go and dance together.

6. Charles – who is Sub Lieut.Strubin. His father and mother are both Swiss, although he is naturalised English. His father owns a shipping firm of cargo ships that go all over the world.

That's all! But they are all very nice to me when I go up there to meals etc., and afterwards we all sit on the verandah and sing. They have other girls in too sometimes.

The junior commander in charge of A.T.S. Company here has gone on leave, and she asked me to look after the girls while she was away. Of course last Saturday, the very first day, I had a report in from the Naval Police about an A.T.S.Corporal, who had signed in in the evening at 11.30 p.m., as she should have done - then at 1 am. a Marine Guard found her just coming in again in a jeep with some friends. She lives in one of the bungalows and not in the flats - some of the girls do - and it is very easy for them to sign in the flats office and then go out again. So she had to be had up on an Orderly Room and be lectured, and you know how I love that! So I got Patricia to do it for me. We went all official and had the girl marched in and I stood behind Patricia, who gave her a bit of a jaw - actually I think I could have done it just as well! You needn't write and say you are sorry for the girl, as she is a Corporal and should set a good example, and also she has been naughty before!

Today I had to pay them all. I went down to the bank in a car with the A.T.S.Sgt. and got the money, and paid them up in the flats at lunch time - I quite enjoyed doing that again - they are mostly very nice girls, about 50 of them. It was quite easy paying in dollars and cents. We had an awful Indian driver this morning - he nearly drove into hundreds of things, and didn't seem to care!

I went for dinner with Christopher Bunch and his friend, Fred Weatherly last night at the Tanglin officers' club. I gave 'em a treat and went in evening dress. It was very nice and I quite enjoyed it - I danced with Christopher. They walked me home afterwards - as it is only about five minutes away from our mess. Christopher is going for three days retreat in Singapore soon - he says they are not allowed to talk at all, and doesn't know how he will manage to keep silent that long! He has asked me over to his mess for a party one day - but I don't know the date yet. He comes to Singapore for a Chaplains' meeting every Thursday, so is coming to have elevenses with me after his meeting next Thursday. I don't think you need worry about him and me! I don't think we are quite each other's styles - although I like him. He says Margaret is liking it at Tonbridge. He is always very worried because Alice has never got married - so I said she still might anyway.

My face has quite cleared up now, thank goodness, but my hands are still in a soil. I saw the doctor yesterday and he has now ordered me to have penicillin cream on them. I have to go down to the sick bay at 4.30 p.m. each day (started yesterday) and have this stuff put all over them, and then have bandages put over as the stuff is so greasy, and I have to keep it on as long as possible. When I got back yesterday evening I wanted to wash my hair, so Harry did it for me, and did hers and we both dried it together on the balcony, which wasn't very good as it was raining on and off! Apparently they should be quite alright in a few days with the penicillin, so I can't see why he didn't give it to me before.

I have sent for another food parcel to be sent to you - so that makes four altogether which should be on their way now. The first one I sent in December, should be with you about now.

Will you tell D.D. I have ordered one to be sent to her - which will arrive sometime in March! It is tea, butter, sugar and jellies, as I know she likes those for her nephews.

I must stop now as I've a little work to do!

Ma's letters are NOT dull and I love having them. We live for mail here.

13th Feb 46.

I got two letters to-day, one from Ma dated 2nd Feb. and one from Boss dated 5th Feb - not too bad, thank you for them. I'm glad the egg situation is so good - I'm not too bad either. We never seem to get them in the mess, but Harry has a friend who buys her quite a lot (I don't know how!) and she always gives me one for breakfast too. We have had one each day for a week now.

I'm sorry, I always forget to ask Frank about Uppers - we don't see him very much in the office – but I'll remember next time he comes in if I can.

I am enclosing that parcel list I use to send you the parcels with* - can't think why I didn't do so before. So will you choose what you would like next - give me several and don't take any notice of the prices. I have already sent you Nos. 19; 10; 13; and 7 and also No.19 to D.D. I am going to write today for one to go to the aunts, and also for one to go to Dug with marmalade, as requested by Boss! - (No.8)

You can buy hot water bottles here I think, and I'll get one - also some sponges, which are plentiful and very cheap. I've never seen an egg timer, but will try.

Dug can pinch any of my Army stuff what he wants - as I shan't want any any more, and I have quite enough shirts, ties etc. here to carry me on until my release in September.

I have made up my mind to have a dress made each for Ma and Boss – but I should like all your measurements over again. I think I have got Ma's in an old letter and will look it up – but send them again in case. I know what sort of patterns you like and he just makes them up from the look of the pattern with the measurements. They will probably be thinnish material, suitable for the summer, but it is so easy to get them made here in a few days – and I have such a nice little tailor – an Indian.

I don't know what made you think Eric is leaving - he isn't but has gone to England just for a few weeks for some conferences. I wonder whether you got the small parcel yet which he took with him, and was going to give Brandy to post.

I'm glad the £4 is regular - mind you get the Bank manager to get you all your dues - I'm sure Dug will manage that.

When we got back to our room about 5.45 yesterday evening, I said I was hungry, and Patricia and Harry agreed - so we opened a tin of baked beans and had them cold on biscuits with H.P. sauce and pickled onions, no plates or anything, it was lovely and we had great fun doing it!

Patricia's family live in Kent, a few miles from Maidstone, and have a farm there. Her mother is only 45 and Patricia has a brother aged 18, who has just now joined the R.A.F. as an A.C.2. I don't think their father is particularly nice, as he seems to carry on with someone else now and again, but still lives at home - so things are rather difficult there, and Patricia is very sorry for her

Ma - who sounds an awfully nice person Patricia is devoted to her.

Harry lives in Birmingham with her father and stepmother, who she likes very much. Her own mother died in 1926 from a mosquito bite - in England.

We all get on extremely well together – none of us ever takes 'offence' which is a great relief.

14th Feb. 9.15 a.m.!

Can't think of anything more to say.

EMPIRE STORES - NEW DELHI.
(All the prices include packing and postage.)

PARCEL NO. 1
1 lb Jam or Marmalade
1 lb Tea
1 lb Sugar
1 lb Butter
Rps. 13.

PARCEL NO. 2.
1 lb Tea (Best Darjeeling)
1 lb Sugar
Rps. 6/8.

PARCEL NO. 3.
1 lb Tea (Darjeeling)
1 lb Butter
Rps. 8.

PARCEL NO. 4.
2 lbs Sweets (Glucose Asstd)
Rps. 8.

PARCEL NO. 5.
2 lbs Glucose Asstd.Sweets
2 lbs Marmalade Imported.
Rps. 12.8.

PARCEL NO. 6.
2 lbs Golden Syrup
1 lb Strawberry jam
1 lb Apricot or Raspberry jam
Rps. 12.8.

Parcel NO. 7.
1 lb Tea
1 lb Butter
1 lb Sugar
1 lb Sweets.
Rps. 13.

PARCEL NO. 8.
2 lbs Jam (Imported)
2 lbs Marmalade (Imported)
Rps. 8.

PARCEL NO. 9.
2 lbs Indian Jam
2 lbs Marmalade
Rps. 6.8.

PARCEL NO. 10.
1 lb Raisins (Selected)
1 lb Sultana (Selected)
1 lb Mixed Peel or Almonds
1 lb Currants.
Rps 13.8.

PARCEL NO. 11.
1 lb Dried Fruit
1 lb Almond (Jordon)
2 lb Sweets
Rps. 16.

PARCEL NO. 12.
2 lbs Boiled sweets.
Rps. 6.8.

PARCEL NO. 13.
1 lb Raisins
1 lb Sultana
1 lb Sugar
2 lb Jam or Marmalade.
Rps. 10.

PARCEL NO. 14.
2 lbs Marmalade Imported.
Rps. 5.

PARCEL NO. 15.
1 lb Marmalade
1 lb Strawberry jam
1 lb Tea
1 lb Sugar
Rps. 12.8.

PARCEL NO. 16.
2 lbs Butter.
Rps. 8.

PARCEL NO. 17.
2 lbs Honey
1 lb Tea
1 lb Butter
Rps. 14.

PARCEL NO. 18.
2 lbs Honey.
Rps. 6.8.

PARCEL NO. 19.
1 lb Jelly crystals
1 lb Sugar
1 lb Tea
1 lb Butter.
Rps. 13.8.

List from Empire Stores for sending food home

14th Feb 46.

I have only just finished writing you a letter but have nothing else to do, so shall try and say a bit more!

I have sent Ar Beat a cable for her birthday, as I thought she'd like it.

I have gone and done something else! I've sent to a place in Calcutta for some rugs to be sent to you! We saw some lovely ones in Karachi, and I have always hankered after sending some home. One is 6ft x 3ft and I have asked for it in assorted colours (flower patterns) or else in blue. Two others are 4ft x 2ft oblong, in green and beige. It is very difficult ordering blind like that, but I don't suppose they'll be too awful. I have said on no account are they to send any very modern designs.

Christopher Bunch has just been in and had tea with me. I have sent a food parcel home to his Mum for him, as he has no bank in India, so I sent a cheque and he has paid me the equivalent in dollars.

I am sending you a silly poem I wrote to Harry the other day*. She is always very generous with her things, and I hadn't thanked her for the eggs for a few days, so gave her the enclosed. She is awfully pleased with it!

Christopher is going into retreat for three days next week, and I am going out with him again on Wednesday week.

I am sorry to hear about Joyce Eltringham – they do seem to be unfortunate with her.

Fancy, after all Verity Orr has done in the ATS – to go and be a common little typist in Kingston. She ought to aspire higher.

I have discovered we are allowed to send home "personal effects" parcels, which are things we brought out and don't want here after all. So I am sending one home - so as to make room in my trunk to bring home what I buy! I am sending my battle dress, some shoes, that summer coat (which Boss can have if she likes) two shirts (khaki) and ties and collars (all of which Dug can have if he wants), and a few books which may interest you. So WHEN it comes, in about two months, please unpack it and sort it out.

I am very disappointed in my black evening dress – I was going to wear it last night, and it seems to have gone too short, or

343

else I am taller! It is about an inch too short now – so I am going to take it to my tailor and see if he can alter it somehow for me.

I have just discovered a Colonel here who had the same trouble with his hands as me, and his are now quite cured, as he had some medicine for his INSIDES. I have told the doctor all along I thought I ought to have something for my innards and that it couldn't be only a skin disease. So when I go to him again on Saturday, I shall insist (if I dare!).

*If you've a drink and all about you haven't
And you know that they would like to have one too
If you've some fruit and others haven't got it
Do you offer both these things to them you do.
If you've got eggs to eat yourself at breakfast
Do you sit down and eat them one by one?
You don't, you give them to your pals, so Harry,
Thank you very much for what you've done.

18th Feb 46.

I got a letter from Ma this morning posted on 8th Feb – thanks. Also I got a large bundle of Sketches from 5th Nov until about 16th Dec, which I enjoy reading very much. It was addressed by Dug - thanks.

At the moment (3.00 p.m. In the office) I am in agony with sunburn on my back. I went on a picnic to Changi yesterday and sat on the beach and bathed in the sea - there is a bit of sea roped off with nets to keep the sharks out - it was a lovely sunny day and I sunbathed hard, and to-day I am very uncomfortable! My back and face, legs and arms are a lovely brown, but my back is very sore, and Patricia keeps putting Calamine lotion on. Harry's is just the same, and we are very sorry for ourselves. I can't wear anything under my shirt to-day at all, and last night after lights were out I took off everything - and just had a sheet over me, bare! I think it will probably calm down in a few days, and then future sunbathing won't affect me.

Paddy Cronin (the Irish major in my office) asked me to his mess to a party on Saturday last, and Harry too. We had a lovely time, danced ate and talked etc. They had a band - about

50 people there. Everybody was so extra friendly and nice. Harry and I both had on dresses made of material we had bought at the officers shop, which was very cheap. Hers was yellow cotton, and mine sort of multicoloured red stuff, stiffish - they said hers looked like sackcloth, and mine like linoleum. They were only teasing, as we both looked very nice, and felt we were quite the belles of the ball.

Patricia's friend John is going back to England soon, and a man has come out to relieve him, and to-morrow we are all four going out to show the new man the sights of Singapore. We are going to Raffles hotel for dinner, I think, and then to one of the 'Worlds'.

We had another strike for one day on 14th Feb. Apparently all the natives had asked for a public holiday to "celebrate" the fall of Singapore, and it was refused. So some of them struck. There were several incidents between those wot wanted to and those wot didn't, and we watched some of it from Patricia's office on the 9th floor, through field glasses. We could see crowds of people and police and bodies being dragged across the road. There was one man killed and 19 injured. There were heaps of troops all going about armed. But everything is quiet again now.*

I have sent Boss a pair of brown shoes with crepe soles, and also a jar of pickled onions (LOVELY ones) for Dug. A girl (a nurse) I know has taken them. She has gone to India first for a month, and then is going to England by boat, so I am afraid you won't get them for about 2 months – but better than never. I do hope they will fit.

My hands are still very soily - and I am going to the dermatologist at the hospital to-morrow morning to see what he says about them. If you get anything wrong in this climate, it is always very difficult to get rid of it.

Frank Owen came in on Saturday and I remembered to ask him about Uppers. He remembers him well indeed, said they belonged to the same club at College, and that he is "a h--l of a good chap"! He said he would like to meet him again sometime, and was interested to know what he was doing. I do hope I shall get my job on the Daily Mail - I haven't mentioned it to Frank lately, as I don't want to harp - but I shall tell him definitely before he goes that I want it - and I am sure he will keep his word. He will be going home when Eric comes back, about the end of this month.

I sent Ar Beat a cable for her birthday to-day and hope she will get it in time.

I went in the town with Patricia this morning in her general's car – and I had my Photograph taken at a shop in the town. She had had hers done before and they were quite good and cheap. So if they are any good, I'll send you some!

You need't worry about your letters to me being rotten – they aren't and I love all the bits of your doings. I am sorry you are so cold there – it is extra specially hot today here, and I have got a white handkerchief round my neck and keep mopping up my forehead with lavender water!

I'm sorry about Eileen's troubles and D.D. I do wish we could have our "amah" to live with us in England. She is sweet - does all our washing, ironing and mending too if we like, and is always so full of fun. She talks in sort of broken, very broken, English and is rather hard to understand, but she laughs over it a lot. We each pay her 12 dollars a month for everything (£1, 8/- a month- not bad).

Got work to do now

* A demonstration on 4th aniv of the fall of Singapore, in memorial to the thousands of Malaysians who had died in defending Singapore. The demonstration was banned and one demonstrator was killed and several wounded as troops confronted them in Singapore.

11th Mar 46.

I have just got three letters from you - dated 24th Feb, 1st Mar, and 2nd Mar - jolly good, the last one was posted on 3rd, and so has only taken 8 days to come. You have no idea how thrilling it is to get mail here - I hadn't had any for 5 days, and felt all squirmy inside when I got these this morning! Thank you for Audrie Vernon's too.

I am so glad you have got that parcel safely - there are about five more on the way - but I am a bit worried over one I ordered for you last week, and also one for Mrs. Haoward, Cissie and Mrs. Harper - as I see in our paper this morning, that they are going to stop food parcels from going out of India, except tea, because of the food shortage. So I don't know yet whether they will ever get sent, I'll let you know when I hear.

Patricia's John left for England yesterday - I went down to the harbour with them, and saw him off on the launch which was taking him out to the ship - the Sefton. He has got your telephone number and may ring you up when he gets back (in five weeks time!) just to say he knows me and that I am okey-dokey. His name is Carew-Jones. Patricia has gone to Saigon to-day - so I shall move into her little room to-night, as I think it will be nice there. Harry will stay in our room, and we can then make the rest of it more into a sitting room.

Yesterday afternoon I went up to Round the Bend - played deck tennis with three of them, and we had lovely curry for dinner. I made a pig of myself and had three helpings, and then was so hot and full I couldn't eat anything else, and had to go out on the balcony before the others to try and cool down! It must look rather funny - as after dinner we all sit out on the balcony on basket chairs - all with our legs up on a table - five of them, and me, and sing songs!

My hands are alright now - and my impetigo is practically gone - the only thing left to clear up now is my ankles. I have to go to the specialist again on Wednesday, so I shall get him to concentrate on them then.

It IS funny old Dug going to that job in Eaton Square - it must be A.W.S.1 he is in.

I know J/Comd.Perry quite well. DO make Dug go up and see Brandy and John Humphries in A.W.S.5. They would love to see him - and they all know my name. I should think Major Griffiths might have gone by now - but I don't know. Also he might see David Snell there too - he would be very interested to see Dug. I am glad he is being a Captain - and it is worth having the Staff pay and Lodging and Ration Allowances etc. I am SO pleased he is in London.

Amusing about Micky – she doesn't sound nearly so nice as Chet.

Of course those mats are for you when they arrive – I only hope they will be suitable to use. It is difficult buying things blind like that.

I am going to lunch at Government House to-day. SAC (Lord Louis) is away, but Betty Crawford (a WAAF officer) who works in his office, and lives in our bungalow normally, is staying there while he is away, with various A.D.Cs etc., and she has asked Harry and me to lunch there to-day - rather nice.

I spent all last Saturday afternoon shopping – on my own – and enjoyed it very much mouching around. It was terribly hot. I bought a sponge to bring back. Do you want any more sponges badly? I also bought a present for Dug – which I won't tell you wot it is yet! I also bought a pair of slipper things for Ma – which she may (OR MAY NOT!) like. I got myself some one day, and they really are comfortable to mouch about in, once you have got used to keeping them on! They are just sort of sole (crepe) with a couple of straps over them, and you just slip in them – bedroom slippers they are. I hope they fit. Of course they may be too cold for your sort of climate!

I have packed up a parcel ready for that Lieut. Whiteing to bring home to you. He expects to go on the Winchester Castle around the 23rd March. I have put in a pair of sandals for Boss – your slippers, and a few bits and pieces of things – and hope they will arrive safely one day. Just in case they don't reach you – the other parcels I have sent by various people are:
1. the violet cardigan I knitted for Ma.
2. pair of crepe oxford shoes for Boss and pickled onions for Dug.
3. two pairs of sandals – one for Boss and one for Chet.

So let me know when any of these arrive. Nos 1 and 3 should be with you any time now – as they were sent home on the Andes – a ship that left here on 13th Feb. and was due back 18 days after that.

Eric isn't back from London yet – but we expect him back about 20th March.

We had burglars in our bungalow the other night - I forget whether I told you. It was on Friday night, and they only went into the room next door to ours, upstairs. It is where Betty Crawford and Elizabeth Eberlie are usually - only they are both

348

away. It seems awfully funny, as they only seem to have taken three counterpanes which were on the beds. The drawers were all left open and a few things taken out and scattered around. But they didn't take a nice clock which was there, nor any drink from the cupboard - and as Betty can see, they don't seem to have taken anything else - so I can't think what they were after.

I hope you'll ask Audire Vernon over one day – I should like to see her again some day.

It's nice - I nearly always get driven to work here every day now. Harry's friend Ted, seems to get a car most days and he calls for her at our mess after breakfast, and takes me too. It is much nicer than our ferry buses, as they get rather hot. Harry and I get later and later for breakfast every day – it is so difficult getting up in the mornings and we usually leave ourselves about 5 minutes for breakfast now!

I saw Hildegard the other day. – she says Philip is being demobilised in a month's time, but doesn't know yet what he is going to do. He was a Major in the Army. Joan has arrived home and her husband. She also said that her father is retiring this summer – so evidently everything is okey-dokey with her Ma and Pa. She says he is 65 and wants to do some other job, as he will have nothing to do, and has no special hobby.

12th Mar 46. 11.30 a.m.

I'll give you a treat & write this instead of typing it!

I went to an ENSA show in the theatre last night - it wasn't half bad, 6 girls & 4 men sang & danced & did sketches etc. The best was when all the lights were out & they played Teddy Bears Picnic, & two skeletons danced about on the stage, it was very cleverly done.

I'm afraid I haven't written to the Aunts for ages – please give them my love & say I really will do so one day.

This is a rotten letter – hardly worth sending – but I said everything yesterday.

I had three Surrey Comets yesterday and two to-day, thanks – one of December , and all Januarys. I was interested to see the deaths of Mr. Sengel, Miss Sanson, and Norris, the man wot sang. What was wrong with him? I remember seeing him in one of Ivor Novello's plays.

It was very funny – in the Trail of the Comet column of January 12th there was a paragraph about a WRNS called Iris Smith, who is engaged to a Dutch officer, and how she used to work in Colombo and is now in Singapore – her parents live in Ewell. So last night I was duty officer at the Wrennery (the flats where all the other ranks live), and I asked the WRNS who was on duty with me if she knew Iris Smith, just for interest. And it turned out that she was her. Wasn't it funny, out of nearly 200 girls, that she should be that one! So I am giving her the cutting. She showed me photographs of her fiancée, who looks very nice indeed, a Naval Lieut., Dutch – they are being married here next month, and going home to her parents at the end of the year, and then she will live in Java with him – such a nice girl.

I went to the skin specialist again yesterday. There is only my ankles to cope with now, and also a few places which have come out on my face again. So he said first he thought I ought to go home - so I said I didn't want to until my time came - so he said would I go to hospital, and I said I wouldn't. So he said I was to go on a fortnight's leave, preferably in the Cameron Highlands - which is north of Kuala Lumpur in the middle of the land on the map - several thousand feet high. So I came back and told the M.O. this here, and he says I definitely must go and will get rid of my diseases he thinks. So I am going to try and fix something up - the worst of it is that I don't want to go alone, and don't know anyone to go with. Patricia has gone to Saigon, and Harry might be able to manage a few days, but not more. Anyway I'll let you know. Of course I still think it is my insides wot cause my ankles to swell and peel and not entirely a skin complaint - so I have started to take vitamin tablets on my own. We eat such a lot of tinned and dehydrated stuff here.

Did I tell you about my lunch at Government House the other day – I can't remember, so you had better have it again!

Harry and I went with Betty Crawford, the WAAF who asked us there. SAC is away in India. We went in a car and went up to her room, which is one of the guest rooms - simply lovely. A huge bedroom with fans, beautifully furnished - a little sitting room opening out of it, and a lovely bathroom, all tiled, and REAL HOT WATER! We kept washing our hands in it. Then we went down (in the lift) (only one floor) to the room which the "stooges" use, and had some cocktails. There was Betty, me and Harry, a Squadron Leader St John, one of the A.D.Cs, another Squadron Leader Devitt (who lives at Esher, and we talked about home), another Air Force officer, who is sort of a permanency at Government House and has been there with the Governors for 25 years (was interned at Changi when the Japs were here), and another man civilian, who is sort of Controller of the household, sees to all the decorating and furnishing etc. All of them absolute birds of the highest degree - such a relief (not that most people out here aren't as they mostly are!)

We had a lovely soup, then sort of meat pudding with mashed potatoes and greens and a horrid pudding - macaroni cheese it looked like, but was sweet - then lovely toast, cheese and butter and coffee. We enjoyed it very much.

I have moved into the little single room leading out of our bedroom, which Patricia had – and like it very much. We haven't had anyone else put in yet, so Harry has the big one to herself – but we have both the doors open and make 'free' with both rooms! Last night when we got back at 5.30 Harry and I had a tin of spaghetti, pickled onions, and pickled gherkins – lovely!

Harry is giving a cocktail party in our bungalow tomorrow night - to celebrate her promotion (same rank as me now in the WAAF), and there are about 12 people coming - then we are going on to the Atomic Club to dance. She and I went into the town this morning and mouched around. We quite often go down for an hour or two, when we can scrounge some transport from the Sgt. In charge. We are both very friendly with him!

I enclose a cutting from todays' SEAC about Bernard Hailstone – he is awfully nice, and I have been up to his studio several times to see his pictures. The one of Lord Louis was awfully good.

It rained hard nearly all yesterday, and was lovely and cool all day – but it is very hot again to-day.

Harry's friend, Ted, has got her a gramophone – lent - through Naval Welfare, which is rather nice. At lunch time to-day we had all Tchaikovsky's pathetic symphony, which Boss knows, and was lovely. – Both of us lying naked on our beds, trying to keep cool!

18th Mar 46.

I had two letters from Ma this morning, one dated 25th Feb. and one dated 5th March – also one from Joyce Townsend. Do you remember meeting her in Bentalls that day, just before I left, and I promised to send her a card. I did send one.

I had a very exciting time on Saturday. Harry's job here is a lot to do with people visiting the H.Q., and people being met who come by air etc. - called Staff Duties Division (Dug should know about it!), and on Saturday she had to go to Kallang airfield to meet Lord Killearn's two women staff. Harry's Major, Bernard Spiridon, asked me if I'd like to go too – so at two o'clock on Saturday, we three went in a V.I.P. (Very Important Personage) (quite an official title!) car to Kallang airfield, and we stood on the first floor balcony of the buildings there, immediately above where all the doings were to take place. About 2.30 p.m. the band of the R.A.F. Regiment marched on, then the guard of honour of the same Regt. – about 100 men and stood ready in front of us. Gradually, all the bigwigs came in their lovely cars – General Browning, Chief of Staff, the C. in C., Sir Miles Dempsey, Admiral Douglas Pennant, Mr Denning, Chief Political Adviser to SAC, and lots of others. (I see all these people anyway quite a lot in the lifts etc. at the Cathay). Then about 2.50 p.m. eight Spitfires went up to meet the aeroplane and went out of sight. About 2.55 p.m. SAC arrived and got out, and he and all the other Generals etc. stood just below us talking and laughing. (SAC himself had only arrived from Delhi by air at 1.30 p.m.). Harry and I were busy taking photographs all the time - I am hoping they will come out very much.

Then punctually at 3 p.m. the aeroplane - a York - arrived escorted by the 8 Spitfires - circled round the airfield, and then the York landed, and the Spitfires went off somewhere else. It was a plane specially built for Churchill once and was beautifully fitted up inside. I didn't see it inside, but the two girls told us afterwards. It taxied right up to in front of the guard of honour, and they got out, and SAC went up and met Lord Killearn, and then they played the National Anthem and we all saluted, and then he inspected the Guard of Honour, and then talked to all the big pots. Press photographers were running all over the place, and there were lots of airmen and odd people all watching. Then he and SAC got into the car - an open one and drove off, with a Military Police escort of a jeep and two motor cycles. Gradually also the other people of the party, about five civilians went off in cars, and Harry and I walked over to the airplane to meet the two civilian girls. They are the ones who do all the cipher signals etc. One of them is out of the bottom drawer and has never been abroad before, and the other one is out of the top but one, and has already served in Italy and Algiers in this war, and lives in Brighton - a very nice girl. We mucked about a bit, and then brought them in our lovely car to our mess, and gave them tea, and showed them their room in the bungalow next to ours. After tea, Harry got a car and we all went up to Government House, and collected their luggage.

Lord Killearn looks absolutely sweet - exactly like Churchill - tall and fat in a light coloured suit and trilby hat, and carried a fly switch - which he kept switching! Not that there are many flys! He looks full of fun. Did you know he was Sir Miles Lampson, the top dog in Egypt. I hope you are interested in all this, but it was very exciting to us.

Ma – thank you for the style you want your dress – but I MUST have your measurements – quickly. I hope you have sent them by now with the drawings I sent the other day.

I had a long letter from Patricia yesterday who says Saigon is very nice - not much gaiety there, quite quiet, but she is enjoying it very much. She also says they do want me to go there, and she has written to General Kimmins to say so - so I am waiting to hear more now. She is living in the same bungalow as the British Consul, and a Brigadier for whom she works. There is only one other women there, a civilian.

Actually, I'm in a bit of a soil as to what to do about leave. The M.O. said I'd either got to go home, or in hospital, or on leave - so at the moment I have asked to be booked for leave in the Cameron Highlands from next Friday for two weeks - but I shall have to go alone, which I am not too keen on, and then I don't know what Eric will say, as we have no clerk in the office, and also I don't know when they want me in Saigon - so as you see I am, as I said in a soil! I shall have to do something, as my ankles are no better, and the peeling - or it is really very dry sort of skin, which itches something awful, is going up my legs and thighs, and arms etc. I wouldn't mind that so much only me ankles are so swolled!

We had a lovely curry for lunch in our mess yesterday. Everyone here is absolutely mad on curry, which we hardly ever get because we are not allowed much rice - so when I come home, can we have some EVERY day please! Or haven't you any rice left either? Anyway we can have curry gravy, and be blowed to my figure from now onwards!

I remember Douglas's Major very well indeed - Major Trethowan - I used to meet him a lot on Sloane Square station, and he also did see me on my motor bicycle. I always thought he was so nice.

Harry had a cocktail party in our bungalow last Friday evening to celebrate her promotion. There were about 20 people there, and we all enjoyed it very much. Our mess are very good, as if we have a 'do' they provide all the small eats for us - sardines on toast, cheese straws, sausage rolls etc. We had the party from 7 to 9, and then six of us went on to the Atomic Club and danced a bit, and got back about 11.30 p.m.. I wore my black velvet evening dress, which looks very nice now.

I made myself a chemise the other day to wear under my evening dresses – out of muslin, wot I bought in Kandy. They say it is good for heat, and I wanted something with a very high back, as that is where I always get so hot, nowhere else. So a friend cut it out for me, and I sewed up the sides.

We have lots of sort of phrases here which everyone says - like Dug's "duffey" I'll tell you a few;

Jolly good oh.

Just the job

I couldn't care less.

I haven't a clue.

I have just been sewing up Paddy's sock which has a hole in his ankle – with white cotton! Just an emergency to keep it from running.

I am sorry to hear about Mrs. Bullen – who will look after Mr.? Also I am very sorry to hear about Ma's asthma – don't let her go out at all. I votes we do go to the South of France next winter if we can.

Municipal Buildings (Padang) with dome roof. Where Surender Ceremony was signed. Building on left under clock is Victoria Theatre where ENSA shows are held. 18th March 1946.

Raffles Place. 18th March 1946.

Bicycle rickshaw. 18th March 1946.

20th Mar 46.

I never know how to start a letter when I haven't had any to thank for – but that's rather clever, as now I have started!

On Monday afternoon I went with two of the Round the Bend officers, Roy Hogg (a new member) and Charles Strubin, to an island near here where they have to go to buy their clothes and stores etc. (Like our officers shop). It is all Navy and Royal Marines there. It is called Blakang Mati (Blanky Matty!) and takes about ½ hr. in a boat to get there from the harbour. I asked Paddy if I could have the afternoon off to go, and he said I could - so we went at 2 o'clock. It was simply lovely on the sea - in a motor boat. When we landed they got transport to take us up to the sort of barracks there where the stores were - I was the only woman anywhere, but no one seemed to mind. There were lots of Japanese prisoners working there. We went in the store, and I got myself some white socks and they bought shirts and shorts etc. Afterwards we went for a little 'drive' round the harbour, and got back about 4.30 p.m. - very nice.

I have moved back into my original bedroom with Harry out of the little room - as it was too hot in there, and the sun streamed in in the early mornings, and started me off too hot for the day.

Last night I went to the ENSA theatre and saw Night Must Fall - it really was first class acting. I think I have seen it before in London, but it didn't matter.

There have been great excitements in Singapore the last two days because that Indian man Pandit Nahru has come on a visit - and all the Indians in the town are wild about it (with pleasure). They were expecting there might be some trouble, and the ferry buses that bring and fetch us to work have been going miles round back streets etc. to avoid the town.

Thursday, 21st March. 9.30 a.m.

(sorry – didn't have time to finish this yesterday).

There were processions and meetings all over the place.

We had such excitements yesterday afternoon. Paddy was at a meeting and I was alone in the office, and at 3 p.m. the telephone went, and it was Eric - who had just landed at Seletar aerodrome - north of the island. He said he could get into Singapore by their transport and would I arrange something to meet him at the Air Booking Office, which is near Raffles Place. So I went down and got a car and thought I'd go and meet him. So I went and waited a few minutes and he arrived, and seemed pleased to have someone to greet him. He left England last Saturday and so only took four days to come - jolly good. I am so annoyed with myself for not cabling you to tell Douglas to get in touch with him - as you could have sent me a message etc. first hand - as he was always in A.W.S.5. on and off. I told him about Dug, and he said what a pity it was that he didn't know he was there. He brought me a letter from Brandy.

Actually, I'm in an awful soil now - as I was going on leave to-morrow to the Cameron Highlands for two weeks - doctors orders - but we have no clerk in the office and Eric says he has masses of work to do, and I daren't tell him about my leave. So now I'm trying to make up my mind what to do. I feel I ought to go to try and get rid of my ills, as my impetigo has started again now under my arms, not badly yet, but its coming.

It was very interesting in the office yesterday after Eric had got back - as Frank Owen came in too, and a man called Ian Coster, who used to be the Editor of Phoenix Magazine, and is in the newspaper world in Fleet Street – and they all talked hard about world affairs etc. Eric had been to see Ernest Bevin while he was in London, about different things.

No more time Eric's just come in.

22nd Mar 46.

I got two letters from Ma yesterday, dated the 11th and 12th – thank you. I am so glad that the three parcels arrived safely from the 'Andes'. That person called Johnson who posted the sandals to you is a man! He was the Corporal clerk in our office - and very nice man indeed, so if he gave his address you might write him a note and thank him for bringing back the parcels. No wonder he wanted to come home - nearly all the other ranks do out here, as they have mostly been here such a long time.

The other parcel with the mauve cardigan and jellies in was taken by an A.T.S. officer for me. That Lieut. Whiting has a parcel which he is bringing, as I told you, and he is leaving here on 26th March on the Winchester Castle, which will take about 19 days to reach England. I am so sorry I was silly, as I bought Ma some sort of slippers, which I think are very comfortable – but I got them for her in a light colour instead of dark. Anyway, if they are any good to her, she can stain them black if needed.

Twice in your letters you have told me that you have got something at Reading that would make my eyes bulge, with pleasure, and I just can't think what you mean. Could you be more explicit, or perhaps Boss can write it to me in shorthand!

I'm so glad Dug enjoyed his Marlborough trip. I do wish he'd call on my old office. Both Griffiths and Hargreaves and Pedrick Harvey have gone now, and John Humphries (that very nice one who lives at Berkhamsted), and Jimmy Lack, the one wot used to be in Italy, are Majors – and Freddy (the one who was a prisoner in Switzerland) is also still there – so DO make him go and see them – also Brandy.

I don't know yet what will happen about that last lot of parcels I ordered from India, Cissies, Mrs. H's etc. – I am waiting to hear whether my letter reached them in time for them to be sent, or whether it was too late.

I haven't gone on leave yet, as you will see. I hadn't the heart to leave Eric without anyone to do his letters, and so I cancelled going today. But I'm going to tell him that he must find someone temporarily, as I must go and get cleared of all my ills. My boosumps are quite alright now - its only me ankles and me impey under me arms again.

I went up to dinner at Round the Bend last night, and we all sat on the verandah afterwards, and I went fast asleep! It didn't matter - the others just talked.

You seem to get my letters awfully quickly. You've got the wrong end of the stick about my trunk! Saying I am sending it back for you to have a pick. I have only sent a small 'personal effects' parcel – which some things in it that I don't want here. There are several shirts and ties etc. in it that might do for Dug. Tell him he can have all my khaki shirts, ties and collars etc. that he wants – as I shall be out of the army when I come home and won't want them again.

Hot potty of Verity Orr to go to County Hall for a job – isn't that just typical! I'll send a card to Mrs. Sturges – only I'm afraid it really means a letter – as you can't buy postcards here! Still I'll try one day. I haven't written to the aunts for ages and feel rather bad about it – so could you make my peace with them, and tell them I'm sorry.

I haven't seen Christopher for a fortnight – I had to put off our last 'date' cos of my ills – and I now hear that his place 'HMS Landawell' has closed down – so I don't know what has happened to him. I expect he will let me know soon.

I am so sorry Ma has been ill again – and do hope she is better now.

I'm sorry that strap for the Sam Browne hasn't come – just like him. Could you ring up Brandy – Sloane 9600, and ask the exchange for A.W.S.5. clerks – and ask her to try and get it for you, as I believe she sees him sometimes (his name is Gale Pedrick-Harvey). Better still, of course, would be for Dug to go and see Brandy in her office – 2nd floor of house 59, room 10 I think – and he can ask her to get it for him. I'm sure she would.

I'm glad the jellies were a success – I sent them because I know that Dug likes them.

They have got four more living at Round the Bend now - I've only seen two of them so far, but they seem to be very nice indeed, quite young though, about 26 and 28. One of them has very fair hair and a beard, and looks so nice!

I'm still not quite sure about Saigon, I may go there yet, and may not. I'll let you know as soon as I do if I am going.

27th Mar 46. 69.I.G.H. Hospital.

I had a very nice letter from Ma sent on 16 March – thanks. I am glad you are getting some parcels & you are to eat the pineapple as soon as you like! - & Boss can lump it - whats the good of saving it up. Anyway I shall be bringing some home with me. What d - - cheek of Mrs H & those socks – I should tell her wot for.

Funny I missed out on the kisses in another letter – I usually try & be so careful of that. The "young" man whose arm I am holding is only Paddy Cronin, the Major in our office, a funny little Irishman. Actually he is my age but looks about 50.

Last Friday when I got back to the office after lunch about 2.30 p.m., there was a Lieut. paratroop waiting for me - & it was Sam Johnston - such a nice looking man - a bit taller than me - & dark eyes & hair - rather like Violet - only better looking - not a bit like Dick. We talked for about an hour - rather difficult as he is a bit shy - & then he said he'd ring me up sometime. He has just come back from Java & is in Transit Camp waiting to go into the middle of Malaya. Anyway - on Saturday afternoon, I got myself a car & went shopping & stopped at one shop & was just getting out of the car - when Sam appeared & greeted me, & said he had been going to ring me up that aft. So he came round shopping with me - & then I asked him back to the mess for tea & then we sat on my balcony & talked etc & he drank beer, & taught me how to learn to parachute - & then he washed & shaved in our bathroom & he & I went to the Phoenix for dinner. He went about 10 p.m. He is very nice - but slightly hard to entertain for long! aged 27. He is longing to be out of the Army & get back to England.

I bought a pair of shoes for D.D. on Sat - & hope they will fit. I may not send them – but will probably keep them to bring back when I come. They are brown lace up shoes with crepe soles – size 6 – is that right?

The Lieut Whiting – who may ring you up – left on the Winchester Castle for home on 25 March – Monday - & will take about 20 days to get home. He has a parcel for you too – so calculate when it might come.

I think my legs are much better today, the Dr thinks so too - my ankles are quite normal - that's cos of lying in bed. Actually we seem to do as we like about staying in bed & can get up & walk about the verandahs in our dressing gowns - or dressed - as we please - but I prefer to stay in bed mostly. I get up for my meals round the table on the verandah - about 12 of us altogether - 6 of our ward & some from the two other wards - they are mostly nursing sisters & FANY's

The food isn't extra good - but we seem to get plenty of eggs – fried - which I like - & anyway I can usually eat anything.

This morning it was the CO's inspection & we all had to tidy ourselves up & have nothing on our bedside lockers. I wore (& am wearing) those mauve pyjamas you made me. I feel rather awful having no decent night clothes at all - as I usually wear those two petticoats you made me - which are miles too big. I had an idea in the night & tried it this morning – to make the neck look nicer. I have gathered it in front & drawn it up & put a few dark French knots on! It doesn't look too bad aft - but I don't know what it will look like on!

The Col. (RAMC Dr.) trailed round about 11 + matron, two nurses, one female Dr & two other male Drs! He stopped & talked to us all - & the female Dr told him I had dermatitis on my legs, & that I am better already - so I'm cheered up now!

The old girl next door to me is a nice old girl - but I haven't talked to her much yet as I believe its difficult to get away - once started & I can't cope yet. She has very pretty white hair – long - which she has in a bun in the day, & at night - two plaits & ties them on top. She seems to wear a vest & flannel nightdress, & in the daytime a flowered blue cotton dress over the top with large white fichu - also layers of knitted shiffs over her knees with bits of elastic round to keep them on! She spends hours talking on & off all these things at night & morning & three times a day she has the bed pan brought & put on her chair - buy an Indian soldier! who is sweet to her. He also puts a screen round - but only one side - & I have full view! if I wanted. I always turn the other way & smoke hard! I feel sorry for the old girl - as she can't move much with arthritis. She is waiting to go back to China & mish' again - but the nurse told me she thought she'd be sent back to UK.

Hildegard Francis came in yesterday to see a FANY in our ward & I had a long talk with her. She was surprised to see me here. I expect Harry will visit me tonight.

When people bring flowers here, they are always in baskets with large handles - beautifully arranged - apparently always done like that out here - there are a lot in our ward.

Do you want me to bring back any hot-water bottles? They are about 10 dollars each – which is a lot – but worth it if ours won't last for next winter. I see in the Picture Post they are making thousands at home now – showed a Streatham factory doing it.

I'll write again tomorrow

28th Mar 46. In Hospital.
I'm still here - but my legs are much better & my ankles are okey-dokey - so I started agitating the Dr. this morning - but she said she wanted them a bit more better before I go out.

Hildegard came in again yesterday & brought me some magazines & chocolate. Harry also came & brought me fruit & bovril & lemon juice. Its rather funny - as there was a draw on in Cathay for some lighters, fountain pens & pipes - as a few had come into the Naafi there. I put my name in for a pen & lighter & have drawn a pipe! Harry brought it yesterday. I expect I shall give it to one of those naval officers of Round the Bend.

We had chicken again last night - bit tough - but not bad. In the mornings there is always a dishful of fried eggs - the others are all sick of them - as they are always cooked hard - but I don't alf tuck in - & have four or five!

When I went to see my specialist on Monday, before coming in here - he noticed I lived at Teddington & said he used to live in Twickenham - & wanted to know where abouts we lived. He is so nice - named Tillman. He hasn't been to visit me here yet - he only comes about once a week I believe.

My impetigo has gone again now - I have got on my legs - olive oil first, to stop them being so dry - then zinc & castor oil!

Its most pathetic - one of the Indians comes round every day & doles us out three cigarettes each! Our ration! Of course I have plenty more. We are allowed to smoke when we like except between 9 a.m and 12 a.m.

I think I shall probably be out in the next few days - it won't be my fault if I'm not!

That looking glass you gave me – the 'Colin' one, is most useful here I have it by my bedside.

We seem to be beside the railway here - & hear trains go by - only about four a day.

I'm glad I'm away from work at the moment - as the lifts aren't working - there was a sort of fire in the lift shaft last Sunday & now they are all out of order - & will be for some time to come.

I'm sorry for poor Lord Killean as he is on the 8th floor! Lord Louis is on the 9th - but is in Australia at the moment.

Birds (sort of sparrows) keep flying into the room & out the other side.

Its amusing at about 4.30 p.m. every day to see people preening themselves ready for their visitors - doing their hair & faces for ages - I just comb my hair & hang on & hope for the best!!

I hope Harry will bring me some letters from you to-night.

31st Mar 46. In my bungalow – 4 p.m. Sunday. I had two letters from Ma yesterday – the latest dated 21 March, & one from Boss – thanks. I wish Ma would send me her dress measurements instead of how she wants it every time! Her pattern wasn't enclosed. Boss may have to have hers of shantung – as that is the cheapest material here – so I hope she will approve. It washes beautifully.

I came out of the hos: yesterday morning. On Friday - on her rounds - the Dr said she didn't see why I couldn't put the stuff on my legs just as well myself - & my ankles have quite recovered & are normal again - so of course I was all for it. So I rang Harry up & she arranged transport for me for 11 yesterday morning - & out I came. The whole thing is not to scratch my legs - which is very difficult - & I have olive oil & also zinc & castor oil mixed to put on every day.

On Thursday evening the specialist came to see his patients - he is sweet & sat on my bed & talked. On Friday evening Paddy Corin (the Major from our office) came to see me & brought me a basket of flowers & talked to me for about ½ hr.

It is funny what people are - just copycats - like Mrs H! On Friday afternoon I spent the whole afternoon in bed making a stupid doll for Pip Carey (the paralysis officer) - as it is her birthday (24) today I made it from a bit of cardboard - drew a face - made some hair & skirt from wool, & plaited some wool for the arms & legs. It was very frail - & so I named it Fragile Fanny & also composed a poem to go with it, a la Hiawatha! Lo & behold, yesterday morning if the WRNS officer in our ward, really a very nice girl - started to make a similar one in wool & also made a pome - aren't I catty?!

Monday, 1ˢᵗ April – 11.30 a.m.. In the office

I didn't have a chance to finish this yesterday - what with tea - and going out to dinner at Round the Bend etc. They have got five new naval officers in that mess - I've only met three of them - two of which are very nice indeed.

I went to the M.O. this morning before I came into the office (as he always starts his day at the flats for the WRNS), and he was very nice, and said I ought now to go away somewhere cool for seven days to finish off my legs. They are much better and I have got proper ankles again - but they swolled a bit last night, and apparently they wont stop doing that until the legs have got quite alright again. So now I am in an awful muck, trying to get somewhere to go.

4.30 p.m. Sorry – I have been doing bits of work for Eric, and also trying to fix up some leave somewhere. I won't go into all the details of how I've been trying, as it won't interest you – but I am going to the Cameron Highlands for a week on Friday. I am afraid that I am going to Saigon after all - I do hope you won't mind., but it really is a terrific op, and I have been told the job there won't last very long - probably only one or two months, and anyway I have GOT to be home sometime in August, as my release is due at the beginning of September.

My worry about leave was that they want me in Saigon on or near the 4th April, and thought they might say it was no good if I didn't go until later. However, funnily enough, this afternoon a very nice Lieut.Colonel came in, and said he had just come from Saigon, and had come to give me Patricia's love, and so I asked him all about it. He has come to go to Penang on sick leave, and he said it would be quite okey-dokey for me to go on leave first, and get quite well, and then go to Saigon on about 15th April, He was very nice indeed, a Lt.Colonel Fuegelsang (?) or something like that. He told me that Patricia loves it there, and it sounds a very nice place. He says there is a hotel where we can go and stay and visit Angkor, which I am looking forward to very much.

I think you had better do something about addressing my letters differently from the minute you receive this letter. My address will be :

SACSEA Inter Services Allied Mission to F.I.C.

Saigon,

French Indo-China.

Sorry it's so long – and I'll see if that is right when I get there, and perhaps get it a bit shorter – perhaps a few initials will suffice!

I spent all yesterday resting on my bed on and off - and in the afternoon Hildegard suddenly arrived to give me back the SMH news letter which she had borrowed. She came in a huge van - which had been used in all the blitzes in England - it had the names of the places painted on the door. She was driving it herself - very well too. She is lucky - had just been told that she is going to Hong Kong - and she has gone on a boat today.

I've got masses more to say – but I think I'll get this letter off to you tonight, and write some more this evening when I get back.

I got two more letters from Ma to-day with her pattern.

2nd April 46.

This is my last morning in this office, as I am going to have to-morrow and Thursday off before going to Cameron Highlands on Friday – and shall do some shopping. I have just written a lot of letters which have been on my conscience for months – Aunt Nelly, Miss Ramsden, Mrs. Sturges. I have also written to that place in India to know whether we can still send food parcels – as it said in the paper that these have stopped. I have asked whether my last lot went off.

I am so glad the weather is warmer at home now – makes all the diff.

I had a nice letter from Ar Beat the other day, which I enclose – as it is so typical! I shall try and write to them to-day.

You've got it a bit wrong about the parcels. You have got all you should have up to now, and I am awfully pleased the sandals fit. That Lieut.Whiting is bringing the next one with the oxford shoes for Boss (no that's wrong – out it out! And start again). Lieut.Whiting is bringing one containing some more sandals for Boss- leather soles - a pair of slippers for Ma which she probably won't like! and a couple of tins of lambs tongues and a tin of grapefruit. He left here on 25th March on the Winchester Castle, and should be in U.K. in about 19 days from then. Another girl called Patricia (I don't know her surname), a nurse, has a parcel containing some oxford shoes for Boss, and some pickled onions for Dug. She left here a long time ago, but is going home via India, so I don't know when she will arrive.

Dr Camps never did write to me about the tea, but I don't mind. He can't retire until after I come home anyway, as he must blow out my ears and cut that thing out of my eye first!

There is a very nice Naval nursing sister living in our little room now, called Ann Ramsden. She was sent out here originally – about two years ago, to nurse senior officers, and she has nursed Lord Louis on two occasions, so knows him quite well. She has been in Java for four months nursing in the hospital there. She is very interesting, as she trained at the Middlesex Hospital, and also went to St Mary's Paddington, and then she had a job with the P&O. Line, and used to go all over on their liners, to Japan, Australia, China etc., as sort of top sister on ships.

That Lt.Col. John Carew Jones, who might ring you up, went on H.M.S.Sefton – a ship, and Patricia and I saw him off on a little boat in Singapore harbour, which was taking him to the ship. I shouldn't bother to ask him over if he rings you up. As he is very shy and it would be rather difficult talking to someone strange. Just talk to him on the telephone. I had a very nice letter from him from Colombo, thanking me for seeing him off, and for all the Irish Stew we had had in our bungalow, usually it was only him and me who ate this in the end!

I had a long letter from Marjorie Fletcher from the Transit Camp, the other day. It has finished there now, and is only a small place somewhere in Hertfordshire. The C.O. has returned from Africa, but has not gone back to the Camp. Marjorie said she had not heard of the R.S.M. for a long time, but had heard that she had resurrected a 'boy friend' – so I expect that is true and is what is the matter, though why she went so queer over it, I can't think.

I liked Boss's testimonial – funny how some people seem to think she is good!! I hope her shoals of letters have arrived from the Ad and that she is picking and choosing. I think she should go back to P.R. in September and save them from extinction.

I am going to the tailors this afternoon with your patterns – as I said, I may get shantung for Boss, and hope it is okey-dokey, as it is only in natural colour. But she can keep it for when she isn't doing dirty work. I may wait until I get to Saigon now for Ma's and see if the material there is cheaper.

I have just been brought in a letter from India, containing postage receipts for all those parcels I sent – so it is alright, and they will arrive eventually – Mrs. Howards, Cissie's, Mrs. Harpers and your other one.

12 noon. I have just been down to the NAAFI canteen to get a few things like notepaper etc., and said goodbye to the boys there, shook hands – they were so pleased! I do it just like Ma, and it doesn't half get you places when you act like her everywhere! Anyway feels nice!

Letter from Ar Beat enclosed Bloom field Cottage, Great Missenden. 15.3.46

My dear Dorothy

Very many thanks for so kindly remembering me on my birthday. I felt quite important for you seem such a long way away – that is why I don't write much or often – as a letter to go that distance should contain interesting news – But there is nothing doing here except the daily round of house chores & grubbing in the garden for me – Jessie is still out a great deal over other people affairs which would not interest you. When she gets new tyres, she is going to take me out some where for our own enjoyment – instead of always helping other people – on which her whole time is spent – of course you know all about Muriel & Douglas coming and distempering the bath room. They say perhaps you will do the kitchen for us!

I have got an extension attached to my wireless for Jessie's bedroom – she listens in evenings to "kitchen front" result we have new & improved cooking. She is very keen on experimenting which is nice.

Our great excitement here is that George Gilmons Thomson, you may remember our white haired handsome neighbour is to be married in May – she is over 50 & he is over 60! Is a widower of a few months when they began courting – so George will just step into the old wife's place & surroundings – who she used to be with – seems extraordinary to me.

Joyce Eltringham has been seriously ill, an old complaint. She is expected to be an invalid always.

The last I heard of Pat Pauton, she was still living with married sister & her children – husband (Pat's) had not retired

You should be having a wonderful time out there. I am glad to hear you may be going to Indo China, as you have gone so far, its nice to see as many places as possible.

We have had snow gales & ice for nearly a month continuously – rather unusual for this time of year – so don't know yet what damage has been done in garden.

Excuse scrappy letter. When I go the promised expedition in car, shall buy some more note paper so may do better next time I write!

Much love from A.B.

5th April 46. YWCA, Kuala Lumpa. Very many happy returns, to Boss. I sent a telegram which I hope arrived. I have started my journey to the "hills" & got here at lunch time today. I have come alone – as Harry has gone to Penang – where her friend Ted is also staying on leave. She has gone to a YWCA there – for 10 days - & anyway I only have a week. The YWCA is the most gorgeous mansion – all beautifully finished – as the occupants had it. They were Chinese & must have been millionaires – huge rooms – enormous verandahs everywhere – grand entrance with pillars etc. There are 7 beds in my room lovely mattresses - its not so bad as I'm only here for one night. The others are QAIMNS or FANYs. I palled up with one at dinner - who is also going to Cameron Highlands tomorrow.

The YWCA woman running the place are very nice & say there will be a truck of sorts to take me tomorrow - another 6 hrs by road.

My actual legs are much better - its only me swollen ankles now, which go down when I rest - so I am determined to spend all my leave on two chairs - legs up all the time!

It's a bit lonely coming on my own - but I know several WRNS officers already at C.H. one of who was in hos. with me.

I haven't seen anything of this place much, just drove through the town on the way here. The station & most of the buildings are white & nearly all with shapes like sort of mosques.

There is a gramophone recital on at the moment downstairs – but I have come up to bed & am sitting under a fan writing this first.

I had two nice letters from Ma on Wednesday – which I'll reply to when I get there.

6th April 46. YWCA. Cameron Highlands. I arrived here this evening at 6 p.m. After driving since 10 a.m. this morning - 155 miles. I came in a station wagon! (Dug will explain that sort of car – I hope!) seats four & is quite big + two drivers. There was me & two army nurses & two Indian drivers. We drove until 11.30 & stopped at a rest house in Tanjong Malim for lunch - soup, steak & onions, chips & greens - then pineapples, bananas & coffee - run by a Malay. There was a notice on the wall by the Civil Affairs Office of the district to say what a nice man the Malay was & how he had helped the evacuees in 1941-42. We left there at 12.15 & drove until 2.30 where we stopped at a rest house in Tapah & had 2 boiled eggs each and tea (my suggestion!) - then left there at 3.30 & went until 4 where we had to wait by a gate in the road until 4.30 - about 12 cars, lorries

& jeeps etc. all waiting to go. The next 50 miles of road is so dangerous with corners that they only allow one way traffic - & it is opened different hours of the day for up & down traffic - men at each end with a telephone, checking the cars off! One driver went terribly fast & we were quite scared! but really he was very good - all hairpin bends the whole way, climbing all the time. This place is just over 4,000 ft high with mountains all round.

The YWCA has five bungalows here for women - all ranks - & the male officers stay in the Cameron Highlands hotel.

That nice WRNS officer Margaret Ripley, who was in the same ward & hos: with me - arrived here yesterday - saw my name on the list as coming & asked for me to share a room with her. So we are in a small bungalow - she & I have one room (upstairs!) & there are only two others staying in the other room - a nice bathroom where I had a real hot bath on arrival (My legs & ankles feel much better already!). Margaret was sweet to me & welcomed me. There is a nice sitting room (where I am now) with a log fire - as it is cold up here!

She & her friend (a Capt., who drove her here in a jeep yesterday) have gone to a dance & so have the other two & I am alone - lovely! I was asked to go too - but refused as my object is not to walk at all and get mended!

We go to another bungalow about 5 mins away for lunch & dinner - have breakfast in bed here & tea in the sitting room apparently. We are taken and fetched by truck to lunch & dinner & I have just come back from mine - best since I left home! First pineapple - then tender chicken, bacon, stuffing - peas - & new potatoes & mint, heaven!

I got back just as Margaret & Donald had just driven out in their jeep - & went into the sitting room & was trying to find the light & they arrived back as they thought I might have difficulty finding the switch, awfully kind of them.

I shan't write any more tonight as I want to put me legs up on the sofa – by the fire!

My letters will probably take a long time to reach you from here – as I believe the mail is not too good from here to Singapore.

7th April 46. Cameron Highlands (Strathiel Bungalow) I have just had the most wonderful curry lunch & am feeling full - two helpings! It really is lovely here. We seem to be in a sort of valley surrounded by hills - the tops of which are misty at the moment. It is quite cool - & cold in the nights - two blankets on our beds. Breakfast was brought up to us in bed this morning – pineapple – porridge - bacon, eggs, toast – tea - & Margaret & I got up about 10 a.m. We then sat outside the sitting room – sort of & talked to her & her friend Donald Cameran (a Lt Col. Who is staying at the hotel) & a Capt & Mrs Ayre. He is stationed at K.L. & she is W.V.S. here. I think they live somewhere here in peace time. At 11 we had tea & biscuits & then they all went out & I sat with me legs up & sewed & read. At 12.30 I walked up to the Lodge – where we eat & started eating & Margret joined me - & now we have come back to ours & are writing letters. I am going out with her & her Donald later on. Its pouring with rain at the moment – keeps doing a bit then stopping.

These bungalows are most beautifully finished - lovely armchairs, cushions etc - & wonderful bowls of flowers – some English ones – nasturtiums, pinks, irises & some queer ones – some shaped like arum lilies only dark red with a white stripe down each petal.

I do wish I had a typewriter I can't manage writing now - & I want to say lots!

There was a piano in the YWCA at K-L & I had a good go at it yesterday morning before I left. I had my music with me in case - & I can still play. I was welcomed in K-L by a FANY who works there & when I gave my name she said she knew Reading & had I anything to do with it – funny.

One of the nurses I traveled here with yesterday was a bird - called Goodchild & her brother was a P.o.W. in No.1. Camp, went with 19th Div, & was a private in the Suffolk Regt - but he never got home - died of tropical - diseases - Does Dug know him?

I have had my tin trunk mended – one of those naval officers got it done for me – also I've had to get two new locks put on my blue suit case – going to cost 10 dollars! But I have to have it done.

9ᵗʰ April 46.

I am quite enjoying myself, spend most of my time eating, sleeping & sewing. I feel very clever - as I have cut out, & made by hand three pairs of knickers! & embroidered the bottoms. Someone cut me a paper pattern & showed me how. They are not very good material – Japanese cotton – but fit alright.

This afternoon, Margaret's friend Donald wasn't feeling well, & she took me instead to the riding stables here - where there are about 10 horses used for anyone on leave - one dollar an hour (2/-4d!). A very nice lady runs it – her face is rather like Miss Ghey's

Anyway we got there at 3 - me in shorts as of course I never brought my slacks up here. S was very worried as there seemed to be too many people. Anyway we all sat on horses ready & then she asked M & me if we'd mind going tomorrow instead - so we got down & went for a walk instead. We are now going at 9 a.m. tomorrow morning & are both terrified! M. hasn't ridden since she was 10 & you know my state on a horse!

My ankles are alright now & my legs are clearing up very well. I only hope they'll stay alright when I get back to Singapore.

When I first arrived here & was giving my name – a very nice looking girl also arrived – a two-pipper in St Johns Ambulance & I thought I knew her face, & she gave her name as Courtenay - & I knew if her name was Angela – she was at SMH "The Lady Angela Courtney" lives somewhere in Devon. Anyway I didn't say anything – but today I met another St John's person who knows her & says she knows she was at school in Brighton so it must be her.

I may call & see her & may not – she is at one of the other bungalows about 5 mins walk. She was never actually at SMH with me – much younger, but she might like to see my News Letter.

I have palled up a bit with an Army Nursing sister from the bungalow where we eat - & she came to my place all yesterday afternoon & evening & we sewed & talked & sang songs & sat in front of the fire. We also scrounged in the kitchen & made some late brew last night. She is very Scotch & has lovely ginger hair –

has been nursing in Java – but one of her ears is wonky now. She was also in hos: with me.

The climate here is lovely – cool – quite a bit of rain & when the sun is out its like a hot English one – doesn't make you all sticky. We are just over 5,000 ft high here – not 3.

I'm longing to get back to get some letters from you – as it wasn't worth having them forwarded here – takes 2 days for them to get here.

We were given 50 free cigarettes & some sweets yesterday.

All the men at the stables helping with the horses were Japanese prisoners - nasty little beasts - I hate seeing them about. But they certainly seemed very nice with the horses. I had a large one to get on & managed to get on it quite easily.

I am wearing that green skirt of mine at the moment & it fits me easily (no corsets!) so I can't be any fatter!

We saw some lovely butterflies this afternoon – all having a game together – 3 yellow 3 bright blue & one lovely large violet one. Also we passed a sort of cottage with three turkeys at the gate – all with their feathers out & red things hanging down - & one white one - & a mum turkey with some little ones! It made me think of Ma.

I do hope Boss had a nice birthday – I'll give her something I want (!) when I return. Did she get my tele?

13th April 46. Singapore

I got back from leave yesterday - after a very good journey by road - staying the night in Kuala Lumpur again on my way back - & I got back at teatime yesterday. It is so hot here after the cool air at Cameron Highlands. My ankles seem to be OK now - I've walked round town & they haven't swollen a bit. I have some nasty spots on my legs – white pimples that turn into spots - & I love bursting them & getting the muck out! I went to the M.O. this morning & he has given me a tonic (at last!) to finish off my legs. So I hope I shall be 'ealthy from now on! Everyone says how much better I look – which makes me angry as I wasn't ill!

When I got back I had 4 letters to read from Ma – the latest dated 1st April thanks. I am going to Saigon next week I think -

but am not sure yet which actual day. I had my injection against cholera this morning, which we have to have for there.

On Wednesday morning at 9 a.m. Margaret Ripley & I went riding at C-H. It was very nice – as her friend Donald was ill in bed & someone else she knew a Major Holford fetched us in the jeep. We found out that he was an ex cavalry man & kept about 20 horses (+ 1 baby elephant!) out here as a side line - at ALFSEA. So we managed to get a horse for him too - & about 10 of us went out - all the others were men - mostly B.O.Rs (ask Dug!). We went to a field & there he gave us a lesson (the woman in charge had asked him to). He was very good indeed - told us how to lead the horse in and out of a stable - how its harness went - & then how to sit, hold reins etc & also get on and off & made us practice that! I had a large horse but managed to get on quite well on my own! Then we walked & trotted etc – but the ground was too wet to do much. Anyway I thoroughly enjoyed it & mean really to do some when I come home – funds permitting!

I had a very nice evening my last at C-H. That nursing sister came to my bungalow & we had tea and sang songs!

We had a good send off after lunch on Thursday - all the Chinese boys came to the door & I shook hands with them all - they were so pleased. Two of them were sweet - brothers, one 15 & one 13 - beaming all the time they waited on us at table. In the same transport there were 3 ATS Cols & a WAAF & a FANY who lives in Saigon in peace time. She has given me a letter to give to her sister who also lives there & has a sugar plantation & says she will show me all the places to buy things in Saigon.

I got the front seat all the way coming back - next to the Indian driver. We stopped at a rest house before K-L & had eggs & chips - pancakes (which I didn't), pineapple, bananas & tea.

I wish I could explain all the interesting things we passed - but it would be impossible. Most of the way down were rubber plantations & the natives lived in homes built on sticks to get away from the wet. Those that have huts on the ground live + chickens, goats, dogs etc, altogether - but on the whole everywhere & everyone is clean.

I'll stop now - as my hand is fair wore out! I'll write another tomorrow.

I am sitting on the balcony of my bungalow writing this. I went into the Cathay on Saturday morning to have my injection and I saw Paddy Cronin & he has asked me to go back to the office tomorrow, until I go to Saigon - as the person who was going to take my job has gone & done the dirty on them & is not coming now - & they are in a soil for someone. So I said I would - but am not that keen - as the lifts are still broken & it means walking up 5 floors.

I marched round the town on Saturday morning & fetched Boss's dress which I had made. I am afraid the material isn't as pretty as it might be, but its not bad - & quite well made. I haven't yet managed to get anything suitable for Ma it all seems to be about $35 a yard – all the stuff wot I'd like to get for her – but I thought I'd see what they've got in Saigon, first. I hope I shall be able to find something nice after all my song & dance over getting the pattern!

One thing I didn't describe when driving through K-L to the YWCA when I arrived there - we passed a Chinese cemetery - & it was evidently some sort of festival - there were heaps of people - all in little family groups - mostly with black umbrellas up (lots of them carry these to keep off the sun and or rain!). They were putting bits of coloured paper with writing on over the tombstones - and lighting joss sticks & leaving them in little jars. Their cemeteries(?) are always built on small hills & are sort of let into the ground - at least all the ones I've seen are - like little door ways.

Outside there were lots of little stalls for buying fruit & the usual little eating stalls - & places to buy the joss sticks (sort of incense).

5.45 p.m. I have been marching round the town again this afternoon & have bought (at least the man is getting them for me by Wednesday) some films for Boss's camera. I can only afford two at present! I have had an enlargement made of that photograph for you - & will send it one day.

Did I tell you I saw that girl who was at SMH - in Cameron Highlands? "The Lady" Angela Courtney – I rang her up & she came to see me - & although she was younger she knew lots of people I did. She was very nice - & borrowed my News Letter – returned it the next day.

Harry & I went to dinner at Round the Bend on Friday & had some lovely curry – 3 helpings for me.

I have packed my trunk yesterday - an awful effort! I got it mended by my naval pals at the docks. I have now sewn it up in canvas & hope it will last the voyage to Saigon & then home.

I am going to try & buy a sheet of crepe to bring home for Ma – which she can have put on to one of her pairs of shoes. I think that will be better than getting any for her here.

I have bought a few pairs of small children's shoes – very cheap – crepe soles. I expect you'd like to give a pair to Mrs Little - & I've got one for Brandy for her niece. What size do Jeanette & Mrs Harper take – as the easiest thing to get them will be a sort of sandal I've found – please let me know.

I have heard, unofficially, that the mission in Saigon will probably end in June - if so I shall come straight home after that. Won't it be wonderful arriving & being met in London by you! (in the car, I hope!) We shall need a trailer for all my luggage as well - as I already have one extra bag - & may have to get another in Saigon.

I took a photograph of our amah this morning - it was so funny - she wouldn't come until she'd dolled up & redone her hair - which anyway is all scraped back into a bun. (They all wear it like that) Then I had to wait while she fetched her daughter aged about 15 who works in another bungalow, & then a third amah arrived & I wanted to take them altogether - but they wouldn't have it - she said the Chinese way was never to be taken three of them! She stood absolutely still - stiff to attention - no smile! but obviously was very pleased.

I am glad the aunts are okey–dokey. Please give them my love – I'm glad you sewed her coat up on April 1st !

I'm longing to distemper all the hall & landing - Dug will have to fix up some scaffolding on the stairs.

That man Donald Cameron - a Lieut Col - who I met in the Cameron H - friend of Margaret Ripley's, had a lot to do with organising the evacuation of the P.o.W.'s last August & September. He was in Rangoon & went & talked to them at the hospital a lot where Dug was. He says the records the prisoners used to keep were invaluable when they were checking all the names etc. The records at Changi - some of them had been buried for safety & have been dug up.

I am sorry I never tried to find Dug's treasure - but I have never had a car available for that sort of thing!

All my love (& to any one who you think you ought to give some to without fibbing!) i.e. Cissie etc!

17th April 46.

I had heaps of letters yesterday – three from Ma, the latest dated 7th April – thanks. You are funny – you ticked me off once for not putting any XXX on my letter, so I apologised in my next, and now you write and say you never noticed I never had!! Doesn't matter! I'm still here, but may go to Saigon at the end of this week.

My legs are practically alright now in the way of spots, but my ankles are still a bit "up" - especially in the evenings. They soon go down when I rest - but I hope that when my skin gets absolutely okay, they will be alright altogether.

I have heard from India that we are not allowed to send any more food parcels - only tea and soap - so I'll send some of that regularly, and try and organise something from South Africa.

3.30 p.m. Frank Owen came in this morning, and I made him and Eric come downstairs with me and I took their photographs – so I hope they will come out. Frank is lucky - he is going off to Burma again to-morrow with a war artist to show him all the battle fields etc., and where all the fighting went on - as he, Frank, is writing some official history of the Burma war for the War Office.

Reference the children in Singapore - they seem to stay up till all hours at night - kids of three running the side streets at 10 and 11 at night. Also when the better class Chinese go out, they are always very well dressed and made up, and also the children are made up with powder and lipstick, from about the age of 1 year upwards!

It was awfully funny yesterday - I went out to lunch at the W.W.C.A. with Charles (he is still here and I see him occasionally)

- as I wanted to go to some shops afterwards and help him buy a pair of shoes, as I knew where the shop is wot keep his size, 12! Anyway, we went in a trishaw (bicycle rickshaw), and you know my size, and he is 6ft. high and quite big and we had an awful job getting in! We both had to sit sideways, and had the giggles. The man on the bicycle was very amused, and we gave him good money for the extra weight!

I bought two more sponges, quite nice ones - for 50 cents and 75 cents, about 1/-2d. and 1/-8d. each! Different from the prices at home!

Its no good – I keep being given work to do now!

18th April 46.

I have come into the office this afternoon "to oblige"! as officially I am having a few days off so that I can pack all my things ready to go to Saigon.

That Lt.Col.Fugelsang, the head of the mission in Saigon came in to see me yesterday, and said everything was changing very quickly there and that the mission might close very soon, and I might only be there a few weeks - on the other hand a new mission might form and I might stay with that a few months, but he didn't know. It would just suit me to go and see the place and then come away! I should then come home, unless I got the chance of a few weeks in Hong Kong - which is EXTREMELY unlikely. I am very sorry that Fugelsang himself is leaving the mission now and going to Java. Patricia says he is about the nicest person there - I told him that yesterday and he was amused!

I packed my trunk the other day and sewed it up in canvas, and today I unpacked the whole lot again and re-arranged everything!

I went shopping early this afternoon and have bought two sheets of crepe rubber to bring home – enough to make four pairs of shoes – so we'll have some made for Ma, or have some of hers covered. It was quite cheap. I also got Boss two films for her camera – which I expect will keep alright until I get back. Nearly all films we buy here are Jap – but they are not bad.

Harry and I went up to dinner at Round the Bend again last night. Its very amusing - they have given their Chinese boys the sack, as they kept asking for more money and got rather unruly - and now they have got four Chinese amahs (women) instead, plus one Chinese male cook. They all look so smart in their black trousers and white pyjama jackets, and wait at table very nicely. They all have black hair scraped back tightly into a bun.

Cont Saturday 20th April. I didn't have time to finish this on Thursday(!) as I was given work to do. We had yesterday & today & tomorrow off as it is Easter.

I tried to pack a bit more yesterday & tidy my things & in the afternoon Harry & I went & marched round the town - I was very good not spending much! At present I am lying on my bed with nothing on - a towel covering all vital parts! Harry is asleep in her bed - I brought some breakfast over for her.

Nearly ever afternoon now, regularly there is a thunderstorm - very heavy rain. I got some papers yesterday - 2 Surrey Comets – Oct 20 & Dec 22! & Norbiton mags for Nov, Dec & Jan.

I see Miss Sauson died - what from? Do you remember your rows with her?! Also Miss Haward & Mrs Duffield. Is the latter the 'puppy' one? I didn't know Miss Walker had died, what was wrong with her and who's got her money?

12 – Just going to lunch & will post this.

Sunday 21st April 5.30 p.m. 46. Easter day
I'm still here & may go to Saigon next week.

I'm thinking of you at the moment & guess you are having your morning brew (11.30 your time) unless you are in church.

I went to the Cathedral this morning for the 10.30 service with two other girls - Naval Nursing Sisters. We got a lift in & got there 9.45 & by 10 a.m. the church was packed and by 10.15 there were crowds standing at the back - & others sitting on stools in the chancels. We got quite nice seats in the middle fairly near the back.

I was rather disappointed with the service - the hymns were not some of the best known & were too slow - the chants were difficult & the sermon not too good - but very dramatic. It wasn't nearly such a nice service as at Christmas. The parsons (2 - one old who preached & one young who took the service) were not too inspiring. I believe the Bishop is in England recuperating from being a P.o.W.

Anyway I am glad I went - it is a lovely Cathedral, there were heaps of the Services there from Generals to privates - also a few Indians & Chinese.

I have bought 3 tins of beef dripping to bring home when I come - also a tin of Christmas pudding!

I went to the Phoenix Club last night & had two catastrophes - the heel came off my shoe & I had to walk and dance with my toe!

Their all the 'boys' had suddenly walked out - on strike because two had been sacked - & we all had to wait on ourselves! Actually it was rather fun.

I'll write again tomorrow

22nd April 46. In the office. 3.45 p.m. I got a letter from Ma this morning dated 10th April – thanks. I have already written to Mr Tate as you asked me to do – did it this morning – jolly good. I have to send letters to all these people, as it is not possible to buy postcards here. I have written him about two pages.

Thank you for Genestes and Hazel's letters. Geneste seems to have forgotten how to thank people! I am enclosing a photograph which may interest you* – it was taken at that SEAC Newspaper mess party I went to about last January. The girl standing next to me is a WVS person. The man (tall one) in civilian clothes with glasses, on the left at the back is a Mr Everson, who is Financial Adviser to Supremo – a very important person, and very nice. SAC can't spend any money without asking him!

The clerk has just brought me in two more Surrey Comets dated Febuary 9th and 16th – getting better.

My Eric is leaving here next Monday - he is going to Ceylon for three weeks and then going home to England, and will be demobbed there. He doesn't know yet whether he is going to America or not - so I've told him that if I don't get that job with Frank Owen, I shall make him get me one! He says he is going to call on Douglas when he goes to the War Office next - about the end of May. He really is sweet.

I sometimes go down into the town at lunchtime now, instead of going back to the mess, and have it in a new officers club, which is open for lunch and tea - and it is in Whiteway and Laidlaw's old shop. I believe the Army are giving it up soon, and it will be given back to them.

22nd April, Top left Mr Everson, financial adviser to the Supremo, Dorothy 4th left

24th April 46.

I got heaps of papers from you this morning - I think they came on the ship Orontes - which has just arrived here and is taking people home again. There were four bundles of Sketches etc. and three Surrey Comets – all ranging from October to February! Very interesting, and I spent the whole of lunch hour lying on my bed naked reading them! And will continue this evening.

I enclose a measly stamp for Boss. I have bought her quite a lot more, which I am keeping to bring home with me. I have also written to Hildegard in Hong Kong and asked her to buy me a set of their stamps and send them to me. Also I hope to get some nice ones in Saigon.

I have sent some money to Delhi and asked them to send you regular parcels of tea and soap – which is better than nothing I suppose.

I went shopping again yesterday afternoon and bought some lovely little bits of china, quite cheap. I got five small soup bowls with coloured dragons all over them - they will be very nice for soup - better than a plate and nicer than a cup!

I also took my camera out yesterday and tried to take interesting things. There were two small girls, about 6 years old at a tiny stall selling fruit etc. I pointed the camera at them, and they immediately ran away and wouldn't let me! I have heard before that they don't like being taken. I did take an Indian with a beard and turban nursing a small child – but it was rather dark and may not come out.

I am sorry I never sent a telegram to congratulate Dug on his promotion - and am so pleased he is a Captain now, so he can take the telegram as read.

This H.Q. is closing down on 31st May altogether, and just leaving a few officers to do the odd bits. Our department will close down altogether, as SEAC is finishing on 15th May, and the films and Radio Station will be looked after by other people.

27th April 46. Saturday. 10.30 a.m.
I haven't had any letters from you for a few days as I expect you are now writing to Saigon. Anyway I hope to be really going there on Monday, so I shall get them then.

The girl has arrived in my office who is taking over my job here - she is a Eurasian W.A.C.(1) (Indian A.T.S.), and is very nice indeed. She lived here before the war, and has just managed to get back here from India, and so is living with her parents and comes every day. I have shown her round everything and how to do the letters and signals etc., and I shall not come back here after this morning. She won't have much to do, as Eric is leaving for Ceylon on Monday, and only Paddy will be here. The whole office will be closing down at the end of May.

Eric is going to Ceylon for two weeks, and is then going to England. I have told him to call in and see Douglas, and he says he would love to, as he will be visiting 60 Eaton Square quite a lot. I am sure Dug will like to see him, as he is so nice, and can tell you how I'm behaving here!! He has a Mum who lives in Llandudno.

My legs are nearly quite alright now. My ankles are very much better and swell only very slightly in the evenings, hardly at all - and will probably be quite okey-dokey in a few days. It is such a relief as it was so difficult finding shoes to wear that were comfy, and now I can wear anything again. I am taking a tonic three times a day to finish off the spots on my legs - two of them the sister said were sort of carbuncles - but they are healed now.

You ask about the flowers we get out here and whether we have daffodils! We certainly don't get anything like that - and I am longing to see some English flowers again. We have a tree in our garden which has white flowers growing in clusters called Temple flowers - with a lovely smell. We often pick some for our room, as they last ages and fill the room with smell. There are lots of trees with flowers on – some of them leading up to our bungalow are just like laburnum - but not quite. One sort of tree which is quite prolific (!) in the town is the travellers palm - called that I believe because the juice can be drunk by people traveling - I suppose! Orchids are all over the place, and also gardenias - grow anywhere and are very cheap to buy - also arum lilies.

I was very interested to see all the pictures of the floods in the Daily Sketches – I had no idea it was so bad – and it mentioned Teddington weir as being dangerous at one time.

I saw the air mail edition of the Times yesterday for April 16th – with two things in wot interested me. Did you see them. One was Edward Whiteaway's engagement, and the other that a Dr. Joane Bowes has a son – she is the first birth in the paper – her hub being a doctor too. She was at S.M.H. with me, and used to live at Ashstead in Surrey – I once went to tea with her there, and I think she came over to Norbiton once to me – a very pretty dark girl, very clever.

I am sending you a set of Jap money, which is quite interesting to keep.

I wrote to Dorothy Aitken the other day congratulating her on her engagement.

I saw General Kimmins again yesterday to say goodbye to him, and he told me that my job in Saigon may only last a few weeks - so I really shouldn't be long before I come home - and am looking forward to it like anything. I shall have to find out something about what will happen if I come back in June and don't get demobbed until September, as I don't want to have a A.T.S. job in England. I could get back on medical grounds saying the heat doesn't suit my spots (!). but I don't want to do that, or they may try and give me a medical board which would be silly. So I shall ask the head AT out here - I think they might demob me as soon as I get back if I ask that. Anyway once I am demobbed I get 56 days leave with pay and allowances, which will be quite good!

I met an awfully interesting Naval Lieut. in the Tanglin Club the other day - he was wearing parachute wings, so of course I asked him what for. He was dropped on the Andaman Islands in 1944 and lived there with another man for six months doing intelligence work and finding out all about the island etc., always being hunted by the Japs. He says they were fed in secret by the natives and by food being dropped by plane, and in the end they were taken off again at night by submarine.

You never told me whether Boss's and Chet's sandals fitted them – please let me know, in case I get anything more in that line for them. Its going to be rather a job bringing back presents for everyone (not the family of course) but people like Aunts. I can't manage shoes for everyone, as I'd never get through the customs. Would Dug like a pair – as I could get him some – if so please tell me his size and whether he'd like black or brown.

One plant I saw growing a lot in Cameron Highlands was interesting - the pitcher plant. (Actually I believe it grows in England too only on a smaller scale). There are a few ordinary green leaves, and the rest is sort of brown bags that hang down and catch insects which the plant eats - they are really disgusting looking things.

I went to one of our private film shows on Friday – and saw a thing called Rhapsody in Blue – the life of George Gershwin (Ma probably won't have heard of him, but Boss will!). The music was quite nice, but I went to sleep quite a lot I do hope you are all okey at home, including the chickens.

I feel rather awful, as I haven't written to you for five days - but lots of things happened, and I thought I'd wait and get meself sorted out. Firstly, I am not going to Saigon after all - and I'm very disappointed. I'd better own up, that I was going by air - as there are no boats going at all except store ones which won't take women - and air is the only way of getting there, and only takes 4 hours. They put in for my air passage on 15th April, but there were so many people wanting to go more important than me, that I have never got a place, although there were three planes a week. Yesterday General Kimmins rang me up and said he was sorry, but as I had not been able to get there - it really wasn't worth while me going now, as the whole Mission is finishing on 15th May, and they are all coming back. So there we are.

My relief is in my old job - but Eric has gone to Ceylon, and she has absolutely nothing to do all day, and if I liked I could get this job back again until it finishes on 31st May. I really don't quite know what to do now.

Last night I went to a cocktail party given by Esme Lawrence - the A.T.S. senior Commander here - to meet Controller White, who is the new Director of A.T.S. We all went in civilian clothes - I looked very nice! (I thought). So I had a talk with the Director, and said if I went home at the end of May would I still have to work in England in the ATS and she said she thought I would for a few months until my demob in Sept. because they are short of officers. So I asked if I'd lose my rank as there are so many Junior Commanders surplus now, and she said she THOUGHT I would not, but couldn't be sure - and I don't want to do that after four years with three pips. So I'm in a soil!

I'd like to come home early in June and get straight out of ATS – but you see my point don't you?

General Kimmins told me to go and see him to see if he could get me something else nice for a few months - so I have come in this morning and been to see him - and he says he will talk to Esme Lawrence and see if he can possibly do anything for me, and will let me know.

My legs and arms are alright now - but I've got two places of impetigo again on my face! one near my eye, which is rather sore, and the other to the left of my chin when I'm facing you! So the M.O. made me go and see the skin specialist again this morning – which I did - but he has only given me some stuff which I have to put on every 10 mins. It is not very bad if it doesn't spread. He had two Indian doctors in there and was teaching them – and showed them my nails which showed when I stopped taking mepacrine – so he said! I could vaguely see it, they are very slightly a different colour half way down. He still thinks that I had a sort of mephachrine poisoning, although he says I didn't show any of the usual signs. The doctor here disagrees with him, and thinks that the climate just doesn't suit me, together with the food not being very good for us – dehydrated and tinned stuff etc., and I agree with him.

In my bungalow: 9.15 p.m.

I didn't have time to finish this before – I sent you a telegram today about my address – as I haven't had any letters from you for a week & I expect you are writing to Saigon. It's a shame as I shan't hear from you on my birthday on Monday now. I have written to Patricia to tell her to bring me any letters - as she will be coming back here.

I shall write tomorrow – as I am going to bed now – I can't write with a pen for long after typing so much! Which is bad, I know.

I have got heaps of papers from you – thank you. Sketches & Comets for Feb & March - & two Illustrated London News – very nice – I read them always.

I do hope you are all okey – its horrid having no letters – so when you get this please send me an E.F.M. cable to say you are all alright – 'cos I shall probably won't have heard by then – although I may.

3rd May 46.

I have come into the office to-day to type some more letters. I am still jobless.

When we were at that ATS party on Wednesday, Lady Killearn* came and was introduced to us all - and I've never seen such a sight. Ma would have stared at her all the time! She had quite a nice dress on - but had a white silk coat just hanging from her shoulders, without putting her arms in the sleeves, and her headgear was just like a brides - a huge spray of white flowers - I think they were false ones too - was stuck straight up on her head. Everyone was remarking how silly she looked. She seems quit young - anyway younger than the old boy.

I was talking to a girl who works here and lives in our mess – a civilian, and discovered she was at St. James College too – only one year after me.

I have got my room to myself at the moment in the bungalow. When Harry knew I was going to Saigon, she asked if she could have a single room in the bungalow next door, as someone there was going home yesterday - and was told she could, so she says she feels awful about it as I am not now going at all - but I don't really mind - as long as I don't get anyone unpleasant with me. Anyway it won't be long as all the bungalows are closing on 31st May, and I shall have to go somewhere else - either to another job out here, or else come home.

I have got my trunk and camp kit, all beautifully done up – I sewed them up in canvas and painted my name and address on in white – and was going to send them home by M.F.O. – and shall probably still do that.

I met two ATS officers at the party the other night – one came and asked me if I had been the Adj at the Transit camp, and she said she remembered coming straight from OCTU, all frightened, and scared stiff at coming to report to me, and I said to her "Have a cigarette, ducky"!! and she felt alright after that!

The other girl cleared up a long standing mystery with me – as ages ago when I was trying to trace Sam Johnston, I got a message through a WRNS officer, that an ATS person had asked if she knew me – because she knew Sam's address, and I was never able to trace her. Anyway this girl came up to me – her name Gregson – and she also knew me at the Transit Camp. Apparently she was in Liverpool with Violet, who told her Sam was out here – although she never actually met him.

After all my fine talk I have not yet had a dress made for Ma – but maybe I shall find some suitable stuff for it soon!

In my bus this morning two girls I know where talking about the F.E.P Division (Far Eastern Propaganda) where they work, and were talking rather disparagingly about someone called Diana Harper – and I think that must be Mrs. Harper's cousin. So I asked what she was like – and they said she could be charming and nice, and sometimes could be a female dog! I haven't met her, and no doubt I could if I tried but I can't be bothered. You had better just tell Mrs. Harper that I have heard she is out here, but she lives in a mess some distance from me, and it is rather difficult to meet her. Don't go and tell her what I've heard!

I've told so many people my new address in Saigon – it is sickening, as I don't suppose there will be anyone there to forward letters on after Patricia leaves on 15th. Please will you tell the Aunts, as I wrote and told them.

Ma – would you very kindly send a few P.Cs for me to these people and tell them that I am not going to Saigon and if they write to send their letters to this address as usual. I wrote to them fairly lately, and I really haven't enough to say to write again now – on the other hand I don't want to miss any possible letters from them.

J/Comd. Violet Johnston, Officers Mess, Hannington Barracks, Formby, Liverpool.

Greyhound – 18, Harrington Gardens, SW.7.

J/Comd. M.Fletcher (she was at the Transit Camp with me) 43, Beaudesert Road, Handsworth, Birmingham.

Thanks!

*Dowager Lady Killearn 1910-2015, second wife of Britain's wartime ambassador in Cairo.

5th May 46. 10 p.m. (Eve of my birthday!)
In my bungalow.

I am having a 'quiet' evening & have been tidying up my drawers & room etc. I keep one 'present' drawer with things I am collecting to bring home. Its awful how the damp gets in. I have a nice tablecloth I bought & it was quite wet.

Its terribly hot - & I'm sitting in my petticoat. I'm still out of a job - its rather nice for a few days - seeing everyone go off to work. I usually go down the town during the day - have lunch with those naval friends at Whiteaway & Laidlaws - which is an officers restaurant - & then march a bit.

My face is very much better - if nothing else develops I shall be a free woman from skin complaints - first time since Jan!

I went to a very nice cocktail party yesterday evening in another mess - a lovely bungalow. I met an RAF officer (I know him quite well) who works in SAC's office & says how busy he is & not enough staff - so I suggested I go and help there. He is going to see about it tomorrow, so I may. If I do - I shall stay until the end of May - & then definitely come home in June. I think that would be nice. I've bought a lovely thermos flask - all Chinese with Old Chiang Kai-Shek on it & Chinese writing - & get it filled with ice cold water in the mess - for lemon drinks during the day.

Excuse awful writing – no excuse!

I haven't had any letters from you for 10 days as they have all gone to Saigon & am longing to hear.

8th May 46. S.R.Division, H.Q.,S.A.C.S.E.A., S.E.A.C. I am so bored with having no job at all, I have come into the office to write some letters – and I think I have almost decided what I will do now if it all works. Paddy says he would like to have me back in this office, as although there is hardly anything to do, I do know my way about things which the new girl doesn't, and she is keen to get a job wot will go on as she lives in Singapore. So what I shall try and arrange is to get back here for the rest of May and then go for a weeks leave in Cameron Highlands from 1st-8th June, and then wait for a ship to come home. Would that suit you – if I arrive back at the end of June?1!! There is a lovely ship going called the Athlone Castle which I might catch - or the Empress of Australia. But I shall have to see whether the head AT will agree to all this. I think she will, as I shall never get rid of my skin diseases out here. My face is practically alright now, but this morning I have two more spot things on my legs, which the doctor says is still another form of impetigo. They are not bad, but I'm fed up with always having to put stuff on me everywhere and taking medicines and pills!

It was lovely - Patricia arrived back unexpectedly from Saigon on Monday with seven letters from Ma dated from 12th to 19th April - thank you for them. I am glad the rugs arrived, but I'm annoyed, as I especially asked for oblong shapes not half moons. I do hope they are really alright. She (Patricia) has gone and got herself engaged to someone else all of a heap and brought him to see me on Monday afternoon - such a nice man. He comes from South Africa, and is a Group Captain in the R.A.F., aged 33, and 6ft.3" tall. I think they are really well suited to each other – more than anyone else she knew. They may get married here quite quickly as if so it is easier for her to get out of the ATS and get home with him - but she also wants to get married in England because of her Ma - so I suggested that they have a civil ceremony here, and then get done again in a Church in England – so they may do that. I spent the whole of yesterday afternoon shopping with Patricia - and we gossiped hard all the time. She loved Saigon and was disappointed I never got there. She said the shops were terribly expensive, and she never got to Angkor - so I don't mind so much now.

Last night I got your cable for my birthday – thank you very much for it, and I am so glad you now know my address again – so I can expect letters regular from you from about the end of this week. Patricia is going back to Saigon at the end of this week, and will bring me any more from there that may have come from you. I am anxious to know whether you got that parcel which Whitney was going to post to you. Charles (one of the other naval officers) had a letter from him in which he said he had rung you up - so you should have had the parcel by now.

I'd love to send you one of those E.F.M. Cables all funny! "Twins born – May you enjoy the Passover" etc. etc!

I went to the theatre on my birthday night and saw a very good play called 'It depends on what you mean' by James Bridie, and a London cast of Ursula Jeans, Roger Livesey, Malcolm Keen. I'm going next week to see the Barrets of Wimpole Street.

I've bought some material to have a dress made for Boss - and it's a twin of one I've had made for myself, so I hope she won't mind - only its such pretty stuff and quite cheap - as they go out here. I enclose a pattern of the stuff, and shall have it made at the

tailors soon. I have also got some white stuff for a blouse for Ma
– don't say you don't want one as I insist on it, and if it doesn't
suit your liking, it will do for someone else. I want it made with a
thing down the front – don't you remember we did nothing but
look for that sort of thing in the shops? I have seen a very nice
pattern in the tailor's book only I'm not sure whether you want
a collar or not. Please let me know in YOUR NEXT LETTER
what you think of it, and if not, please draw me what you want.
I think it would go well with your coat and skirt. Why don't you
have a coat made and skirt at Strutts? I shall be able to help you
with some coupons when I come back, as I shall get about 100 to
start me off with.

You ask me what I think about leaving Bush. I think you
should – as he seems to have a very low stock in things wot we
want. Only mind you go somewhere where you can creep under
the counter! What about Stephenson and Rush? Or the Co-op!!!

The other day I got a very garbled telephone message about
a J/C. Munro (who I know quite well) who was in hospital, and
would I see Riley Carr!! So yesterday I went to the hospital (the
one I was in) to see another ATS officer and also a nursing sister
who are both ill, and then I asked about the Munro person, and
no one had heard of her – then who should come down the
corridor but old Riley! And it was him that was in and he had
met this Munro visiting someone else, and asked her to let me
know he was there and would I go and see him. We had a long
talk – it was rather pathetic, as he was SO pleased to see me. He
said how lovely to see someone from home and I don't think he
has anyone to visit him. He had just come from Borneo, and has
a bad knee and has to have the cartilage removed, and then will
probably be boarded out and sent home. So I promised to go and
see him again sometime, as he will be in for about three weeks.

I told the Amah it was my birthday on Monday, and in the
afternoon she appeared with a huge bunch of flowers for me -
wasn't it nice of her.

I am getting on very well with my new room mate Hilda
Stiven - she is such a nice girl - our type! She is quite tall and
large. She lives at St Georges Hill, Weybridge - so must be quite
well to do. Her Ma and Pa's pictures look very nice and quite

birds! She says she thinks she has heard the name Staniland, but didn't know him.

I suddenly remembered Christabel's birthday to-day, so I have sent her a cable, and I shall write to her one day.

I bought myself a lovely pineapple to-day - I wish you were here to help me eat it! I have also bought myself some embroidered Chinese shoes for the evening.

Thank you very much for the nice Easter card.

Did that parcel ever arrive with my 'personal effects' in? It was sent off in Febuary, so should soon..

10th May 46. 4.15 p.m. in the office. I have definitely decided to come back into this office, and the Chief AT is going to find the other girl another job. Then I shall leave here at the end of May, and hope to go on leave for a week to the Cameron Highlands, and then come back in June. I haven't asked yet whether I can come back in June - but I shouldn't think there will be any bother, as the doctor is always saying I should be in a cooler climate for my skin diseases.

I'm quite free from any skin trouble at the moment.

I went to a cocktail party last night given by the new "Flag Officer of Malaya and Forward Areas" (known as FOMFA)! He is an Admiral, and is sort of in charge of all the Navy in Malaya - very grand. He lives in a wonderful bungalow, and they have decorated the garden with coloured lights. I didn't know many there, as they were mostly Navy high-ups - Captains, and Admirals and Commanders, and a few high-up Army types. Ursula Jeans, the actress, was there, and Lady Killearn, with her queer sprig of white flowers stuck on top of her head in front! I quite enjoyed it as I palled up with a mere Sub-Lieutenant and we talked together all the time and know each others family histories! He was at school in Christs Hospital, lives in Tonbridge Wells, and is an engineer! It was a wonderful sight to see everyone - all the Naval officers dressed in white, with some of them with gold braid hanging round their shoulders - means they are flag Lieuts. or something! There were about 80 people there. The admiral greeted us all and shook hands.

I had such fun with Hilda this morning, at lunch time. I bought a chair yesterday from the officers shop. It is one in a bag, which fits together with canvas for the seat and back- and I have bought it on purpose for the boat coming home, as I know how short they are. I never once managed to get one coming from Kandy here. So we started to try and put it up to-day, and every time we got two legs in the others fell out - and this went on for ages and we were crying laughing! Then she suddenly discovered that all the parts are numbered and fit in to each other quite well when put in the right places. It is up now, and most comfortable - and will be very nice for the garden at home.

I shall have to stop now, as Paddy has dared to give me a bit of work to do.

13th May 46.

I have come back to the office today - & actually have been working all day - which is sickening - as I have no time to write to you! This is just a short note to let you know I'm OK!!

I got some Sketches & a Comet today & the Illustrated of 2 Mar with that lovely picture in it – thank you – I'm going to have it out & framed.

I played tennis yesterday - very hot in the blazing sun - but nice - & am rather stiff today. I'm going to see the Barrets of Wimpole Street tonight with Roger Livesey, Ursula Jeans etc.

I've got no ills at the moment except prickly heat all over my back! but that comes & goes quite quick.

I'm def coming back sometime in June – I haven't asked yet – but am sure it will be alright – so get tidy!!

I'll write better tomorrow.

14th May 46. 11.45 a.m. In the office.

I have just got your first letter from you addressed to this place again - dated 7th May - and it is most tantalising, as I haven't had anything since 19th April. The rest are still in Saigon, and I have just sent them a signal to forward everything here – but I don't suppose anything will come for about another week and am longing to hear all the 'in between' news! I gather from your letter Alice Bunch is engaged! Who is the man?

I am so glad Boss got that parcel of shoes and the onions. I was afraid they might spill on the shoes - as they had a long journey. The parcel was taken by a nurse who left here last January to go home via India - jolly decent of her. I am glad the shoes fit. I wonder if you got the other parcel Whitey brought back with the sandals and tongue etc. I expect you have and that it is in your letters in Saigon.

Harry had a telephone call from Patricia from Kuala Lumpur last Friday to say she was getting married at 11.30 on the Saturday morning there and could we possible go. So Harry wangled us on to an aeroplane, and we got up at 3.45 a.m. On Sat morning and went to Changi - had a nice breakfast there at 6.30 - got on the plane, a Dakota, and took off at 7.10. At 7.30 the pilot turned back and landed us all again at Changi, as he said the weather wasn't going to be good enough! So we never got there. It was so disappointing for us as well as for Patricia, as we couldn't let her know in time. Apparently she was married in white - had a dress made in 24hours - but that is all we know at present. She has gone to Bangkok for her honeymoon and the will go back and collect her luggage etc from Saigon, and then I think will come back here on her way home. I still have her trunk in our room. She has married a very nice man indeed, but I think she should have waited much longer before getting 'done' as they have only known each other about two months. He is 33 and she is 22. DON'T be worried, as I shall not be flying anywhere again!

For Dug's benefit they have built a large new airstrip at Changi - I think the Japs started it. They have got one of the Jap suicide planes there as a souvenir, a tiny little thing.

Harry and I and another girl are going up to Round the Bend for a curry dinner tonight, so I shan't eat much lunch to-day to prepare for it!

I haven't done anything more about coming back yet. What do you think? Shall I come in June, or shall I get a job at ALFSEA for two months and get back in August? I can't make up my mind – sometimes I long to get back and sometimes I think its silly as I may have to work in the ATS in England for two months and may be sent anywhere - perhaps the north of Scotland - which would be just as bad as being away from you here! Please give me your views.

We have had some terrific thunderstorms lately in the night. Last night I had to get up and shut all the windows as the wind was blowing everything all over the room, and the rain was coming in hard.

Does Dug want any films for his camera? If so what size? I have got Boss two 116 and will get her some more before I come back.

16th May 46. 10.30 a.m.
I have written to Mr. Walmsley, and also to Major Percy!

I enjoyed my work in the office yesterday more than I have done since I came out here - as Paddy had to do his mess accounts, and I helped him work out the balance sheets! Of course they wouldn't come out easily. Which was all the nicer – and I thoroughly enjoyed it. I think I should like to get a job as a bookkeeper or accountant! We got so keen on it, that we had lunch here together in the Phoenix and came up again straight afterwards to finish the thing!

I got a telegram from Douglas for my birthday yesterday – sent from you on 5th May! I don't know whether he got the address wrong, or whether it was a mistake by the post office people, but apparently they had a job finding where I was as it was sent to S.R.Division Singapore. I was very amused by it – thank you – and loved the last line!

Harry has got another job here, as she finished soon - and will be going back to Australia in September, lucky girl. Did I tell you that I think I could have got a job in Tokyo, only it would mean signing on for another year, and I don't want to do that. I still haven't made up my mind whether to come back in June, or whether to wait until August. I don't want to have a job in the ATS in England.

Has Douglas discovered my War Office Despatch case yet?

I don't know where it is – probably in my cupboard or a drawer, but please do use it if you want to.

I had an 'acc' the other day. I was walking to our ferry bus in the car park to go back to lunch and passed behind another car –

and didn't notice that it had a back window what sort of opened, and I went bang into a jutting out piece on my forehead! It bled all over the place from a smallish cut, and I have quite a big lump there now – its not bad, but I make quite a lot of it!! A la Boss!

17ᵗʰ May 46. 3.15 office

I got a letter from Ma today dated 10ᵗʰ May & the one from Mrs Howard, please thank her. I hope you have heard from me by now about Saigon.

I went to the hospital yesterday visiting several officers I know there from our mess. I also bought a few grapes & gave them to that old Mish: from China - who is still there. No one ever goes to see her & I was sorry for her. She was so pleased with the grapes & also 3 eggs I got for her.

I went to see Riley Carr who has had the 'op' on his knee & is in bed. He has been told he will be there for six weeks. He was very pleased to see me.

I also had a long talk with the WAAF officer who has infantile paralysis. She has been there about two months & was in the iron lung but is much better now. She can only move her right hand - her left arm & legs are quite paralysed - but will probably get better in time. She finds it a little difficult to breathe too - & is dreadfully thin. She is going home on a hospital ship on Monday - which will do a lot of good, as apparently half the cure for that complaint is wanting to get on.

I am longing to hear more about Alice's engagement & who he is.

I went to the pictures last night & saw Robert Donat in something not bad "Adventures of Tartu" a spy in Germany in this war.

I'm going to see the head ATS on Monday & arrange what to do after this job ends.

20ᵗʰ May 46. 3.15 p.m.

It was lovely this morning – I got all the mail forwarded from Saigon – about 14 letters altogether – lots from Ma, up to May 2ⁿᵈ – one from Ar Beat and one from Ar Jessie, Dug, Mrs. Harper,

Cissie, Hildegard, and Brandy. It took me a long time to read them all – and at lunch time I read some of them again!

Please thank Chet for her letter – I am so sorry the sandals were too big, and I'll certainly get her some more now I've got her size. I'll also get Dug some shoes – he doesn't say what colour, so I expect I shall get brown.

I went to see Esme Lawrence this morning – the chief AT here. (She was at Staff College with me, and is now a Chief Commander – Lt. Col). She was very nice and friendly (as I know her very well), and talked about what I should do. We have decided that it is not worth my while to get another job out here for just a few months, but she said that I was entitled to 28 days leave out here, and that we are allowed to spend that in India if we like. The snag is that I don't want to go alone. There is another girl Sheila Drake, who was also at Bagshot with me – one of the nicest girls there – and she is also going home soon, so Esme rang her up while I was there and asked her if she would go with me to India, and she seemed quite keen. So we are finding out more, and hope it will come off. Of course our dream is to go to Kashmir! but that may be too far to go to. Also we shall have to see about having enough money. So if I go to India I shan't be home until about the end of July – but if I don't go, I shall be home about the beginning of July – so get READY!!

Paddy and I have moved into Eric's old office, which was next door to ours, and we have a fan there going all day, also a private lavatory, and a wireless! We used it before, but have installed ourselves in it properly now, as another department wants our other room.

I had a nice letter from Hildegard from Hong Kong. I asked her to get some stamps for Boss, and she says she will, but wants to know whether I want them used or unused, and I don't know which Boss would like, and I can't ask her for both sets as I know she hasn't much money. So I shall write back and ask for an unused set and hope Boss will agree. She'll have to, anyway.

I am so glad John and Whitey rang you up. John has a lovely voice, and he is very good at acting and reading Shakespeare etc., and also conjuring tricks. But I shouldn't ask him over really now, as Patricia has married this other man and it would be rather difficult. I am glad you got the parcel from Whitey and that the sandals fit Boss. I shall get her some more with crepe soles, but I'm afraid they are all open at the heel here and she'll have to like that. We all wear them that way here – it is much cooler and more hygienic.

Charles Strubin (that Swiss naval officer) is getting me a camphor wood chest made - instead of buying any more trunks or suitcases. They have lovely chests in the shops here, all of camphor wood, or teak, and beautifully carved. But they are rather expensive, and I don't think it is worth while, buying one. The one he is having made will, of course, be quite plain on top, but made of nice wood and will have locks fitted. I have bought a 6 lb tin of margarine to bring back, so shall need a lot of room!

Yesterday I got "recreational" transport! Which means a station wagon - a sort of large car only more like a truck, with quite comfy seats! If we want it on Sundays we can apply for it, and usually get one. So I went for a picnic with another girl and a man called Alan Flint and Charles Strubin (both from Round the Bend) and we went to Johore, and then on to those reservoirs where I went once before - just like a huge lake with hills all round. We took lots of food, tinned stuff mostly, Irish Stew, sardines, eggs (which I bought in the market and two of which were bad!) and bread and butter and lemonade, and ate it on the grass by the side of the lake, but the ants and animals were awful which rather put us off eating! Then we went for a little walk round the lake and then came back. It was very nice. We had a nice Indian driver. They have their morning meal about 9.30 or 10 and not anything more until 5.30 in the evenings, so their meals are easy.

We have got to move from our bungalows at the end of May - all the ATS and WAAF and go to the Tanglin barracks where ALFSEA are. They live in bungalows there (the officers), and I shan't be there very long, so I don't mind so much, but it's a fag, as I am hoping to go to the Cameron Highlands again on 29th May until about 6th June, so I shall have to move before I go. Esme Lawrance says I can dump all my things in her bungalow before I go. It is not very far from where we live now, about 1 mile away.

I am glad Dug saw his old batman. What about his wife?!

Thank you very much for all the birthday cards and wishes. Please thank Cissie for hers and for her nice letter. I am glad you have got Mr. Love to do your shoes for you – I hope he will be able to put some crepe on some of Ma's when I get back.

I am still free from all ills at the moment, except prickly heat a bit on my back, but that doesn't worry me.

Do you remember I asked W.H.Smith to send me a book through you called Georgian England? I have had a letter from them returning my cheque, saying the first edition is sold out already, but they will be having another lot in the autumn, so I am asking them to keep me one for then.

To Boss

21st May 46.

I am only writing this because I thought you & Dug (& of course DD) would like some real Chinese toilet paper!! (or it may be Jap – I don't know). I got it from the theatre yesterday.

It was a rotten show – variety - absolute bosh. Isabel Jeans and Roger Livesey sat just in front of me & I'm sure they were bored too - but they were so nice & clapped everything. Lots of people went out - & at one rather dirty joke everyone hissed.

I'm so glad the sandals and shoes fit you. I want to buy 1000000's of pairs of shoes - it breaks my heart to pass any shoe shop - & nearly every shop has some in!

I'm still toying with the idea of some leave in India & have been told of a place called Naini Tal - somewhere north east of Delhi in the hills - which is supposed to be lovely - or of course there's always Kashmir which is everyone's dream out here. But I don't know! I should have to go to Calcutta first by sea - 5 days, & then train - about 2 days. I feel its an "op" not to be missed - I wish you could come too. There are YWCA's at all these places to stay at. I think you'd better go back to P.R in September – would you like to? Would Uppers like a bottle of Angostura Bitters?

22nd May 46.

I got a letter from Ma this morning dated 3rd May (I've already had hens dated 10th) I apologise about the "Kisses question" & quite agree that Ma is in the right!!

After you get this letter – please address everything to me at: H.Q., A.L.F.S.E.A. TANGLIN Barracks Singapore & put J/Comd D M H ... A.T.S. & then I'll be sure of getting them – as I have to move in there on Monday next - & finish work here next week.

I had lunch at Round the Bend today and then their truck came to my bungalow and fetched my trunk and camp kit and one of the officers there, a newish one is going to have them crated for me and then get them sent home by the M.F.O.

Did my "personal effects" parcel ever arrive home? I sent it in Febuary and hope it has. If not it may be lost & I hope it isn't. It had my battle dress & a fawn coat etc. in it. Let me know.

23rd May 46. 4.0 p.m. S.R.Division, H.Q.,S.A.C.S.E.A.,
Tanglin Barracks, Singapore.

There's not much to say, but I expect a letter with nothing in it is better than none at all.

I don't think I shall be going to India, as there seems to be many difficulties about getting there and about getting home from there afterwards, so I am going to Cameron Highlands again on 29th May until 6th June, and then returning here. Then I shall either come home, or try and have another few week's leave somewhere out here. What I hope for, which I don't think will come off, is to be invited to stay at Port Dickson on a rubber estate for a bit. I expect you remember me telling you about Archie Dunlop - well his wife Eve has just arrived out here and gone straight there. Unfortunately I didn't know she had come and missed her, and she, of course, thought I was in Saigon. (She was that Sgt. With the grey (blue) hair and blue eyes). So I've written to her to-day and said how nice it would be to see her etc., hoping she might invite me there. If she doesn't I might try and go to Penang for a week - and then come home. If none of that

400

comes off, I shall come home on the next available boat, maybe in the middle of June – so are you getting TIDY??!!

I'm in a misery now trying to think of presents for people! I know you say don't bother, but I must bring something for the aunts, Cissie, etc. as well as you lot! Of course the easiest thing is shoes, but I can't possibly do that for everyone because of the packing and the customs. I am dreading the thought of the customs already – although I've really no need!

I think the Empress of Australia sails on about 18th June - so I MAY come on that, but don't bank on it. Hilda my room mate, came back from Penang yesterday and says it is lovely there.

Thank you for the Norbiton Magazine – I am glad about the memorial to Daddy, and I think it would be nice to give something from us.

It's rather sickening as I shall miss a few things next week through being on leave – but it really doesn't matter. Next Tuesday the H.Q. here is giving a cocktail party for Supremo and Mrs Louis in the Phoenix restaurant here - but everyone has to contribute towards it $5 - so I don't mind missing that! Then on Thursday next Supremo is giving a cocktail party for all the H.Q. in Flagstaff House - where he now lives, as the Governor lives in Government House - and I have been invited to that. But as there will be about 300 people there, I don't really mind, I suppose. Then on Saturday, June 1st one of the A.T.S. Officers of ALFSEA is getting married, and I have been asked to the wedding, but I don't know her very well, and have never met the man at all, I suppose I don't mind that either!! Anyway I'd rather be on leave! But it's a pity they all come at once.

I bought a photograph album yesterday and am sticking all my photos in it with those corners. They look quite nice, and will be easier to show you all stuck in.

I am sending you a letter I had from Cissie for my birthday – which was very kind of her. I thought you'd like to see it.

Paddy and I have got to move our office before Saturday – sorry I've told you that one!

I'm glad Dug enjoyed his regimental dinner.

25th May 46. S.R.Division, etc. 11 a.m.
(forwarded to Hotel Montpelier,
Montpelier Rd, Brighton, Sussex)
I have just had a letter from Ma and one from Boss dated 15th
May, and also Boss's card from Brighton. Thank you very much, I
am so glad you are all going away and hope you'll enjoy it.

I had a letter from Ma yesterday as well. I am rather annoyed
that you got jam and treacle from India, as I sent that parcel
to you when you asked for marmalade, and asked for a 2 lb jar
of marmalade to go. I suppose they hadn't any and sent treacle
instead. But I suppose you can make use of it.

It really is agony looking round the shops here and seeing so
many lovely things which you can't get no how in England. It is
just impossible to buy everything - but its awful not to! I'm sure
I shall never be able to pack everything I have now! I think it
is quite wrong the way we can buy masses of tinned food stuffs
- which all seem to be imported from America and Australia.
They should be sent to England. We can buy from four NAAFI's
- quite legitimately - practically anything in the food line in tins
- fruit, meats, peas, beans, fish plenty of biscuits, Lux, Rinso,
Starch, sauces and pickles of all kinds - even whole tinned ham -
tinned to match the shape of the ham, and weighing about 15 lbs.
I would love to bring one back, but I really couldn't manage it.

Paddy and I moved our office yesterday to the lower ground
floor, only half a flight away from the Phoenix Restaurant and
the NAAFI. We are in Freddy Jaque's old office (the one wat was
engaged to Miss Edwards of the Transit Camp – and he has gone
ill), and we look out the other side over the harbour. Although
we are lower ground, we are still very high up from the ground
outside as we are on a hill, if you can understand that! Its lovely
seeing all the ships. We are only here for a few more days and
close down finally on 31st May – and Paddy is letting me go on
29th to Cameron Highlands.

It was quite amusing last night - I went to one of our private
film shows, and afterwards I stayed talking with Lt.Col.Hickley,
who is in charge of the film section, and Major Thomas, who is
under him. I know them quite well, as we have quite a lot to do
with them with work. I talked to Hickley all the time, and he is

all Yogi and reincarnation and stars. He has lived out in India all his life and loves it and is all mystic etc. He really was very interesting and much more scientific about it than Olive is, and I came away with four books I have borrowed. He also worked out all my stars for me and given me a book to work out the meanings of the various planets I was born under etc! I don't understand much! He also talked a lot about dreams and how the astral body detaches itself from the physical body, and floats above it, and how, in your astral body, you can see your body lying on the bed! He says it happened to him once, and he couldn't get back into his other body for a long time! DON'T worry I'm going all pyschic (?) because I'm not, and can't understand how sane people can understand such talk - but I do like to hear all about it. He talked about the 4 dimensions - 1,2 and 3 are breadth, height and depth, and the fourth is space-time! Anyway we talked until 1.15 am., and then Major Thomas drove me home. I told him Ma was interested in it, but didn't say in what way.

I have got to pack all my things and move to Tanglin Barracks on Tuesday – and Esme Lawrance says I can just dump everything in her bungalow until I get back from leave. I MAY go on to Penang for a week after Camerons from about 7th June to 13th, and then I shall start to think about coming home. There is a ship, the Empress of Australia going on 18th June, which I may try and get on. But I shall see Esme first and find out whether there is still any chance of going to India. I don't think there is much, and I really don't mind, as I hate having to arrange everything for myself, and the other girl can't go, and I don't know anyone else to go with.

I've got no ills at the moment.

Tell D.D. I have already bought her some shoes like Boss's lace ups, and I might get her some more. I don't mind the money with these things, - it's the packing to bring home, as shoes take up so much room. However I'll manage somehow. I'll also get Dug some.

27th May 46. S.R.Div

(but Tanglin address for you.) 4.15 p.m.

I have had two letters from Ma to-day, dated 20th and 21st May – the last one only six days ago – jolly good. Thank you for them.I am pleased the bis has sold so well, and that you'll have a bit more money. The stocks look quite good to me. You know how much I know about that sort of thing! Do you remember how we used to long for Douglas to do the income tax rebate for us when he was a P.o.W?!

I do feel rather awful about promising you a dress and then coming down to a blouse – but it's the material wot is so difficult. There is no tweed or wool stuff at all under 25 dollars a yard! and the silk materials aren't really your style. But I may find some yet and have one made. Of course I never waited for you to send that blouse pattern back, but went in and told him to do it, and then saw another pattern which was more what you wanted once, and chose it – so I do hope it goes down okey. I may have another one made too if I can't get the dress stuff.

I am going to leave on Wednesday, and shall finish buying presents when I come back. I have also taken Boss's pink stuff to be made up, but can't remember the pattern I chose!

I am having an awful job at the moment in the bungalow trying to pack. I have to pack some things to take on leave, and pack all the others, get transport (somehow) and take them to Tanglin Barracks and dump them to-morrow, ready for when I come back - as we have to be out of our present bungalows by 31st May.

I had a lovely day yesterday - I swam at the Tangin Club in the morning with two of those Naval Officers - had curry lunch in our mess - played tennis in the afternoon, and then swam directly afterwards again, which was lovely, as it is terribly hot playing tennis. The pool has been shut for a long, time, and is only just open again - and the Club is only about three minutes walk from our mess.

I am glad the rugs are satis. Shall I get a couple more – I am toying with the idea? LET ME KNOW ABOUT THIS, as I should have to order them from here while my banking account is in India. I think it would be quite a good idea.

I am sorry the chicken 'wot' has been ill, and hope he (or she?) is better now!

29th May 46. 12. Noon. YWCA, Kuala Lumpur
I arrived here about an hour ago & am staying the night - as there is no transport to Cameron Highlands until tomorrow. The other YWCA hostel has closed & this one is a block of flats - very nice indeed. I have a room to myself (1 other bed - nobody in it) & bathroom & lavatory leading out. It is beautifully furnished & lovely bowls of flowers everywhere.

My bottle of iodine has leaked over one of my white blouses - but feeling Pollyannarish (!) I am only too thankful it hasn't gone on anything else! The people who run these places are so nice always & help in every way they can. Many of them are New Zealand ones.

I packed all my things at the bungalow on Monday & yesterday - such a job. Charles Strubin (naval officer) had a crate made for me at the docks - a sort of wooden trunk - to my measurements - but I asked for it much too big. It's absolutely enormous 5 ft X 3 ft X 2 ft and weighs a ton! I daren't put anything too heavy in it - & haven't even been able to fill it!

Anyhow I got packed & got transport yesterday at 2 & 4 coolies & we managed to hoist it on the truck with my other cases & I took it all to Tanglin Barracks & dumped it in a bungalow there. They are lovely large bungalows there – but I haven't actually been given a room yet until I return from leave.

I am staying in Cameron H until 7th June & then I've booked in a hotel in Penang until 12th - but if I like it there, I may stay longer. Then I shall go back to Singapore & start trying to get home by ship – maybe on 18 June – the Empress of Australia – but I DON'T KNOW yet.

Its very hot here – seems worse than Singapore & I'm longing to be in C-H tomorrow I've got no ills at present.

From Martyn Walmsley, Kingston on Thames, to Dorothy

31st May 1946
It is very nice of you to write to your 'man' I am glad to hear that you are well and happy.

Your letter took I suppose about seven days to reach me. Its very wonderful. Your man is a much older man. During the last year or two he has given up several activities e.g. (that's meant for 'such as') Education Committee and gardening, I miss them. The former brought me in contact with a lot of interesting people, Harper & I were close friends, but he now has so much to do that I feel I dare not walk into his office and take up his precious time.

I was told last week that he had broken down!

As for gardening, spells of about an hour are long enough. Happily we have a gardener one evening a week. There are no apples alas!

Do you hear of Faith Watson?

I think she was rather fond of me. We had one day a meal quite daintily served in her room – the girls were in their shelter.

St Peters Rose show is to take place on June 29 Mrs H Watson and the bishop are to be there.

Cyril has seen Douglas. Douglas looked much better than I expected after what he had gone through.

It's a job to write on this paper it must be greasy.

The boys are well. Guy work a partnership in an accountants practice.

The difficulty is to find a house to live in.

Do you think Princes Elizabeth should have so many frocks?

This may not reach you before you start for home. It will be no great loss, except that I want you to know how much I appreciate your letter.

From H Percy, Kingston upon Thames, to Dorothy

1st June 1946

I was delighted to hear from you, to learn where you are, and to know you are having a good time and enjoying yourself. You were I think always anxious to go out, and there you are. After Ceylon, Singapore may not be such a pleasant place as regards climate. I have always heard that the Straits Settlements, as that part of the world was formerly called was a bad place for Europeans, but it must have improved when Singapore became an important Naval Base. I can understand your having a gay time. It is the usual method of Englishmen in their exile and often is very irresponsible.

One could not say that we in England are having a gay time, far from enjoying the fruits of Victory our condition is even worse than during war time, and according to the broadcast tonight there is quite a possibility of bread being rationed in the near future. People expected a lot from this Socialist Govt, they are being disillusioned.

I cannot thank you enough for your help in the somewhat distant past. Nor shall I cease to remember Johnston who assisted in the scrubbing out of the Commandants Office until she moved to join the hierarchy of the A.T.S

I have handed over all connection with the Comforts fund, and with it a credit of £2600, which amount, I hope will be used to help those Prisoners of War who were in Japanese hands whenever they need it.

It is needless to say how pleased I shall be to see you on your return to England. The School may have altered in it's constitution by then, for the Governors may be altogether different, and I celebrate my 76th birthday next month, so it's time I retired from active work. Meantime my best wishes go to you and if you desire to become slimmer then that is also my hope.

From Dorothy to Mother, Boss & Dug

2nd June 46. Cameron Highlands

I feel awful I haven't written for three days! No excuse – just laziness.

I came here on Wednesday – got to K-L about 11 and was going to stay the night there in the YWCA – which is very nice - & had a double room given me – to meself. They said if I waited until Thursday there would probably be transport coming up here – otherwise it meant another 6 hrs in a train to Tapah, & then 2 hrs in a truck. So I had lunch at the YW - & at 2 the person said the ration truck had arrived & if I could be ready in 2 minutes I could go all the way in it. So I was & I did! It was very amusing. An Indian Lieut drove with a WVS woman next to him - (I had met her before - not bad, quite old). In the back were two Indian soldiers & me, & sacks of rations & crates of beer etc.

407

Not much room, & it wasn't very comfy - but better than train. We stopped for tea at a rest house - & didn't get here until 9 pm.

I am in a bungalow called Kochoon (?) high up over the golf course & very nice - a double room - but I'm by myself which is nice. It is lovely being cool again, & the food is very good! I have spoken to quite a lot of people.

I shall stay here about a week, & then go to Penang for a week, & then come home! Lovely. When we had tea at the rest house I had it with the WVS person & the Indian Lieut - who had a big moustache, & he drank his tea just like Aunt Beat drinking soup - magnified ten times! (Don't show her this letter!)

It's a lovely view from this house - a valley below - all golf course - a few bungalows - & the jungle all round on hills.

3rd June 46. 10 a.m. Monday,
I wrote you a mouldy letter yesterday & will try & do better now!

I am sitting on the verandah outside the bungalow – with hills & jungle all round – the weather is not too good here – it rains quite a lot, & the clouds come right down all over the place – but the air is lovely & cool - & you can always hear water rushing all the time – waterfalls in the hills – rather like Switzerland.

Charles Strubin – one of the Naval Officers of Round the Bend - has arrived for a few days & is staying in the local hotel for officers - the Cameron Highlands Hotel - so on Saturday I went to a dance there - not bad. It was an all ranks dance & they had Paul Jones, Palais Glide & things like that. I danced in a Paul Jones with a little Private - & afterwards he came & asked me for another & said something funny - meant to be a compliment. He said how funny it was that girls who looked as though they couldn't dance always could - & those who looked good were like planks to take round. I presume I looked bad but could dance good!

I spent nearly all yesterday doing a jigsaw puzzle with another girl a WAAF officer, quite nice.

It was funny – on Sat. at the dance I was introduced to the WVS person who runs the hotel (It is purely a leave place for officers), & when she heard my name she asked the usual question about Reading! It turned out that she lives at Sonning

& her name is Player. I can't remember the name of that person who owns our villa in Cannes – as I thought she might know her.

Then I met a man there – Army Officer in a Parachute Battalion, so I asked him if he'd ever come across Sam Johnston - & he is in the same Battalion & knows him well - & has also met Violet – isn't it funny. He is on sick leave here - & says Sam is now in Siam (!) & they are there to 'put down' the bandits.

There is a large jar of geraniums in front of me now, & a tiny little bird has just come & sat on it – a most peculiar one with a very long beak..!!

A RAF officer who is staying here on leave, went for a walk in the jungle the other day & has never returned. Apparently it is very easy to get lost in them. A little while ago two nurses went & got lost & were out 3 days & nights in the jungle - but they were found & are getting better in hospital. Lots of search parties have looked for the airman. Don't worry -I've no intention of walking in it and getting lost!!

We had a lovely curry for lunch yesterday - two helpings for me! Everyone in this bungalow walks to the one next door for meals – just down a hill.

I went to a film on Friday evening – with some of the others. The cinema is part of the local hospital & we sat on benches. It was Sonja Henie in a skating film – not too good.

I do hope you have enjoyed your stay in Brighton. I don't know what to do when I come back – I shall have a good leave first! Esme Lawerance (chief ATS) told me that a new thing has come out to say that if our jobs have finished - we can go home & be demobilised straight away - which is nice - as I shan't have to stay in until Sept now.

I don't know whether I'll ever get that job with Frank Owen now - I know him much better & think he is the sort that makes all sorts of promises & offers that don't come to anything. I wish Boss & I could set up something on our own & be our own boss! It's the only way to make any money.

There is a piano here in the bungalow next door – where we eat - & I have played it several times.

I'm longing to get home now - & can't realise its so near
Get tidy!

Clean my mo bike

Clean out the moths

I expect the ship I come on will land at Southampton & I hope to be met in London if you've any petrol when I come back.

5th June 46. 10 a.m.

This is my last day here – which is a pity. Its lovely just lazing about! I am going back to K.L tomorrow – by transport to Tapah & from there I've got to go by train to K.L – 4 ¾ hrs to go 90 miles! Which I didn't like the idea of - but if there aren't many people going – they won't send transport all the way. I have to start at 6 a.m. because the 'road' is only open early in the morning for down traffic. I shall get to Tapah about 9 a.m. & then have to wait until 1p.m. for the train. I hope there'll be someone in the truck to pal up with - & we shall have to march round Tapah (quite a big place – a large village) & eat in the rest house until the train goes.

I am sitting on the lawn in front of our bungalow writing this in lovely sun.

Yesterday afternoon I went for a walk with Charles - I should never have dared go alone or with another girl as we went into the jungle. We walked for about ½ hr & then turned up a small path & soon got right into the jungle - all along a very small track going up all the time. It was very frightening! (I thought so anyway) & we didn't go very far.

That airman who was lost for 4 days was found yesterday - I don't know any details yet. There are notices up everywhere now to say no one is allowed to go climbing in the jungle unless in an organised party or with a guide.

There is still a wild tribe of people who live in the jungle - & I saw two of them. They still use blow pipes & arrows - but are quite friendly towards everyone.

There's nothing more to say I've done nothing only eat & sleep! Going to Penang on Friday.

7th June 46. 4.30 p.m. Kuala Lumpur

Here I am again for two days & am hoping to go to Penang tomorrow.

I have never been so hot in my life as I am at the moment. I think I feel it more after the cool in Camerons. All my prickly heat has come up again - & I'm longing to be in England!!

I had a fairly decent journey down yesterday - by truck from Camerons to Tapah Road & then a 4 ½ hr train journey here - as I was the only girl coming so there was no transport all the way here. I came with a Sub Lieut (Navy) & Charles Stubin & a flight Lieut in the RAF. We got to Tapah about 12 & went to the rest house & had some soup, fried fish, roast beef, carrots & boiled potatoes, fruit salad & coffee - very good food - only $2.50 each.

Then we went to the station. The train was supposed to go at 1.15 but didn't come in until 2, I'd love to explain how amusing all the people were & what they were like at all the little stations on the way down, but I think I'll tell you in the next letter, or when I get home for three reasons (a) There is a piano just behind me waiting to be played. (b) I'm very hot (c) It's easier to type a lot than write a lot.

All the rest of my little lot went on to Singapore last night – so I have been marching round K.L. today on my own - got Boss some stamps & her & me some rubber sandals - which will be lovely for hosing the garden. I've got mine on now - very comfy & cheap.

Must stop for reasons above!

11th June 46. (Put ATS after my name)
Tanjin Barracks, H.Q. ALFSEA, SEAC
I am so sorry I haven't written since last Friday – but I've done so much since then (& yet so little!) that I haven't written.

I can own up now that I shall never do it again - that I flew to K.L. & back each time I went on leave in a Dakota. It took 1 ½ hrs by plane, & by train it took 12 hrs - all night. So do you blame me?! Anyway I'm not flying any more.

I didn't go to Penang after all as there were no planes for 3 days cos of Whitsun & I couldn't face the train journey there from K.L. 9 p.m. to 11 a.m. next day. So I flew back here on Saturday, got here at 7 & came to my new bungalow & got a bed for the night. On Sunday another girl came whose bed it was - as they hadn't expected me till Wed; So I was in a muck as it was a holiday for everyone - so I took a towel & nightie & went back to my old room & slept there with Hilda Steven & stayed two nights & came here today.

Wed. 12th June. 4.p.m.

I'm sorry I just can't get down to writing. I've still only a bed & no furniture yet & am living in a suitcase which is horrid & its very hot - & I'm fed up cos I haven't had any letters from you since I came back & I know there must be some. I told them to forward them here & I've tried everyone & can't find them – I'm going to Cathay Buildings to-morrow to 'create' until I find out where they are.

I spent this morning with Patricia who has just come back from Saigon with her husband. They are going home on the Empress of Australia - which leaves here somewhere about 20-25th June. I have asked to come back on it too - but don't know yet whether I am.

I don't have any work to do now & am busy trying to shop & get things ready to come back.

I sent a cable yesterday 'cos I hadn't written.

I'll try & write better in a few days.

16th June 46. At/sea Sunday 3.30 p.m.
Don't write to me anymore from now on !

I haven't written for several days again - & am very sorry. Its because I have nothing to do! Anyway by the time you get this I shall have sailed for home in the Empress of Australia! I'm getting very exited & rush around all day trying to buy things.

I have spent all this morning & afternoon sorting out things in my room. But I can't start packing yet, as one of those Naval officers of Round the Bend is having a sort of chest made for me, & it won't be ready till Tuesday.

I do hope it won't be rough on the sea! & that I get a nice cabin.

Patricia & her husband are on the same ship which is rather nice. The ship is due here on Wed. 19th June - & I may leave on 21st. On the other hand – it may stay for 5 days here for boiler cleaning. I shall know later. Its useful as Charles Sturbin is in Sea

Transport & arranges all the ships sailings etc. & so I know all the latest news every time.

I have my bedroom to myself now, & have two chests of drawers & also a fan – which is lovely & keeps the room cool.

I'm glad that parcel came – the clerk in our office wrote the address for me – with 'effects' I left it as I thought it didn't matter!

The amah from my old bungalow came here to see me this afternoon to say goodbye. She says she loves me & I love her!! Her name is Ah Nya!

The ship should take about 23 days to get home.

I got four letters from Ma yesterday enclosing Violets, Plain Smith's etc – thanks. I am glad you enjoyed Brighton & I am sure its nice to be home again.

It's really a very good thing I'm coming home – as my health – although good – is liable to break out again! I have awful prickly heat, & still get a few impetigo spots on & off, & now I have gone & found an alopecia patch on the side of my head – fairly Large.

So I went & had my hair permed on Friday at the Officers Shop which covers it well & looks quite nice.

I went on a launch round the harbour yesterday - & steered the boat for quite a long way in & out of aircraft carriers etc!!

I am not sure yet when I shall actually leave Singapore. The ship should take about 23 days to get home. So if I leave 21st June - I should arrive on or about 14th July - or perhaps 5 days later. I don't yet know whether its Liverpool or Southampton – but will tell you more details later.

Longing to be home again.

Get TIDY!!!

Telegram returning home. 19th June 46.

    Expect to be home soon don't write further

    Writing in detail

    Love to the best mother in the world.

    Dorothy Heelas

19th June 46.

I went to say goodbye to Paddy yesterday & found he had heaps of mail for me - at least five letters from Ma dated between 23 & 29 May. I don't know whether you wanted me to cable my sanction to something about the stocks or not – but I'm sure if you think its 'OK' that I'll agree.

I had a very nice letter back from Major Percy & also rather a peculiar one from Walmsley – which I enclose!

I am annoyed at not getting the letters sooner - as I had an "invite" to stay with Eve Dunlop & her hub at Port Dickson & now its too late.

You will have my cable by now that I am coming home on the Empress of Australia (Canadian Pacific Line) We are embarking on Saturday 22nd June - & I have nothing packed yet as my crate hasn't come that I am having made by one of those naval officers (Jim Read – new name to you – but quite a nice man).

I have bought a LOVELY pair of sandals for Boss & am very jealous of them – as they were the only ones in the shop & are just too big for me – so should fit her. I've bought Chet's sandals & Dug's shoes. I spend most of my days shopping in the Town.

Thursday. 20th June.

The ship has come in but has got to have the boilers cleaned & I shan't sail until Tuesday or Wed next. It will take about 23 days from then to get home.

I had another letter from Ma yesterday dated 8 June. I am glad the kids went to see the processions. They have had it all on the news reels here – but I haven't been to see them yet.

I'm getting very excited at coming back. I shall land up in Liverpool, Southampton or Tilbury – but will try & find out before I leave & let you know. I want to be met in London if poss – but don't know how you will know when I arrive. I expect there'll be some means laid on to let you know.

Just going into town with another girl – 11.15 a.m. See you soon.

24th June 46.

My heavy luggage has just gone, a large wooden box & a small tin trunk. The box was terribly heavy - the four Japs who took it downstairs had a job getting it down.

We are embarking on Thursday & will sail next Friday 28th June. I am very exited & wish the voyage was over.

My first night back I only want the family and DD without fail. I believe we can post letters at Suez - so I shall be able to tell you more then.

I have got two alopecia patches, so ask Dr Camps to get a cure ready for me. Actually the voyage will probably do me good.

I can't think how I shall carry all my hand luggage onto the boat as we are supposed only to take into our cabins what we can carry - I have two suitcases, two holdalls - a chair in a bag & a large coolie hat! not to mention cameras, haversacks etc!

Nothing more to say. I wish I could buy masses of things to bring back – but am limited by money & space!

Nothing more to say – I might write again – but might not – It takes about 23 days – so if we leave on 28th June – I should be back about 26 July.

I sent a card to Mr. Price.

23rd June 46 BET between Charles Stubin & Dorothy Heelas (Newson)

    THAT she will not get
married within two years
from 27th June 1946
Stake £5 to be paid on
27th June 1948
Signed C P Stubin
Dorothy Heelas
23rd June 1946

Telegram
Sailing on Empress of Australia 27th June

1st July 46. Empress of Australia

Here I am on my way home – so get tidy & excited. We sailed last Friday, & reach Colombo tomorrow morning. We are supposed to arrive on about 19th or 20th July - probably at Liverpool. I hope to be able to send you a cable before we land - & say when I shall reach London. It would be nice if you could meet me there.

DD must (repeat must) be present on my first evening, even if it's a Saturday - her beastly bridge will have to go hang that night. If she isn't there – she won't be given the 2 prs shoes I've got for her! I don't want anyone else except the family – unless Chet can come – I should like her – or will it be holidays.

My tin trunk went home last May on the Athlone Castle - & should arrive soon.

It is funny - there is a Lt.Col. Bill Rowett on board - I've known him on & off for sometime - & once he asked me to go out with him. I was going, but something nicer turned up & I wrote & asked him to change the day - then he got posted to K.L. Anyway I was talking to him the other day & discovered he is Betty Chiddell's husband! They live in Wimbledon and have 5 boys ages 10-2! Kitty has a daughter. Avelyn's husband is a vicar in Weybridge. John is unmarried & is with the Austrian Control Commission.

This boat is terribly crowded - nearly 3,000 & I am in a cabin with 9 others, all Red Cross & WVS etc., ENSA types. I keep myself to myself. There was a bit of a muck up when I arrived on Thursday to get on board - the Transit Camp hadn't got my name and so I had to wait till the end to get on - other wise I should have been with the other ATS and Patricia, which is sickening.

I'm fed up with the voyage - It has been quite calm except yesterday was rather choppy & I laid down for a bit! But I still ate my food. One girl in our cabin (Dutch) looks about 16, is sick every morning.

I have my meals at second sittings, which is the best time & sit at a table with 10 RAF officers & 3 other girls - not bad. The food is very good.

There are lots of ENSA on board & also the Anglo - Polish Ballet Company. I always wondered what the men dancers look like off stage - now I know!

I hope this will get posted at Columbo.

I'm longing for it to be over & to get home.

27th June 1946 Singapore

I offer you this humble token as on this sad day we part,

Please never let our love be broken and keep me always in your heart.

Whenever, darling, this bracelet you wear. Think of your Charles and Singapore.

What lovely days we spent together there, and memories that will live for evermore.

True love such as ours is love that cannot die, and I'm afraid that suffer, suffer terribly we will.

One alone knows the answer to the questions why.

Fate is cruel and our love we cannot fulfil.

Life will go on for you and for me, with its ups and downs, work and play.

But a hope in my heart there will always be, that the time will come when we'll be one, for ever and a day.

With all my truest love for you and you alone, my dearest beloved Dorothy, From your Charles.

4th July 1946

I should have written you long before this, my dearest, but I'm afraid I just haven't been able to, you see I've been in bed since last Friday, and until today have been feeling really ill, today I have been able to sit up and take a bit more notice, although still in bed, the doc reckons I should be OK to return to the office about Monday (8th). It was my tummy, of course, and it turned out to be dysentery. I had an awful time until about Tuesday, but am feeling a bit better now and hope to get up tomorrow.

I do hope this letter will catch you up alright at Suez, darling, please forgive only an airograph, but I promise there'll be two or three thicker ones awaiting you when you get home.

I was so miserable last Thursday evening when I left you, I can still hardly believe that you are not in Singapore, Dorothy my darling, and I need hardly tell you how much I am missing you and longing to see you again, to talk to you, to hug you, to kiss you, to love you, just to go on from where we left off in Singapore, even in the short space of a week I have realised more and more how much I do really love you, Dorothy, my darling. I am just longing to follow you home and to see you again in London, my dearest one.

How are things on the ship, dearest? Not too bad I hope. Have you managed to rig your chair alright? (Wot! No Charles and Hilda!) and find a space for it up on deck? I hope you have managed to chum up with a few nice people, it will make life so much more pleasant for you, darling (I hope there aren't any "Montys" tho, sorry darling, I am a beast saying that after your very sweet letter, aren't I), thank you so very much for that letter my sweetheart, it was so sweet of you to write it to me, I am just longing for your next one, sweetheart.

I'm sorry this letter is such a jumbled mess my sweetheart, please forgive me, but I'm writing it in a very awkward position in bed with an attaché case for a table!

Well Dorothy, my dearest one, life is very empty at the moment and I'm just living for your next letter, please write as often as you can always darling. I expect you are getting more and more excited now as you are getting nearer and nearer home.

Dorothy I could kick myself for being such a beast on Wednesday night, I'm sorry really I am, it was horrid of me.

Cheers for now Dorothy darling, All my love for you and you alone, dearest, From your Charles

28 Sept 46. On board M.V. "BRITANNIC", Approaching Suez. Dorothy, my dear

I was very surprised indeed to receive your last type written letter from London. I am sorry you did not receive any of my letters from Singapore, I can understand the ones I wrote you c/o the "Empress of Australia" going adrift, but I wrote two to your home address, one on about 5th August and the other round about 31st August and on receiving no reply, concluded that you didn't wish to write me anymore, I do hope that you really didn't receive them and this was not the case.

Anyway Dorothy, be that as it may, as you can see, I'm on my way home at last, this is a very fine ship in every way, good food, plenty of entertainment and a very good mixed bag of passengers - the only thing is, that being a Western Ocean ship, we are finding it very hot here in the Red Sea.

So you're off to Italy now – well, well, I wonder whether your appetite for travel will ever be satisfied! I hope, anyway that you enjoy your holiday in dear old Switzerland first, & then find a congenial job awaiting you in Italy.

Do write c/o Railway Hotel, Bourne End, Bucks. If this reaches you before you leave , I should very much like to see you once again (rem Sat 2nd Nov, I haven't forgotten) in any case, I will send or take your hold-all and electric iron to your home address.

Well Dorothy, I will close for now, If I don't see you again all best wishes for happiness in Italy & hope to see you again "sometime". Please do write, Cherio for now.

Best Wishes Sincerely, Charles

Chapter 11

Dorothy goes to Italy

From Dorothy to Mother

10th Oct 46. 3.0 p.m. Thurs. Kui Hotel Warmbad,
Villach, Switzerland

Its my first opportunity to write you a letter & it is so cold with
no heating at all in the hotel that this may not be much good!

I'll tell you about the journey so far - I am still only half way
- & leave here tonight - hoping to arrive in Naples on Saturday.
There are still a few things I made a note of to tell you – from
home.

1. The key of the house, garage & coal house (which I
padlocked) are in Dug's desk.

2. Boss's fur gloves are wrapped up in top left hand drawer of
my chest of drawers.

3. The chickens misled you & laid 3 more eggs on Sunday
& none on Monday morning. I had two for tea on Sun & 3 for
breakfast on Mon I gave Kathie 2. + 3 oranges.

4. The Steps & Hoover are in boot-cupboard.

5. I darned 7 prs of Boss's stockings & put them in her top
right hand drawer!

I had a lovely dinner on Sunday – 3 rashers, 3 sausages, an
egg – toast – apple & tea.

I pottered & darned in the afternoon with a fire – At 7 I
had a tin of soup. At 9 Mrs H. came & talked & took the silver
back. At 10 Kathie came & had an orange & I had tea & bread
& marmalade. We went to bed about 11.30. She wouldn't have
breakfast & went at 7. I got up at 7.30.

The musical box is behind screen in drawing room. Mrs H.
has my wireless & also Ma's.

I was going to put the 5 watt bulb in the study – but after thinking about it & talking it over with Mrs H. decided not to for various reasons. Cissie is going to draw study & dining room curtains everyday & back in the mornings.

If I ever get left alone again, I shan't bother with Kathie – I didn't mind it a bit - & went all over the house at night & wasn't the slightest bit frightened – funny?! (I fed the chickens every now & again!)

Anyway I had plenty of time for finishing things on Monday & the taxi came at 9. & followed me to P.s. where I left the car with the list & said you would collect it on 21st Oct.

I got to Victoria at 9.50 & waited on the platform with a whole collection of others & got the train at about 10.15. There were lots of women going to Germany. ATS & Central Commission - the latter are an awful looking lot - & they wear navy blue uniforms with berets & large badges on them – so Boss will look fine! I was the only ATS officer - & a few males were there including 3 Colonels. One Col came & talked to me - Col Stephens of AWS 3 (Dug Knows him) going to Germany for a few days - A very nice old boy. I was in a carriage with 3 other males to Dover. There we waited around for sometime - the women were all given two blankets each - which I was very glad of in the train. We were in a very small boat & it wasn't as calm as it might be - & I never turned a hair! We went up & down & side to side & I liked it!! I sat on deck all the time with Col Stephens & talked to him. He lives in Truro & knows my Claude's relatives – was in the last war with his father – he says they are a very old & good family there.

At Calais all the Germany people went straight on in there train & there were only six females left for Italy - 3 Nursing sisters, a Red Cross person (who came back on the Orduna when Dug did) & Mrs Hedley - Dug's Help Society woman!! Who I palled up with. At least she palled with me & stuck to me - & I should have preferred the Red X person really I think!

We were met at Calais by an ATS truck which took us to a Transit Camp - just outside the station. I still had my luggage with me which was nice (& I still have her) Porters were easy to get - all the foreigners love cigarettes as tips.

We got to the transit camp at 4 & had to change our watches on to 5 - had a wash & a good dinner at 5.30 - served by French girls - & then sat in front of a nice stove & waited till 8.30 - had a cup of tea - & were driven back to the station.

We had 3 carriages allotted for the 6 of us – two to each so we had a whole seat each - I shared with Mrs Hedley. It was a very long train - About 400 troops & in our coach about 9 males (officers) & us six. The males also only two to a carriage. I was sorry for the troops who only had a seat each.

We left about 9 p.m. Next door to us, was a Col Riddell & a Major Mc Kenzie (the latter & I am sure we've met before – but can't make out where). They were very nice & friendly & Mrs H & I went in & sat with them & had some of their drink until about 10.30 - & then we retired for the night.

It was very cold - but we had two blankets & my rug & my pillow & slept fairly well.

Funny – Major Mck: has been over here before for some time & was in Bologna & knows Katherine Stewart quite well – (I was at school with her, & she married the Mayor of Bologna). He has been to her house several times.

We stopped at 9.00 the next morning at Pagny-sur Moselle - where there was a large camp by the station. We all got out & had breakfast there - not too bad & then washed. In one place there was a row of basins - all German helmets!! & - hot water. The DD/GS house seats were also in a row - & nothing to screen them from each other - so we went one at a time!

We passed through Nancy at 11.30 - I knitted & read & looked out all day. We were given haversack rations each day at breakfast for our lunch - & I had three eggs & apples & choc.

We passed lots of bombed places on the way - especially German stations.

At 5.30 we stopped at Karlsruhe for dinner - just outside the station in a large restaurant. All the ORs were downstairs - & the officers on a balcony above them - & there was a band (four of them) playing and a girl sang - all German!! It was rather nice & the troops loved it.

We left there at 7 p.m. Mrs H & I had our sit with the Col & Major & went to bed about 10. During the night we passed through Munich & at 5.30 a.m. - we stopped for breakfast at a little place called Trounstein (in Germany) - in a hotel which had been requisitioned. We left there about 7 a.m. We passed thro Salzburg - the station of which was in ruins - & and then some lovely country - mountains with snow on - & rivers & things just like Switzerland.

At 12.45 (noon) yesterday we reached Villach (which is in Austria).

Us women were met & driven to this hotel - which is a place where you "take the cure". There are two lovely swimming pools in the grounds - one open & one closed & the water in them is radio-active! Apparently you can't stay any longer than 20 mins as it does things to you! It is in a lovely huge park & lots of soldiers seem to do a lot of riding - lovely looking horses.

Mrs H and the red X person left us here & have gone to a place called Klagenfurt - about 25 miles away on a huge lake. So I've palled up with the 3 nursing sisters - who are very nice - 2 Scotch, 1 Irish.

We had lunch here & washed - & later on I went the office & they asked me to go in & see the chief ATS officer here – a Senior Cmdr – as she knew me. It is a girl called Kathleen Cooper who was at St Marys Hall! She was in the ATS as an Ambulance Driver at Kingston when I was there as a Private! She is so nice, & I had tea in her office with her - & later on she asked if I would like to spend the night with her in her flat in Klagenfurt. So we left at 5.30 p.m. & dove there in her staff car - all by a lovely lake with young mountains all round – about Burgenstock or a little higher height!

She has a very nice flat – 2 bedrooms, sitting room & usual offices! First we each had a hot bath. Then about 7.30 we went up to her mess for dinner – two male officers - Afterwards she took me to the local Garrison Theatre & saw "There's Always Juliet" quite well acted by 'Stars in Battledress' but most unsuitable for the troops, who didn't enjoy it a bit.

I slept very well - had an early morning cup of tea by an Austrian woman, a hot bath again, breakfast in her mess & we left at about 8.45 a.m. & came back here.

At 10 a.m. I was driven by truck into Villach (about 2 miles) to the Field Cashier where I changed my Austrian money into lire. There was a very nice Capt there doing it, & he gave me coffee & cakes! After that I walked round to find the Post Office to get Boss some stamps - & I was such a fool I evidently didn't find the right entrance - & thought it was shut! All the shops were shut as it is some sort of holiday. Anyway they say hardly any of them are ever open as there is nothing for people to buy here. So I've bought some Austrian stamps for Boss in this hotel but couldn't get the whole set. I shall probably be able to get a set on the way home. I had lunch here – sat in the lounge here all aft & had tea & am now writing this. We leave at 8.30 tonight for Naples & should reach there on Saturday. What a journey!! I am longing to hear how you got on. It's terribly cold here & there is no heating of any sort – the hotel – as in peace time it is a summer place. It is run here for all the women's services as a Transit Camp, & also for the Italian & Austrian wives & children of the services going to UK.

I do hope you get this letter safely – as I could never manage to remember all this again!

I hope you are having a nice time. I shan't send any more letters to Switz;

The Austrian people seem very nice – lovely feathers in the backs of their hats! One QAIMAS has a birthday to day & she brought a cake (iced) her Ma made her in a tin (made with eggs & very nice)which we had for tea today.

13th Oct 46. Sunday, 9.30 p.m. In my room. A.W.3.
(Broadcasting), G.H.Q., C.M.F.

I arrived here yesterday evening and am more or less installed alright. I'll tell you from where I left off in my last letter first. I hope you got that one alright – I am now going to start numbering them.

We left Villach (Austria) at 10 p.m. on Thursday night (me and the three sisters). I was going to share a carriage with them as there wasn't much room - but that Major Mackenzie (who was in the other train) had got a carriage on his own & so I shared with him & had a whole seat to myself. It was terribly cold in the night,

& I spent a lot of it looking out the window - most lovely scenery through Austria into Italy - mountains etc - & bright moonlight. We got to Padua at 8 a.m. & had breakfast - & Maj Mck left there as he had to report to someone there - so I was thrilled to get a carriage to myself. However a few hours later at a station a girl got in. I had long talks with her after – she came to Naples - & felt awfully sorry for her. She was Swiss (from Zurich) married to an Englishman - who was killed in the war. She got caught in Germany with her parents in 1939 & they were all interned - & now she can't find any trace of her parents. Her only sister is in China & she has great difficulty in making enough money to live in Italy - & she can't get out - apparently it is very difficult for these sort of people to leave any country. Anyway she seemed very pleased with me - almost cried when I gave her an apple - said she wasn't used to people being so kind to her.

We stopped for lunch at Bologua. All stations we passed in Germany & Italy were very badly bombed (by us) & also all the bridges were temporary ones - with lots of men at every one making new ones - also lots of bomb craters by the side of the line.

At Bologna lots of Poles (Army) got in, & one came in our carriage, such a nice looking man, but he spent a lot of time in the corridor. We talked a bit to him. We stopped at Rimini for an evening meal at 5.30 p.m., & at 6.30 were told we'd have to wait there for 5 hours, as an ammunition dump had been blown up 5 miles down the line & would burn for hours! So I sat with the nursing sisters, & we played silly card games - & knitted. We had another meal at 10 p.m. & left at 10.30.

At 3.30 a.m. at a station, another Pole with an Italian wife got in. She sat on my side & I moved my legs up, & she immediately stretched full length on my seat. I was so angry! & had to put my legs over the other seat! Anyway they found another carriage quite early in the morning.

At 10.30 a.m. on Saturday we reached Rome & had a meal - station very badly bombed. We left there about 11.30 & reached Naples at 5.30 p.m. There I went to the R.T.O., who of course knew nothing about me. In the end he managed to ring up the welfare HQ, who sent a car for me & took me to a huge building - the welfare HQ - where there were just Military Police in charge.

I told them my trouble & they rang up Maj Bennett (who is to be my Boss) in "A" Mess. He was away, but Lt Col Lewis spoke to me & said he'd fetch me at once. By this time it was 6.45! He arrived in a car & brought me here. He is a very nice little man & I've had long talks with him yesterday & this evening. His father was a parson, he is a barrister (evidently very clever) & he plays the piano beautifully & is an ARCO, he is 29 & is organist at a church in Cardiff! We spent a long time this evening discussing religion. Anyway he was very welcoming & took me up to his mess – which is a lovely house where we all eat, & some of the male officers sleep above. We had a nice meal – Italian servants - & most lovely furniture – polished tables etc. About 10 p.m. I came to where I shall live - it is just around the corner - the top story (about 6th floor!) of a block of flats. Maj Bennet (who I haven't seen yet) a Maj Cottrell, & 4 of us women live in it. The other women are a J/C. Marsh (who I knew before – she came to visit the War Office a few weeks ago), a very nice girl who was Y.W.C.A. & now broadcasts – and a WAAF officer who is away at the moment. I've got a lovely room looking over the sea - Isle of Caprie, Vesuvius etc. Its large - & has a wardrobe – chest of drawers, two arm chairs – a nice table – two small cupboards & a very comfy bed. There aren't really many drawers anywhere – but I manage.

Of course for the first time ever - I need some sheets & blankets. The others have lent me some, & I shall buy some more at the Officers shop.

(I forgot to say that all through the journey in Italy we never left our carriages unguarded as the Italians steal luggage whenever they can. So the nurses & I ate in two shifts everywhere we stopped!)

I went over to breakfast this morning & then came back & unpacked everything. I went & had lunch alone as the others were all at the Broadcasting Station & went back to the flat, of course couldn't get in – as I hadn't got a key, & our Italian maid had gone! So I went for a walk for about an hour - & went back for tea & tried to get in again, & couldn't. I found out afterwards that May Cottrell was in & was asleep & didn't hear – but I was rather annoyed as I wanted to write this letter then.

I spent the rest of the time in the mess reading & playing the piano & from 7-8.30 talked to Col. Lewis. He is engaged to a girl he met in Rome. She is English & lives there with her parents. She is ill in hospital at the moment.

It is funny - we live quite near Parkers Hotel which I passed on my walk today. It is the Headquarters of the Americans over here – only about 200 yards from our mess.

It was a simply lovely day today – very hot. But they say the weather has been quite cold lately.

There is quite a nice dog which lives in our flat a sort of foxhound – called Ally. He divides his time between the flat & the mess – finds his own way - & is supposed to guard us.

I'm longing to hear how you got on - & am hoping there'll be a letter in the office tomorrow.

22nd Oct 46 To Ar Beat and Ar Jessie From Dorothy,
A.W. H.Q Army Welfare Services, C.M.F.

I have been meaning to write you a proper letter for sometime - so here it is. I had a very good journey out here - left England at 11 a.m. on Monday 7th October from Victoria. I crossed from Dover to Calais on a smallish boat - a troops one - and although it was fairly rough I didn't mind a bit, and palled up with a Colonel I knew from the War Office, who was going to Germany. At Calais, after a rest of about 2 hours in a women's transit camp. we started our train journey. I was very lucky and only had one other person in my carriage, who belongs to the Sailors, Soldiers and Airmen Help Society, and whom Douglas had a lot to do with! We travelled through France, Nancy and Strasbourg, and then Germany, Karlsburg, Salzburg and Munich, and then Austria. We reached Villach in Austria on the Wednesday afternoon, and there went to the Women's Services Hotel for the night.

There were six women travelling to Italy, three nursing sisters, one Red Cross, the Help Society person and me. At the Hotel, which must be a lovely place in peace time, and has two large swimming pools with radio active water (where people take the cure), I found the chief A.T.S. officer running it to be a girl called Kathleen Cooper, who was at St.Mary's Hall with me. She was very nice indeed to me, and drove me to her flat that night, which was in Klagenfurt about 20 miles away, by a lovely large lake. She brought me back to Villach the next morning, and I had a mouch round the town, which is very small. The Austrians all seem very poor and nearly all the shops are shut. as there is nothing for them to sell. The land is all very well cultivated.

On the Thursday evening we left by another train at 10 p.m., and I had a Swiss girl in my carriage - and later on two more people got in, a Pole and Italian woman, wife of a Pole. I had long talks with the Swiss girl, who had had a very bad time and was very depressed. She had been married to an Englishman, who was killed in the war, and her father and mother and she were caught in Germany at the beginning of the war, and interned there all the time. Her Pa and Ma both disappeared and she cannot trace them at all, and now she has no friends or relations, only a sister in China, and she has very hard work to make a living. I felt very sorry for her. She wants to go back to Switzerland , or Germany where she has a house, but is not able to get out of the country.

(It is now 5.15 p.m. in the office, and Tuesdays are lightless days in Naples, to save the electricity, so I really cannot see a thing I am typing!)

All through the night when we left Villach we came through Austria in to Italy through the most lovely country all mountains and gorges etc. It was terribly cold, and so I looked out at the scenery most of the time - and it was bright moonlight. We came through Padua, Bologna, Rimini and Rome, and reached Naples about 5 p.m. on Saturday evening. Our meals, breakfast and supper each day were arranged at Stations on route, where we were also able to 'wash and brush up'. Our lunches were given to us in sandwiches. All the railway stations in Germany and Italy were very badly bombed, especially Bologna Station.

I live in a mixed mess here, about 16 people altogether, four of us are women, another A.T.S. officer, a WAAF and two majors live in a lovely flat 6 floors high. I have a large bedroom to myself overlooking the bay, with the Isle of Capri opposite, and Vesuvius on the left. We work in a large building in the town.

Early next month the whole of this Directorate is moving to the north - as the Headquarters has already moved to Padua. We (the Welfare people) are going to a little place called Abano

Termi, about 15 miles south west of Padua, where there are hot springs, where people take the cure in peace time. All the hotels are centrally heated by these springs, so it will be rather nice in the winter time. Also it is only about 3 hours journey to winter sports places, which will be lovely.

The shops in Naples are absolutely full of everything - even better than Singapore!

The weather just now is lovely - with the sun out all day, but not too hot.

Could you please let my family see this letter, as I think I have told you more details of my journey, than I told them, and I'd like them to know it all.

2nd Nov 46.12.30. In my room. Rome, Italy
I have just come in from a march round the shops. I went down the Via Nationale – turned to the right & walked through a tunnel to the Via T.... - & have enjoyed it very much.

I bought a needle (packet) & stuff to mend stockings with - when I asked for needles she brought out buttons at first! Then the old boy who kept the shop came & asked me what something was that he had - & I said it was a bomb! Looked just like one - then I discovered it was an American thing for killing insects - mosquitoes etc - & it works like a mills bomb! He said would I like it - & I had to carry the beastly thing all the way back - & was scared in case it was a bomb & he was fooling me!! But it is alright - as it is covered with instructions in English.

I then bought myself a pair of stockings - first time as I always thought I couldn't get any large enough. I could only get 9 ½ and have just tried them on and they are lovely. But they'd never fit Boss which is a pity.

I bought Ma a brooch – rather a pretty one.

5.30 p.m. I had lunch at 10 on my own and at 2.15 Mack called for me with a vehicle - a station wagon (ask Dug!) & we set off to see Rome. He doesn't know much about it – although he has been stationed here for three weeks – so first we went to the Coliseum – then via St Peters & the Vatican – where we didn't stop – to a high place called – Mario which is the Observatory –

very high up so that we could see all Rome below – a wonderful view – I wonder if you went there.

We drove back & had tea at the C.W.L. Club (Catholic Women's League – sort of YWCA)(Roman Catholic – they mean!) There I met Mack's Colonel – whose name is Blunt – thinks he's related to the Bishop of ? Bradford. He was not bad. Then we went into their Gift shop, where I sent a box off to D.D – with almonds, raisins & walnuts in – so please let her see this.

There was a very nice RC Padre in there – who belongs. He showed me some lovely Xmas cards – all animals, which he had just bought & there were no more left – so he let me have his.

I have just come back to the hotel to wash etc - & Mack is going back to the CWL at 6 to meet a man who wrote a Guide Book to the Vatican & St Peters – to see if he can get us into the Vatican Museum tomorrow altho' its shut so I hope he can.

We are doing St Peters & the Vatican tomorrow morning.

He is calling back for me later & we are going to an officers Club for dinner.

I have bought Boss some sets of stamps – 4 lots & will send them separately now & again!

When I told you about 'Dead' day in another letter – it really meant that the Italians keep 1&2 Nov as Remembrance Day for the two wars - & the chrysanths are symbols of death out here.

I never told you how difficult it was yesterday driving out of Naples – as our way led past the cemetery - & there were all the people going with their flowers (all chrysanths - all colours) to put on the graves. I've never seen such a conglomeration of traffic - taxis, lorries full of people, horses & carts, donkey's & carts & crowds walking. The traffic jam was awful.

It was horrid as the taxi in front of us ran over a small black dog & I think, killed it - but we saw it all happen. Anna, the Italian wife, of our driver, cried about it - & I felt awful!

I think this is a wonderful place - nicer than Naples - except for the sea.

I have no idea yet how I'm going to get back – I go round trying to find people returning by car to cadge a lift – but haven't got one yet.

You'll be glad (?) to hear that my heel has quite recovered – I can't think what went wrong with it last night – as it was awful bad all thro' the night – perhaps I needed exercise!

I'm no fatter yet - in fact slightly, very slightly thinner I think!

19th Nov 46. Rome

We are here in Rome at last after many adventures. I had two letters last night from Ma after I had finished one to her, and am very sorry to hear about the illness and very worried, as I know M. and B. means people are really ill. I do hope you are better now, and I rely on Boss to tell me the truth about Ma's illnesses. DO be careful, and never go out again this winter. I'll take you out in the car next Spring when I come home.

I left off my last letter, which will be posted at the same time as this one, when I was waiting in the flat for things to happen. Leo and Yvonne found Mary Meredith in a bad state and took her to the M.O. who said she must go to the hospital at once as she had acute tonsillitis. So Leo rang me up in the flat yesterday at lunch time to tell me this, and he and Yvonne drove her over to the hospital at Caserta, about 30 miles away, as she was so upset at being left behind. Anyway she has been put in the isolation ward, and we are very much afraid she may have diphtheria, or something like that, as the M.O. was so grave about it. At 3.45 the truck arrived at the flat ready to fill up with our luggage (it was supposed to come at 2.30!), and I started organising things with a corporal and two Chetniks. (The later are Yugoslav prisoners who were on the other side to Tito – very nice men). About 4.45 Leo and Yvonne came back and he helped stacking all our luggage in the truck, which is a five tonner Studebaker, belongs to our broadcasting station in Graz in Austria, and came down to help us move. We got it all packed up with our luggage and it went to our Naples broadcasting station garage for the night.

About 6.45 Leonard Yvonne and I left the flat for good and went and parked all our things in the Oriente Hotel in Naples, which is a military hotel for officers and their families. At 7.30 we went and saw the C.S.E. (formerly ENSA) show in the local theatre, which was quite good. The best thing was an Italian visiting singer from the Opera house in Milan, who sang some things from Pagliacci etc., and was simply lovely. We got back to the hotel at 10.30 and had dinner, which they had kept for us, and then went to bed. I had a very nice room.

This morning we went at 9.30 to a meeting place in Naples where we met three huge trucks which were going with us. – all to do with our broadcasting stations. We arranged that Leo and Yvonne and Luigi (our driver) should go in the P.U. (the small little van thing) with our hand luggage, then a Cpl Mac Veigh and me in an enormous Studebake 5-tonner (which had been loaded with our heavy kit yesterday) then a 3-tonner Bedford lorry with trailer, with a Corporal driver and Louisa (our Italian maid - a sweet girl), then another Bedford with two English soldiers in it, carrying a load of generators and furniture etc. for the broadcasting station. We stood around the trucks sorting things out, and then got in to start, and one of the Corporals said to me, I will get my bag out of the front of the truck, and it wasn't there. It had been pinched while we were standing there. It was a haversack with his night things and camera in it. I believe I have told you how awful they are in Italy thieving things everywhere.

We then went on to the petrol point and filled up, and then started off. Leo and Yvonne in front, then me on our truck, and the other behind. Soon after we had got out of Naples, we had lost track of the last truck with the two British soldiers in - so gave them up. We went on, and about 1 p.m. we all stopped at a place called Formia, right on the coast by the sea, with mountains behind, and had lunch and found that a box containing rations and cigarettes had been pinched out of the truck behind us - so we shared out all our sandwiches.

We started out again and did not stop until we got to Rome about 5.15 p.m. where Leo and his lot were, and me and my man there. There was no signs of the second truck behind us, and we had given up hope of the third one! So Leo and Yvonne and I came to our hotel and settled in. I have a very nice room (in the we Continental where I was before), and my driver and truck went on to the C.R.s transit camp for the night.

About 6.30 we heard the second truck had arrived and Leo went to see them, and found they had to stop to see to the engine of their truck on the outskirts of Rome and found their truck had been slashed open behind and lots of their kit taken! About 7.30 we heard the third (missing) truck had arrived, and there's also had been slashed open, but nothing taken, as it only contained a generator and furniture. Isn't it awful, the thieving. It is all done by kids of about 13-18, and so skilfully done, that one never can catch them, even though we think we are being careful. Yvonne and I are terrified at the thought of our kit in my truck, although it has steel doors and locks. – and are hoping it will be alright tonight in the camp.

We are spending all to-morrow in Rome, and Yvonne is taking me to the Vatican in the morning, and are leaving here on Thursday.

My driver, Cpl. Mc Veigh is a sweet little man, comes from Newcastle, and was all through the Battle in Italy, Cassino etc., where he got shot in the foot and had to go to Hospital. I light cigarettes for him while he is driving the truck, and he is a wonderful driver.

I have a very nice room in the hotel here, on the fourth floor, and Leo and Yvonne are also on the fourth floor quite near.

We have just had a very good dinner, and I am on the point of going to bed.

I have borrowed Leo's typewriter for this letter, and am expecting complaints from next door all the time I am writing this – it is a senior Commander ATS next door!

I am interested to hear Dug had lunch with Miss Tyrwhitt the head ATS woman – she was the head of Egham when I was there on a three weeks course once, but she wouldn't know my present name. She might remember me if Dug told her who I was, as I didn't do too badly on that course, and I liked her very much indeed.

I am glad you liked my photograph – but I have got rather a nicer one that Mac took in Rome, which I will send you in my next letter. I shall ring him up to-morrow and ask to see him, and get the negative, and get some done for you, as it is quite good of me smiling.

Another quite interesting thing happened tonight – Leo, when he was out in the street tonight met two people, a man and woman – civilians - who accosted him and asked if he spoke

English. It turned out that they were a man and wife who had been sent out here by the War Office to see their son, who is seriously ill in Naples, and they arrived in Rome (flew here) and did not know where to go, or how to get to Naples, and asked Leo to help them.

He was very kind and has fixed everything up for them to go by train at 6.30 tomorrow morning, as if they had been sent for, it means their son is dangerously ill. It had been fixed by A.W.S.1 - tell Dug - and I think they are disgusting not telling them how to do everything once they got to Italy. All they were told was to get in touch with the Army Welfare Service in Rome - which means nothing to them, and poor things were quite distracted when Leo met them. Anyway, he has arranged their journey for tomorrow, and they are staying in our hotel, and happened to sit next to us at dinner, so we talked to them. Leo also told our waiter to give them a bottle of wine, on him - which they didn't realise had come from him, but they seemed to enjoy it, and were so grateful to him for helping them, I do hope their son recovers.

I do hope Ma is recovering quickly and will be quite O.K. soon. I am glad that Dr Mayston is nice. I feel I should like to come home soon, and shall be back in Febuary for certain. I can't do with you being ill when I'm not there, although I know Boss is a wonderful nurse – much better than I should be!

I've lost my fountain pen too – must have dropped out of my pocket.

22nd Nov 46. Hotel Vienna, Riccione, Italy

We haven't aft 'having a time getting here! It would take me years to tell you all the little details of our journey, but I'll tell you as much as I can. I last sent a letter to you from Rome on Wednesday night after all our robberies. I have got those straight now. We are (in our little lot), first Leo, Yvonne, and Luigi the driver (although Leo usually drives), in the P.U., the little utility van – then me and my driver, a Cpl. MacVeigh – a dear little chap from Newcastle, and a very good and careful driver – in a five-ton Studebaker, with a trailer containing a generator. Our vehicle is well built in, with doors at the end wot lock, and all our heavy luggage is in there, and is quite safe – so far. Then came a Ford

3-tonner, which contained another generator and furniture from the broadcasting station – with two British drivers, very nice men. Then came a Bedford 3-tonner, with a trailer, and in the back of that van was all the men's kit, plus my mackintosh cape, which I put in there at the last minute. They fastened up behind with huge canvas door affairs. In front were the British driver and Louisa, our Italian maid.

First of all, we quite lost touch with the Ford with the two men in – and they did not arrive in Rome until 9.30 – to find when they stopped that their doors were swinging open behind, and a lot of rations – sugar bully beef, and 300 cigarettes – had been taken.

The Bedford, with Louisa in arrived in Rome about 7 p.m., about an hour after us, and while they were booking in with the Town Major in Rome, the canvas at the back of their truck was slashed, a huge hole made, and all their kit taken - including my mac. I don't mind much, as that is the thing I can lose most easily of all my belongings. But all the men's clothes have gone. I simply hate all Italians now. Lots of other trucks going north have had things taken too. Of course in a way - we know what they are - and should be even more careful than we are, although we always think we are guarding our things every minute. Also, when Lousia and her driver found their truck slashed behind, they both ran to the back to look, and Lousia just turned round in time to see some beastly kids making off with her coat and bag, which she had left in the front seat! Fortunately she called out and an Italian policeman ran after them and got the things back!

Another thing these youths do, is - the whole way along the roads, they stand, either alone or in groups making signs with their hands, pointing their thumbs down, hoping the lorries will stop and 'flog' (sell) petrol to them, for which they pay. It makes me so angry, and today I put my tongue out at one of them. But usually we ignore them.

Anyway, we all met at the petrol point yesterday morning, just outside Rome, ready to start off again, hoping to reach Riccione last night - which we ought to have done. A whole lot of people we knew from Naples were also getting petrol - including the staff from our mess - the sgt, and batmen and cooks etc.

We left there about 10 a.m. And away we went. After a few miles, Leo's car stopped and we all stopped - and they found they had water in their petrol. So my driver (who is a mechanic) tinkered with it, and we went on. This happened three times every few miles, so in the end they emptied out his tank, and filled it with petrol from some cans we had. Afterwards we found out that heaps of other people's lorries and cars had the same trouble, and it must have started from the petrol point in Rome. Either the rain had got in, or it had been done deliberately - which has happened before. The beastly Italians are up to any tricks, and if they can get vehicles stranded - especially when its dark - they just hold the people up and steal the vehicles. As they are allowed to buy old Army vehicles, it is quite easy for them to get away with them by altering the numbers, and painting them etc. That's another thing they do when they ask for petrol - they sometimes just make off with the trucks and leave the driver standing - so we never stop for anything near them.

About 12.30 we all got going well, and Leo went on ahead and was soon out of sight, and so did the Ford with Louisa in. But the Bedford, going up a step hill, started to boil at the top, and we had to help it. For three hills we came to, my driver put the towing rope in and towed it up, as by then it would hardly move even up an incline (shades of us going to Bournemouth!). He got fed up with that, that at one hill, we went behind, put out nose on his tail and helped push it up - it worked well, but dented our nose!

After about an hour of this, we came across the other van, with Louisa in, stuck on a hill, with the petrol trouble. So we righted that and it went on ahead again. Then after a few minutes, (by now it was about 2.45), the Bedford stopped suddenly, made awful noises, and it was the back axle broken. That was what had been going wrong gradually with it. Fortunately there was a R.E.M.E. Recovery Point 4 miles on (ask Dug what that is), and me and my mate went there, and they said they'd tow the van in, and would have to tow it back to Rome for mending. So that was the end of the Bedford and it's drivers!

We then went through the most lovely scenery - all in the mountains, up steep hills and hairpin bends with rivers and

436

waterfalls everywhere. All the trees are turning golden, like our Autumn, and it was a lovely day and evening. By then - about 3.30 we knew we couldn't get to Riccione that night, so decided to stop at Foligno, the next petrol point, which we should reach about 5. About 4, in the middle of the mountains, we passed Louisa and her van, but they were all right, only having a rest.

The worst part was that Leo had all the sandwiches in his car, and we had nothing to eat, except two apples! We got to the petrol point about 5.15 and found a message from Leo to say that they were there, and we were all stopping the night there in the only place there was, an O.Rs transit camp. So we found it - and spent the night there. It had been an Italian lunatic asylum! Yvonne and I shared a room in the Sgts quarters, as they didn't cater for women.

3 p.m. (in Abano) 23rd Nov.

We had very nice food indeed - but the washing was most amusing. We had to wash in the O.Rs place - just a long sink with a tap in the middle! After food, we went into the room where there was a bar, and sat with all the O.Rs and had some beer.

Next morning, we went out about 9 a.m. to go to Riccione. Again - it was a lovely drive, right over the mountains, and through a gorge, called the Fulso pass (I think). Leo went on miles in front, and just after we had got down to the level of the valley, the other side of the mountains - in a tiny hamlet where the road was very narrow, our lorry stopped. We had been the only ones who had had nothing wrong so far - and had been boasting how good we were! It turned out that we had got so terribly hot in the engine that the rotor arm had broken, and the distributor head had also broken in three places. An UNRRA van came up and helped too, and our other lorry. We managed to get a new rotor arm out of the generator we were trailing, and they fastened the distributor head round with wire and tape, and after about an hour we went on and met the others.

Practically every bridge the whole way here had been blown, and there are temporary ones everywhere, and we had to go over awful narrow little places now and again to get along.

After we caught up with Leo, we went for about another hour, and came to Fano which is on the coast, and from there we drove along by the sea to Riccione. It is the Adriatic Sea -and looked lovely. If you look at a map of Italy, it is quite interesting to see where we drove from Naples here - I can remember a few places, and will give them to you.

NAPLES – Capus - Formia – Terrachina – ROME.

ROME – Terni – Narni – FOLIGNO.

FOLIGNO - (can't remember any here!) - Fano – RICCIONE.

RICCONE – Rimini – Ravenna - Ferraro – ABANO.

24th Nov 46. Sunday, 10.30 a.m. Abano Terme (at last) I haven't yet finished my last letter to you – but I am mouching round the town of Abano, and have found our H.Q. and our offices, and also this typewriter in our clerks office, and thought it a good opportunity to continue writing to you. There is no one else in – everyone is just wandering round the town etc., seeing everywhere.

On Friday evening in Riccione I went out to a café cum bar with Leo and Yvonne about 6.30 - and while we were there, a Lieut.Foster, who is the M.T.O. of our place - also on his travels to here - came in with some friends of his, and we all joined forces and had dinner in an Italian restaurant, quite nice. We had spaghetti then pork chops with fried eggs and chips, then apples.

We all left Riccione about 10 a.m. yesterday morning, and all went well until about 1.30 when we stopped by roadside and had lunch. It was quite an interesting drive at first as we came through Riccione, Rimini (which all sort of joins on - all along right by the sea), Ravenna, and they were all terribly badly bombed, as the battle passed right through those places. All the fighting in Italy is called The Battle. It would be lovely to go for a holiday in Riccione or Rimini, as the hotels and lovely houses are built right on the beach - which is very nice sand. The sea is full of little fishing boats, with coloured sails. We all kept within sight of each other all the morning - Leo and Yvonne in front, then me in my lorry, then the other lorry with Louisa and her driver. About 2 p.m. just as we got to a place called Ferraro, our lorry conked out again. The rotor arm had broken, and the distributor cap had come apart again in three places, where it had been tied up with wire and tape. So we hooted hard at Leo, and after a few minutes he gathered we weren't behind and came back. After cogitations, we decided that he would go on and try and get REME to send something back to help us, and mean while the other lorry would start towing us. It towed us for about a mile through the outskirts of the town - very slowly, as we were too heavy for it being a five tonner. Then came THE CROSSING OF THE RIVER PO! We got to the bailey bridge which has been put up temporarily - with notices all over saying how careful everyone had to be as it wouldn't stand very heavy loads, and everything had to be spaced out etc. and the river is terribly wide, about twice the width of the Thames at Kingston. Anyway, we got just to the beginning of the bridge, and the lorry towing us stopped with petrol trouble! After about half an hour they got it going and we went over the bridge at about 1 mile an hour, I was terrified it would give way! but of course it didn't. They have another bridge built on boats about a quarter of a mile away for traffic coming in the other direction.

Well - we'd crossed the PO - and what a PO - and got on the road the other side, and stopped a bit, and then came along Lieut. Foster and his little lot. He was in an ambulance - a glorified car really - and also had a three tonner. They stopped to see if they could help, and couldn't, and then came along an A.K.C. van - and they stopped, and they had a new rotor arm wot fitted our lorry. So that was put in, the distributor head tied up again - and Foster gave us some bread and butter and sausage to eat, and about 4.45 we started off again. But in a few miles ours stopped again - as the distributor head wouldn't keep on. So they fixed it again, and in another few miles we stopped again! So Foster said he would take Louisa and me in his car, and we would leave my lorry and the other one of ours to get on as best they could. As it was nearly dark by that time - it was the best thing to do. So we came on in the ambulance and got here about 7 p.m.

(11 a.m. - Leo has just come in to the office and told me both lorries have now arrived - but I don't know any details yet. I am glad they've come, as all our luggage is on the one I was in.)

You are probably fed up with our journey by now - but the bon bouche of happenings occurred last night! I got to our hotel, which is called the Orrelogio, and found Rhona Marsh (the other ATS officer, who came a week ago). She was angry, as it had been arranged that she and me and Yvone and Leo and Douglas Cottrill (the other Major) would sleep in the Due Torre Hotel, just up the road, where ten bedrooms are allotted to our mess, and feed in the Orrelogio, and she had been doing that for a week. But yesterday the Colonel said we would all go to the Orr: hotel for sleeping as well - as we have taken the whole of that hotel, for our mess also, and also all married families. It seems that one side of the hotel has all been redecorated, and is lovely, but lots of the rooms haven't been done yet - and Rona and Yvonne and I were put in mouldy rooms - dirty wallpaper and looked rather moth-eaten. However, we thought when we'd got more furniture and stuff it wouldn't be so bad. So I unpacked my little bits I'd got and went down and had dinner with Doug and Rhona. Then she and I went up to bed. After about half an hour she called out to me (next door) and said would I go in quickly. (By the way, we each had our own bathrooms cum lav - lovely ones). So I went in and she was practically crying and all over her bed were bugs - absolutely filthy. They were the little kind. She had been asleep and woke up itching and of course looked on her sheet and there they were. So she put on her dressing gown and went and fetched Doug and he came up - and Leo and Yvonne, and we all cogitated. I then went and looked at my blanket and found it covered all over with moth cocoons. I hadn't been in bed, but I expect mine would have been buggy too. Apparently the hotel had been used by Polish officers before. It seems the manager of the Hotel had told the Colonel that the rooms were not fit to be lived in until they had been redecorated, but he wouldn't listen - so he isn't half going to get it now by all of us.

So Doug and Leo raised H-LL, and Rhona and I moved into a newly done room, which is for another Colonel and his wife when he comes, and Yvonne was also given another room for the night. So now we are awaiting events, and decent rooms.

The hotel is otherwise very nice - good food, and central heating and hot water. The central heating is all right – but it seems very sort of stuffy to me at nights.

Just outside our window is a large sort of swimming pool affair, which is all hot and boiling, and everywhere in town you see steam coming from the gutters, and baths in all the gardens and courtyards of hotels. There is one just outside this office, and I can see it all boiling underneath. It is all the natural hot springs.

This looks a very nice little town – with quite a number of shops, which I shall investigate when I go back to the Hotel. Our H.Q. where I am now, was a hotel too, and I have a nice little office. It is only about five minutes walk from where we live.

When I get settled in a room, it won't be too bad here, I think.

In our dining room they are all small tables, and Doug and Rhona share one, Leo and Yvonne another, and Rhona has arranged for me to sit at one with 6 male officers! She says she thinks I shall be a Mum to them, as they will all be new arrivals from UK. Only two have arrived so far! But as I had dinner with her last night, and came down to breakfast after everyone had finished, I haven't met any of them yet!

3 p.m. I didn't finish this this morning, as Leo and Yvonne came in and I went and had some coffee with them at the local café – very nice. We also went and saw some of the springs, which are just across the road. You can see the steam rising all the time – looks rather like fog. I am glad to see there are quite a lot of hills round this place.

Our two trucks arrived here at 3.30 a.m. last night! The other lorry managed to tow mine as far as Padua, where they got at 12 o'clock, and they went to our broadcasting station there, and got one of their vans to tow them in here - as by that time the second lorry had run out of petrol. In a few minutes they are going to unload our luggage - and put it all in our broadcasting workshops, until we have our rooms to put them in properly.

The Colonel saw Rhona Marsh this morning - and apologised to her about last night - and they are doing something about giving us decent rooms to ourselves.

I had a very nice lunch, and two of my table companions came in – they are very nice looking youths, only arrived from England last week, and work in the Legal Aid part of the Welfare Branch here. They know the Legal Aid people where Dug is.

I'll finish now, and go back and finish the one I started in Riccione!

I don't know when I shall get any letters – as they will all have to be forwarded from Naples. I think you'd better address your next ones to me: A.W.3 Broadcasting, H.Q. Army Welfare Services, ABANO TERME, N.Italy

> 6th Dec 46. A.W.3 Broadcasting,
> H.Q.Army Welfare Services, C.M.F.

I honestly don't know about my correct address yet – but I think you'd better stick to the one above, as you have been doing, as I seem to get your letters okey-dokey. It is now 4.30 p.m. in the office.I can't think why you haven't heard from me lately – as I have written a lot – at least every other day, and sometimes daily.

I have at last been able to move my room to one where there are some drawers! It is two doors away from where I was - much bigger and has a nice wardrobe, with long glass, with three drawers fixed on the side of it. I moved all my things in there the day before yesterday and in the evening when I got back about 5.30 I started to unpack my trunk, and had everything all over the table - including a bottle of lemon squash. Then about 6 I had a telephone message from Naples to say that Mary Meredith, our ATS clerk, was arriving at Padova that night – so I had to go and ring up all sorts of people – RTO and our broadcasting station etc., to get her met and brought to us. When I got back to my room about 6.45, Rhona Marsh (the other ATS officer) came in and said could I lend her a little lemon juice - so I said yes and went and picked it up, and nearly dropped the whole bottle on the floor - IT WAS COVERED WITH ANTS!! Then we found the whole table was crawling with them, all over my things - absolutely disgusting. They are not as big as ours on the front door step at home - but smaller. They were wonderful to watch, as they were coming from underneath the radiator, just near, and going in one long line, single file on the table. It was rather funny really, as one ant was going the other way, and instead of going above or beneath the long line of them, it bumped into them all on its way!

Anyway, fortunately I had that insecticide bomb that that man had given me in a shop in Rome (wot I told you about), and Rhona fetched Doug Cottrell, and he opened it and sprayed them all, and they were all deaded - then Rhona helped me shake all my things and clear up the mess. I sprayed under the radiator for hours after that into their hole, and I haven't seen any since.

I can't write much now, as I think I might do some work. Our station commander from GRAZ, Peter Hesketh is here at the moment in Leo's office next door. He used to be in my job here – such a nice looking man, with lovely fair curly hair. He is only here for the night.

I'm going shopping in Padova to-morrow afternoon again and shall buy some more fruit to send you for Christmas. They have got some glacé cherries and crystallised fruit, which I shall get if I can find anything to put them in, as they sell them loose.

25ᵗʰ Dec 1946. B6 Army Broadcasting Station, UDINE.
CHRISTMAS DAY. 12.30 hours
I've nothing to do for the moment, so shall write a bit to you.

This morning about 8.30 Ken, Alec Oulianine and Sgt Agness, who is a very nice man, all arrived in my room with my tea and chanting A Happy Christmas and presented me with a cigar! Then they all sat down and had tea as well – it was amusing with me in bed.

I didn't get up until about 10, and came down, and we didn't have breakfast until 10.30, as some of them kept being 'on air'. We had a lovely breakfast – sausage and two rashers, two fried eggs, tomatoes and beans. Ken had put a present on all our plates from him – which was very nice of him – but of course I haven't got anything for him. He gave me quite a nice looking fountain pen – which was what I wanted, as I lost my best one the day I left Naples.

I have been mucking about all the morning – doing some typing for them, making a stencil for the men's Christmas dinner, and tying up cigarettes as presents for all the men etc. Everything here is very sort of free and easy – everyone wandering about all over the place. I usually park myself in the Station Commanders office where I am now, and where everybody wonders in and out!

I have been listening in to the wireless – too – as they are going all over the place, all the time. We had a very nice service relayed from the church in Trieste. We heard the carol service this morning from the BBC from Kings College choir – I expect you did too.

It is a simply lovely day to-day, sunny and dry, but quite cold out of the sun.

In case you are muddled up with the people I keep talking about, they are:

Captain Ian Woolf – who is the station commander here. He is tall and dark, and rather peculiar – half Russian, half French I think, but is British born and so has no accent at all. He is married to a Dutch girl he met in Java (where he was dropped by parachute during the war there) – a most attractive girl. The only place where they were able to live here is Grado, which is 30 miles away on the coast, so it is an awful long way for him to come every day. He used to be in charge of the station at Naples, and has only recently come here.

Captain Alec Oulianine – the Russian prince man – who is very nice.

Captain Kenshole – who has been acting station commander until Ian arrived. He will eventually be my boss in Abano, when Leo decides to take his release. He has a large black moustache, and is very nice. He is very kindhearted.

There are also two Sergeants who eat with us – both broadcasters – Don Agness , and a RAF sergeant Lawlor.

Boxing Day 12.30

I started a letter to you yesterday, which I have left upstairs and can't be bothered to fetch – so I shall start again on this one from where I think I left off!

Alec Oulianine had a friend who came in for most of yesterday an Italian girl, who is sweet, and I like her very much. At 1.50 we all gathered in the entrance hall to give away presents from the tree. Ken had asked me before if I would present them, but I suggested that Jeanette (Alec's girl friend) should do it – as she is a pretty little thing and I thought the men would appreciate her more than me! So she did it, and very nicely. All the men seemed very pleased with their presents – all small things like combs, diaries etc. I got a bottle of Eau de Cologne and some chocolate – which I expect will find its way to you in my next parcel home!

Then about 2.15 all the men (22 of them) went to their mess, which had been nicely decorated. It is a sort of large Nissen hut in the grounds, with the cookhouse next door. We all served them with their food, which we fetched from the cookhouse next door. It is wonderful how they do their cooking, in a very old fashioned sort of stove affair – rather like ovens they bake bread in – and all heated by wood – and nothing else! They had a very good meal – even I couldn't have eaten so much. Soup; a plate filled with turkey, stuffing, potatoes, peas, and cabbage; then a plate of pork with apple sauce; Christmas pudding and tinned milk, like cream; pears and cream; then apples and oranges and coffee. We didn't finish them off until 3.30, and then we sat down to have our meal and one of the men waited on us. We had the same – but I didn't eat the fruit part. We listened to the King while eating, and we didn't finish the meal until 5 p.m.!

It had been 'laid on' that a lot of WAAF girls had been asked in about 7 to make a party for the men. They are girls who are touring in a CSE show and they said they would like to come. Anyway they never arrived, and we discovered they had gone to an RAF place for lunch and never returned. It was very mean of them not even to telephone – as our studio here had been got ready for it, with heaps of drinks and eats for them. So we did the best we could for the men – played musical chairs, and one of them played the piano a lot – beautifully – all sorts of things – even Boss couldn't have beaten him, as he really professionally good.

It was very funny, about 10 one of the men came in, and he had had one over the eight, and wasn't nastily tight or anything, but just very amusing – went round talking to everyone and saying the funniest things. We were all in fits of laughter.

I went to bed about 11 and so did most of the others.

6.30. I keep writing this in patches.

I got up for breakfast today about 9.30 and had a lovely one. They certainly have very good food here. About 11 I went for a mouch round the town on my own, as they were all more or less working here. The materials in the shops are lovely – and I kept nearly buying some – but it is very expensive, and I know we can't get it made up at home. I might get some in Padua and have a dress made for Boss like I did in Singapore. If you think that is a good idea, perhaps she will send me her measurements. I can't get any woollen stuff as that is the most expensive of all, but the cotton isn't too bad. They have some lovely corduroy velvet here – in blue and green, but although it is the same as in Naples, it is 500 lire more a yard.

We had a very good lunch here to-day – kidneys and boiled potatoes, and I had two helpings!

About 4 to-day Alec and Jeanette and Ken and me went out in the jeep into town, and went to a lovely tea-shop and had the most gorgeous tea. We had coffee with cream on, and meringues with real cream in – exactly like the ones we used to get in Christchurch, only smaller, and we all ate five each! They were absolute 'heaven' only Ma says I mustn't say food is heaven!

We came back here about 5 o'clock and had another tea which was ready for us in the mess here – tea and toast and butter and jam. Since then I have been sewing Ken's medal ribbons on his 'blues' jacket for him, and putting a white collar inside round the neck. He and me and Alec and Jeannette are all going out tonight to the officers club for dinner.

I seem to write you an awful lot of rot in these letters, but half the time I am writing them, people are in the room and keep talking, and I never know exactly what I am putting down!

I went round to the CSE hostel this afternoon to see that other girl, who I nearly came up here with for Christmas – to see when she is going back so that I can go with her. They say I am to stay as long as I like here, but I feel I really ought to go back to work.

I went to the men's dormitory this afternoon to see some puppies wot were born yesterday – seven of them, absolutely sweet.

I do hope you all had a nice Christmas with all the different Aunts.

12th Jan 1947 Sunday In my room. 6 p.m.

My darling All,

I really have got quite a lot to tell you in this letter!

I got a nice long letter from Ma on Friday evening, thank you – posted on her birthday (I think I must have thanked you for that on Friday – so I'll go straight on!)

On Friday evening I went to dinner with the Colonel and his wife name of Coe. A Lt.Col Mowbray went too from here, and took me in his Jeep, which was jolly cold. I went in my best uniform and looked quite nice. They have a very nice house about 3 miles away along a country lane – with one enormous room where they sit one end with a lovely fire for logs, and a smaller dinning room leading out. We all had a drink first and then went in to dinner.

Mrs.Coe is a very nice little thing – she is Belgium – but speaks English fluently with a nice accent. Aged about 40, and I think he is 49. She is mad on cats and has two of them – one a tabby and the other one pure white all over – a lovely animal. She had evidently dressed to suit the cat on purpose – as she had a long red velvet dress on with long sleeves – down to the ground – the most lovely colour – and of course with the white cat on her knee it looked lovely – and I said so – and she agreed with me!

They were both extremely friendly and natural. We had some sort of savoury thing to start with – its an Italian vegetable looking rather like celery, with a sort of sauce on, and was lovely. Then we had some lovely chops and the most gor mashed potatoes, all light – soufflé or something. Then my troubles started – I got a coughing fit and could I stop??!! They got me some hot milk which helped a bit, and I stopped eventually just after the meat course was over. It was sickening. The Colonel gave me two helpings of everything, which I managed to eat. We had Christmas pudding afterwards with sauce with rum in, which was good. They had a German to wait on us and they have a German cook.

Afterwards we all went and sat and talked - about everything. I told the Colonel how I wanted to go to Cortina, and he said they are going next Thursday, and if I can get off then, he'll take me up in his car! So I am going to ask Leo if I can go then. One of the things the Col and Mobray were talking about was how sad it was about a man called Brigadier Matthews, who died suddenly. (You'll see why I mention that later on!) We left there about 11 p.m. and came back.

Then yesterday morning, David Rees was going to Riccions and said he would go via Bologna and drop me off there – the truck would take him on and call for me on its way back here to-day. So we started about 9.30 - in an ambulance. It is really a long sort of car – all closed in, so very warm. David sat in front with the Italian driver, and I sat just behind on a seat, which had been put in the car – and his luggage was behind me. After we had been going about half an hour the roads started to get awful – we had known they might – they were covered with snow and ice – quite thick and terribly skiddy – so we went very carefully. Then outside a place called Ravigo, about 25 kilometres from here, we had a little acc. It was entirely our drivers fault – he was going round a corner on the wrong side, saw a charabanc coming, but darn't put his brakes on because of the ice – so had to go into it. Both of us were going so slowly, it was a very gentle bang. Our car – being all steel – wasn't hurt a bit, but the charabanc had the radiator all bent, the bumper, wing and headlight all smashed. There were about 30 Italians in the bus, nearly all men, and two drivers, and they all got out and all started talking and gesticulating – you can imagine the hullabaloo! David Rees was very good indeed with them and quietened them down a bit. Anyway they said they wanted the carabineiri to come and take measurements. We had to agree, as they might have turned nasty on us if we'd tried to go on – although they had all our particulars.

So we waited for about an hour while someone went to fetch the police – only from about 200 yards away – and they never came. So David got angry and went off himself to fetch them. While he'd gone, three police arrived – and started to write all the particulars down – then a bit later, David arrived back in a police car with the commandant of the whole district with him! He was such a nice looking man and most friendly. In a few minutes he had fixed it all up and away we went. I stayed in the car the whole time to guard our things – and they all kept coming to look at me through the windows.

David and I both had lost our confidence in the driver by that time and made him go very slowly all the rest of the way – as the roads got worse and worse – and it was horrid going along on a high bit of road with the river Po on one side, and a drop into fields on the other.

However, at about 1.45 we got to Bologna and found the officers hotel. There outside it were heaps of cars, and officers standing about, and we found it was this Brigadier Mathews funeral just going to start, as he had died in Bologna in that hotel, where he was living. I had no collar and tie on, only a red spotted hankie round my neck, so I went into a shop doorway and quickly did up my greatcoat collar!

We went in and went straight into lunch, as David had two more hours drive and wanted to get off. So he left me about 2.30, and I went to my room, which was quite nice. It was an awfully gloomy sort of hotel – rather like a cathedral – with high ceilings all painted with pictures – but the food was quite good.

After lunch I got a map of the place from the porter and found that Kitty Stewart's house was only a little way away – so I set out for there about 3 p.m. I found it quite easily, and rang the bell and a maid came – and then Kitty came out to meet me.

She knew me at once, and I knew her too, and was delighted to see me. She was just preparing for a birthday party for her smallest child – who was 6 yesterday – and was very busy getting the tea ready etc. She had their dining room with two tables in it spread with the usual cakes etc. , and then took me into her room for a short talk. She asked me to stay but I wouldn't and she asked me to go back there for supper – which I said I would.

She has two children – girls – one of 12 and the other 6, Barbrielle and Carlotta. The little one was very pretty, with lovely curly hair, and the elder girl, is very tall, with straight hair, and a really nice face. They had such nice manners, and when they shook hands they did a sort of little curtsy at the same time!

The kids & hub are RC – but Kitty has stayed C of E & goes to the English Garrison Church there.

I talked to Kitty for about 15 minutes and then left, as I knew she was very busy – and I went out and started mouching round the shops. I hadn't gone very far along a street, shop gazing, when a major in front of me stopped and said did I know my way round the place – so I said I didn't and he said would I like him to take me round! (what you call a real old pick-up!) As he was a bird of the highest degree and about 45 – 50 I agreed, and he was very nice. He was a Major Lucas, in charge of the OR's transit camps in Bologna and Riccione, and had come over for Brigadier Matthews funeral, which was just over, and he had nothing to do.

I stayed with him all the afternoon – we kept going into different cafes and tea places and having coffee and cakes at some, and drinks of vermouth in others – as he showed me places were people eat at nights – lovely very old places – one underground in sort of a cellar. We went to one very smart tea shop, where there were all the elite of Bolgona society – most interesting, as I have seldom seen any high born Italians.

The only things I bought were some liqueur (?) chocs for Ma, and a box of dates and some sweets for the children (Ma's children I mean – and I'll send them soon.)

He took me back to my hotel at about 6.30 and waited for me for about 5 minutes, and then walked me all the way to Kitty's and left me there, which was nice of him. He knew Kitty too – she seems to know all the English officers in the whole place!

She has a very nice house inside – with rather a peculiar entrance through a courtyard. She has one enormous sort of baronial hall – about at least 6 times as big as our drawing room – a smaller room where they eat. Even that is about 3 times as big as our dining room – full of paintings, as her hub is a connoisseur (?) of them. They have about three bedrooms – very nice.

When I got there about 7, the party wasn't quite over, and the children – about 25 of them – were seeing a film in the big hall place – shrieks of laughter going on in there. I went into the smaller room and talked to Kitty, and Parents kept coming to fetch their kids away – all wealthy Italians – very interesting to see them. Of course Kitty gabbles away 19 to the dozen in Italian – she has lived out here for 14 years now. I was introduced to her hub. I can't make it out why she married him – he seems at least 15 years older than her, and very ordinary looking man – but seems very nice indeed, and they all seem a very devoted family to each other.

After everyone had gone, about 8.30, we had supper – quite nice and then the kids went to bed, hub went out of the room and Kitty and I talked hard for ages! Her husband used to be the Mayor there, but now there is a communist one. He is a lawyer. They evidently had a very difficult time, especially just before Bologna was liberated by us, as the Communists turned nasty, and they had to hide in different places in case her hub got caught by them. Then at the beginning of last year she was able to get home, as her father was ill – she took her youngest girl with her and stayed in England for four months. She got home just five days before her father died. He was the vicar of Lillingstone, near Stowe School, in Bucks.

About 11 p.m. they both walked with me to the hotel. After breakfast this morning I went round there again, and talked a bit more and took their photographs and came away about 12. They were going to spend the day in the country about 3 miles out – they walk there, as they have no car now – and every Sunday go to a children's orphanage (100 of them) in the mountains near – as her husband is the president of it, and likes to visit them, and they go and eat with the matron there. He seems to do very good works sort of man in the life of the town.

I have promised to send Kitty's mother some dried fruit etc. as I can do it cheaply, and she is going to pay me for the stuff. I gave her some cigarettes, which she was very pleased with. She says it is terribly expensive living there.

I had lunch about 12.30 as I had told my driver to call for me at 1. Afterwards it got to about 1.45 and he hadn't come, and I went outside the hotel and saw a lovely car there with two British soldiers putting luggage in and asked whose it was and where it was going, and they said Major General Wood, and it was going to Treviso through Padova. So I went inside and waited in the hall until he came out of lunch, and braved him and asked for a lift back to Padova! He was very tall, about 6 ft 3", about 48, and very nice, and said he would certainly give me a lift and would be glad of my company! So I left messages for my driver in case he came, and about 2 we set off. He and I sat at the back of the most comfy car, with blankets all around us, and the two drivers in front. I felt very grand – as a Major General is something! He was very interesting as he had seen my SEAC flashes, and he had been in Northern Malaya himself, and was in with Lord Louis etc. He knows General Grover very well indeed.

He is the boss of the board in CMF which examines officers who want to take regular commission in the Army – and he told me to tell Dug, that if he wants to do that he must apply VERY SOON indeed, as it may stop quite quickly – so if Dug wants to get a regular commission, he'd better do it right away – as I know this man knows all the latest dope. He has been in Bologna as the very same Brigadier Matthews had been a very great friend of his, and he had had to arrange everything for the funeral, and then see to the wife, who was out here. He was taking her luggage back in the car to send it home for her from Venice. Mrs. Matthews is going to stay with his wife in England for a few days too. He lives in Oxford and has a girl of 18 and a boy at prep school in Oxford – the Dragon School. It seems very sad about this Brigadier dying as he was only about 50, and had arranged to retire and go back to England any day when he suddenly took ill and died in three days – from blood pressure and over work. It was funny how I came across him and his death with everyone I met!

Maj Gen Wood was extremely nice in the car – we talked quite a lot all about Malaya and Singapore etc., and he was very interested in our Dug. He is going to Egypt soon to hold boards there, and then returns to England.

I had expected to be dropped in Padova, but he insisted on driving me right back, and I asked him to come in and have tea, and he said he would. Fortunately, just as we got in the hotel, I met the chief Sgt here, and asked him to get tea ready and to see to the two drivers having some. Then I brought the General to my room(!) and shoved him in my bathroom, while I quickly changed my trousers into my skirt. I had been wearing my red spotted hankie again instead of a collar and tie, and apologised to him for it, but he didn't mind. It was a good thing, I had a bad coughing go in the car – so he could see it was necessary I didn't have anything high at my neck!

We went to the dining room and a lovely tea was brought to us straight away, and I fetched him a bottle of lighter fuel, as he said he couldn't get any, and I had a new one. He was very pleased with that. All the other people at the other tables were looking very interested at me with a Major General! After tea he went and I went down and saw him off and thanked him etc. I had only told him my name once at the beginning, but he remembered it. He didn't mention having seen it although I told him my people originally came from Reading!

After he had gone I went back into the dining room, and some of the people were very amusing. A man called Jack Le Traill, and his wife (he is head of AKC) stood up and saluted me every time I walked to them – just teasing me, as I had consorted so high.

A few things I had forgotten to say earlier ..... Mrs.Coe's mother lives in Belgium, has a Siamese cat – and I think I shall write to Michael Joseph's and get him to tell him that I dined with Colonel Coe, as they know each other very well indeed.

As I have expended so much energy over this letter, will you let me know if you get it alright! I have taken a carbon copy in case, to send to you, in case it gets lost!

Please impress on Dug again, that if he wants a Regular Commission through the present method, he must apply now according to my man – and I am sure he knows.

14th Jan 1947 From Charles Strubin Railway Hotel,
Bourne End, Bucks. to Dorothy

Dorothy my darling

I have been meaning to write to you for a long time, but things have been very difficult at home with one thing & another.

I realise, now, Dorothy my dear, only two well that little can now come of anything between us (altho' God knows, I want it to!)

Please excuse this very short note – I'm in an awful rush – off to Switzerland tomorrow for a month or so.

Must see you again when you come home; Dorothy ....
(The George in the Strand!)

Please don't write to the Rly. Hotel any more – causes a bit of bother!

Please write:-
Chas Strubin, JUNIOR.
Chas. Strubin & Co., Ltd.

27 Creechurch Lane,

Leadenhall St, London E.C.3.

Your girl-friend phoned me last Saturday night –

(Please don't do that anymore either – more trouble than that!!)

Hoping to hear from you in Feb. & see you later end of that month.

Please excuse me Dorothy, darling – must dash.

Cheerio, now,

All my love,

Charles

XXX

P.S. I'm just longing to see you again, believe me darling

Chas

From Dorothy To Mother

21st April 1947 Monday 9.30 p.m

From: The Danieli Hotel, Venice

I came here for the weekend - & I'm absolutely dark brown with the sun & burning all over! (pen's just run out & I'm in my room – so no ink) I got a lift in on Saturday morning by doing a job for Major Molyneux (who works with my John). I had to pay some money into the bank here for him – nearly a million lire, I went over to his office on Saturday morning & counted it all – 917,500 lire! & then came in his car – an open one which was lovely – with a German driver & an armed escort! A soldier with a gun all ready to fight for me! We got to Venice about 11 a.m. & had a special little launch ready waiting for us - & it took us up all side canals to the steps of the Bank of Napoli. I was about an hour there paying the money in.

In the Office – Abano – Tues morning 10 a.m.

I was just too sleepy to finish this last night!

To continue – As I was going to be so long in the bank I told my soldier escort to go back to the launch and take my suitcase round to the hotel and then he could go – as I knew it wasn't far for me to walk. I didn't get to the hotel until 12.30 and no suitcase had arrived. So I was in an awful state, and the porters etc were very nice and said two lots of luggage had arrived that morning – but both for male officers. So I rang up Major Hooper who is Welfare Officer in Venice who had provided the launch and asked him to find out from the man wot had driven the launch wot had happened. I hung about the hall and about 1.15 one of the porters discovered my case had been put in another man's room by mistake. So I was okey!!

I went down to the Lido on Saturday afternoon, all Sunday and all Monday and lay out all day long and am now very brown – or red – everywhere where my bathing dress wasn't. I'm a bit sore on the shoulders and chest! I palled up with that Senior Commander Thelma Oxnevad – I've told you about her before – and she was there with quite a lot of friends and they were all very nice to me. We had a cabin each day where we could change etc. They are very posh cabins, sort of young cottages – and six of these are taken by the military for which we paid (I didn't) 500 lire a day – about 5/-. There are hundreds all along the shore, and the Italians have to pay 900 lire for theirs.

The sea was gor – quite warmish, and they had nice little raft affairs with seats on and oars. Yesterday I started to row one and Thelma and her pals tried to upset me, and succeeded – so my hair is in an awful state now!! But it doesn't matter.

This morning we all had breakfast at 7.30 a.m., and then got the military ferry, and Thelma had a car to meet her and she gave me a lift back here, as she lives about 5 miles beyond Abano. Ken and I are going to dinner with her tonight. She works at O2E which Dug will explain to you what it is! (If he has enough time off from his girl!!)

I had my meals (breakfast and dinner) alone in the hotel – I didn't want to force myself on the others and actually I preferred it alone so I didn't have to be polite – as I carefully went in at different times. I had scampis extra with my dinner each night – only cost me 150 lire – they are fried prawns in batter with tartar sauce and lemon – gor.

For lunch each day we walked along the front at the Lido to the other end to the Excelsior Hotel – which is taken over by the Americans, and they had invited any British officers to lunch there any time they liked. It was very good food.

I think our weather has now really started to be hot – as it is lovely again to-day.

I got two letters from Ma waiting for me this morning – thanks. That parcel you've got is evidently the second one I sent. I send one each month – and there is another one on the way, as I sent three altogether. I don't suppose you'll ever get anything back on the first one – so I shouldn't bother. I don't think it is worth doing anything my end, as I expect the things were stolen.

There is a parcel of rice and tea on the way – or should be – which I sent about 10 days ago, I do hope you'll get it alright, as the post corporal here has never given me the registered slip for it – says he lost it – and I'm not sure that I trust him very much – as he has already lost one of Ken's parcels. So let me know as soon as you get it if you do – and if you don't I'm jolly well going to create about him here.

Thank you for opening the Post Office book – I don't want it here, so please keep it for me safely. It is a shame about my gratuity – as I was only a Sgt for 5 ½ months, so I get paid for my other rank service as a Cpl, as you have to have held the rank for six months to get the higher rate. Still I suppose it isn't too bad. I owe Boss £20 and Ma £12 out of it which you will both get one day!

I got back here about 9.30 this morning and Ken was very surprised to see my face – which is brown and red. I expect there will be lots of remarks about it later when people see me.

My John had to go to Florence for the week-end with his Colonel, and is not returning until to-morrow.

I can't see how I'm going to get the Vogue for my tailor in Singapore – can you? I'll write and try and get it , and if not, I'll buy him some fashion magazines and send them from here. The Italian fashions seem very peculiar – so maybe they will be like Vogue's!

I had a very nice room at the Danieli in Venice – it was on the 4th floor, but there was a lift, and I was sort of on the side of the hotel, and had a little balcony and could see the grand canal from there. The bed was very comfy – and all the proper conveniences were opposite my room – very convenient! The chambermaid I think must have been a bit cracky – she seemed to love me at once and kept coming to talk to me, and said she was going to a job in Brunnen (Lucerne) in June, and then wanted to go to England so she could get to New Zealand where she had a 'boy'. She was about 50 in the shade and kept giggling.

Must stop – got to work.

Reference Letter for Dorothy 29th September 1947
Lieut. Col. I.B.Lewis MBE
Assistant Director Army Welfare Services
GHQ CMF
TO WHOM IT MAY CONCERN
Sen Comd D.M.HEELAS (223895) ATS.

The above named officer was appointed Staff Captain in the Broadcasting Section of Directorate in October 1946, and since that time I have had ample opportunity of judging her character and ability.

Of her work I cannot speak too highly. Before being appointed to this Directorate she had already graduated from Staff College, BAGSHOT. This training, coupled with her natural aptitude for grasping essentials, has made her one of the most efficient staff officers with whom I have worked. Of a most pleasing personality, she can be relied upon to make sound decisions and to carry out her duties without supervision. Her tact and loyalty, both to superiors and colleagues, are of the highest order.

For several months, and in addition to her normal work, she undertook the duties of Personal Assistant to the Director and to myself. In this capacity, her speed and accuracy as a shorthand-typist, reduced the pressure of work to an unbelievable extent.

Her promotion and appointment as Chief Broadcasting Officer, CMF, necessitated her return to full-time work with the Broadcasting Section. As Chief Broadcasting Officer, her insistence on sound administration quickly became evident throughout the radio networks under her control. The termination of this appointment is due solely to the close down of this Theatre.

I am only too happy to recommend her for any future employment where the qualities I have outlined above are the main requirements. Furthermore, I shall be pleased to answer any questions with regard to this officer in connection with any appointment for which she may be considered.

I.B.Lewis Liet. Colonel.

Chapter 12 Muriel

Teaches In Switzerland

From Muriel, Chatrlard School, Les Avants, Montreux, Switzerland.

12th May 1948

I am sorry I haven't written much, but I seem to be very busy. I can't think why, but I love it here! First I had better tell you about the journey. My pal and I got on very well. She lives with her Ma and Siamese kitten at Dorking. She is a Roman Catholic and has a her brother who is a Monk at an R.C. Public School. We had coffee and food on the train, then we got on the boat, the Invicta, where we had lunch straight away. We nearly finished before the boat started. The sea was quite calm, and we mooched about on deck. We had reserved seats on the train to Paris, and for our companions had an international Lawyer of unknown nationality, and also a filthy Portuguese, who traveled in sardines and oil! He would try to talk to us in Spanish, but we ignored him, and chatted to the Lawyer. We got to Paris about 7.0, stuck our luggage in the booking office, and took the Underground to the Champs-Elysees, where we saw all the decorations and flags and grand stand erected I presume for Elizabeth*. We found a nice little café near the Arc de Triumph and had Omelette and soup and beans. When we finished we found 'a la Dar' that we were still hungry, so we had it all over again. It came to about 10/- each. We kept trying in French to find a bus back to the station, but either there wasn't one, or they couldn't understand us, so we had to go back by underground. We still had about two hours to put away and it was pitch dark, so we went to one of those cafes opposite the Hotel we stayed outside the Gare de Lyon, and had coffee and I had a hard boiled egg. Then we went about 11 p.m. got our luggage and got into our train. We found a compartment to ourselves, so we tried to go to sleep.

My companion spent nearly an hour getting her make up off, and then when I woke in the morning about 5.0 a.m. found her spending hours getting it on again!

Unfortunately in the night another man got in and sat by my side, so I couldn't stretch out properly. We woke about 5 a.m., and about 7.a.m. we stopped at Vallorbes, and when the customs man had been we were allowed to get off and have breakfast. It was lovely, and I bought two slabs of chocolate. Then we arrived at Montreux at 9.40 a.m. There was no one to meet us, so we went and had coffee, and then caught our little mountain railway up here. Our registered luggage was at Montreux waiting for us.

It takes half an hour by mountain railway, and is quite steep. We are very high up indeed. There was a porter to meet us at the station who took our luggage, and we nervously arrived at the school. The headmistress had flown to London that day, so we haven't seen her. The senior secretary took care of us, and we had to go straight into the common room for a cup of brew. It was terrifying. All the staff seem about 18 years old except for three terribly old ones. As far as we can gather they all seem to be ill! One doesn't go home for holidays, and another one talks about her Dr in Engleberg, so we don't quite know what to make of any of them. They are rather unfriendly, so I have to keep my pal. We get on all right, but she isn't quite my sort. The nicest of them all is the senior secretary, who looks about 40. Her brother is a master at Charterhouse, and she is a keen stamp collector, so we get on very well. There is also a new Secretary, and she and I work together. She is quite young, but I think rather inefficient.

To-day I had to start teaching shorthand. I had four girls who are quite good, and can do it 40 words a minute. Then I had two others – one who is a Belgian Countess (I must tell Miss Phillips that one), who doesn't know anything, and another who knows so much and can write at 90 words a minute, and wants to know less, for she is afraid that if she is too good she won't be able to go to a secretarial college, which she wants to do. I have to teach type writing to-morrow.

I have been kept very busy, for the senior secretary, Miss Malaher, (she is English, and a bird of the highest degree) keeps giving me letters to do. We seem to have Office hours. One day we are off from 2-4, and the next from 4-7. Girls come in at all hours asking things. One of the jobs is to go to the Post Office which is just opposite and get all the letters and sort them out, so I get yours nice and quickly. Miss Malaher was very jealous of the 1d stamp that Douglas put on your letter. What was it, and could I have a few more unused please. We have never seen one before.

Of course the building is absolutely perfect. It is an enormous hotel, and evidently they have bought all the contents with it. I have a lovely bedroom and the bed is lovely also. The common room has an enormous balcony, all opposite the snow mountains. I don't really know what this place is like compared with where we have been. There are snow mountains in one direction and high hills all round. It is a wee village with 6 shops, and we are next door to the station. There are three restaurants, and my pal and I went to one last night and spent the evening there. I tried to talk to the waitress in German, and there was an awful looking man who wanted to get in with us, but we weren't having it.

I shall have to do something about my French. When I am on duty alone I keep having people in who can't speak a word of English, and once a week I am supposed to sit by the telephone from 8 to 10 in the evenings to answer it! I don't seem to have any free time yet, for it takes me so long to prepare my shorthand lessons. I am longing to go to Montreux, where it looks a lovely town, but it is not worth while going unless we have a long time there, as it takes a good time. Also until the headmistress comes back we don't quite know how much money we are going to have in Swiss. Needless to say I have consumed a great quantity of chocolate. I fear that it isn't allowed to send any, but I will try and find out more definitely one day.

I do wish you chaps were here. It is absolutely beautiful. The only thing we don't like is the staff. My pal (Miss Watkins) and I keep a list of the staff, and tick them off as to whether we think they are birds! Meals are terrible. We have to wait in the passage for all the girls to go in, and then file in afterwards. There are two staff tables, and if we are late, we are supposed to apologise to the most senior of them. I was late to-day, but I am dashed if I am going to apologise, so I didn't. I also went to Prayers this morning. The secretaries don't usually go, but I like trying everything once.

All the girls (about 160) sing-song out "Good Morning". I nearly bust with laughing.

I must stop, as I am supposed to be working. Don't forget to try and get your money allowance to come out here. The term ends on the 18th July, as they say it gets so hot here it is unbearable. Being Secretary I expect I shall have to stay longer.

I have now got to go across the road and collect the letters. The wretched postmaster can't talk a word of English or German, and there always seem to be complications, so hope I shall be able to manage.

I am sorry if the typing is bad. On Swiss typewriters the "z" and the "y" are changed round, so it is very awkward.

I hope you are getting on all right. Come out to Switzerland soon. In the meantime I am enjoying myself! Thanks Dug for getting me off. To Dar: I have hung up all my dresses all on coat-hangers!

* Princess Elizabeth and the Duke of Edinburgh visit Paris May 1948 while pregnant with the now King Charles

14th May 1948

Thank you so very much for your second letter, also for Dug's stamps. It is very kind of him to bother, and I am most grateful. I was very proud, as I received mine first, and there are other staff keen on stamp collecting.

I still like it here very much. The staff are much more friendly now. They are (about 10 of them) very young, most of them with degrees and straight from College. They never seem to stay more than a term or two. The majority are leaving again at the end of this term. I don't know why. I don't think they are keen on the headmistress, and they find it dull, as this place its shut away from civilisation. The only things I don't like are that the office and my bedroom have no sun, also I reckon we don't get enough food, but that is easily remedied at a price! It is a lovely large office – the usual one in hotels by the entrance hall, and this is a nice Underwood typewriter. There is another one, but the other Secretary who works with me likes that best, and I like the Underwood best.

My bedroom is very nice, with a big armchair and bedside light. I spend all my free time trying to learn French, I have also had a go on the piano.

I am having to sit and answer the telephone to-night from 8.0 to 10 p.m. I had one awful French call, so had to get someone in, then someone who could speak English, and now the head mistress has just rung up from England to speak to the head secretary.

I went for quite a long walk up a young mountain this afternoon. It took an hour. To-morrow I have the afternoon off, and am going to Montreux to look at the shops. I am getting a bit short of money, but I believe they will advance money to new-comers. If you want me to write lots, could you please sometimes buy an international reply coupon for 6d. That means I can exchange it for a stamp to write to you with! We have to send all letters by air-mail and pay 0.40. One of the young staff has been talking to me for about an hour, and she tells me 14 of the staff are leaving this term. I have a terrible lot of work to do, and heaps of shorthand and typewriting classes. I teach a Belgian, two Indians, an American, English. The girls are quite nice. They won't allow us to send any food parcels (not even chocolates) except those shop ones where you pay £2.

I think I had better stop, as it is 10 o'clock, and I can go to bed. We generally go and booze up at a restaurant at night, not to mention the chocolate I go to bed with. I will send you a book of pictures of the school to-morrow. I shan't put a letter in, as it is cheaper without.

Sunday.

I am sorry I never got this posted, yesterday we went to Montreux. It is absolutely beautiful. We mouched round the shops, had tea complet, & then went on the lake (Geneva) by boat to Vevey (about ½ hr) Montraux is to Geneva what Fluelen is to Lucerne. We got back too late for supper at the school, we had eggs & bacon at a local restaurant up here.

It is Sunday morning & I have just being playing tennis. It is the only time the staff can play. They only have a service here in the evenings. I have heaps more to say, so shall have to continue another day.

I am on duty from 2-7 to-night. There is always too much work to do as well.

Could you please send me a Sunday paper sometimes. I have only seen one paper since I have been here & there don't seem to be any wirelesses.

Must stop again.

1st June 1948

Thank you very much for some more letters, also I forget to thank for the last International Coupons.

I have just been trying to type out some remarks on the Staff, but they aren't very good or full. My days seem so full. Fortunately it is wet to-day, so I thought I'd try and write a decent letter to you. On Saturday I went with three others for a long hike up a young mountain. They gave us some grub to take, which we had with a drink in a little hut. Unfortunately it started to pour with rain, so instead of going up higher we had to come down. The weather is terrible, always raining, but it makes the mountains look nicer, and it has snowed on them. I worked most of Sunday.

The flowers here are gorgeous. According to Letti this place is noted for narcissi, and the fields around are covered with them. They sell boxes, and all the girls pick them and send them to England. I ought to have done it, but I didn't realise till they were over.

They don't seem to go in for music here at all. Two people come over from Lausanne once a week to teach. But none of the girls learn any instruments, and they don't seem to have any singing.

The parson is a funny little man. They tease me for he gives me his copy of the Times each day, instead of to Miss Malaher, to whom he used to give it.

My lot have joined a tennis club, just by. We can only play on the school courts on Sunday, as the girls use them the rest of the time. I went to Montreux yesterday, as it was my half day. I went to the pictures, as it was pouring with rain. I hoped it would improve my French, but I couldn't understand a word, so went to sleep.

There is a man in the village who is very keen on singing. He comes up here to get someone to play for him, so I have done it. He has a lovely voice.

I am sorry to hear about the strawberries. You ought to ask Aunt Jessie what has happened to them. We have found some chess men, and I am going to play to-night with Malaher.

I would love to come back to see you all for a bit, and also the garden. I want badly to know what has and what hasn't come up. I am glad the tomatoes are having every attention.

I hope you are all well. Also are you doing something about coming to Switzerland?

Descriptions

Miss Malaher. She is head Secretary, and has been hear since 1934. She has auburn hair, and always dresses in green. She is a bit of all right, and what Miss Mead was to Dar, so is she nearly to me.

Miss Lovegrove. She is the above's pal. Very quiet, and I don't know much about her.

Miss Watt. She teaches History. Is 22, and looks my age. She has a spotty face (very), and was at Cheltenham College, and in Masters House for a term.

Then there are two Gym mistresses – wet – and they are friendly with the other Junior Secretary. Her name is Miss Church. I share an office with her. We get on quite well. She is about 30'ish. She now does most of Miss Braginton's letters, while I do most of Miss Malaher (which suits me). Miss C. is a bit wet too.

Now we come to the 'gay lot' and into which lot I have fallen.

Stephanie Wright. She is 23, very good looking, and heaps of character. I string along with her, she is the one that drags me at dead of night to play jazz in the Assembly Hall for her to ballet dance to.

Sanders. She is another gay one, and also comes balleting. She is much older.

Miss Fielding. She has a degree in French, and also takes part time music. She has a Swiss boy friend, and so is definitely not approved. She is very good looking, and about 22.

Miss Watkin. She is the one I traveled out here with. She is a funny mixture, but we remained friendly.

Then there are a few foreigners. One is a

Fraulein Gottstein. (Swiss). She hates newcomers, and so was not a bit nice to us. She dislikes me still, for I was enquiring about the gambling at the Kursaal. She objected to it most strongly, although I pointed out that there was a notice outside the Kursaal to say gambling, in spite of her declaration that gambling wasn't allowed in Switzerland.

Miss Stephenson. (I've remembered some more English ones). She is quite old, and has been here for a long time. Every time she speaks, she laughs. She is quite a nice old girl, and plays Bridge.

Miss McClaren. She is older still, and has been here ages. She keeps herself to herself, but is quite pleasant.

Miss Poole. She is the Froebel mistress. She is quite nice.

4th June 1948

I haven't had a letter from you for about three days, so hope I shall get one to-morrow. I had an ordinary letter (3d) only from Aunt Jessie, and it only took the same time to come as yours do by AirMail. So why not try it and save tuppence!! I will let you know if they take longer.

It is my telephone duty now. Last week one of my pals rang up from the local in French, just for a trick on me. She asked for herself. I rather suspected it, and so when I was trying 'Parlez-vous Anglais' on her I heard her giggle, so knew it was her. Then about 11.30 p.m. a message came for me to go and see Miss Braginton. Needless to say I thought she had overheard our conversation and giggles on her telephone, so was a bit worried, but she only wanted something out of the office, so I was very relieved.

I have already been poking my nose into the Matrons part. They have a most stupid clothes list, and wanted me to type some more. So I redesigned a decent one, which was very much approved of.

It has rained all and every day for ten days now. The snow is lovely on the mountains, but it is so cold, and I have quite run out of winter dresses – or rather sick of the three I brought with me.

I had another awful telephone in French the other day. There was no-one about to help, so I had to cope. All I could gather that something or someone was coming up on a train that arrived in at 2.30. I thought it sounded like 'fleures', but when I told someone to go and meet some flowers at the station, they thought I had the wrong end of the stick entirely, so they went to the station prepared to meet a person. Anyway nothing arrived, but afterwards I heard that some flowers had come up, so was jolly pleased I was right !

I am sorry my letters are so poor. I was never good at it!

We just had a draw for the Derby – 1 franc. I have drawn Hope Street and Speciality. Have you had a flutter?

15th June 1948

I am sorry I haven't written a decent letter for such a long time. Miss Malaher (head secretary) has been away for the weekend & Miss Braginton has kept me busy. She is always ringing up (she has her office on the 1st floor). The sort of thing that goes on all day is this: she rings up to say there is someone knocking on her door, would I send them away. Five minutes later she wants to see one of the staff, so I dash round the building, generally up 4 or 5 floors. By the time I get to the top of the building, I hear her ringing again, so I dash down, she wants some letters done. I take them down for about an hour, start typing them, after about 10 minutes, she rings again, wants to talk to me, so I sit & listen to her chatter, generally about nothing, then I start typing again, & she rings for me to show someone round the school, so it goes on.

We had a lovely time in Geneva on Saturday. It took nearly 5 hours on the lake. Then we spent our time looking at the shops. I had to buy some shoes, as the soles had fallen off mine, & we had a terrible time as we couldn't speak French, & we went from shop to shop trying them on. None pleased me, so all we could manage was "Je regretted" & ran off as hard as we could. I got some nice ones in the end.

I'm with Dar that it is impossible to save money. Although I never buy much, it all goes. I have to have a "nightly" cig occasionally, & then we like going to have a cup of coffee at the local about 10 p.m., so we are starving & have a cake or two, & the money just goes.

I have next week-end off from Friday – Monday night. I don't think I shall go away. Three of them went to Venice last week-end.

We had an awful thunderstorm last night, & it has been pouring with rain & thundering all this afternoon, but it is very hot.

The parson gave me some flowers he had picked t'other day. He is terribly "wet" & very small. He has meals alone in his room, but is always coming to the office for a chat. Last week I was dragged off the tennis court to play for a service. There were only 17 girls & a terrible harmonium.

I saw a rubber mouse in the shop. I will bring one home. The postage is so dear, for everything has to go by Air Mail, & the mouse was solid rubber, & so heavy.

I'm so pleased Doug is looking after the garden. Tell him on no account to pull up the runner beans. The black fly rarely get on the beans themselves. Anyway I don't suppose he will pull em up, but just in case.

I long to hear which departments Dar gets to in the BBC. Have you had any raspberries? Didn't any of the strawberries come up? I do hope you are well & having decent weather.

The letter which you sent with only 3d on which you posted at 7 p.m. on June 7th reached me at 3.0 p.m. on June 9th. It seems to be just as quick as those ones which you send by Air.

20th June 1948

Thank you very much for your letters and newspapers. Also Dar's nice letter received yesterday.

This is supposed to be my free week-end, but it has done nothing but pour with rain. It is a pity, as me and another were going out to Champery, near Chamonix, and it is not worth while. Also I never brought a mackintosh. It is like tropical rain it is so heavy. I played the piano most of yesterday, then we went and bought cakes and strawberries, and had a posh tea in our rooms. Then there was a crises in the Secretarial line, and the other Secretary, who is an absolute fool, got all het up, and came to see if I would help. So of course, I couldn't refuse. Miss B always has these crises, which generally consist of having to send circulars to the 150 parents, and do them and get them off in an hour. Anyway Miss B. thanked me very nicely, as she realised it was my free week-end. The head Secretary was out. I am sorry for Miss B, for it was given out a few months ago that there would be no more allowance for Education abroad, and so of course no new girls were entered, and then in May it was announced again, but by then parents had fixed up their girls elsewhere, so I believe there aren't very many new ones coming, and lots leaving.

I went to the pictures in Montreux the other night with Miss Malaher to see Henry VI was so interested to see the French translation written at the bottom (as it was spoken in English) that I forgot to look much at the pictures. Anyway we had to come out before it finished, as the last train up to Les Avants is at 11.15 p.m. They don't have continuous performances out here.

Last night I had to go and play for the girls to dance to. They dance together every Saturday, and happened to see me. I hope Dar will send me a bit more jazz. They keep wanting a polka. Could you please send that book of miscellaneous jazz dances. It doesn't matter really.

There is a place called Caux near here, which is the permanent headquarters of the Oxford Group. I always intend to hike there one day, to see if John Chidell is there. I wonder if Dar knows?

I am getting very good at speaking French. We go to the local every night, and the female keeper of it generally comes and sits with us, and talks, and ticks us off when it is wrong, so it is a great help.

There isn't really much news. It has been raining solidly for nearly a week now.

There are two others with me also writing to their parents. There is a room with four typewriters in it. So we are having a good chat over it. We have been sitting over our breakfast this morning till 10.30. a.m., with heaps of pots of brews.

We do ourselves very well here. Five of us always go about together. There is Catherine (Miss Watkin) who came with me. One called Stephanie who is very nice. Then one called Robin, who definitely has a "Village Boy". We go to the local in the evening, and there all sit together with them and their Village Boys. Miss Watkin, who is a bird of the highest water, and I were horrified at first at the commonness of their village pals, then we realised that they are also most common. She and I have a test now, as to which of the staff aren't common. Nearly all of them have failed, either by saying "pardon" or by licking their fingers when they turn over!!

Term breaks up a month to-day, but I suppose I shall have to stay a bit to help to do the accounts. Everything has to be done in francs and English money, according to where the girls live and how they pay. Quite a lot of them are kids of consuls and things like that. Miss B. wants a bookkeeper next term who can speak French, and she is reorganising the secretarial staff again. I don't know whether she will keep me. She thinks I am much too good just to do her letters for her, and so I may leave, but Miss Malaher says she won't make up her mind, and most probably will tell me if she wants me back, just as I leave for the holidays. I don't mind one way or another, although I rather like it here. None of 'em seem to know if they are coming back or not. Miss B. always gets her staff the way she got me.

I must stop. I am sorry I never seem to answer your questions, as I never have your letters by when I type. I am glad Dug is keeping the garden going. Who will be chief gardener when I come back?!!! Thank you also for the stamp coupons. Also I do hope your asthma is better.

1st December 1948

I hope you are /or have enjoyed yourselves in Torquay. It sounds very nice. I did not write to Torquay, except once, as we heard how everywhere was foggy, so thought you wouldn't be able to go. I hope you got my two cards from Italy! I will tell you all about it.

First of all last Thursday, I went down to our Abgle Swiss Club, as Percy Scholes was giving a lecture, and I asked him for his autograph, which he was very pleased to give me. I missed the lecture, as I wanted to come back here early, and if I stayed, I wouldn't have got in till midnight.

On Friday morning at 9.0 Watkin and I set off for Milan. We took 12 eggs, two boxes of cheese etc. We went to say good-bye to Miss Braginton the night before, and she said I must take her Meta stove to bathe my tooth in case it ached, and she also lent us heaps of books on Italy. We went through the Simplon tunnel, and got to Milan about 4.o'clock. We parked our bags at the station, and went by tram to the town to try and book tickets for the Scala Opera, but of course it was shut until 7th December. Then we went back to the station and tried to get a hotel. The first place we tried would only let us have a double room. Then we tried another, and they would let us have two single, but when we went to get our luggage I thought I didn't like the look of it, so we went to another hotel, much posher, and booked a double room there. Then we went and eat spaghetti, and the more we thought of our double room, the more we hated it. So Watkin was brave enough to go and cancel it, and we went back to the place where they had earlier offered us two singles. Then we went to the town and looked at the shops. They were magnificent-far better than Switzerland. We got back to our hotel about 11.0, and were scared to find an Italian had followed us in. We wished then that we were sleeping together! Anyway we locked the doors, and had a secret knock for each other. The hotel was one without food, and very nice and clean. Running hot and cold, except that no water ran out of the hot, and there was no stopper in the basin. We did as we did last year – had breakfast in our room, and on Miss B's Meta stove we made ourselves a drink, so it was very useful. On Saturday we spent the whole time looking at the shops and eating. At 6.0 we were worn out, and went to our hotel, lay down a bit, and then fed at about 9.0 started for the night life at Milan. We thought we would try a dancing place that we had the address of. We asked one man the way, and he insisted on taking us to have a cup of coffee first, and paid for it, then he took us to the Dancing place. When we tried to go in they said we couldn't without a 'cavalier'. So the man told us to wait while he got us two. Then it dawned on me that we would have to pay for them, so we took to our heels and ran! We went to another place where they had music, and the men that made eyes at us was manifold. We went to bed about 12.o'clock.

On Sunday, Watkin being R.C. wanted to go to Mass at the Cathedral, so we went about 10 o'clock. She stayed all the time, while I wandered around, and looked at all the side shows going on there. Then we went to see the church with The Last Supper in. There were pictures of how the bombs during the war had knocked down one of the walls, and half destroyed something next door, so we came to the conclusion that we ought to mention that Watkin was half Italian, in case they had a grudge against the English. Every time we told them that as everywhere we went, we had eyes made at us, and heaps tried to talk, they burst forth into Italian at her.

Then we went Sunday mid-day to a small restaurant, and had lunch, and the manager sort of man said his friend could talk English, and would like to speak to us, so he came and sat by us all the meal. He was a prisoner of war in Manchester for three years, and said he couldn't understand our English accents. Then he asked us to meet him again at 8.30 p.m. We then went off by train to a place called Vertosa di Pavia, an hour in the train, as there was a famous Carthusian monastery there, where they put Mussolini's body, and it was famous for its liqueur. We found a guide taking people round, so we tacked on to them. It was very interesting. Then we had an hour to wait for the train, so went into the local, and there were about 12 Italian men only. Of course they stared and tried to speak to us, and we got off quite well with two of them. The only language we could ever manage was French, so it was hard work. Unfortunately they were going back to Milan, so we had to go with them. The train was packed, and the doors would hardly shut. There was me with one Italians arm around me, and Watkin had one each side. When we got to Milan, two of them wouldn't let us go, unless we promised to meet them that evening. We didn't know what to do, so said we would. Then we had a Fair near our hotel, Watkin went on roundabouts while I gnawed delicious nougat. She got cheered by a group of Italian soldiers every time she came round. Then we rested on our beds and ate till 8.30 p.m. We thought we would keep a date with the Italian from the train, as he was rather sweet, so we went, but got off the tram at the wrong place, and was half an hour late, so couldn't find him. So we went and drank at a café where they

472

had music, and there was an Italian who beckoned to us to go to him, but we wouldn't. Then the waiter brought us a card from a Dr. Daniel, and it said in English that he would be pleased if we would join him at his table. So we went. He had a friend, and they were Iraq (or Iran), and talked English quite well. We sat and drank with them – they were most amusing. They wanted us to stay most of the night with them!, but we insisted on going back at 12.30 p.m. On Monday we left Milan early, and went to Stresa which is one of the places on Lake Maggiore. It would have been nice, but it was misty, and most of the place was shut. We got talking to an old man who came to meet trains for his Hotel, and he spoke a bit of English. He used to work at the Carlton Hotel in 1903, and when we started talking about the food, I said it was all rationed now, he thought we said Russian, and went forth into a long tirade against the Russians. Watkin has an awful habit of giggling, and can't stop, so I have to behave on those occasions.

We got back here about 9.45 p.m. We found that the sort of porter man, who did odd jobs, and had been here many years, had died that morning all of a heap, from a stroke. Unfortunately I happened to pass his room just as they were taking the stretcher in to take him out.

I forgot to tell you, in Milan I went into a shop with Watkin to enquire something (it sold typewriters) and the man talked English, and when we had finished speaking, he turned on a thing, and he had recorded the whole of our conversation on a new American invention. He stuck the microphone in front of us, and made us talk again. They were thrilled with us, so we went back later, as we wanted to know something. The man then who spoke English had gone off somewhere, and so they sent some bloke round on a bicycle to bring him back to talk to us, while we had to sit down in chairs.

Then yesterday, Tuesday, being our half day, we went to the Kursaal, where they had tea and speeches for the British Colony out here in honour of the New Prince. We paid 2.00 francs, and it was beautifully decorated with Union Jacks and flowers on every table. I should think there were 150 people – nothing younger than 90. And we had speeches by the British Consul in Berne, and an orchestra. Then I spotted Percy Scholes again, so I had an idea that Dar might like his autograph for her Oxford Dictionary of Music. So Watkin went with some cock and bull story invented by me, that she was jealous I had his signature the other night, and could she have it. So he did it, and asked for her name, and of course she didn't think and started saying her name. I poked her just in time and said Dorothy Heelas, so he wrote Dar's name down. Now I am jealous, as hers is much better than mine, for he didn't put my name on mine! I will send hers next time I write, if I remember.

Our Italian trip didn't cost even £5. The train fares are very cheap indeed. It only costs 13/- return from Milan to Venice. I wanted to go, but the cold was terrific, and our hotel was so nice and warm, we thought we were best staying put.

Last night it was one of the mistresses birthdays, and we all played silly games, and then she gave us a feast of meringues, shortbread, sweets etc. Tonight I am going to play Bridge. In the meantime I do a little work!

I sent my shorthand class a card from Milan, and wrote it in shorthand. It hasn't yet arrived, and the others we sent have arrived, so I hope they don't think it is some sort of a secret code!

Longing to hear how you liked Chets, and whether you are back home again, and how your asthma and Douglas is. My tooth is completely cured, also my cold. Please don't forget to make an appointment with Cyril as he gets so booked up, and I wouldn't let the dentist take my tooth out here.

Only three weeks more. I am a bit fed up with it.

Chapter 13

Dorothy and Muriel on a Trip from Australia

From Dorothy

Monare Hostel, Cooma North, N.S.W. 30th November 1958 (STARTED)

Muriel has ordained that a letter should be written about our recent travels – but has no intention of writing it herself – so I will do the best I can.

The Moderator of the Presbyterian Church in New South Wales came to see us off – it sounds very grand, but actually he is the Presb. Minister in Cooma where we work, where Muriel has been playing for services – and he has been made Moderator for a year.

We set sail on Wednesday, 27th August on the "S.S.NELLORE" of the Eastern and Australian Line – which is an offshoot of the P. & O. It is a cargo ship of 10,000 tons and carries 12 passengers, with Australian officers and a Chinese crew and stewards. It also has on it a large Siamese cat – which is about 9 years old and rather bad tempered!

Each morning we were called with tea and toast about 7 a.m. and soon afterwards the Chinese 'bath' steward used to come and say our 'barberly' was ready which we soon gathered meant 'bath'. At first we used to argue and say it was too early to get up – but he took no notice, so in the end we also took no notice and went along much later and just put more hot water in! My cabin steward was called Wong and Muriel's was Foon – they were always clean and smiling and happy looking – they also waited at the table for meals. We had breakfast at 8.30, beef tea or lime juice at 10.30, lunch at 1, afternoon tea at 4, dinner at 7 and supper at 9 – and the result is that I am now 2 stone heavier than when we started!

The other 10 passengers were very nice and we got along well with everyone. Their ages can be guessed as Muriel and I were called "the girls"! There were two married couples - retired – one spinster person of nearly 70 who intended getting off in Japan and then trying to go to China by herself to see the great wall. She was a retired hospital matron.

- a widower who was a Customs officer in Sidney
- a widow of 66, who, last year, was returning to Australia from Europe in a P. & O. ship called the Chillon, with 6 passengers, when they collided with another ship and hers sank and she lost everything,
- a female of just over 40 from Tasmania, with a lovely singing voice, but who was rather odd and a nymphomaniac.
- a female over 50 who was the first woman to fly from Australia to England in 1933 in a single seater plane. She was very wealthy and most interesting.
- the doctor's wife who was extremely nice. The doctor was retired and occasionally gets jobs on ships. He was counted as one of the crew.

We all had single cabins (except the married couples who had double ones). They had a sort of couch as well as a bed, h. & c. water, wardrobe and chest of drawers and a fan, table, and lots of shelves and a porthole. Muriel and I were the only 'pomies' on board. (That means English!).

We used to sit on deck, play deck quoits or golf, or just sit. In the evenings we played cards or scrabble or house, or when it was very hot, just sat on deck. We had a nice saloon with tables and chairs and a small library of books – and a bar.

The cargo on board was mostly wool, and steel (for China) and an ex-army landing barge which was tied on deck.

Friday, 29th August – we sailed up the Brisbane River – with pelicans on the banks – and docked in Brisbane, where we spent the day ashore, leaving again the next morning.

The weather got quite warm and they erected a swimming pool on the deck – which had fresh sea water flowing in and out all the time. We used to bathe about twice every day. On Wed. 3rd Sept. at 4 a.m. (the middle of the night!) we all got up and went on deck as we had stopped just outside Thursday Island to unload the landing barge and leave mail. We couldn't see the island in the dark, but they sent out a launch for the mail and lowered the barge into the water. It had its own engine. Some company on the island is going to use it for getting bauxite – whatever that is. On Friday, 5th Sept., before breakfast, we passed very near a solitary island – looked like an extinct volcano and was called Manuk – or Bird – island. As we passed by the ship sounded its hooter and thousands of birds of all sorts flew up and flew around us. On Sat. 6th Sept. Muriel and I discovered we were swimming in the pool as we crossed the Equator – which sounds rather good!

Mond. 8th Sept., about 8 a.m., we arrived at Tarakan, which is an island about 20 miles off the coast of Borneo – on the right hand side as you look at a map. We stopped there for oil for the ships engines. There was a long jetty with about 4 huge pipe lines and the shore was littered with oil tanks and derricks. Muriel and I were invited to go in a taxi round the island with Mrs.Bonney (the airwoman passenger). We were not allowed any sort of money there and she paid partly in US dollars and partly in cigarettes – which they were very pleased with. There was no real town - just queer little shops – all the people were interested in us, especially the children who stared and giggled all the time.

We drove round to an open space, with jungle all round, and a building which they said was a temple nearby – although it looked like an ordinary house. We bought some bananas and all round us were monkeys – wild ones – about 50 of them – who come to be fed by visitors. Some of them were tame enough to snatch the bananas out of our hands.

On the way back we stopped while a small boy climbed up a tree to get us some coconuts. It was very hot and humid all day.

On Tuesday, 9th Sept. we passed heaps of islands all day – the Philippines – and were told there are 7,000 of them, and some of them are still inhabited by pirates who raid and loot small ships passing by.

We arrived at Manila early on Thursday, 11th Sept., and some of us shared a hired car (a Cadillac!) and went all round to see the sights. It is a huge city – had a lot of bomb damage which is still being repaired – and it was very very hot. They are very keen on education and there are 8 universities in this one city. We saw an organ in an old church with pipes made of bamboo. There were hundreds of vehicles in the streets which had been made from the jeeps the Americans had left there – all converted into small buses, brightly painted and called 'jeepneys' – we went in one in the afternoon. They also had sort of rickshaws drawn by horses.

We were taken to see the President's Palace and shown round by one of the soldiers guarding it. It was a wonderful place, built by the side of the river.

Late in the afternoon of Sat. 13th Sept. we arrived in Hong Kong. The Captain invited us all on the 'flying' bridge to see the ship enter the harbour. That is a small deck just above the bridge. It was a wonderful sight – with heaps of islands dotted around and many Chinese junks. As soon as we docked the ship was invaded by swarms of Chinese all trying to sell their goods, such as tablecloths and embroidered things and also giving us cards to tell us where their shops were. We just went ashore for a walk that night. I know all places and harbours look lovely at night with the lights on – but Hong Kong beats the lot, I think. We actually were in Kowloon which is on the Chinese mainland, but for about 24 miles behind Kowloon it is British territory, then it becomes Red China. Hong Kong island was opposite, and took about 5 minutes in the ferry, and they run continuously – as soon as one ferry left another one filled up to go.

The airfield is in Kowloon and they also have red double decker buses like London = all mixed up with men pulling rickshaws and heaps of cars. The place seems very crowded. They have put up enormous apartments, very high, and nearly every window has a bamboo pole sticking out of it with the family washing on! Some of the back streets had little shacks down them with families living in them. I think now they have stopped the refugees from coming in as they can't cope with more people. All the big banks and Government buildings etc. are on Hong Kong island, where there is a very high hill called The Peak which we went up in a cable car one day.

The next day, Sunday, 14th, Muriel and I met a girl and her husband who had been at school with me in Brighton, and I had not seen since 1928! She used to live in Japan, but now her hub is Manager of the H.K. and Shanghai Bank in Kowloon. They took us to lunch in their house – waited on by Chinese maids. She had a little boy of 8, called Jeremy, and last year he was killed falling off some scaffolding he was playing on – which was very sad. In the afternoon they took us for a drive, about 30 miles – and they call – that district – the New Territories, (don't know why). We had tea with some friends of theirs who had a beautiful house overlooking the sea and more islands.

About 9 in the evening Muriel and I went to a little tailor – who had been recommended to us – and were welcomed with lemonade while we chose some material to have dresses made. They made us dresses for £4 10/- each – which included material and making and were beautifully made.

Monday, 15th – we spent the whole day 'doing' shops – which are wonderful. We ordered a large camphor wood chest for our doctor here (he had asked us to get it for him). It was very tiring as the heat was awful. We got on board again about 5 and sailed at 6 p.m.

For the next four days we were at sea sailing towards Japan. While passing Formosa the ship had enormous Union Jacks draped from one deck to the other, on both sides and many times during the days American aeroplanes used to fly quite low over us to see who we were. (This was because of the trouble with the Chinese islands.) Our ship was registered in London, that is why we had English flags – apparently because Australian ships can't have Chinese crews. Muriel and I were very pleased about the flags, as they were always teasing us about being 'pomies'! The Chief Engineer found out I had been an officer in the ATS and kept pretending to salute me!

On Saturday, 20th Sept. we got to the first Japanese port. There were heaps of Jap men all waiting on the wharf to unload cargo and I hated the sight of them – they all looked like the pictures we used to see of the guards of the Jap Prisons. The place was called Yokkaichi, and we were only there for two hours – and it took us all that time to get our money changed in the local bank. Later in the morning we arrived at Nagoya – a huge industrial town and the ship stayed there for two days unloading wool.

Muriel and I went with two other passengers in a taxi to see some of the sights, but it wasn't very successful as the driver could not speak any English and did not seem to have any ideas of where to take us. We had a map and found a castle and a shrine mentioned, so pointed them out to him and he took us to those places. At the shrine we had our first taste of what we had to do many times in the future – the 'shoe game'. This involved sitting on the steps and taking off ones shoes before going into the temple or shrine. (In Japan they have Buddhist temples and Shinto shrines. If you want to know what Shinto is you will have to read about it! It is too difficult to explain and hard to understand – as it is a sort of religion and yet it isn't (!) as you can be a Buddhist and a Shinto as well). Anyway they had a huge Buddha in this shrine, with about 20 arms on each side of the statue, and they all had a thick layer of dust on them – I longed to get a duster and get cracking on it! Just near the 'alter' there was a door leading out into a big room and there, all round the floor, were men squatting playing mahjong, talking, laughing, and being served with tea and saki by women! Funny goings on in a temple!

After that we got the taxi man to leave us in the town near the biggest shop, which was a large store. We went with another female passenger into the restaurant there and asked for 1 cococola and two lemonades – and we got one coffee and two hot lemon drinks!

In the streets there were quite a lot of women wearing kimonos with huge sashes called 'obis' tied at the backs in sort of square bows, and padded with small 'cushions'! We also saw many women with their babies carried on their backs – tied there with long pieces of material.

The next day, Sunday, 21st Muriel and I got a tram into the town from the ship – all the people were most interested in us. Women are very much the 'under dog' in Japan and no Jap men would dream of giving them a seat in a train or tram – in fact I saw one young Jap woman get up and give her seat to an older one, while plenty of youths just sat. We went and had a cup of coffee in a Jap restaurant – and they give you a little bamboo basket with a wet flannel in it, either hot or cold, for you to wipe your face and hands with, and also a glass of cold water, then they take your order. They are so clean in those ways – but their lavatories!! Just a hole in the floor – and usually a smelly hole at that!

We left Nagoya that evening and next morning arrived at Yokohama, Mon. 22nd Sept. The Orsova was in the berth next door, on the point of leaving and was being seen off by hordes of Jap schoolchildren, and a Jap band playing Waltzing Matilda, as it was crammed with Australians on a cruise. We were thankful we were on a small ship!

After breakfast we were met by car by my two school friends – who I hadn't seen since we left school in Brighton! One of them, Frances, lives in Yokohama, is married to a Norwegian, and has a boy in school in Norway, and twin girls who are at our old school in Brighton now! Her husband has his own shipping firm and seems to do quite well as they have a beautiful house overlooking the harbour, two maids and a chef! And two cars. Her mother lives with her too; she is 76 but goes out every day teaching English to 'high born' Jap women – as she speaks Japanese fluently. Both my pals also speak the language well – so it was always nice going out with them. In the afternoon – although it was pouring with rain – Frances took us to a nearby village called Kamakura to see a huge Buddha, which was in the open, very old and very large, made of bronze. Its eyes alone were 3 feet long, each eye!

The other sister, Phyllis, actually lives in Kobe, but had been to Yokohama for a few days to meet her son of 11. He has been at a prep school in England for two years, but was not doing at all well, so he had flown out to Japan again and was going to a school near their home to be coached up in lessons, so that he will be able to pass his common entrance examination for a public school – a nice little boy. On Tuesday, 23rd. Phyllis and her little boy went off to kobe.

Frances took Muriel and me in to Tokyo. We went by train which took about 25 minutes. The ship was in the harbour and Muriel had to go out to it in a small launch – and that was the last I saw of her until 20th November, when she arrived back in Sydney! I hope she will be writing her 'memoirs' to add to this letter.

My friends thought I ought to see something of real Japanese living, and so on Sunday, 28th Sept. they saw me off at Kobe on a ship called the Sansui Maru at about 10.30 in the morning, about 2,000 tons, going through the Inland Sea to a place called Takamatsu on another of the Jap islands – Shikoku. I was the only European on board (they call everyone who is not a Jap a 'foreigner', but in other places in the East they are called 'Europeans'), which was rather difficult as I could not read any of the necessary notices! Then I discovered a couple of Japs who lived in Honolulu who spoke American and they helped me! I was given a cabin – don't know what for as the trip only lasted until 5p.m. – but I sat on deck all the way. At lunch time I went into a tiny saloon with two tables – the Honolulu couple were at one and me at the other and I had some lunch. Then afterwards the waiter cleared away and just lay down on a couch in the window and went to sleep – in the first class saloon!

I went and sat on a seat on the deck where there were some Jap schoolgirls. (Everywhere one went in the country there were always hordes of schoolchildren being taken sightseeing too. They always looked so nice – the girls in white blouses and navy skirts and coats and the boys in rather military looking uniforms – with their heads shaved – always). Anyhow I asked if I could take these girls' photograph and they all giggled and laughed and I took it – and no sooner had I done so when I was surrounded by the whole lot of them - about 25 boys and 25 girls all aged 14 to 16. I sat on the seat and they all just stood in front of me staring and giggling - most embarrassing! Then after much poking from the others one girl asked me some questions - 'what is the time; have you a son; have you a daughter; do you like Japan; where do you live' etc. etc. I explained I came from London, England, and then some of them produced notebooks for me to sign my name in.

I then asked if I could take the boys' photographs - and in a flash they were all posed, kneeling in front and standing behind - but unfortunately it did not come out - my one failure in photographs. Then one of the bigger boys started drawing me and when he had finished he presented me with it with a low bow - a very unflattering, but rather good drawing. They were all most polite and friendly. Then the girl who could talk English came and gave me her address and said would I be her friend and write to her - which was difficult as I had to explain my address was in Australia, when I had told her I came from London! However I have sent her a Christmas card. When we got near the end of the journey they all bowed and said goodbye.

The scenery through the Inland Sea was lovely - hundreds of islands, all sizes and shapes. We got off the boat at Takamatsu and went to a Japanese Inn for a meal to wait for my next ship. There I saw some geisha girls, and some business men all dressed in kimonos, who were having a party.

At 11 p.m. I got on the next boat - a bigger one and had a cabin to sleep in, with a tiny sitting room leading off it overlooking the sea - with no deck between and the view in the moonlight was wonderful with all the islands. We got to Beppu on the island of Kyushu about 11 the next morning, Monday, 29th Sept.

There were a lot of men holding flags with Jap signs on, on the wharf - from the different hotels - but one little man came up and asked if I was Miss H...s and he was the manager of the hotel I was booked into and had come to meet me in a car! The name of the hotel was the Hagone Inn - quite Japanese - and I was shown into my room, after playing 'the shoe game' at the front entrance! My room was bare, with the special matting on the floor (can't remember the name - but it is inset into the floor in strips and quite springy), and one table about 12" high and one cushion. In the corner was a scroll picture and a 'flower arrangement'. There were windows all along the length of one wall and a little verandah with two proper armchairs and a table. Outside there was a small garden and lily pond and an aviary with birds in. The inevitable green tea was brought and the manager sat on the verandah and talked to me - was delighted to air his English and kept telling me he had another English man staying there and he was most anxious we should meet.

In the afternoon I went for a bus tour round the district – which was rather nice – all hills – and thousands of hot springs and mud pools and geysers, which I got rather sick of. The Jap hostess on the bus gave all the commentary in Jap so I couldn't understand a word! There were three American females, otherwise they were all Jap tourists. I had some tea in the town of Beppu after the tour and asked for an egg sandwich – which turned out to be an omelette in between bread and butter! Then after 'doing' the shops I went back to the Inn and met the Englishman at the 'shoe game'. He was an engineer for a shipping line in Hong Kong and was taking some leave in Japan. About 6 I was 'sent' to my room for the evening meal – they don't have public dining rooms and everyone eats in their room. The manager solemnly informed me that he had arranged for the largest kimono they had to be laid out for me! (he wasn't being rude – just helpful!) and I got into it, as it seemed to be the thing to do. Then two waitresses came in – in kimonos – with my food. A huge bowl of rice and lots of little dishes with queer stuff in. I was supposed to kneel and then sit back on my heels to eat – like they do, - but I ended up sprawling on the floor. Then the two waitresses squatted in front of me to watch me eat! And kept giggling when I made faces over the food – which was horrid – and had to be eaten with chopsticks!

Afterwards I dressed properly again and went and sat in a sort of lounge place – there were arm chairs, a piano, a shop and a ping pong table all in the one room! There I met the Englishman again and he asked if I would like to go to the local museum with him – so we did and it was quite interesting.

When I went to bed about 11 p.m. the table on the floor had been cleared to one side and the bed made on the floor – two or three mattresses and one tiny very hard pillow, and some stuff burning on the floor – which was to keep mosquitoes away. The bath was wonderful – a private one thank goodness – as I think sometimes everyone bathes together. I went into a small room where there was a basket for my clothes, then down some stairs into quite a large tiled room where there was a basin where I had to wash, and then get into a sunken bath – about 4 ft. deep, boiling hot – as it was hot spring water – and the most wonderful feeling.

It really was quite comfortable sleeping on the floor. Next morning I had an English breakfast (bacon & eggs) on the verandah, and the manager came to see me off on the train back to Kobe, Tuesday, 30th Sept. It took until 5 pm to get back – the train stopped at Hiroshima for a time but I could not see much of the place.

On Thursday, 2nd Oct. I left kobe again for Yokohama by train – took all day again and this time I saw most of Fujiama – all except the top of it, and got some quite good photographs through the train window. I had lunch in the train restaurant with two Jap men opposite me. One spent the time sniffing and picking his teeth – the other ate, very noisily, his soup, steak and beer all at the same time – most interesting!

The national flower of Japan is the chrysanthemum and is used on all sorts of ornaments etc., but only the Emperor is allowed to have sixteen petals.

My friend, Frances, met me at Yokohama and took me back to her home. Next day, Friday, 3rd Oct. she took me to Tokyo again and we spent the day 'doing' the shops along the Ginza – a very famous shopping street.

On Sat. 4th Oct. Frances took me to the station at 7 in the morning and saw me off to Tokyo on my own. There I joined a bus tour of about 23 people – mostly Americans – to go to Nikko – a famous place for tourists. First we went by train for 2 hours to Nikko. I sat in the front seat of the train – with a glass front, just like going by car! Next to me was an American (not one of our tour) who came from the missile testing place in Florida and the man with him was the second in command of the place – they were quite interesting – had been stationed in Japan after the war and had come back for a holiday there. At Nikko we were taken by a coach to a huge hotel for lunch – which I had with two Canadian lady teachers. Then we went to see some famous shrine, a huge waterfall and up a cable car railway to 4,000 ft. The hills there were lovely – just like those 'misty' pictures you see of Japan. I went back to Yokohama by bus and train and bus again – and got a taxi up to Fances' house. Fortunately she had written her address in Japanese for me to show to the taxi driver,

The taxis in Tokyo are awful – they tear along as fast as they can go. They are all just ordinary cars and the prices vary with the size of the car – the smaller the cheaper.

Next day, Sun. 5th Oct. it simply poured with rain all day, but Frances and her husband drove me to a place called Miyanoshita high in the mountains, where there was a beautiful hotel where we had lunch.

At 10.45 at night Frances drove me – still in the pouring rain – to the airport, which is between Tokyo and Yokohama. Her mother came with her and they saw me off on the plane to Hong Kong. It was a B.O.A.C. Britannia – no noise, no vibration – a wonderful plane. The stewards and stewardess were English – one from Staines and one from Chiswick and the plane was going to London. I was tempted to stay on it! I had a seat right at the back and was paying tourist fares. But the seat was too small for my behind! Both armrests touched me which was rather uncomfortable. The steward was most amused and as there was no one next to me he put down the armrests and I had three seats to myself for the night, which was nice!

On Mon.6th Oct. we were woken about 6 and given breakfast and landed at Hong Kong (Kowloon really) at 8 a.m. We were taken to the Peninsula Hotel – which is enormous and very expensive – but next door is the Y.M.C.A. (takes females!) where I had booked to stay, and which was very comfortable.

I stayed in Hong Kong until the following Sunday. Muriel was due to arrive on the Saturday and I was going to meet her, see her ship off, and then leave on Tues. 14th for Darwin and Sydney. I spent all the mornings shopping and every afternoon going for bus rides to different places. I also went to a few meals with my friends. Then on Friday, 10th Oct. I heard Muriel's ship had been delayed and wasn't coming in for another week. I just couldn't face staying there much longer alone. I had not much money – it was very hot – and I had 'done' all the sightseeing places. So someone suggested I should go to Bangkok, only 4 hours away by air and only £12 more in fares. I had a very busy time being booked on planes and getting a visa from the Thai Embassy – but I got off on Sunday, 12th Oct. in the morning by an Air India plane. (By this time – due to my size and the seats' size I had paid – at least I still have to pay – the extra for first class! The man next to me in the 'plane looked a typical RAF Englishman – but turned out to be a wealthy businessman from Melbourne, who had been doing business in Japan and was going to Bangkok for three days holiday. He suggested we should do the tours together – and it was very much nicer for me than going on my own. He was an extremely nice companion.

We got to Bangkok about 4 – but it was 2 by their time – pouring with heavy rain and hotter than I thought it could ever be anywhere!

It rained there every afternoon for about ½ an hour, then suddenly cleared up. We were both booked in at the Oriental Hotel, which is by the river. I won't go into all the details of the next three days – we saw heaps of temples on conducted tours. We were taken to a snake farm and saw cobras and king cobras being milked – the men had to be most careful doing this. The snakes are 'milked' for their venom every week for snake bites. We went for a wonderful trip in a motor boat up the river and up the rivers little alleyways – early in the morning to see the 'floating market' – selling things from little boats. I only saw one Siamese cat! But four dead dogs floating in the river! We went for rides on trams and buses, all very crowded and dirty and went to a night club and saw some classical dancing. My one disappointment was that we could not get to Angkor Wat, which is in Cambodia and takes about an hour to get to by plane and is a regular tour. But there was no room to come back – so I couldn't go. (This an ancient city which has recently been discovered buried in the jungle). Not many people could speak English – so it was a bit hard getting around. My pal paid for everything except my hotel bill – which was a great help!

On Wednesday, 15th Oct. we left in the afternoon on a Cathay Pacific Airways plane (British company from Hong Kong) for Singapore – took 4 hours and we arrived there about 8 p.m. and went to Raffles Hotel. I could not have stayed there for longer than one night as it was terribly expensive! Next morning, Thurs. 16th Oct. I spent some time fixing up my air tickets as the BOAC strike was on and they put me on a QANTAS plane instead, leaving that evening, as I had to be back at work on Monday 20th. We just wondered around Singapore – it was most interesting to see it again, as I had been there in 1946. I left the airport there at 7 p.m. (my pal saw me off), got to Perth for breakfast at 5.30 a.m. next morning, Melbourne for tea, and reached Sydney at 6 p.m. on Friday, 17th. John met me there and I stayed at the Y.W.C.A. for two days and then flew back to Cooma on the Sunday evening, 19th, and HATED the whole place!

Somehow I don't think this is a particularly interesting letter – but I hope parts of it are not too boring. I've done me best!

Con't Muriel – her rout back from Japan to Australia.

I, being a non-flyer, stayed on the cargo ship to go back to Australia, and on 26th September I left Dorothy in the hands of the Japanese and set forth on my own. Fortunately, to keep the English up, a new passenger, a very nice young English girl joined the ship and we were buddy's for the entire journey.

'Ida", a typhoon was approaching, so instead of heading into the open sea we (the ship!) went through the Inland Sea, which Dorothy mentions, dodging in and out of the 3,000 odd (actually, I have heard since 4,382) Japanese islands. This route is not generally taken, as it means having the expense of a pilot on board for the day or so that it takes to dodge the islands. It was lucky for us as it was all very beautiful. The ship had to get to Shanghai by 28th September or bust. This was due to the fact that on the 1st October there were 'Red' celebrations to take place to celebrate the beginning of the 2nd Five Year Plan. We had two day's worth of cargo to unload, so should have been and left Shanghai by then. On the 28th September we duly entered the Yangtze-Kiang River, all yellow. The Purser had to lock up all our money, binoculars and cameras, as we weren't allowed them. Security officers then boarded the ship. We all had to stay in our individual cabins, while the security men made a search. I had a grumpy women, with two short pigtails, gazing at my passport, while the security men went through all the drawers, cupboards, and even looked under the bed in my cabin. The only thing they seemed interested in was an innocent looking Woolworth torch, which wouldn't go. So I showed them nothing was hidden inside! We stayed then in the Yangtze River for 27 hours. Then a pilot came on board, and we turned down a tributary called the Whampoa River, and finally on the morning of 1st October, we stopped at the wharf at Shanghai. (The Yangtze is some 3,500 miles long and navigable for 2,000 miles). A security officer, stayed on our ship, snooping around everywhere, the whole time.

Unloading began at once – mostly great steel sheets from Australia. We watched them doing it: women as well as men. We heard that as it was the celebration holiday, everyone had to turn to and work for nothing. There were University students, teachers and nurses all carrying and helping the men. When that was finished they started loading pigs (cut in half) – I mean, two halves made a pig, into the freezers of our ship. These were for U.K., and were going to be unloaded in Hong Kong. By this time, us 9 passengers were ramping to go ashore, but the Tourist Department officials came and said that we weren't allowed to go by ourselves, but only escorted by them, and they had so many passengers off other ships that we couldn't go for a few days. All the officers and crew were allowed off, much to our disgust. I suppose it was because they were 'workers' and we weren't. But on 3rd October, the Tourist people called to take us for a day's outing to Shanghai, so we went: first by launch to the shore, and then by bus all around the city. We were now allowed to have cameras with strict instructions that we mustn't take photographs on the waterfront. The city was most interesting. It once must have been lovely, but now very shabby, and there were bits of red flags and stuff stuck all over the buildings as decorations. Very interesting posters everywhere anti-America and England. We went to see the things that the Chinese wanted us to see – a wonderful Sino-Soviet Friendship Building – enormous, and built in ten months: an exhibition with samples of all their export things in it: one of their Theatres, open at the sides, with hard seats, and which seated 13,000 people. We went to, as usual, to see Buddhist temples and Jade Buddhas, shoes off again!! We were driven around their Workers building estates, and all the time in the bus we had thrust down our throats how wonderfully well off everyone was since liberation. We went to, what must have been once, wonderfully posh hotels to eat. They were empty except for a few Indian and an odd visitor or so. We ate the most horribly grand Chinese food with chopsticks only! This food seems to bear no relation to the Chinese food one gets in restaurants in England and Australia. I was hungry that day. I was glad I couldn't catch much with my chopsticks! The streets seemed full of Chinese men and women ALL dressed alike in blue trousers and tops – hardly any other colour. Everywhere we went, we had crowds (generally children) following us, and we felt like royalty as we just had to push our way through these crowds to get to the bus, after we had been in buildings and places. Whether it was because they never see Europeans (in Shanghai there are 7,000,000 people, and 20 Europeans) or because we wore coloured clothes, I don't know.

The funniest part was to see the roads empty, as there were hardly any cars at all. There were buses, and rickshaw things drawn by a man riding a bicycle in front. I believe they are called peda..(forgotten the rest of the word!). To end the day we were allowed to go into a big store called The Friendship Department, where prices were reduced for people off ships. It was the only shop we were allowed in. I bought myself a mouth organ. Both in Japan and Shanghai abacus's are used for all accounts in the shops. (look it up in the dictionary if you don't know what they are!) They are used very skilfully, for multiplication and every sum under the sun instead of machines.

That mouth organ was a boon. The English girl had a ukulele which she hadn't learnt, so from now on we spent all day on the ship trying to learn and play songs. The other Passengers took our noise very well indeed, and never complained. We had to get them and the officers and captain to sing to us songs they knew so we could learn them by heart to play. Days and dates meant nothing to any of us. China seemed to have forgotten all about the 'Nellore' stuck in the middle of the Whampoo River. The security men seemed to have taken charge of the Captains place and the ship. Occasionally the Captain got impatient, and went ashore to see the shipping agents, who wouldn't come to him, to see when we could get loaded and back to the wharf. By this time, the Chief Engineer, started to have Carol (other English girl) and me into his private sitting room each evening to play canasta and other games with him. (Also till Hong Kong there was another English girl who joined in too). So the days passed pleasantly with music during the day, and games at night.

A ring of the bell summoned the Chinese steward and brought sandwiches and tea about 9.0 p.m. for us while we played cards. We were told secretly we were known as the Chief Engineer's harem! Sometimes the Chief Mate and Captain had us to their rooms to listen to gramophone records. One day we moved back to the wharf and loading began. We also had another day ashore – again escorted – more temples and things. All day long hundreds of junks passed our ship – once I counted 100 just by us, taking cargo up and down the river. I don't think there was one of us who didn't manage to get some pictures from our portholes when the security man wasn't about! Carol and I nearly got copped, which gave us some anxiety! On 14th October, after 17 days instead of 2, we were ready to leave. We now had more security men snooping around for 12 hours till we were practically out in the open sea once more.

We had two days sailing before we reached Hong Kong. First we had to go a bit longer way round to dodge another typhoon, and then we came across a ship called 'St Christopher' with 45 people aboard by the Philippines whose engine had failed, so we had to tow it for six hours at 1 ½ knots an hour to somewhere in the Philippines. (That's wrong – that happened between Hong Kong and Borneo)!!! To go back, we spent four days in Hong Kong and then via Philippines to Borneo. Borneo was lovely. We had now unloaded all our cargo at Hong Kong, and the ship was more or less empty. Our first stop was Labuan – an island, and Carol and I had a lovely time ashore. We discovered that there were quaint buses – not much more than bits of wood stuck together (no windows) taking the native people to their homes right amidst the jungle, and we patronised these. Each ride took about two hours, quite off beaten tracks and no roads. One bus we were in we got so fed up being thrown on the floor, that we ended up by sitting on it! The native people all had their shopping with them. Mostly fish (not wrapped up) stuck on a hook and laid on the floor. One women next to me had an enormous hamper, with stuff at the bottom covered by a big leaf. She also had a bag full of ducklings. The latter fell over, and when we stopped to help pick up the ducklings, I noticed enormous live black crabs which made their way to the top of the hamper and crawling about. I was terrified that would fall over also! One passenger, a boy about 11, was singing 'Frere Jacques' in French, and then proceeded to whistle 'Colonel Bogey'. I never thought they'd teach that in native schools. When we weren't going on bus rides (when one had finished we changed to another bus and went off again) we went swimming in the sea. It was so hot and we enjoyed it. While we were gadding around logs were being towed by launch to our ship which was anchored in mid-stream to take back to Australia.

Labuan was lovely with all its tropical bananas and cocoanuts and what-have-you. 'Sparks', the radio officer, had a friend who lived there and we spent a nice evening dancing etc. at his house. After Labuan (two days) we moved to Sandakan, Carol and I still did our bus rides and bathing. Here, there was also a hotel where in the evenings some of the officers and Carol and I went for a bit of frivolity. We were there two days. Then we moved to a place called Kennedy Bay. There was only about six people living there, so we didn't even get off the ship, but the Chief Steward lent us a fishing line, and while logs were being loaded, we fished! I managed to catch two – very good looking, one was with a green stripe down it. I couldn't bear to eat it, but Carol did! We then moved to Bohinan Island – still getting more and more logs. Once again there was no place for us to go ashore, but we were taken for a launch trip to see the coral in the water. We then went to Tarakan to fill the boat with oil, and went once more to see and feed the monkeys. Then our last stop in Borneo called Wallace Bay. Here there was a very small town, and a few Europeans who had a swimming pool to which we were invited to bathe, and which we did. We were always warned that even 10 yards walk in the jungle and we were liable to get lost for days, so we didn't go far. We were, in all, playing around Borneo for a fortnight, and the ship got fuller and fuller with logs, or rather tree trunks. There were over 2,000 of them with an average weight of 2 ½ tons each. They were, in the end strewn all over the decks and piled high, and so back to Australia, a nine day without a port journey. Here, I disgraced myself by being ill. To cut it short, most of my breathing went – I don't know where or why. Fortunately there was an extremely good Doctor on board, who only just managed to keep me breathing till Brisbane, by giving me adrenalin injections every few hours. He even had to radio for fresh supplies to be brought on the ship by launch from Thursday Island. Then in Brisbane he dashed ashore and got me some cortisone, and after that I got better very quickly. If I hadn't, I was going to be stuck in the hospital there. We stayed nearly two days in Brisbane, while I got better and better, so I was allowed to stay on the ship until we reached Sydney. By that time I had quite recovered but was very weak. Dorothy had been telephoned for from Brisbane to meet me there, and it was lovely seeing her and our car on the wharf all waiting for me! It was very sad saying goodbye to everyone. It had all been so enjoyable and interesting. My greatest disappointment was not seeing more of Japan, (but I might one day) and China. I arrived back in Sydney on 20ᵗʰ November after three months on the ship!

We motored back to Cooma and on the 24ᵗʰ November I presented myself back for work after being well over five weeks later than I said I would be. I was warmly welcomed back, which was lucky.

Everywhere we went we took coloured slides with our camera, so no doubt you will be all made to look at them when we return to England!!! They are very good, we think!

§

Mabel their mother to whom most letters are written passed away on the 3rd November 1950

On 29th June 1960 Dorothy and Muriel sailed on the Caledonien bound for Marseilles on their way back to England.

Dorothy had been suffering from asthma on and off and was prescribed a new drug. She died on the 11th October 1960 shortly after her arrival in England.

Douglas was ordained a priest 29th May 1963 by the Bishop of Southampton.

Douglas's wife Jean died on the 9th May 1985, affecting Douglas very badly.

Douglas Heelas died on 11th July 1985, peacefully, at home, after a short illness. He was 65 and he lived in Ludgershall. His funeral was on Thursday 18th July at Ludgershall Parish Church

Muriel died in August 1985.

Abbreviations

A.C.2 Aircraftman 2nd Class

A.D.C Aide – de – Camp

A.K.C. Army Kinematograph Service

A.I.M.N.S. Army Institute Medical Nurse Service

A.L.F.S.E.A Allied Land Forces South East Asia

ARCO Associate of the Royal College of Organists

A.T.S. Auxillary Territorial Service

A.W.S. Army Welfare Service

B.O.R.s Battalion's Other Ranks

C.O. Commanding Officer

C.P.R. Canadian Pacific

C.S.E. Combined Services Entertainment

D.S.R. Division Section Reception

E.F.M. Expeditionary Force Message

E.N.S.A. Entertainments National Service Association

F.A.N.Y. First Aid Nursing Yeomanry

F.I.C. French Indo China

G.H.Q.C.M.F. General Headquaters Central Mediteranian Forces

L.M.G. Light Machine Gun

I.G.H.69 Indian General Hospital. Singapore

M.F.O. Military Forwarding Office

M.O. Medical Officer

M.T.O. Motor Transport Officer

N.A.A.F.I. Navy Army Air Force Institute

N.C.O. Non Commissioned Officer

O.C. Officer Commanding

O.C.T.U. Officer Cadet Traning Unit

O.H.M.S. On His Majesties Service

O.R. Other Ranks

P.O.W. Prisoner Of War

P.U. Pick-Up truck Commer light truck based on Hillman Minx Sedan

Q.A.I.M.S. Queen Alexandra's Imperial Military Nursing Service
R.A.M.C. Royal Army Medical Corps
R.A.S.C. Royal Army Service Corps
R.C. Roman Catholic
R.E.M.E. Royal Electrical Maintanice Enginers
R.S.M. Regimental Sergent Major
R.T.O. Regimental Transport Officer
S.A.C. Strategic Allied Command
S.A.C.S.E.A Supreme Allied Comand South East Asia
S.E.A.C. South East Asia Command
SMH St Mary's Hall School for girls Brighton
S.R.Division State Reorganisation Division
U.N.R.R.A. United Nations Relief & Rehabilitation Admin
V.A.D. Voluntary Aid Detachment
W.A.C. Womens Army Corps
W.A.A.F.S Womens Auxillary Air Force
W.R.E.N. Womens Royal Naval Service
W.R.N.S. Womens Royal Naval Service
W.V.S. Womens Voluntary Service

BV - #0006 - 050724 - C0 - 229/152/28 - PB - 9781915972279 - Gloss Lamination